The Politics of Interna
International

The Politics of International Law and International Justice

Edwin Egede and Peter Sutch

EDINBURGH
University Press

© Edwin Egede and Peter Sutch, 2013

Edinburgh University Press Ltd
22 George Square, Edinburgh EH8 9LF
www.euppublishing.com

Typeset in 10.5/12.5 Sabon by
Servis Filmsetting Ltd, Stockport, Cheshire, and
printed and bound in Great Britain by
CPI Group (UK) Ltd, Croydon CR0 4YY

A CIP record for this book is available from the British Library

ISBN 978 0 7486 3471 2 (hardback)
ISBN 978 0 7486 3472 9 (paperback)
ISBN 978 0 7486 3473 6 (webready PDF)
ISBN 978 0 7486 8452 6 (epub)

The right of Edwin Egede and Peter Sutch to be identified as
authors of this work has been asserted in accordance with the
Copyright, Designs and Patents Act 1988.

Contents

Acknowledgements   vii

Introduction: International Law and International Justice   1

1 Introduction to International Law	1 Segregation and De-segregation: IR, Law and Ethics	10
2 Sources of International Law	2 Normative Authority and the Sources of International Law	46
3 The Subjects of International Law	3 Justice in a World of States: The Moral Standing of Legal and Natural Persons	98
4 The United Nations and International Law	4 The Constitution of the International Community: Justice, Power and the United Nations	134
5 The Protection of Human Rights and International Law	5 Justice and Injustice in the Age of Human Rights	178

Contents

6	Diplomatic Communications	6 Diplomacy and Justice	214
7	The Ethics of Coercion	7 Sanctions and the Use of Force in Contemporary International Affairs	256
8	The Law of the Sea	8 Justice and the Common Heritage of Mankind	306

Conclusion 344

References 347
Index 375

Acknowledgements

This book project actually begun when I started to work with the Department of Politics, Cardiff University. I must say that writing this book has been a very exciting and stimulating journey – a journey enriched by interesting and thought-provoking conversations shared with my colleagues in the department. I have also had the unique privilege, as an international lawyer, of teaching international law to international relations (IR) students at both undergraduate and postgraduate levels, who, one way or the other, have contributed to my appreciation of areas of international law that are of interest to students of IR.

I indeed owe a debt of gratitude to a number of people, without whose encouragement and support this book would never have reached the point of publication. Special thanks to my darling wife, Hephzibah, for her support, encouragement and patience during the time it took me to write this book. Further, I wish to thank various international lawyers, such as professors Boisson de Chazournes, William Schabas, Robin Churchill and Akin Oyebode, whose eloquent and clear presentations on various international law issues at one forum or the other have over the years helped to shape and sustain my interest in international law as a discipline. I would also like to express my gratitude to all my colleagues in the Politics Department, Cardiff University, especially Peter (my co-author), Professor David Boucher and Dr Christian Bueger, who have helped me to scrutinise international law through the 'lenses' of international politics. In addition, I thank the anonymous reviewers who initially read the proposal

Acknowledgements

for this book for their critical, insightful and very helpful comments. Grateful thanks also to the team at Edinburgh University Press, especially Nicola Ramsey and James Dale, for their help in making this book happen.

Finally, I wish to thank and dedicate this book to Prince Emmanuel – my main inspiration. You are a Friend who sticks closer than a Brother!

Edwin Egede

* * *

Writing this book has been an intellectual journey that has taken me to new places, encouraged me to work with and learn from new people, and enabled me to teach new courses. In each part of that journey I have incurred debts and forged friendships. This journey, like most in my career, started in the Politics Department, Cardiff University, and I need to thank my fellow political theorists for their unfailing willingness to engage with ideas I found interesting and to share their broad experience and insight. Peri Roberts, Bruce Haddock and David Boucher have all played a significant role in the formation of this work. I also need to thank the lawyers who put aside their initial bemusement at my approach to their world to engage with this project. Edwin, my co-author, joined the Politics Department at Cardiff and started the series of encounters that would lead to this book. Urfan Khaliq, of Cardiff Law School, made it possible for us to teach law students and IR students together (although I am sure we learned more than they did), and I look forward to continuing that partnership. Cardiff University made it possible for me to try out aspects of the argument in many conferences and workshops. I am particularly grateful to Christof Humrich, who organised the panel on normative political theory and international law at the ECPR workshops at Muenster where I first aired the thought that legalisation had important implications for theories of international justice, and to Graham Long, who worked with me on the Just War since 9/11 project at the workshops in Political Theory at Manchester that sharpened my thoughts on the relationship between the laws of war and just war theory. I am also grateful to the University for allowing me research leave in the spring 2011 to work on this project and to Swansea Law School for enabling me to work as a visiting scholar in a very welcoming environment. Many of the ideas in this book have been worked through with students on the undergraduate and postgraduate IR programmes at Cardiff. Their enthusiasm and occasional confusion have

Acknowledgements

been very important to the development of this book. I would also like to thank that team at Edinburgh University Press who have made every step of this process work smoothly. All shortcomings in the text, are my own. Finally, I would like to thank my family who have supported my obsession with this project as they have always supported my journey in political theory. Nicola, Victoria and Matthew, the finished product is dedicated to you.

Peter Sutch

Introduction: International Law and International Justice

This is a book about public international law, and about the relationship between law, politics and ethics in global affairs. International relations (IR), more than any subfield in political studies, has disputed the relevance of the law and of the idea of justice to its scholarly project. This book is premised on the argument that there is a palpable and increasing need for students of IR to understand the nature of international law and its place in international politics, and that doing so requires a full engagement with questions of justice. As law becomes ever more central to the practices of global politics, we also believe that it is essential that lawyers look beyond the horizons of their profession to consider the political and ethical dilemmas that constitute the contested parameters of international law.

One of the distinctive features of post-war international politics is the way that actors increasingly use international law as a key resource in their international dealings. As the law becomes an established medium of international politics, we find that it is increasingly difficult to understand IR without understanding international law. Equally importantly, we find we cannot understand international law without understanding the politics of international law. The legalisation of world politics (a key concept we explore below) does not imply the transcendence of politics. Rather, it points to new modes of 'doing' politics, a new vernacular, a distinctive mindset, a new range of tools and, vitally, a new set of normative (social and moral) commitments. Increasingly, global debates concern the justice of acts, institutions, policies (and so on) where justice is measured, in part at least, by the lawfulness of the act, institution or policy. This measurement is not always, perhaps not ever, a straightforward matter of demonstrating that policy X complies with the relevant law. Sometimes it is a matter of choosing between a range of potentially applicable rules and pressing the case that best suits a preferred policy outcome or selecting the rule that best coheres with the core values that the agent wishes to promote. In other cases, it is a matter of arguing that an act or policy is just or legitimate because it was performed in the spirit of the law or because it is consistent with the community values the law was meant to further. In others, it is a matter of arguing that a novel challenge requires the reform of existing international legal regimes or governance mechanisms, or the construction of new ones. In each case claims about the lawfulness of acts, policies or institutions merge with claims about the justice or moral desirability of the act, policy or institution. The authority of these arguments depends partly on the skill and power of those making them, and partly on the extent to which international actors have come to accept that legitimacy and justice are closely linked to international legal standards. There is, as David Kennedy notes, an important sense in which the legalisation of world politics has led to a transformation in our understanding of international law. Law is no longer (only) a clear set of rules, promulgated by an appropriate authority. It is a tool of normative debate, part of the vocabulary of politics where persuasiveness is as important as strict legal validity.[1] This in itself generates opportunity and risks, and we need to understand them if we are to understand some of the most urgent and fascinating debates in contemporary world affairs.

Both the study of law and the study of ethics and justice have been labelled 'utopian' or 'idealist' by one of the most formative and significant approaches to the discipline of IR. The classic expressions of this position are to be found in two texts that established the direction of the study of IR after the Second World War. Both E. H. Carr, in *The Twenty Years Crisis: 1919–1939*,[2] and Hans J. Morgenthau, in *Politics Among Nations: The Struggle for Power and Peace*,[3] questioned the power of law or ethics to override or transcend the struggle for power that is the true essence of international political affairs. Their purpose was not to deny the relevance of law or ethics, but to urge the newly emerging political science of IR to focus on the underlying power relations between states that provided, they argued, the foundation for the observance or otherwise of legal rules and moral principles.[4] Their argument was to have a profound effect on the development of IR as a discipline. It provided its subject matter and founded its methodology. Realism is still a powerful force in IR and has much to offer in a consideration of the politics of international law. Nevertheless, there are many reasons to think that the study of international law and international justice is increasingly vital to the study of IR. The key reason we ought to revisit the traditional disciplinary boundaries between IR, law and ethics is found in the claim that international affairs have become increasingly legalised. The term 'legalisation' emerged out of a series of academic debates published in the journal *International Organization* at the turn of the millennium. Its precise meaning is contested, but in broad terms it refers to the ways that agents increasingly use legal instruments and institutions in their relations, and to the growing ambition that is evident in the reform of existing norms and institutions and in the creation of new ones. It also refers to the claim that a legalised international plane is distinct from earlier global political practices, where less emphasis was placed on the role of international law, that the character of international politics has been (or is being) reconstituted by the turn to law in global affairs.

There are many distinct approaches to these issues. Some commentators argue that nothing has really changed. International law is simply the newest mask for power politics and that, at its root, international law is epiphenomenal on the interests of states.[5] Others argue that everything has changed (or should do so immediately), and that we must remake international society to give more complete expression to core humanitarian and human rights concerns (see our discussions of the liberal cosmopolitan tradition below). Between these (admittedly stylised) poles are a broad range of analyses that seek to present key features of the politics of a legalised world order in a manner that helps us to comprehend the benefits and burdens and the opportunities and challenges it presents.

In the following chapters we argue that this complex relationship between politics, law and ethics gives contemporary international society a distinctive character. If we are to understand the power of specific claims (poverty is a human rights violation for which the international community is responsible; unilateral humanitarian intervention is just; the United Nations should be reformed; head of state immunity should not apply where international crimes are committed; nuclear weapons should be illegal) then we need to understand the nature of our legalised international society. This is the case because the relative power of such claims is tied to broader claims about the core values of the international political order and to how those values are (or ought to be) given institutional form. In some cases, the globalised nature of international crises (such as the potentially devastating consequences of nuclear or environmental Armageddon) or the universal value of humanitarian principles or human rights lead to claims that we need more international regulation and governance, a greater hierarchy in or even the constitutionalisation of international politics and law. Yet international society and international law is historically pluralistic and increasingly fragmented; it is heterachical rather than hierarchical. Famously, international society has been described as the anarchical society.[6] International pluralism, it is argued, protects the sovereignty of states, which itself protects the social, cultural and political freedom of the peoples of the world and promotes order in the political relations between them; justice, at the international level, requires the preservation of this pluralism and a respect for the sovereign equality of states. The politics of the legalised world order has thrown up a series of challenges to this traditional view of international society. These challenges, many of which we explore in the following chapters, ask questions about the justice or the desirability of a further move to legal and political hierarchy; of the continuing fragmentation of law as competing legal regimes or institutions generate and institutionalise different approaches to international law; of a continuing respect for pluralism. How these broader questions are answered has significant implications for how we respond to specific global challenges. The legalisation of international affairs contains the seeds of pluralism and of constitutionalism, and both present costs and benefits that weigh heavily when we consider the international response to specific crises and opportunities.

In large part the debates in the legalisation literature concern an empirical question. 'How, if at all, has the increasing legalisation of international politics changed the nature of international affairs?' The word 'legalisation' is found more often in IR scholarship than legal scholarship. This is hardly surprising – law students turn up expecting to study a legal order, but IR students are often told that the study of politics, especially international politics, is distinct from the study of law. In both disciplinary literatures law and politics are often defined in contrast to each other. International politics is anarchical, unregulated, based on interest and power, and is thus subjective. International law is ordered, formally constituted and objective. The rules and techniques of power and law are said to be different. Indeed, one very powerful and long-standing metaphor for international politics is that of a state of nature that exists prior to, or outside of, the establishment of law and morality. This image of the separation of law and politics, reinforced by the practice of disciplinary territoriality in the professions and in the academy, belies the interrelation between the practices of law and politics in international affairs. This is not to deny that we can benefit from the enormous range of expertise developed independently by social scientists and by lawyers. Rather, it is a claim that the rigid maintenance of these disciplinary borders masks both the legalised nature of international politics and the political nature of international law.

In this book, while we refer to the growing body of work that is designed to aid students of politics trying to understand how international law relates to international politics, we set out to explore a related set of questions concerning the idea of international or global justice. The basic premise of this endeavour has two related parts. The first is that arguments concerning global justice are important to, and have normative authority in, international affairs. The second is that the increasingly legalised nature of international politics has significant implications for considerations of global justice: that arguments about justice are now stronger when they are related to arguments about the politics of international law. An interest in international, global or humanitarian justice is a crucial aspect of moral and political decision-making in international affairs. In contemporary IR it is a matter of exploring and applying the critical techniques of asking whether a particular policy or action is good or bad, right or wrong, just or unjust. These are questions of ethics and of morality and, like questions of law, they were explicitly excluded from the agenda of the post-war science of IR. The legalisation of world politics offers new opportunities for the consideration of questions of justice.

Justice is not an easy concept to define. Indeed, disputes about the nature of justice have driven political theory for millennia, just as disputes about what justice and injustice requires have driven humanity to revolutions, wars, riots and rebellions. It is the illusive content of the idea, as well as its incendiary properties, that makes many scholars and political actors wary of it. Theories of justice are concerned with those elements of social life that can and ought to be politically governed and regulated. They seek to determine the appropriate scope and means of governance. These debates are morally complex and deeply political. At their heart they are normative debates. Normative debates consider how we ought to act or how we ought to legislate or govern. When faced with new political challenges, or when we come to view existing challenges in a new light (so requiring a modified response),

Introduction

normative questions inevitably arise. A significant part of the politics of international law concerns disputes about how we ought to apply law, or to create new rules, in response to global challenges. It is vital, then, that we learn to critically assess normative claims about justice and the politics of international law.

Most legal scholars use the word normative in a narrow sense to refer to rules that have binding legal force (or quasi-legal force). Law and justice in some regards are expected to be complimentary, which is why in legal terminology the phrase 'court of justice' is sometimes used interchangeably with the phrase 'court of law'. However, in reality not every law is just and history is replete with unjust laws. For instance, the laws passed during the Nazi regime in Germany authorising the horrific genocide of Jews could not by any stretch of imagination be regarded as just laws.[7] Over the years, this issue has resulted in two main schools of law: the naturalists, who believe that law must have a moral and just content, therefore, there is a crucial need to determine what law ought to be; and the positivists, who believe that law, morality and justice, while they may sometimes overlap, are totally different concepts and are thus interested in the law as it is. This raises the question of whether justice plays a key role in international law? Is there a moral content to international law that requires it to be an instrument of justice? Some scholars and jurists appear to take view that there is. According to Judge ad hoc, Dr Ecer, in his Dissenting Opinion in the *Corfu Channel* case (*UK* v. *Albania*), referring to the role of the International Court of Justice, the principal judicial organ of the United Nations, as an instrument to accomplish justice:

> The International Court's task as the juridical instrument of the United Nations is more far-reaching than that of a domestic court. A national court is called upon strictly to apply the law, and nothing more. The cohesion of the national community is provided for by other means. The decisions of national courts have not the same importance for the cohesion of the national community as international justice has for the cohesion of the international community. The International Court's task is therefore to help to strengthen the cohesion of the international community. The instrument of cohesion of the international community is the United Nations Charter. It is true international law, with its source in the new requirements of international life and the juridical conscience of the peoples.[8]

Blackstone in his definition of international law appears to suggest that a key function of international law is 'to insure the observance of justice and good faith'.[9] There are also various instruments that attempt to associate international law with justice. For instance, the United Nations General Assembly Millennium Declaration states: 'We are determined to establish a just and lasting peace all over the world in accordance with the purposes and principles of the Charter. We rededicate ourselves to ... resolution of disputes by peaceful means and in conformity with the principles of justice and international law.'[10]

In political theory the word normative has a broader meaning. Normative claims are 'ought' claims. The power of a legally normative claim is tied up with the fact that we ought to follow a particular rule because it is a rule of law. In Chapter Two we investigate the sources of law and, in doing so, critically explore those features of a legal rule that are commonly said to give it normative authority. We go on to show that there are many claims to normative authority that lack or transcend these features that nevertheless have traction (or exert a compliance pull on actors) in international affairs. Here we explore the relative normative authority of appeals to national self-interest, to the rule of law and to ethical claims relating to human rights, humanitarianism, equality, fairness and so on. As IR becomes increasingly legalised there is a tendency to think that actors have moved beyond politics and ethics – to the objective realm of law. But law, especially international law, is intrinsically political and the practice of critical reflection, of standing in critical relation to international politics and law, of asking 'is this a good, the right or the just thing to do?' is essential. In political theory the search for the sources of normativity[11] extends well beyond the question of the sources of legal normativity and beyond questions of justice to the source of moral and ethical value more generally. A detailed exploration of these claims is beyond the scope of this book. However, in exploring questions of justice alongside question of international law we intend to show how political and ethical judgement are an ineliminable element of a legalised world order.

Different approaches to international justice are essentially different approaches to the question of which issues or reasons count as compelling or authoritative in the construction of an argument about justice or injustice. In essence, they are specialised or focused arguments about the source of normative authority. In what follows we will encounter arguments about the weight of reason, culture

Introduction

and history in the construction of normative orders. In many of the traditions that we explore in this book there is also a claim about the relationship between moral claims, legal claims and political claims. These normative orders provide the context in which values, claims to legitimacy, to legal authority and to justice are shaped and contested. It is vital that we explore these, not because we can find a 'right answer', but because it encourages us to continually expose and to question many of the often hidden, reified 'truths' that support normative claims and political justifications in contemporary IR. The politics of international law is at its most vibrant when the validity or utility of established rules, regimes and institutions are contested. The sort of arguments advanced to support, for example, a doctrine of preventative self-defence or of humanitarian military intervention (see Chapter Seven) challenge both treaty and customary international law. Other claims, especially by those who argue for the reform of international law on the basis of the overwhelming priority of human rights claims (see Chapter Five), challenge the very idea of a consent based legal order, while others, concerned with the preservation of sovereign freedoms, challenge the rapidly expanding normative authority of human rights claims themselves. In each of these engagements, crucial policy issues, such as when to use military force or how to approach the challenges of global poverty, are debated in moral, political and legal terms. Understanding the force of any particular argument is a matter of discerning and analysing the relative merits of the different normative claims in play. For these reasons (and more) this book takes the reader on a search for normative authority in law, politics and ethics.

One of our core arguments is that moral and ethical criticism is simply a part of 'doing' politics, rather than being something external to it. Questions of international and global justice are embedded in the routines and practices of world affairs, and each of the arguments that we explore advances a version of this claim drawing on political, legal and moral argument to make their points. In the history of political thought this account of the sources of normativity is highly controversial, with a variety of metaphysical and philosophical traditions claiming normative foundations external to the practices of international society. While those debates are far from settled there has been a clear move in contemporary political theory towards an account of the social and political nature of normativity. In what follows we focus on a broad range of distinctive political and philosophical traditions that argue that normative debates in politics and law are inherently socially and historically informed. The form of reasoning we explore can be described as social or institutional moral reasoning. We explore the place of this form of political theory in the following chapter as we explore the relationship between the disciplines of international law and international relations as they developed after the First World War.

Notes

1 Kennedy, D. *Of War and Law*, Princeton, NJ: Princeton University Press, 2006.
2 Carr, E. H. *The Twenty Years Crisis: 1919–1939*, London: Palgrave Macmillan, [1939] 2001.
3 Morgenthau, H. J. *Politics Among Nations: The Struggle For Power and Peace*, Boston, MA: McGraw Hill, [1948] 2005.
4 See especially Carr, *The Twenty Years Crisis*, Pt 4, and Morgenthau, *Politics Among Nations*, ch. 18.
5 Krasner, S., 'Structural Causes and Regime Consequences: Regimes as Intervening Variables', *International Organization* 36(2) (1982): 185-206; Mearshiemer, J., *The Tragedy of Great Power Politics*, New York: W. W. Norton, 2001; Goldsmith, J. and Posner, E. *The Limits of International Law*, Oxford: Oxford University Press, 2005.
6 Bull, H., *The Anarchical Society: The Study of Order in World Politics*, 2nd edn, Basingstoke: Palgrave Macmillan, [1977] 1995.
7 Robertson, G., *Crimes Against Humanity*, London: Penguin, 2003, p. 30.
8 *Corfu Channel* case (*UK* v. *Albania*) [1949] ICJ Rep. 4, at p. 130.
9 Blackstone, W., *Commentaries on the Laws of England*, vol. 4, Chicago, IL: University of Chicago Press, [1766–1769] 1979, p. 47.
10 Paragraph 4, A/RES/55/2, 18 September 2000.
11 Korsgaard, C., *The Sources of Normativity*, Cambridge: Cambridge University Press, 1996.

CHAPTER ONE

Introduction to International Law

Segregation and De-segregation: IR, Law and Ethics

This chapter sets out to introduce the reader to some of the essential characteristics of international law and the politics of international law. We demonstrate that, even at the most fundamental level, the nature of international law and international justice is contested, and we aim to provide an overview of the core issues at stake. Each of these issues will be taken up and further developed in later chapters as detailed argument about the nature of international society and international law provide the context in which questions of justice are contested. We begin with a seemingly basic question 'what is international law?' and explore some of the issues that make such a basic question complex. In the second part of the chapter we offer an introductory examination of the politics of international law and some critical questions that form the essential core of our intellectual and critical enterprise.

What is international law?

Hedley Bull identified international law as one of the vital tools of interaction in the international system.[1] What then is international law? A number of jurists have over the years sought to define what international law is. Among the most cited we find Westlake, Oppenheim, Brierly and Lauterpacht, who define international law as follows:

International Law, otherwise called the Law of Nations, is the law of the society of States or Nations.[2]

Law of Nations or International Law . . . is the name for the body of customary and conventional rules which are considered legally binding by civilised States in their intercourse with each other.[3]

The Law of Nations, or International Law, may be defined as the body of rules and principles of action which are binding upon civilized States in their relations with one another.[4]

International Law is the body of rules of conduct, enforceable by external sanction, which confer rights and impose obligations primarily, though not exclusively, upon sovereign States and which owe their validity both to the consent of States as expressed in custom and treaties and to the fact of the existence of an international community of States and individuals. In that sense International Law may be defined, more briefly (though perhaps less usefully) as the law of the international community.[5]

Several issues arise from the above definitions. First, is international law applicable solely to sovereign states or is it also applicable to non-state actors? Second, what exactly is the most appropriate terminology for these body of norms: is it the law of nations, international law, or some other terminology?

Is international law applicable only to states?

Initially international law was thought to be applicable to states, particularly states that were the so-called 'civilised states'. At this time, an era that may be termed as 'classical' or 'traditional' international law, not much significance was attached to non-state actors.

However, with the establishment of the United Nations (UN) in 1945, international organisations and other non-state actors began to assume more prominence in the international system. For instance, the emphasis in the UN Charter on the promotion and protection of human rights highlights the role of individuals as subjects under international law. This therefore brought to the fore the need to redefine international law to reflect its application not only to states, but also to non-state actors.⁶ This led to an era that could be termed as 'modern' or contemporary international law.⁷

It is, however, important to point out that the traditional–modern divide of defining international law does not necessarily depend on the period when the definition was constructed. Yet, as earlier stated, it would not be wrong to propose that quite a number of the earlier authors of international law, especially pre-1945, tended to adopt the more traditional definition. However, there are exceptions to this proposition. For instance, William Blackstone (1723–80), the renowned author of the *Commentaries on the Laws of England*, in his definition as far back as the eighteenth century, recognised that international law was not only applicable to states. He defined it as follows:

> a system of rules, deducible by natural reason, and established by universal consent among the civilised inhabitants of the world; in order to decide all disputes, to regulate all ceremonies and civilities, and to insure the observance of justice and good faith, in that intercourse which must frequently occur between two or more independent states, and the individuals belonging to each.⁸

The sole role of the state in international law under the classical view, and its main role even under the modern view, could be traceable to the Westphalian system of international relations. Slaughter and Burke-White point out that the 'foundation of international law reflects the principles of Westphalian sovereignty', and Gross states that 'the Peace of Westphalia was the starting point for the development of modern international law'.⁹

The shift from the 'traditional' or 'classical' definition of international law to the 'contemporary' or 'modern' view also raises the issue of what is the appropriate terminology to describe this body of norms. Early scholars described it as the law of nations. In the eighteenth century the more widely used terminology, international law, was coined by Bentham in 1789, who defined it as the 'principles of legislation in matters [between] nation and nation'.¹⁰ He proposed the change of the terminology because he was of the view that the term law of nations did not adequately represent the discipline. He stated:

> The word international, it must be acknowledged, is a new one; though it is hoped, sufficiently analogous and intelligible. It is calculated to express, in a more significant way, the branch of the law which goes commonly under the name of the law of nations,

an appellation so uncharacteristic that, were it not for the force of custom, it would seem rather to refer to internal jurisprudence.[11]

But is international law any different from the law of nations? First, these two terminologies would appear to focus more on state actors. This excludes the growing number of non-state actors, such as international organisations like the UN and European Union, multinational corporations and even individuals, that are regulated by this body of norms.

Is another terminology therefore needed to describe this body of law? Some scholars would appear to think so. For instance, Jessup suggests that transnational law would be more appropriate, since what is presently known as international law is merely a body of law, 'which regulates actions or events that transcend national frontiers', and also regulates 'the complex interrelated world community which may be described as beginning with the individual and reaching on up to the so-called "family of nations" or society of States'.[12] There are other suggestions as to the appropriate terminology. Should it be called cosmopolitan law? Although Kant appeared to regard international law and cosmopolitan law as separate norms, the modern definition of international law and its growing interest in the individual as a subject of international law in areas such as human rights would appear to be in line with Kant's perception of cosmopolitan law.[13] Other suggestions as appropriate terminologies include the law of the world community,[14] world law[15] and the common law of mankind.[16] Despite the possibilities and arguments for and against the appropriateness of one terminology or the other, the authors of this book have chosen to use the term international law. We go on to explore some of the implications of the statism (or otherwise) of international law in Chapter Three.

Is international law really law?

Perhaps instinctively most students of international law, especially those from highly developed domestic legal systems, think of law in terms of the structures with which they are familiar in their respective domestic systems.[17] They would usually look out for some centralised legislature (e.g., parliament, congress, diet, national assembly, etc.) with powers to make the laws. In addition, they would probably look for an executive body that implements and enforces these laws, as well as a judiciary with compulsory jurisdiction to interpret the laws and, in the case of domestic systems with a supreme constitution, with the ability to strike down any law or action contrary to the constitution. They are often disappointed when they fail to locate such a centralised system in international law. The absence of these core institutions has generated debates on whether international law is really law.

Some, notably John Austin, the eighteenth-century positivist legal philosopher, have argued that international law is law 'improperly so called' and is merely 'positive international morality'.[18] However Franck, writing in the twentieth century, argued that modern international lawyers have departed from the traditional inquiry of whether international law is law to other inquiries such as: is international law effective?; is it enforceable?; is it understood?; is it fair?[19] While this is no doubt a fair assessment of some questions with which modern international lawyers are engaged, these questions are in reality merely fallouts of the core question: is international law really law? The question as to whether international law is really law is as real now as it was when Austin identified it as law improperly so-called. Some modern jurists, though perhaps now hopefully in the minority, still take the view that international law is not really law. For instance, John Bolton (the former US ambassador to the UN during the presidency of George W. Bush), in an article written relatively recently stated as follows:

> Simply because treaties are not 'law' does not mean that States are not in some sense bound by them, or that States may dismiss or ignore treaty promises without consequence. Nor does it mean that failing to consider treaty as law unleashes anarchy upon the world. Consider three sentences about treaties:
> Sentence One: The United States is morally bound by its treaty obligations.
> Sentence Two: The United States is politically bound by its treaty obligations.
> Sentence Three: The United States is legally bound by its treaty obligations.
> ... First, these three sentences say three different things. Being morally bound is not the same as being politically bound, and being politically bound is not the same as being legally bound. Second, Sentences One and Two are true, while Sentence Three is false. There is no legal mechanism – no coherent structure – that

exists today on a global level to enforce compliance with treaties, a fact international law advocates flatly ignore.[20]

With views such as the above, it is therefore apposite to explore various arguments on whether international law is really law. The crux of the debate on this appears to rest on varying views on the question: what is law? – an intriguing, but rather intricate, question that has engaged the attention of jurists over the years.[21]

One of the most devastating arguments against international law being law was put forward by John Austin, who defined law as a command of a sovereign that 'obliges generally to acts or forbearances of a class', and is backed by sanctions if commands are disobeyed.[22] He points out that a sovereign is a person or body receiving the habitual obedience of the members of an independent political society, who in turn does not owe such obedience to any person. According to Austin, international law does not fall within the ambit of this definition, therefore, it is law 'improperly so called' and is merely 'positive morality'.[23] The Austinian conception of law appears not to be buried in the annals of the eighteenth century, as modern jurists, such as Bolton, support this view of what is law. He stated:

> We understand 'law' to be a system of commands, obligations and rules that regulate relations among individuals and associations, and the sources of legitimate coercive authority in society. These are the forces that can compel behavior and enforce compliance with rules.[24]

The question is whether all types of laws, even in the domestic setting, fall within the ambit of Austin's definition. Some argue that the Austinian definition is rather narrow and certainly does not cover all types of law.[25] For instance, in England there is the common law, which originally emerged as unwritten law based on common customs and usages in England. Over the years this law has been applied by the English courts and is now known as case law, a law developed by the judges through decisions of courts and not the legislature. Common law, which does not fall within the ambit of Austin's definition of law, has been accepted as law. If under the domestic setting there are laws that fall outside the ambit of Austin's definition, it could be said that international law, which operates in the international setting, is a law though it does not fall within this rather restricted definition. In any event, since it operates in international society which is decentralised, unlike the domestic setting, and applies horizontally, rather than vertically, international law could be said to be have a peculiar type of nature that is in many ways distinct from domestic law.

Some are sceptical about the law nature of international law, because international society lacks proper governmental structure such as that in the domestic setting. For instance, there is no legislative body in international society like the legislature within a state. Much as the plenary UN General Assembly may look like some sort of parliament, it is not one and certainly has no powers to enact international legislation, since its resolutions are generally merely recommendatory. Also, there is no international executive arm like the executive within a country – no cabinet, no police force to arrest people and send them to jail when they violate the law. Despite the enormous powers of the UN Security Council, when the Permanent Five (P-5) finally agree to act, it is certainly not an international executive arm of international society. Neither is it a sort of 'world policeman', similar to the policeman in the domestic setting, though the Security Council has been so described in some texts.[26] In addition, there is no compulsory judicial system in international society similar to courts within a country. The judicial system under international society is based on the consent (explicit and tacit) of states. The crucial question is whether the existence of an organised and formal structure of governance is what determines the law-like nature of rules in a society? For instance, there are certain less developed societies that do not have the formal structures that we find in the United Kingdom or the United States, and yet these societies have customary laws that regulate interactions therein. The mere fact that international society lacks formal structures like developed domestic societies does not in itself remove the law-like quality of international law, but merely confirms that international society is perhaps a different kind of society that is less developed than the municipal legal systems with which we are familiar.[27] Recently, we can see certain developments in the international system that suggest a move in certain areas towards a more formal type of structure. For instance, ever since the Nuremberg and Tokyo tribunals, especially since the end of the Cold War, there is a trend to set up international criminal tribunals, such as the International Criminal Tribunal for the Former Yugoslavia (ICTY), the International Criminal Tribunal for Rwanda (ICTR) and the International Criminal Court (ICC), which are in some respects similar to domestic criminal courts. These international criminal tribunals have the powers to try individuals for crimes against international law and actually have the powers to convict and send to jail those found guilty of committing such offences. Although there is this trend, there is no suggestion that the international system would eventually have governmental structures exactly like the domestic system. The international system by its very nature is different from the domestic system, and to expect these two systems to have exactly the same type of governance mechanism would be unrealistic. While, undoubtedly, there would be further institutionalisation in different areas of the international system, there is no expectation that this would lead the international system to have a governmental system identical to the domestic system unless there is a radical overhaul of the state consent basis of the international system.

Another argument raised is that international law is not law because it is unenforceable. Again, this is tied up with the Austinian definition of law as a command accompanied by sanctions that in essence enforce the law. How, argue those who support this point of view, do you enforce international law against states, especially powerful ones like the United States? Some international lawyers, such as Fitzmaurice and D'Amato, question the necessary interrelation between enforcement and the law nature of international law.[28] There are examples of domestic laws that are not enforced, but yet cannot be denied being characterised as law.[29] For instance, the fact that the United Kingdom Hunting Act 2004, which criminalises hunting wild mammals (including fox hunting) with dogs, is hardly enforced does not make it cease to be a law.[30] D'Amato points out that the character of a rule as law is not determined by its enforcement, but rather because of compliance by the majority of the society in which the law applies. He argues that such compliance can be seen in respect of international law.[31] Fitzmaurice asserts that 'we obey the law [international law] not because we necessarily think that the law is just, but because we believe it to be just to obey the law'.[32] According to Slaughter and Burke-White, quoting Abram and Antonia Chayes, maximising compliance with international law 'is a task more of management than of enforcement, ensuring that all parties know what is expected of them, that they have the capacity to comply and that they receive the necessary assistance'.[33] On the other hand, some authors say that international law has an enforcement mechanism, albeit not as sophisticated as the developed domestic system, but, nonetheless, a type of enforcement system. For instance, some point to enforcements of international law through countermeasures (an illegal act that is rendered lawful as a response to a prior illegal act), retorsions (unfriendly, but lawful, acts by a state in response to either an unlawful or lawful, but unfriendly act of another state) and exclusion of erring states from common entitlements.[34] In addition, there is the Security Council power to make binding resolutions using its chapter VII powers,[35] and to use economic and military sanctions to enforce compliance (see Chapter Seven). Although military action has been rarely used against states due to its highly controversial and political nature, its use against Iraq for the invasion of Kuwait contrary to international law shows that this power has considerable bite as an enforcement mechanism.[36] Further, there is the power, which has so far not been used, of the Security Council to enforce judgments of the International Court of Justice. Article 94 of the UN Charter states as follows:

1. Each Member of the United Nations undertakes to comply with the decision of the International Court of Justice in any case to which it is a party.
2. If any party to a case fails to perform the obligations incumbent upon it under a judgment rendered by the Court, the other party may have recourse to the Security Council, which may, if it deems necessary, make recommendations or decide upon measures to be taken to give effect to the judgment.

In addition, with the establishment of various international criminal tribunals, such as the ICTY, ICTR and ICC, we see enforcement of international criminal law in an identical fashion as domestic law.

Opponents of international law as law argue that it is more honoured in breach than in observance. They point to the various wars/conflicts, breaches of treaties and oppression of weak states by more powerful states that appears to confirm the fact that 'might is right'. Supporters of international law, on the other hand, argue that a law does not cease to be law because of this. They point to examples of domestic systems with a high crime rate, breaches in the law, breakdown in law and order, etc., and point out that this in itself does not make the applicable laws cease to be laws. While there may be support for the position that the laws in such domestic systems are ineffectual, it certainly would not be correct to say that these laws are not laws. Further, they point to the fact that the breaches of international law are usually publicised, while the various aspects of international law that are regularly observed and obeyed by states are largely underpublicised. According to the oft cited quote by Louis Henkin, 'almost all nations observe almost all principles of international law and almost all of their obligations almost all of the time'.[37]

Supporters of international law as law relying upon the Roman maxim *ubi societas ibi jus* (if there is a society, law will be there), argue that there is an international society and therefore there is law (international law) that regulates relations between members of the society. Opponents of international law as law argue that even if this maxim is accepted it raises the further debate: is there really an international society?[38] The English School of international relations insist that there is an international society of states. It argues that the Treaty of Westphalia 1648, which introduced the modern state system with attributes such as sovereignty and legal equality among states, established some sort of international society. It is an anarchical, decentralised and horizontal international society with a body of norms – international law – to regulate interaction between members of the society. According to Hedley Bull:

> A society of States (or international society) exists when a group of States, conscious of certain common interests and common values, form a society in the sense that they conceive themselves to be bound by a common set of rules in their relations with one another, and share in the working of common institutions.[39]

He asserts that the modern international system is also an international society.[40]

It has been contended that, among other things, there are two crucial conditions that are required for a rule to be regarded as law. First, there must be in existence a political community and, second, there must be recognition by its members of the settled rules as binding upon them as law.[41] Is this the case with international law? Is there really an international political community? If so, do the members of that community recognise international law as law? This is a crucial feature of the debate, as it concerns both the nature of international law and the relationship between international law and international politics. Before we turn to the political arguments it is worth exploring some of the answers to these questions found in legal practice.

It would appear that there is a generally held view that there is actually an international community.[42] The ICJ has referred to an international community in some decisions, for example, the *US Hostages in Tehran* case.[43] The United Nations, in its Declaration on the Occasion of the Fiftieth Anniversary of the UNGA, has also referred to the international community.[44] Article 53 of the Vienna Convention on the Law of Treaties 1969 states that *jus cogens* is a peremptory norm of general international law 'accepted and recognised by the international community of States as a norm from which no derogation is permitted and which can be modified only by a subsequent norm of general international law having the same character'. While these are clear references to the international community, it is not clear what exactly the scope of this community is. Such community clearly is no longer limited to any particular civilisation and value system, but rather is a multicultural one. This community extends beyond states and includes other non-state actors that play a role in the international system. de Wet rightly points out that:

> the community is composed predominantly but not exclusively of States, which still remain central to the process of international law making and law enforcement, international and regional (sectoral) organizations with legal personality, such as the United Nations, the World Trade Organization (WTO), and the European Union (EU), however, also participate in the membership of the international community. In addition, individuals also constitute members of the international community to the extent that they possess international legal personality, for example in the context of international or regional systems for the protection of human rights.[45]

The 1995 UN Declaration on the Occasion of the Fiftieth Anniversary also acknowledged this, and went on to include non-governmental organisations (NGOs) and other actors of civil society by stating:

> We recognize that our common work will be the more successful if it is supported by all concerned actors of the international community, including non-governmental organizations, multilateral financial institutions, regional organizations and all actors of civil society. We will welcome and facilitate such support, as appropriate.

A key question concerns whether there are common values in this so-called international community to justify it being designated as a community? It is contended that there are common values such as the prohibition on the use of force, the obligation to respect fundamental human rights and protection of the environment. de Wet points out that the 'international value system concerns norms with a strong ethical underpinning, which have acquired a special hierarchical standing through state practice'.[46] The strength and depth of this value system is a key element of our exploration in all that follows.

The members of international society recognise international law as law. For instance, virtually all states have legal office manned by lawyers to advise on international law. For example, in the United Kingdom the Foreign and Commonwealth Office, which is the main centre of expertise in international law within the government, is manned by lawyers who provide legal advice on international law.[47] In the United States, there is the Legal Advisor's Office, US Department of State, also manned by lawyers, that provides legal advice on international law.[48] In cases where states are accused of violating international law, they do not dismiss it as mere international morality, rather they seek to justify their actions on the basis of international law. For example, when the United States, the United Kingdom and the other members of the so-called 'coalition of the willing' were said to have violated international law in the 2003 invasion of Iraq, they sought to justify their actions by arguing that the invasion was in line with international law. Various officials of states or international organisations treat international law as law and not as international morality. For example, the UK Iraq Inquiry (the Chilcot Inquiry) to identify lessons that could be learned from the Iraq conflict certainly regarded international law as law to be obeyed by the government of the United Kingdom.[49] Also, the president of Russia in a 2008 speech to the meeting with Russian Ambassadors and Permanent Representatives to International Organisations urged them 'to identify and resist the attempt of national or group interests to ignore international law. After all, this is the set of rules that has been and remains the most solid foundation for relations between nations'.[50] In addition, the municipal courts apply international law as law. There are several examples of municipal courts doing so in various countries. A ready example is the *Pinochet* case (see Chapter Six).[51]

It can be argued that the whole debate about whether international law is law is a consequence of a rather limited conception of what law actually is grounded in the 'domestic analogy'. Law is a rather complex concept and has been subject to diverse definitions.[52] Strictly speaking, law goes beyond norms enacted by a centralised legislative body, enforced and implemented by an executive, and interpreted by a judiciary with compulsory jurisdiction. International society is clearly different from its counterpart in the domestic setting, and in reality it would be rather illogical to use the domestic analogy to seek to determine whether the law that applies to international society or the international community is actually law. It is easier to appreciate international law as law if we come on the basis that this is a law that regulates relationships in the international system, which is different and primordial in comparison with the domestic analogy that most of us are used to.

Public international law, municipal law and private international law

International law must be distinguished from municipal law (or national or domestic law). The latter is the law of a state, which governs the relationships of individuals, juridical persons, groups and entities within that state. While the former, as pointed out above, is the law that regulates actors, both states and non-state actors, within the international community. In addition, the discipline of international law (more specifically public international law) can be distinguished from another discipline, private international law (or sometimes called conflict of laws). The latter has been defined as 'a body of rules which determines whether local or foreign law is to be applied and if so, which system of foreign law'.[53] For instance, if A and B, citizens of the United Kingdom and France, respectively, enter into a contract for the importation from France to South Africa certain pharmaceuticals with an a clause stating that payment should be made into a Swiss bank account, there is the possibility in any eventuality of a dispute that different laws, including those foreign to the parties, may apply. Would it be English, French, South African or Swiss law that would apply? Private international law (or conflict of laws), which is actually a part of municipal law, is the discipline that determines which of the numerous municipal laws, would apply in this situation and not public international law; the latter being the subject matter of this book. Although, in theory, the distinction between these two disciplines is clear cut, in practice there is sometimes an overlap. For instance, there may be treaties between states that deal with the issue of conflict of laws. An example of this is the Convention for the Settlement of Certain Conflicts of Laws in Connection with Bills of Exchange and Promissory Notes (1930). Which is why some have suggested that the way to avoid such conflicts is to do away with the terminology – international law – and adopt the term, transnational law, which would make the distinction between these two disciplines redundant.[54]

International law and municipal law interact at different spheres.

Over the years, this has raised theoretical debates on which of these two systems are superior. It has also raised practical issues for actors in the international system on how international law may be applied in the domestic system and the reverse, how is municipal law to be applied in the international arena. Some practical examples that may arise are as follows:

Scenario 1: Is the European Convention on Human Rights superior to the domestic law of the United Kingdom? What happens if there is a conflict between the Convention provisions and domestic legislation, which prevails? How can the provisions of the European Convention on Human Rights be applied domestically in the United Kingdom? Does it apply automatically or must there necessarily be an Act of Parliament in place?

Scenario 2: How does an international court deal with an issue of whether or not an individual is a national of a state that purports to act for such individual before the international court/tribunal? Should it look at the national law of that state to determine whether the individual fits into the definition of a national under such national law?

How do we classify the above examples? Scenario 1 deals with issues of international law in a domestic system,[55] while Scenario 2 deals with national law before the international legal system. There are two main theories on this: monism and dualism.[56] The main points of controversy between the two theories are whether international law and domestic law are two separate legal orders or merely parts of the same order; and which of the two is superior to the other. Monism theory points out that international and municipal law are merely two components of a single legal order, and if there is a conflict between the two international law will always prevail. This will obviously augur well for areas of international law, such as international human rights, so international law can trump domestic laws that violate human rights. Dualism theory argues that international law and domestic law are two separate independent legal orders, in cases of conflict domestic law prevails. It points out that international law regulates relations at the international plane, while domestic law regulates relations at the domestic plane. As a result of the superiority of domestic law, for international law to be applicable in domestic plane it must first be 'transformed' into domestic law. Another view states that the monist–dualist controversy is unreal, artificial and assumes a controversy where there is none. The controversy assumes that they both have a common field, which is not the case. Therefore, there can be no conflict; neither is there an issue of one being superior to the other. It is just like arguing about whether English law is superior to French law or the other way around. This is simply not an issue as both laws apply in different spheres.

In actuality, state practice does not always reflect the clear demarcation between monism and dualism in national legal systems.[57] In national legal systems, international law may be applied either by way of incorporation or transformation. The doctrine of incorporation, which appears to be a monist viewpoint, asserts that international law becomes part of domestic law automatically, without any need for express adoption either by the legislature or the courts. It is said to be 'incorporated' into the domestic legal system. For example, in the old case of *Buvot* v. *Barbuit*,[58] Lord Talbot said that: 'the law of nations, in its full extent was part of the law of England'. On the other hand, the doctrine of transformation, which appears to be a dualist viewpoint, asserts that international law can become part of the domestic system only if it has been expressly adopted by the state authorities, usually by way of legislation. It is said that international law has to be deliberately 'transformed' into national law. For instance, Lord Atkin, in *Attorney-General for Canada* v. *Attorney-General for Ontario*,[59] said that, 'Within the British Empire there is a well-established rule that the making of a treaty is an executive act while the performance of its obligations, if they entail alteration of the existing domestic law, requires legislative action.' Most continental countries operate a monist type of system, whereby international law is incorporated automatically in the domestic system and trumps other domestic laws. In most common law jurisdictions, on the other hand, while customary international law (CIL) applies automatically, treaties have to be transformed. The incorporation–transformation distinction may not always be straightforward. For instance, Article VI, Clause 2 of the United States Constitution states that:

> This Constitution, and the Laws of the United States which shall be made in Pursuance thereof; and all Treaties made, or which shall be made, under the Authority of the United States, shall be the supreme Law of the Land; and the Judges in every State shall be bound thereby, anything in the Constitution or Laws of any State to the Contrary notwithstanding.

Over the years the US courts have made a distinction between self-executing (automatic domestic application) and non self-executing (requiring domestic legislation) treaties. Paust, on the US situation, argues that this is a judicial invention and rather subjective in its application.[60] For instance, in the case of human rights treaties the US courts have at times said that they are self-executing and, at other times, non- self-executing.

The politics of international law

Many of the themes surveyed in this brief overview of the nature of international law come to prominence in our exploration of the politics of international law and of questions of international justice. In particular, they arise as questions concerning the normative authority of international law. In order to preface a detailed exploration of questions of international justice as they emerge in the contemporary period we need to start with a brief overview of the ways in which these issues led to a situation in which the study of international politics and law were separated from each other and from questions of ethics. We also need to get a clearer understanding of the key features of the legalisation of international affairs and a broad outline of the different arguments about how we might begin to (or why we need to) think about ethics, justice or morality as a part of thinking about the politics of international law. This approach is intended to offer an overview of the theoretical tool-kit that has been developed in IR theory and normative international political theory. We then turn to a detailed exploration of those elements of public international law that we consider vital to questions of international justice.

Theory plays an important part in the analysis of any phenomenon. Political theory and IR theory have established canons and traditions that help us group similar approaches to the subject together and to glean general insight into these distinct approaches. In the next section we do not offer an exhaustive overview of these approaches. Rather, we explore those traditions that have offered particularly important insights into the questions of normative authority and the politics of international law. These theoretical approaches have stood the test of time because they highlight key features of the global legal and political order. The basic traditions will be familiar to most students of IR. Realists show how important it is that we recognise the role that power-politics plays in the practices of states that constitute the international legal order. Liberal institutionalists show how, over time, the process of legalisation alters the patterns of international politics and forces us to think about complex interdependence among actors. Constructivists and English School theorists focus on the normative evolution of international society, showing, for example, how the increasing importance of the rule of law alters the nature of the actors themselves, leading them to, in the words of one of the tradition's leading contributors, pursue justice with increasing normative ambition.[61] Liberal-cosmopolitans show how reflecting on the morality of the politics of international law drives us to challenge some of the most fundamental institutional practices of the international order. Critical theorists challenge us to understand the pervasive hegemony of the power relations inherent even in a legalised world order, and to stay clear of those assumptions that entrench inequality and domination. There are, of course, many variations within each theoretical tradition. If we are to benefit from theory we need to be able to understand the working parts of each argument to understand their subtleties and to be able to recognise where insight gives way to limiting assumption. We also need to stay clear of the drive to simply pick one tradition and to fetishise it, to defend it come what may. We can, and must, learn from each approach – from each insight and each error – as we seek out normative authority in the international legal order.

IR is a relatively young academic discipline. The first chair (professorship) explicitly in international politics was the Woodrow Wilson Chair at Aberystwyth University, established in 1919. This does not mean that what we now think of as international relations were not previously the object of philosophical enquiry. In fact, there is an extraordinarily rich tradition of scholarship in politics, ethics and law stretching back millennia. However, the modern discipline was born in a reaction to catastrophic world wars, with a passionate desire to renounce what it termed 'utopianism' in the analysis of world politics, and to inject the scientific rigour that these early 'realists' thought necessary to prevent another descent into global conflict. Central to our endeavour is to understand why international law and morality were viewed as the utopian problem rather than the solution.

Among the most famous exponents of what was to become the realist tradition in IR are E. H. Carr and Hans J. Morgenthau. Writing either side of the Second World War, these scholars (the former a diplomat at the Paris Peace negotiations in 1919, the latter an international lawyer) provided the foundation both for the rejection of the liberal institutional project as represented by the League of Nations and the separation of international politics from international law. The realist rejection of the utopianism of the liberal aspiration to bring international affairs under the rule of law is often caricatured (portrayed as the denial that there could possibly be any such thing as law in an anarchical system or dressed in the parsimony of later neo-realist claims that law is merely an epiphenomenon of political power structures). In fact, the treatment that both scholars offer the politics of international law is subtle and detailed. The key to their rejection of the potential of law to overcome the conflictual nature of world politics stems from a particular insight into the relationship between law, ethics and politics. The ambition of Woodrow Wilson's liberals was to achieve international peace and security through the institutionalised acceptance of the rule of law as the actual rule of conduct among states.[62] For Carr, the failure of this experiment was not simply a product of Japanese or Italian aggression or the decision by the United States to remain outside the League of Nations, rather it was the thoroughgoing utopianism that made liberals oblivious to the ways in which the political nature of the international community limited the ability of law and ethics to mitigate the challenges of an international system populated by sovereign (but radically unequal) states. For Carr

> politics and law are indissolubly intertwined; for the relations of man to man in society which are the subject matter of one are the subject matter of the other. Law like politics is the meeting place for ethics and power.[63]

Carr had no truck with the inadequate 'half-truths' of the legal naturalists, who believed that law is somehow 'more moral than politics', or of the legal positivists, who argued, following Hobbes, that law exists only at the command of a powerful leviathan. Law is not inadequate in itself, because it does not exist in itself; power and ethics are both part of the equation. But, crucially, law is a function of a community, and the international community was, he argued, 'embryonic'. The international community he was writing about was populated by relatively few states. The inequality of states was magnified by that fact that some of the most developed states were the recently vanquished states and that it was the victors who were proposing these new terms of social cooperation. For Carr, this meant that the development of general rules, applicable to all, was a particularly difficult enterprise and, therefore, this 'makes international law more frankly political than other branches of law'. Institutional underdevelopment (the lack of a judicature, an executive and a legislative body) might contribute to the weaker nature of international law, but the inevitable consequence of the social underdevelopment of the international community was the real key. Under these circumstances 'rules, however general in form, will be constantly found to be aimed at a particular state or group of states; and for this reason, if for no other, the power element is more predominant and more obvious in international law than in municipal law'.[64] For Carr, nothing was more expressive of the utopianism of the League of Nations liberals than the fact they could not see that the dominance of the liberal way of thinking after the First World War was a consequence of their military victory. How could they not see that the emphasis they placed on the rule of the law entrenched *their* law? Respect for international law, argued Carr, 'will not be increased by the sermons of those who, having most to gain from the maintenance of the existing order, insist most firmly on the morally binding character of the law'.[65] The utopians, he argued, had an inadequate grasp of law and ethics because they overlooked the third key ingredient: power.

After the Second World War, Morgenthau cemented the insight that the study of power should become the exclusive concern of IR. Like Carr, Morgenthau realised that international law was a significant part of international politics. He pointed to the imposing edifice of 'thousands of treaties, hundreds of decisions of international tribunals, and innumerable decisions of domestic courts' that had regulated the relations among nations since the Treaty of Westphalia that ended the Thirty Years War and stands as the totemic 'starting point' for modern international relations. In most instances, he argued, these rules are scrupulously well observed. Nevertheless, he also pointed to the dramatic failure of the more 'spectacular instruments of international law', those such as the Kellogg–Briand Pact, the Covenant of the League of Nations and the Charter of the United Nations, that attempted to fundamentally alter international politics and, inevitably, failed to do so. The inevitability of this failure stemmed from the pattern of power relations in a decentralised world order. Power, rather than law, is the key. Where states share interests (in establishing the status and rights of diplomatic representatives, for example), or where there exists a balance of power, then law can exist. But where interests diverge or power is distributed unevenly then the one truly objective social force – power defined in terms of interest – wins out.⁶⁶ The student of international affairs (who was inevitably drawn to the high politics for which law was not suited) was therefore instructed to focus attention on this objective social force. The science of IR was to be the elaboration of general rules about the nature and function of power.

> Intellectually, the political realist maintains the autonomy of the political sphere, as the economist, the lawyer, the moralist maintain theirs. He thinks in terms of interest defined as power, as the economist thinks in terms of interest defined as wealth; the lawyer of the conformity of action with legal rules; the moralist, of the conformity of action with moral principles. The economist asks: 'How does this policy affect the wealth of society, or a segment of it?' The lawyer asks: 'Is this policy in accord with the rules of law?' The moralist asks: 'Is this policy in accord with moral principles?' And the political realist asks: 'How does this policy affect the power of the nation?'⁶⁷

There is, of course, a series of important insights in the work of Carr and Morgenthau. We simply could not understand the nature of international law if we did not seek out the role of power in the international system. This insight is as central to contemporary critical theorists and constructivists as it is to realists. But the way that realists (as Morgenthau and those that followed him called themselves) built their science of international politics from this starting point entrenched the segregation of IR as a discipline from considerations of ethics and law. In part, this was a bid to establish the disciplinary identity of IR. IR studied power. It was different from the study of law and from the study of domestic politics. This difference, it was claimed, was necessitated by the anarchical conditions of global affairs. In a bid for ever greater rigour, the realists honed the ways in which they measured and theorised power in world politics. If the focus on power pushed IR away from the study of law, the aspiration to objective social science and the influence of the emerging positivist approach to social science (an approach that focuses exclusively on observable, empirical data) led to the segregation of ethics and international politics. In this positivist IR had a collaborator in positivist international law.

Positivism is a key feature of contemporary IR and international law. They are distinct from each other and reinforce the divisions that have been commonly thought to exist between the two disciplines, but, as Armstrong *et al.* note, there is 'a certain irony' in the mutual antipathy between them.[68] Both disciplines sought objectivity. IR realists found it in the abandonment of utopianism and in reliance upon empirical and testable scientific method. Their method excluded normative questions as a matter of ontology and epistemology. An ontological claim is a claim about the fundamental nature of existence. Epistemological claims concern how we might come to know about the world. Foundational to the positivist method is the claim that normative principles do not exist in a fundamental sense. They are subjective principles, contingent and, because we cannot test them against reality, we cannot come to know them with any certainty. The resistance of normative claims to scientific study reduced them, in the words of A. J. Ayer, to the status of 'nonsense' and they were to be excluded from the discipline.[69] Lawyers found objectivity in the abandonment of natural law theory (the idea, prevalent throughout much of human history, that international law was one aspect of universal law emanating from a metaphysically true source, usually God) and in the assertion that law is the product of human will. Here positivism takes many forms. At one extreme we have what is known as the command theory of law or the Austinian handicap (see above). A more usual contemporary positivist position argues that normative authority in international law rests on the consent of states (rather than on the merits of the law itself). This positivist doctrine makes it possible to discover what law is through the examination of what states have or have not consented to – something we turn to in the next chapter, which explores the doctrine of sources.[70]

The turn to positivism in both disciplines rests on the claim that it is possible to discover the objective truth about politics and law and a further claim about how to do so (the development of a positivist methodology). The totalising nature of these claims, the exclusion of ethics and the separation of law and politics have come, and continue to come, under severe criticism. It is not that their basic insights (that power or consent matter) are misguided. Instead, critics have focused on the ontological and epistemological assertions that they ally to such insights.[71] The scientific 'discovery' of the enduring character of the sovereign state, or of international anarchy, or of state consent as the source of law, or of the subjective or illusory nature of ethics is built into the assumptions of both sets of positivists and then placed beyond critical scrutiny. These assertions are both theoretically suspect and politically damaging. They limit our understanding of the content of and the potential for justice in a legalised world order.

The re-emergence of interdisciplinary thinking about law and politics has two primary springs. The first is a series of political and legal developments that feed into the concept of legalisation. Familiar concepts in contemporary IR scholarship include globalisation, transnationalism, institutionalism and complex interdependence. All explore the multi-layered nature of contemporary international organisations. In cross-disciplinary legal scholarship the emphasis on transnational legal processes and transgovernmental networks, the emergence of non-state actors as both the subjects and the creators of law, and on the effect of legalisation on compliance with global norms offers good reasons to reconsider the importance of international law to the globalised international community. The image of a globalised and legalised world order fundamentally challenges some of the core assumptions of the realist–positivist disciplinary divide. A new, but now largely empiricist, liberalism (neo-liberalism or liberal institutionalism) described legalisation as a particular form of institutionalism. Legalisation, argues a classic expression of the genre, varies across institutions but can be observed along three dimensions:

> *Obligation* means that states or other actors are bound by a rule or commitment or by a set of rules or commitments. Specifically, it means that they are *legally* bound by a rule or commitment in the sense that their behavior thereunder is subject to scrutiny under the general rules, procedures, and discourse of international law, and often of domestic law as well. *Precision* means that rules unambiguously define the conduct they require, authorize, or proscribe. *Delegation* means that third parties have been granted authority to implement, interpret, and apply the rules; to resolve disputes; and (possibly) to make further rules.[72]

Despite wide variation across these dimensions in various regimes and institutions each example 'represents the decision in different issue-areas to impose international legal constraints on governments'.[73] This reinvigorated liberalism challenged the view that the high politics of nation-states should be the sole focus of analysis, showed how partially globalised laws and institutions altered both incentives and preferences in global politics,[74] and pointed to the normative ambition inherent in a legal order drawn from a plurality of formal and informal sources.[75] Updating the classic epithet of IR, several authors proclaimed that 'law is the continuation of political intercourse with the addition of other means'.[76]

The liberal legalisation approach has a well-developed and

established literature. The debates are still extremely fruitful and the major contributions are well presented in a number of essays and textbooks.[77] Globalisation and the rise of neo-liberalism form an essential background to our project in this book. But, like realism, neo-liberalism was a largely positivist approach to IR.[78] Its insights were essential to the possibility of an inter- or transdisciplinary approach to the politics of international law, but it did not have the tools to support an exploration of international justice. We should be clear: positivist approaches to IR and international law are still strikingly dominant, especially in the US academy. Nevertheless, the last few decades have also seen fundamental challenges to the claims, in IR and international law, that objective descriptivism was necessary (or possible).

The insights gained from the study of globalisation and legalisation did not simply entail a remapping of the processes of international relations. At a rather more abstract, but more fundamental, level the assumptions of positivist IR were challenged by a range of approaches loosely grouped together under the title reflectivism.[79] Reflectivism is a term that covers a broad range of contending theoretical approaches to IR. Under this umbrella we find social constructivism, post-modernism and critical theory (and their many variations). In a classic essay on the rise of reflectivism Ole Waever, citing three of the leading figures in the emergence of the debate, presented the shared basis of reflectivism:

> Reflectivists, according to Keohane, are characterised by emphasising interpretation, the reflections of the actors as central to the institutions. Norms and regimes cannot be studied positivistically but have to be seen as inter-subjective phenomena only researchable by non-positivist methods (Kratochwil and Ruggie 1996). Institutions are not something actors rationally construct following from their interests, since they act in meta-institutions (such as the principle of sovereignty) which create the actors rather than the other way round. Institutions and actors constitute each other mutually.[80]

Reflectivism, also known as post-positivism, has had a significant impact on the study of IR and international law. The shared view that institutions and actors constitute each other challenged scholars to review assumptions about the nature of both actors and institutions. Recognising that institutions such as sovereign states, self-help and power politics are not natural or essential aspects of anarchy famously led Alexander Wendt to argue that 'anarchy is what states make of it'.[81] The idea that the political and legal horizons of the world were not fixed prised open a vital space for normative reflection. Post-positivism has both radical (or critical) and constructivist traditions. Some post-positivists wage 'post-structuralist guerrilla war against the system'.[82] Here post-modernists and critical theorists show how legal norms and institutions, as well as the dominant modes of studying them, control the social agenda and hide the hegemonic realities of law and politics under the veil of universality.[83] The deconstruction of the established truths of theory and practice moves the focus from 'problem-solving theory' to 'critical theory'.[84] Studying the existing system accurately and learning to apply existing norms strategically is not sufficient. Instead, we are urged to ask how that system came about, what inequality it entrenches and how it might be otherwise. Other post-positivists are not committed to the project of deconstruction, but are thought of as social constructivists. Recognising the socially constituted nature of international politics and law, constructivists show that the dynamics of both are therefore different from that presented by the rationalists. The social constructivist project has been described as a 'middle way' between the positivist and post-positivist approach.[85] In some cases this is appropriate because the project is to show how existing norms and institutions arise and evolve through socially constitutive processes. Alexander Wendt shows that 'causal depth' requires that we embed an account of the law 'within broader historical contexts that construct its elements (preferences, beliefs and so on)'.[86] In the legalisation debates Martha Finnemore and Stephen Toope show that the institutionalists capture only what they term 'legal bureaucratization', and argue that legal normativity is to be found beyond the institutional, as narrowly defined, in the practices, traditions and beliefs of societies.[87] Their 'richer view of politics and law' urges us to look beyond treaty law to customary law, to consider law as process and to take account of interstitial law: 'the implicit rules operating in and around explicit normative frameworks'.[88] The requirement that we seek legal normativity in broader social normative enquiry is simply to acknowledge 'part of what is going on in institutional design'.[89] But there is, as most (if not all) constructivists recognise, a third use of the term normative involved in the analysis. A focus on social norms leads us to a discussion of 'normative desirability',[90] to think about legitimacy and justice: the normative in the moral or ethical sense. As Finnemore and Toope point out:

Legal claims are legitimate and persuasive only if they are rooted in reasoned argument that creates analogies with past practice, demonstrates congruence with the overall systemic logic of existing law and attends to the contemporary social aspirations of the larger moral fabric of society.[91]

The politics of international law is intimately tied up with the debates surrounding the right, the good, the just, the legitimate. Indeed, Wendt's critique of the rational design model of international law points out that all the really interesting political questions are closed to the rationalist. Exploring the question of institutional legal design Wendt wrote:

(1) Who should be the designer? In most cases states are the designers. Is this a good thing? What about those affected by international institutions? (2) What values should states pursue in their designs? Wealth? Power? Justice? (3) For whom should states pursue these values? Nations? Civilisations? Humanity? (4) What should be their time horizon? Should states care about future generations, and if so at what discount rate? (5) Should institutional designs focus on outcomes or procedure? In sum what constitutes 'the good' in a given situation to which designers should be aspiring?[92]

Wendt acknowledges that these questions fall outside the domain of social science and fall into the realm of normative political and international theory, but he also acknowledges, as every constructivist or constitutive theory must, that such a separation is seriously problematic.[93] Political theory is not an alternative to political science; rather, the exploration of the normative is essential to a complete understanding of the social and political. Christian Reus-Smit argues that paying attention to the social norms that underpin the constitutional structure of international society underwrites a renewed focus on normative and ethical issues that enable us to move towards a more emancipatory or critical constructivism.[94] It is here that this book makes its contribution to the debates. Exploring the claims to justice and injustice enables us to think critically about normative desirability and normative authority.

The critical approach to normativity that the turn to reflectivism underwrites is too diverse to characterise simply. Critical theorists, post-modernist, constructivists, feminists, post-colonial theorists, analytic normative political theorists and the English School have all returned to questions of normative desirability and authority. These arguments form the substance of our examination of the law in the following chapters. The normative turn encourages those interested in politics and law to regain a critical perspective on the structures and practices of world affairs. But this return to questions of justice and ethics more generally does not imply a return to the traditional preoccupations of moral philosophy or natural law theory. The critiques of positivism were simultaneously critiques of foundationalism. Most contemporary theories of justice are resolutely post-foundational or post-metaphysical. The core of the critique of positivism was the recognition that positivism made some crucial assumptions and effectively hid them from view. These assumptions were epistemological, but they had significant political implications, offering partial or biased starting points. However, the modernist 'heroic practice' of hiding politically significant predicates in the foundations of an argument was attributable to most of the moral and political traditions of modernity.[95] Many traditions fell foul of the anti-foundationalist analysis. Their premises were shown to contain untested and often culturally or politically biased concepts. Historical perspective enables us to understand the influence of, for example, the European conviction that there was a God-given duty to take religion and civilisation to the new world. The critique of bad foundations in social science goes further to show how so many of the 'truth' claims we make entrench bias and inequity. The force of this recognition is central to the continued rejection of many of the moral and ethical–legal arguments that were characteristic of the pre-positivist era. Instead of returning to natural law theory or to enlightenment philosophy, contemporary political theory (a term that embraces a multitude of positions) self-consciously attempts to ground normative claims on arguments that are not partial or biased. One approach to this task is common across the range of ethical and political traditions, and creates further links between international law and international political theory.

While we must recognise that international law is just one more mode of social interaction (and that its claims to normative authority must be critically appraised as such), we must also recognise that it has distinctive characteristics that are enormously significant for this enterprise. As Reus-Smit points out:

> recognising that politics has constituted the international legal system, but is in turn transformed by that system, is crucial if

we are to comprehend one of the most important features of international law – its discourse of institutional autonomy. The fact is that international political actors behave as though the legal realm is separate from the political . . . [this] has encouraged states and non-state actors to imagine a realm of institutionalised action in which certain 'political' types of behaviour are foreclosed and other 'legal' types are licensed and empowered.[96]

The politics of international law is the crucible of moral and political debate. Positions within this debate are more likely to be considered valid if they relate to the institutions, doctrines and practices of the existing international legal order. The further a claim to normative authority or desirability gets from established claims the harder it is to defend and justify it. This does not mean that we can read the just out of the established legal order. It will become clear in the remaining chapters that many of the most fundamental ideas in international legal doctrine are coming under severe pressure as their desirability and authority is questioned. The ways that the international community responds to this pressure also require critical scrutiny. Attempts to modify or amend the law or ad hoc, unilateral action by powerful states can be just as dangerous as attempts to rigidly enforce existing law. It is clear that we need to develop the critical tools to help us to make these judgements.

A key reason why IR scholarship and international law scholarship has a limited interest in questions of justice is found in the well-established view of international society, and thus of international law, as a rather primitive, or immature, form of society and law. Thomas Franck, in an article titled 'Is Justice Relevant to the International System?', argues that:

> the exposed role of legitimacy and the minimal role of justice distinguish the international rule system from its domestic counterparts. It is not entirely an agreeable task to argue that justice is largely irrelevant to the international rule system, but it is necessary to do so if the dynamic of that system is to be understood, studied and gradually reformed.[97]

His argument, which resonates with much of the constructivist and English School literature, is that the principal agents of international society (states) prioritise certainty, predictability and order over justice. He argues that there is a greater incidence of voluntary compliance with rules that are perceived as emerging through legitimate process than with rules that are based on normative claims concerning justice or injustice. Justifications based on legitimacy and justice share a common structure. The extent to which a rule exerts a compliance pull depends on the strength of the shared communal standards that underpin those claims. However, 'while there is considerable agreement on what makes an international rule or institution legitimate, a common measure of justice is still in its most rudimentary stage of evolution in the global community'.[98] This set of ideas has significant support in the literature. Key debates in the English School centre on the relevance of order versus justice to international actors.[99] Constructivists, although recently engaged with the idea of international society, still appear reluctant to engage with questions of justice rather than legitimacy.[100] Even political theorists, whose primary interest is in questions of justice, present questions of international justice as 'perplexing and underdeveloped',[101] and, most famously in contemporary political theory, as distinct from questions of domestic justice.[102] Very little of this literature denies that justice is a relevant category or standard. Nevertheless, the intransigence of the international system in the face of urgent claims about justice and (more often) injustice is thought to be an unfortunate, but inevitable element of the study of international affairs.

Recent developments in constructivist and English School theory and in normative international political theory offer to strengthen the relationship between the theory of international society and international law, on the one hand, and the theories of international justice, on the other. For scholars such as Andrew Hurrell, Richard Falk, Christian Reus-Smit or Terry Nardin the international rule of law has matured to the point where moral and ethical considerations have an essential, although not dominant, role in the analysis of the justice and legitimacy of the international legal order.[103] Their work opens an important dialogue with both IR and international law scholarship. More boldly still, political theorists, such as Fernando Téson or Allen Buchanan, argue that the international legal order has to respond to the centrality of human rights claims, which have come to be seen as the core of a justice-based account of institutional legitimacy.[104]

Key to these projects is the relationship between claims about law and arguments about ethics. Ethical claims gain traction because they relate to the institutional practices of a shared international sociopolitical project. For Andrew Hurrell 'tackling the problem of moral accessibility' means that:

arguments need to be related to the values, patterns of argument and normative structures of both international society and global society as part of a broad process of public justification and persuasion.[105]

Importantly, this point of view is not restricted to the constructivists of the English School. Buchanan's neo-Kantian cosmopolitan theory also accepts the discipline of working within the normative structures of international society. In setting up his moral theory of international law he argues that:

> The requirement of moral accessibility signals that ... ideal theory's principles can be satisfied or at least seriously approximated through a process that begins with the institutions and culture we now have.[106]

What gets these theories off the ground is not an abstraction from the legally and sociologically normative, but an active engagement with the norms of international society. Indeed, normative justification is itself the product of what Buchanan refers to as 'social moral epistemology'. For Buchanan, the interplay between norms and institutions is not a matter of 'mere legalization'[107] or merely consequentialist. Writing in the context of an argument about human rights norms and the legitimacy of global governance institutions Buchanan argues that:

> the justification of claims about the existence of human rights and the legitimacy of efforts to implement human rights is not a once-and-for-all feat of abstract philosophical reasoning; it is an ongoing process in which institutionalized, public normative reasoning plays an ineliminable role.[108]

The essence of a political theory of international law is the claim that starting from within the discourses of international society gains the theorist of justice access to what Hurrell terms 'a stable and shared framework for moral, legal and political debate', as well as 'a stable institutional framework for the idea of a global moral community'.[109] Buchanan, writing in a very different philosophical tradition, suggests that what he terms institutional moral reasoning is an essential corrective to abstract moral theorising, on the one hand, and the conservative positivism of most international law, on the other.[110] Not only can this engaged conception of moral accessibility connect international political theory with the legalisation scholarship, it offers us good reason to think it desirable to do so. The need to ground a view of normative desirability and authority in shared institutional reasoning requires us to think hard about what Reus-Smit called the institutional autonomy of international law. While it is clear that law is not separate from politics, it is nevertheless the case that a legalised politics is distinct from a non-legalised one:

> Because international law is a normative order, casting claims in the language of law associates interests and strategies with the norms of international society, conscripting the power of social opinion to one's cause. And because norms are a guide to action, defining a problem or issue as legal reduces opportunity costs by invoking standardised, socially sanctioned solutions.[111]

If normative claims are going to rely, in part, on socially sanctioned solutions, then significant work must go into critically exploring the socially sanctioned nature of key claims. In the following chapters we explore key claims concerning justice and injustice in international affairs and show that despite shared agreement over how ethical claims ought to relate to the international legal order there is still vigorous dispute over what is and is not normatively desirable and authoritative in international affairs.

Notes

1 Bull, *The Anarchical Society*, p. 71.
2 Westlake, J., *International Law*, vol. I, Cambridge, Cambridge University Press, 1904, p. 1.
3 Oppenheim, L. and Roxburg, R., *International Law: A Treatise*, vol. I, London: Longmans, 1920, p. 1. This definition has been updated in more recent editions. For instance, in Oppenheim's *International Law*, vol. 1, eds Sir R. Jennings and Sir A. Watts, 9th edn, Oxford: Oxford University Press, 1996, p. 4, international law is defined as 'the body of rules which are legally binding on States in their intercourse with each other. These rules are primarily those which govern the relations of States, but States are not the only subjects of International Law.'
4 Brierly, J. L., *The Law of Nations: An Introduction to the Law of Peace*, ed. Sir Humphrey Waldock, 6th edn, Oxford: Clarendon Press, 1963, p. 1.
5 Lauterpacht, H., *International Law, Collected Papers*, ed. Elihu Lauterpacht, Cambridge, Cambridge University Press, 1970, p. 9.

6 Slaughter, A. and Burke-White, W., 'The Future of International Law is Domestic (or, the European Way of Law)', *Harvard International Law Journal*, 47(2) (2006): 327–52.
7 Koh, H., 'Why do Nations Obey International Law?', *Yale Law Journal*, 106 (1996/7): 2599, at pp. 2607–34.
8 Blackstone, *Commentaries on the Laws of England*, p. 66. See also at: http://avalon.law.yale.edu/18th_century/blackstone_bk4ch5.asp, accessed 10 November 2011.
9 Slaughter and Burke-White, 'The Future of International Law is Domestic', p. 328; and Gross, L., 'The Peace of Westphalia, 1648–1948', *American Journal of International Law*, 42(1) (1948): 20, at p. 26.
10 Quoted in Janis, M. W, 'Jeremy Bentham and the Fashioning of International Law', *American Journal of International Law*, 78(2) (1984): 405, at p. 408.
11 Janis, 'Jeremy Bentham and the Fashioning of International Law', p. 408.
12 Jessup, P. C., *Transnational Law*, New Haven, CT: Yale University Press, 1956, p. 2.
13 Téson, F. R. 'The Kantian Theory of International Law', *Columbia Law Review*, 92 (1992): 53–102; Kaldor, M., 'The Idea of Global Civil Society', *International Affairs*, 79(2) (2003): 583, at p. 590.
14 Shaw, M. N., *International Law*, 6th edn, Cambridge: Cambridge University Press, 2008, p. 121.
15 Corbett, P. E., *The Growth of World Law*, Princeton, NJ: Princeton University Press, 1971; Berman, H. J., 'World Law', *Fordham International Law Journal*, 18 (1994/5): 1617–22.
16 Jenks, C. W., *The Common Law of Mankind*, London: Stevens, 1958.
17 Scott, S. V., *International Law in World Politics: An Introduction*, Boulder, CO: Lynne Rienner, 2004, p. 2
18 Austin, J., *The Province of Jurisprudence Determined*, ed. W. E. Rumble, Cambridge: Cambridge University Press, 1995, pp. 112, 123–4, 171 and 175.
19 Franck, T. M., *Fairness in International Law and Institutions*, Oxford: Oxford University Press, 1995, pp. 4–6.
20 Bolton, J. R., 'Is there Really Law in International Affairs?', *Transnational Law and Contemporary Problems*, 10 (2000): 1, at p. 5.
21 Aust, A., *Handbook of International Law*, Cambridge: Cambridge University Press, 1995, p. 3.
22 Austin, *Province of Jurisprudence Determined*, p. 25.
23 Austin, *Province of Jurisprudence Determined*, p. 20.
24 Bolton, 'Is there Really Law in International Affairs?', p. 2.
25 D'Amato, A., 'Is International Law Really "Law"?', *Northwestern Law Review*, 79 (1985): 1293, at p. 1296; Hart, H. L. A., *The Concept of Law*, 2nd edn, Oxford: Oxford University Press, 1994, pp. 18–49.

26 See, for instance, Malone, D. M., *International Struggle over Iraq: Politics in the United Nations Security Council 1980–2005*, Oxford: Oxford University Press, 2007, p. 55.
27 Hart, *The Concept of Law*, p. 3.
28 Fitzmaurice, G. G., 'The Foundations of the Authority of International Law and the Problem of Enforcement', *Modern Law Review*, 19(1) (1956): 1–13' D'Amato, 'Is International Law Really "Law"?', pp. 1293–4.
29 D'Amato, 'Is International Law Really "Law"?', pp. 1293–4.
30 Hunting Act 2004, *Laws of England and Wales*, ch. 37.
31 D'Amato, 'Is International Law Really "Law"?', pp. 1293–4.
32 Fitzmaurice, 'Foundations of the Authority of International Law and the Problem of Enforcement', p. 13.
33 Slaughter and Burke-White, 'The Future of International Law is Domestic', p. 339.
34 Kelsen, H., 'Sanctions in International Law under the Charter of the United Nations', *Iowa Law Review*, 31 (1945/6): 499–543.
35 Article 25 and chapter VII of the UN Charter.
36 See generally de Wet, E., *The Chapter VII Powers of the United Nations Security Council*, Oxford: Hart, 2004.
37 Henkin, L., *How Nations Behave*, 2nd edn, New York: Columbia University Press, 1979, p. 47.
38 Williams, G., 'International Law and the Controversy Concerning the Word "Law"', *British Year Book of International Law*, 22 (1945): 146, at p. 155.
39 Bull, *The Anarchical Society*, p. 13.
40 Bull, *The Anarchical Society*, pp. 23–50.
41 Jennings, R. and Watts, A. (eds), *Oppenheim's International Law*, vol. 1, 9th edn, New York: Longman, 1996, pp. 8–16.
42 For more on the international community, see Tomuschat, C., 'Obligations Arising for States Without or Against their Will', *Recueil Des Cours*, 241 (1993-IV): 195, at pp. 209–40.
43 [1980] ICJ Rep. at 43.
44 Resolution No. 50/6, UN GAOR, para. 17 (1995).
45 de Wet, E., 'The Emergence of International and Regional Value Systems as a Manifestation of the Emerging International Constitutional Order', *Leiden Journal of International Law*, 19 (2006): 611, at p. 612.
46 de Wet, 'The Emergence of International and Regional Value Systems', pp. 612–13.
47 See UK Foreign and Commonwealth Office, Our Legal Advisers, available at: http://www.fco.gov.uk/en/about-us/who-we-are/legal-advisers, accessed 16 August 2011.
48 See US Department of State, Office of the Legal Adviser, available at: http://www.state.gov/s/l, accessed 16 August 2011.

49 The Iraq Inquiry was established by Gordon Brown, the UK Prime Minister, on 29 July 2009 under the chairmanship of Sir John Chilcot to consider the United Kingdom's involvement in Iraq from the summer of 2001 to the end of July 2009, including the way decisions were made and actions taken, to establish, as accurately as possible, what happened and to identify the lessons that could be learned.
50 See President of Russia Official Web Portal, available at: http://archive.kremlin.ru/eng/speeches/2008/07/15/1121_type82912type84779_204155.shtml, accessed 17 August 2011.
51 *R. v. Bow Street Metropolitan Stipendiary Magistrate, ex parte Pinochet Ugarte (Amnesty International Intervening)(No. 3)* (1999) 2 All ER 97.
52 Williams, 'International Law and the Controversy Concerning the Word "Law"', pp. 146–63.
53 Lipstein, K., *Principles of the Conflict of Laws: National and International*, The Hague: Kluwer Law, 1981, p. 1.
54 Jessup, *Transnational Law*, p. 2 and Koh, 'Why do Nations Obey International Law?', pp. 2624–9.
55 Thomas, K. R., 'The Changing Status of International Law in English Domestic Law', *Netherlands International Law Review*, 53(3) (2006): 371–98.
56 See Starke, J. G., 'Monism and Dualism in the Theory of International Law', *British Year Book of International Law*, 17 (1936): 66–81.
57 See Egede, E., 'Bringing Human Rights Home: An Examination of the Domestication of Human Rights Treaties in Nigeria', *Journal of African Law*, 51(2) (2007): 249–84; Egede, E., 'The New Territorial Waters (Amendment) Act 1998 – Comments on the Impact of International Law on Nigerian Law', *African Journal of International and Comparative Law*, 12 (2000): 84–104.
58 Ed. (1737) Cases t. Talb. 281.
59 [1937] AC 326.
60 Paust, J. J., *International Law as Law of the United States*, Durham, NC: Carolina Academic Press, 1996, p. 51.
61 Hurrell, A., *On Global Order: The Constitution of International Society*, Oxford: Oxford University Press, 2007, p. 304.
62 See the Preamble to the Covenant of the League of Nations.
63 Carr, *The Twenty Years Crisis*, p. 165.
64 Carr, *The Twenty Years Crisis*, p. 165.
65 Carr, *The Twenty Years Crisis*, p. 176.
66 Morgenthau, *Politics Among Nations*, pp. 283–6.
67 Morgenthau, *Politics Among Nations*, p.13.
68 Armstrong, D., Farrell, T. and Lambert, H. *International Law and International Relations*, Cambridge: Cambridge University Press, 2007, p. 69. See also F. Kratochwil, 'How do Norms Matter?', in M. Byers (ed.), *The Role of Law in International Politics: Essays in International*

    Relations and International Law, Oxford: Oxford University Press, 2000, pp. 37–43.
69 Ayer, A. J., *Language, Truth and Logic*, New York: Dover, 1936.
70 For a brief introduction to these debates see Neff, S., 'A Short History of International Law', in M. Evans (ed.), *International Law*, Oxford: Oxford University Press, 2003, ch. 1.
71 Smith. S., Booth, K. and Zalewski, M., *International Theory: Positivism and Beyond*, Cambridge: Cambridge University Press, 1996.
72 Abbott, W., Keohane, R. O., Moravcsik, A., Slaughter, A.-M. and Snidal, D., 'The Concept of Legalization', in R. O. Keohane (ed.), *Power and Governance in a Partially Globalized World*, New York: Routledge, 2002, p. 17.
73 Goldstein, J., Kahler, M., Keohane, R. and Slaughter, A.-M., 'Introduction: Legalization and World Politics', *International Organization*, 54(3) (2000): 1, at p. 2.
74 Keohane, R., *Power and Governance in a Partially Globalized World*, London: Routledge, 2002, ch. 6.
75 Koh, H., 'Why do Nations Obey International Law', in O. Hathaway and H. Koh (eds), *Foundations of International Law and Politics*, New York: Foundation Press, 2005, p. 17; Reus-Smit, C. (ed.), *The Politics of International Law*, Cambridge: Cambridge University Press, 2004.
76 Abbott *et al.*, 'The Concept of Legalization', p. 149.
77 For a very useful and comprehensive overview of the literature see Beck, R. J, 'International Law and International Relations Scholarship', in D. Armstrong (ed.), *Routledge Handbook of International Law*, Abingdon: Routledge, 2009, ch. 1. Accessible annotated anthologies include Hathaway and Koh, *Foundations of International Law*; Simmons, B. and Steinberg, R. (eds), *International Law and International Relations*, Cambridge: Cambridge University Press, 2006. Textbooks suited to IR students, include Armstrong *et al.*, *International Law and International Relations*; Cali, B., *International Law for International Relations*, Oxford: Oxford University Press, 2010.
78 Waever, O., 'The Rise and Fall of the Inter-Paradigm Debate', in S. Smith, K. Booth and M. Zalewski (eds), *International Theory: Positivism and Beyond*, Cambridge: Cambridge University Press, 1996, pp. 149–86.
79 Keohane, R., *International Institutions and State Power: Essays in International Relations Theory*, Boulder, CO: Westview, 1989. See also Smith *et al.*, *International Theory*.
80 Waever, 'The Rise and Fall of the Inter-Paradigm Debate', p. 164.
81 Wendt, A., 'Anarchy is What States Make of It: The Social Construction of Power Politics', *International Organization*, 46 (1992): 395.
82 Waever, 'The Rise and Fall of the Inter-Paradigm Debate', p. 169.
83 Paulus, A., 'International Law and International Community', in

D. Armstrong (ed.), *Routledge Handbook of International Law*, Abingdon: Routledge, 2009, pp. 44–54.
84 Cox, R., 'Social Forces, States and World Orders: Beyond International Relations Theory', *Millennium: Journal of International Studies*, 10(2) (1981): 129.
85 Checkel, J., 'International Norms and Domestic Politics: Bridging the Rationalist–Constructivist Divide', *European Journal of International Relations*, 3(4) (1997): 473–95; Adler, E., 'Seizing the Middle Ground: Constructivism in World Politics', *International Relations*, 3(3) (1997): 319–63.
86 Wendt, A., 'Driving with the Rearview Mirror: On the Rational Science of Institutional Design', in B. Simmons and R. Steinberg (eds), *International Law and International Relations*, Cambridge: Cambridge University Press, 2006, pp. 403–25.
87 Finnemore, M. and Toope, S., 'Alternatives to "Legalization": Richer Views of Law and Politics', in B. Simmons and R. Steinberg (eds), *International Law and International Relations*, Cambridge: Cambridge University Press, 2006, pp. 188–204.
88 Finnemore and Toope, 'Alternatives to "Legalization"', p. 188.
89 Wendt, 'Driving with the Rearview Mirror', p. 413.
90 Wendt, 'Driving with the Rearview Mirror', p. 418. See also Hurrell, *On Global Order*, p. 85.
91 Finnemore and Toope, 'Alternatives to "Legalization"', p. 195.
92 Wendt, 'Driving with the Rearview Mirror', p. 442.
93 Wendt, 'Driving with the Rearview Mirror', p. 442.
94 Price, R. and Reus-Smit, C., 'Dangerous Liaisons? Critical International Theory and Constructivism', *European Journal of International Relations*, 4(3) (1998): 259–94.
95 Ashley, R., 'Untying the Sovereign State: A Double Reading of the Anarchy Problematique', *Millennium: Journal of International Studies*, 17(2) (1988): 227–62.
96 Reus-Smit, *The Politics of International Law*, pp. 36–7.
97 Franck, T., 'Is Justice Relevant to the International Legal System?', *Notre Dame Law Review*, 64 (1989): 945.
98 Franck, 'Is Justice Relevant to the International Legal System?', p. 947.
99 Bull, *The Anarchical Society*; Hurrell, *On Global Order*; Jackson, R., *The Global Covenant*, Oxford: Oxford University Press, 2003; Foot, R., Gaddis, J. L. and Hurrell, A. (eds), *Order and Justice in International Relations*, Oxford: Oxford University Press, 2003.
100 Reus-Smit, *The Politics of International Law*, ch. 1.
101 Nagel, T., 'The Problem of Global Justice', *Philosophy and Public Affairs*, 33(2) (2005): 113–47.
102 Rawls, J., *The Law of Peoples*, Cambridge, MA: Harvard University Press, 1999.

103 Hurrell, *On Global Order*; Falk, R., 'The Grotian Quest', in S. Mendlovitz, F. Kratochwil and R. Falk (eds), *International Law: A Contemporary Perspective*, Boulder, CO: Westview, 1985, pp. 36–42; Reus-Smit, *The Politics of International Law*; Nardin, T., 'International Pluralism and the Rule of Law', *Review of International Studies*, 26(5) (2000): 96–110; Nardin, T., 'Theorizing the International Rule of Law', *Review of International Studies*, 34 (2008): 385–401.

104 Téson F., *A Philosophy of International Law*, Boulder, CO: Westview, 1998; Buchanan, A., *Justice, Legitimacy and Self-Determination: Moral Foundations for International Law*, Oxford: Oxford University Press, 2004; Buchanan, A., *Human Rights, Legitimacy and the Use of Force*, Oxford: Oxford University Press, 2010.

105 Hurrell, *On Global Order*, p. 303.

106 Buchanan, *Justice, Legitimacy and Self-Determination*, p. 38.

107 Buchanan, *Human Rights*, p. 91.

108 Buchanan, *Human Rights*, pp. 5–6.

109 Hurrell, *On Global Order*, p. 303.

110 Buchanan, *Justice, Legitimacy and Self-Determination*, pp. 14–70.

111 Reus-Smit, *The Politics of International Law*, p. 38.

CHAPTER TWO

Sources of International Law **Normative Authority and the Sources of International Law**

Most introductory texts on public international law will have an early chapter on the sources of law. To a reader coming from outside the law, particularly a reader interested in the grand questions of global affairs, this may seem a little formal. On one level it is. The doctrine of the sources is very much a professional vocabulary, an attempt to formalise and standardise international law.[1] We will return to this as a description of the doctrine of sources below. On the other hand, an account of the sources of law is also a description of the object of our study – not just of international law *per se*, but of the community in which this law is developed and applied. Think about the questions the concept of sources asks us. As we ask 'where can we find the law?' we are beginning to learn the techniques necessary to understand the law. But when we link this question to another and ask 'who makes law and how?' we are doing something more. We are thinking about what H. L. A. Hart termed the secondary rules of law – the rules that tell us how law is created and altered.[2] Legal rules are authoritative because they arise in a certain way. At the most basic level the doctrine of the sources tells us that rules arise primarily from the consent of states as expressed in treaty and custom. The rules of treaty and custom are themselves the subject of detailed analysis and specification. It is certainly the case that there are disputes about elements of treaty law and of customary law, but the idea that there are authoritative sources of law is an attempt to specify the legitimate authors of law and legitimate law-creating practice and to rule out other illegitimate sources.

State practice and state consent create law. Other social practices, religious, moral, cultural or political do not.

In our brief overview of Article 38(1) of the statute of ICJ we see the dominance of this standardised view. In our exploration of treaty and custom, of soft law and superior norms, in the role of courts and non-state actors in law creation we find this doctrine challenged in many subtle ways. Broadly, these challenges arise because the description of the international community that the formal doctrine of sources relies upon is very stylised. The doctrine of the sources appears at a very specific period in the history of international law in the immediate aftermath of the First World War. Article 38(1) of the ICJ was taken from Article 38 of the statute of the Permanent Court of International Justice (PCIJ) that was established under Article 14 of the Covenant of the League of Nations in 1920. This articulation of the sources of law was a statement of intent, a claim about what the law should be in a post-war order. Spiermann, citing Allot and Anghie, notes in his exploration of the rise of the international judiciary, that:

> In Professor Philip Allot's view the Permanent Court was one among 'many previous attempts at international pseudo-constitutionalism'. But, to use the words of another commentator, 'somewhat ironically . . . [state-sovereignty] was upheld and celebrated by institutions [such as the Permanent Court] that had been created in the hope that they could somehow curtail sovereignty'.[3]

The doctrine of the sources combined conservative elements (entrenching a 'Westphalian' conception of sovereign equality at the root of international law) with the ambition of making international law formally identifiable, determinate and, above all, distinct from politics and philosophy. The specification of sources is intended to determine the basis of a rules' legality. However, the place of law in society means that specifying legality without regard for other crucial social factors, such as legitimacy, power or justice, or for the historical context renders the project problematic.[4]

Sources of international law

In any society the sources of law are determined by a sometimes complex political process. For instance, in most domestic systems there is a legislature that enacts the law, an executive that implements the law and a judiciary that interprets the law. While this is a general model for modern domestic societies, this is not always so, especially for less developed societies which may not have a formal institutional framework demarcated into the three arms of government. Nevertheless, these less developed societies have their own equally complex lawmaking process. This section seeks to determine who or what the law-creating organ is for the international community. It demonstrates that although international society is embryonic in comparison with most domestic societies, it does have a law-creating mechanism perhaps more akin to that of less developed societies. It also examines specific sources of international law including treaties, customary international law and general principles of law. Here we look at the legal and political processes that result in their emergence as international law, especially the central role of states in the making of international law. We also explore the role of the courts, and non-state actors such as international organisations, NGOs, multinationational corporations (MNCs), etc. in the development of international law.

Traditionally, the starting point for discussing sources of international law is Article 38(1) of the Statute of the ICJ, which states:

> The Court, whose function is to decide in accordance with international law such disputes as are submitted to it, shall apply:
> a. international conventions, whether general or particular, establishing rules expressly recognized by the contesting states;
> b. international custom, as evidence of a general practice accepted as law;
> c. the general principles of law recognized by civilized nations;
> d. subject to the provisions of Article 59, judicial decisions and the teachings of the most highly qualified publicists of the various nations, as subsidiary means for the determination of rules of law.

However, over the years it has been suggested that there are other sources of international law not mentioned in Article 38(1).

Generally most international law textbooks seek to distinguish between formal sources, which deal with the legal procedures and methods for creation of international law, and material sources, which deal with the contents and substance of international law.[5] Dixon sought to explain this distinction by stating as follows:

the function of formal sources is to create law, the function of material sources is to identify the substance of the obligations which become law. In this sense, state practice, the practice of international organisations, the practice of non-state actors, judicial decisions, the writings of jurists and General Assembly resolutions are all material sources for they indicate what a state's obligations actually are, rather than the method by which those obligations became legally binding. Similarly, treaties may be material sources if (and this is controversial) they create 'obligations' rather than 'law'.[6]

Brownlie, however, alludes to some difficulties with maintaining this distinction.[7] Rather than adopt the above distinction we take the view that it would be clearer and more helpful to deal with the sources of international law by exploring three crucial questions: who creates international law?; where can it be found?; and how is it made?[8] The first part of this chapter will therefore adopt this format in exploring the sources of international law.

Who makes international law?

Although currently there is a plurality of actors in the international system, states are regarded as the core subject.[9] They therefore play a dominant (some would argue perhaps a sole) role in the creation of international law. A perusal of Article 38(1), referred to above, reveals that with regard to the main sources of international law – international conventions, customs and general principles – states have a preponderant role in their creation. International conventions are entered into mainly, though as we will see subsequently not exclusively, by states. The 'general practice accepted as law' that is required for a custom to be formed is the practice of states. Of course, the general principles are those recognised by states. With the crucial role of states in the formation of international law it is not surprising that realists like Carr have argued that international law is the reflection of the 'policy and interests of the dominant group in a given State at a given period'.[10]

Non-state actors, however, do play some role in law creation in international law. For the sake of clarity we distinguish between international organisations and other non-state actors. International organisations (IOs), which are key non-state actors, have a role, albeit a limited one, in the creation of international law. For instance, when permitted either explicitly or implicitly by their constituent instruments they are able to enter into treaties with states and other international organisations. According to Alvarez, 'In the standard account, the power of IOs to make law is limited by how this comes about: IO law-making power is only as extensive as those who delegated their sovereign power want it to be.'[11]

In addition, IOs also indirectly contribute to the creation of international law by acting as facilitators for the states as they exercise their law-making powers in the international system. For instance, they may establish internal organs that assist states in creating law. A ready example is the UN International Law Commission (ILC), which has as its object the promotion of the progressive development and codification of international law, and has contributed immensely in putting together draft treaties for states to consider.[12] Further, IOs may facilitate creation of international law by convening conferences attended by state representatives and other non-state actors to deliberate and negotiate in respect of certain areas of concern to the international community. For instance, the Law of the Sea Convention 1982 was the product of the Third United Nations Conference on the Law of the Sea (UNCLOS III), a conference under the auspices of the United Nations.

Also, it has been argued that certain internal organs of some IOs exercise legislative powers and therefore contribute to creation of international law.[13] For instance, with the adoption of the Security Council Resolution 1373 (2001) to combat global terrorism, certain scholars have sought to discern some sort of legislative power by the Security Council.[14] It has been argued that some General Assembly resolutions, such as the Universal Declaration of Human Rights, have normative effect.[15] However, it is contended that a closer scrutiny of this and the practice of these organs would seem to suggest that any so-called legislative tendencies of such internal organs is actually that of states acting collectively through these organs.

Some non-state actors, such as sub-states, may have treaty-making powers if so permitted by the sovereign state of which they are a part.[16] For instance, it is possible for a sub-state in a federal sovereign state to have some treaty-making powers if the federal constitution makes provision for the sub-state to have such powers. Other non-state actors, such as NGOs, MNCs and individuals, do not have a direct involvement in the creation of international law – they are unable to enter into treaties and neither do they contribute to the necessary elements for a norm to emerge as customary international law (CIL). However, these non-state actors do have an indirect influence on the creation of international law through their involvement in the adoption of soft laws, which may sometimes crystallise to hard law.[17] Examples of such soft laws include the Stockholm and Rio Declarations, adopted at the Stockholm Conference on the Human Environment 1972 and the Rio Earth Summit 1992, which have played a crucial role in shaping the development of international environmental law, and the Universal Declaration of Human Rights 1948, as well as the subsequent Vienna Declaration and Programme of Action adopted at the World Conference on Human Rights 1993, which have both played a crucial role in the development of international human rights law. While the Universal Declaration of Human Rights could be said to be mainly initiated and adopted by states and their representatives, the other declarations had a huge input from NGOs. For instance, at the Rio Earth Summit and the World Conference on Human Rights about 2,400 and 800 representatives of NGOs, respectively, were present.[18] Also, we see an involvement of multinational corporations in norm-setting for the international community in the United Nations Norms on the Responsibilities of Transnational Corporations and other Business Enterprises with regard to Human Rights, which was adopted in 2003 to provide an authoritative guide on corporate social responsibility, including the responsibilities of these business entities with regard to international human rights.[19]

Further, these non-state actors may be indirectly involved in making international law through their participation and input in major conferences that are convened with a view to adopting treaties. An example is the UNCLOS III where various non-state actors made their input either directly at the conference or through acting as consultants to government representatives. Although individuals are not in any way formally involved in making international law, they may do so informally. As states and international organisations are merely social constructs, they have to act through individuals, some of whom are able by sheer weight of personality to push forward certain positions on how international law should be developed. These charismatic individuals acting as norm entrepreneurs push forward certain norms that eventually emerge as part of international law.[20]

Subsection (d) of Article 38.1 of the Statute of the ICJ refers to the decisions of courts and the teachings of highly qualified publicists. The clause is qualified by Article 59, which reads: 'the decision of the court has no binding force except between the parties and in respect of that particular case'. This is intended to limit the creative power of the court. Is there a role for the courts in international law-making? Some have argued that since the sources of international law are located in Article 38(1) of the Statute of the ICJ, international law could be defined as what the International Court of Justice (ICJ) would apply in a given case.[21] Implicit in this is the point that the courts have a crucial role in the formation of international law. Higgins, however, argues that the view that international law is simply what the courts apply is rather narrow, and insists that international law should be identified by reference to what the actors, mainly the states, regard as such, even without the input of the ICJ.[22]

Traditionally, it is said that the courts do not make laws, but rather merely interpret and apply existing laws.[23] However, in reality the courts do sometimes make laws under the guise of interpreting and applying existing laws. For instance, arguably the courts, in determining whether a norm has emerged as customary international law, may sometimes end up actually creating such customary international law norm. For the court to accept that a norm has emerged as customary international law it has to be satisfied that the required twofold element exists, that is, the required state practices (objective element) and *opinio juris* (subjective element). However, in actuality the courts would merely explore the practice of a few states, especially those that have documented their state practice, without necessarily carrying out a wide survey of the state practice of the generality of the member states of the international community to arrive at a decision that such customary international law exists.[24] Arguably, in so doing the courts are actually imposing their view on what is customary international law. Further, in interpreting ambiguous treaty provisions the courts are meant to discern the common intention of the parties. In so doing, the courts may sometimes superimpose their views on the intention of the parties, their own notion of such intention and thereby implicitly make laws.[25]

Although, the phrase 'highly qualified publicists' is nowhere defined, it could be said to refer to jurists and academic scholars who write on international law. In the formative period of modern international law jurists, such as Grotius (who has been described as the 'Father of International Law'), Selden, Vattel and Vittoria played a significant role in its creation and development. However, presently highly qualified publicists have an almost non-existent role in law-making. Publicists merely interpret what states do.[26] However, there is no doubt that such interpretation may sometimes influence and guide states in their decision as to whether a norm of international law has emerged.

Where can I find international law and how is it created?

As has been mentioned above, it is important to also know where international law may be found and how it is created. This process is tagged by Rosalyn Higgins as 'the identification of international law'.[27] This section will examine the identification of the various sources of international law. It is pertinent to point out at this stage that the traditional view is that international law; especially the two main sources – treaties and CIL – are created as a result of the consent of states, explicit in the case of the former and implicit in the latter case.[28]

Treaties

Treaties, as one of main sources of international law, are described in Article 38 of the ICJ statute as international conventions, whether general or particular, establishing rules expressly recognised by the contesting states. The Vienna Convention on the Law of Treaties (VCLT) 1969, which has been rightly described as 'the treaty on treaties',[29] defines in Article 2(1)(a) a treaty as 'an international agreement concluded between States in written form and governed by international law, whether embodied in a single instrument or in two or more related instruments and whatever its particular designation'. This particular treaty, which was directed at regulating treaties between state actors, limits the definition to an 'Agreement between States'. However, Article 2(1)(a) of Vienna Convention on the Law of Treaties between States and International Organisations or Between International Organisations, adopted in 1986, but not yet in force, applicable to international organisations, defines a treaty as an 'an international agreement governed by international law and concluded in written form (i) between one or more States and one or more international organizations; or (ii) between international organizations, whether that agreement is embodied in a single instrument or in two or more related instruments and whatever its particular designation'. There are numerous examples of treaties entered into not only between states among themselves, but also those to which international organisations, such as the United Nations and the European Union, are parties. All that is required is for such international organisation to have the power, either explicitly or implicitly under the treaty setting it up (i.e., its constituent treaty), to do so.[30] Examples of the latter includes the Agreement Between the United Nations and the United States Regarding the Headquarters of the United Nations, signed 26 June 1947, approved by the General Assembly 31 October 1947, and the Cotonou Agreement Between the European Union and a number of African, Caribbean and Pacific States since 2000.[31]

What is clear from these definitions in the two 'treaties on treaties' and the reality of international politics is that a treaty may be either be between two or more states, between one or more states and one or more international organisations or between international organisations. Further, it does not really matter the designation of the treaty (it may be called a treaty, convention, charter, agreement, pact, covenant, etc.), as long as it is in writing either in a single document, or two or more related documents, and is intended to be governed by international law, it would be regarded as a treaty. Clearly, from this an oral agreement cannot be a treaty. In addition, an agreement whether between states, or between one or more states and one or more international organisations, or between international organisations, which is intended to be governed by domestic law is not a treaty under international law. For instance, an Agreement between the United Kingdom and Saudi Arabia for the sale of Military Jets, which is intended to be governed by either the domestic law of the United Kingdom or Saudi Arabia or some third state, would fall outside the scope of a treaty.

Treaties may be either bilateral or multilateral. Bilateral treaties are treaties between two parties, while multilateral treaties are between more than two parties.[32] Some scholars also make a distinction between treaties as mere contracts and law-making treaties. Brownlie points out that the former are treaties that create legal obligations that dissolve with the observance of such obligation. He provides the example of a treaty for jointly carrying out a single enterprise.[33] Law-making treaties, on the other hand, in his view 'create general norms for the future conduct of the parties in terms of legal propositions, and the obligations are basically the same for all parties'.[34] If the aim and purpose of the treaty, whether bilateral or multilateral, is for such obligation to disappear after the observance by the parties it is necessarily contractual. On the other hand, if it is intended to put forward general norms to regulate the future conduct of the parties for as long as it is in force, then it is legislative. Treaties that are contracts are usually bilateral; those that are law-making are in most cases multilateral.[35] Examples of the latter are the Law of the Sea Convention 1982 and the Vienna Convention on the Law of Treaties 1969.

Dixon, however, points out that the distinction between treaties that impose obligations (i.e., treaties as contracts) and those that create laws (i.e., law-making treaties) is unhelpful in certain respects, since the legal effect of all treaties, whether as contracts or law-making, are the same as only parties to such treaties are bound.[36] He, however, acknowledged that such distinction may sometimes be helpful if the idea is merely to identify the purpose and aim of the various types of treaties.[37]

Treaties are obeyed as a result of the customary international norm, *pacta sunt servanda*, which many acknowledge has attained the status of *jus cogens*. Kunz, in an article written as far back as 1945, said:

> *Pacta sunt servanda* is a customary norm of general international law, a constitutional norm of a superior rank, which institutes a particular procedure for the creation of norms of international law, namely the treaty-procedure . . . These treaty-created norms, like the contents of a contract in municipal law, have the legal reason of their obligatory force not in the manifested concord of the will of the states, but in the superior norm *pacta sunt servanda*, which orders that the manifested concord of the will of the states shall produce, through the treaty procedure, valid norms of international law.[38]

This norm has since been codified in Article 26 of the VCLT, which states that: 'Every treaty in force is binding upon the parties to it and must be performed by them in good faith.' It has been pointed out that the good faith requirement of this norm requires states not only to perform their obligations under treaties to which they have become parties, but also to refrain from acts which would defeat the object and purpose of such treaties, even prior to the coming into force of such treaties.[39]

Usually treaties are initially negotiated. This negotiation may be bilateral or multilateral, usually through diplomatic conferences. An example of such a diplomatic conference is the Third United Nations Conference on the Law of the Sea (UNCLOS III), a marathon multilateral negotiating conference that began in 1973 and finally ended in

1982 when the treaty, the Law of the Sea Convention, was adopted. At this negotiation stage a draft treaty is usually drawn up by the negotiating parties.[40] When the negotiations are completed the relevant parties adopt the draft treaty, a process called adoption. Aust points out that the 'term adoption is not defined in the Convention [VCLT], but is the formal act by which the form and content of the treaty are settled'.[41] Although the adoption of a treaty is generally not synonymous with the authentication of, or consent by, the parties to be bound by it or the entry into force of such treaty, it may sometimes be the case that the adoption of a bilateral treaty may simultaneously indicate the consent and entry into force of such treaty. According to Aust:

> Adoption of the text of a bilateral treaty is often done by initialling, though even then it may not always be easy to establish the precise time at which the text can be said to have been adopted, since the text is often not finally settled until shortly before the treaty is to be signed. In that case adoption is, in effect, by signature, which will often express also consent to be bound. This telescoping of the stages of treaty making is normal for bilateral treaties, but rare for multilateral treaties.[42]

Adoption is usually followed by the duly authorised representatives of the states at the conference appending their signature to the draft treaty.[43] The signature stage is usually followed by the consent by the state or international organisation, as the case may be, that seeks to progress to being parties to the treaty. Treaties are important to international lawyers because they provide an important and clear evidence of the consent of states to international law.[44] This consent is usually by way ratification. It is done when the competent officer sends to the depositary of the treaty (usually a state or an international organisation) its instrument of ratification. The ratification process provides an opportunity, after the signature, for a party to positively affirm its consent through its competent officer. For states such as the United Kingdom and Nigeria, the ratification is done solely by the executive arm of government. However, other states, such as the United States, share the ratification power between the executive and the legislature. In the United States, although the president and not the Senate ratifies the treaty, the former may only do so with the consent of a two-thirds majority vote of the Senate.[45] In the case of bilateral treaties, ratification is usually by the exchange of the instruments of ratification.

However, more recently for most bilateral treaties this ceremonial exchange of the instruments of ratification has been replaced by a mutual notification of the 'completion of internal or constitutional procedures'.[46]

Apart from consent by ratification, the VCLT recognises that there are other ways to express such consent: accession, this method of consent is usually used instead of ratification by a state or international organisation if for one reason or other it is unable to sign the treaty when it is adopted and such treaty actually permits accession; signature; and exchange of instrument constituting a treaty or by any other means agreed to by the state parties.[47]

After the consent stage the treaty still needs to come into force. For instance, the VCLT was ratified by the United Kingdom on 25 June 1971 and the Convention came into force on 27 January 1980.[48] Bilateral treaties usually enter into force either on signature, or on exchange of instruments of ratification, or when the parties have notified each other that all the necessary initial procedures required for the entry into force have been completed, or if the treaty provides for a particular date, it comes into force on that date.[49] Multilateral treaties make provisions on how a treaty would come into force. Generally, this is done by requiring a certain number of ratifications. The Law of the Sea Convention 1982, for example, states that: 'This Convention shall enter into force 12 months after the date of deposit of the sixtieth instrument of ratification or accession.'[50]

As a general rule treaties are only binding on parties to the treaties and not on third parties.[51] This is based on the principle of *pacta tertiis nec nocent nec prosunt* (i.e., treaties do not impose any obligations, nor confer any rights, on third states). This principle has been endorsed in various decisions of the international courts. For instance, as far back as 1925 in the *German Interests in Polish Upper Silesia* case, the Permanent Court of International Justice (PCIJ), the predecessor of the ICJ, said that a 'treaty only creates law as between States which are parties to it; in case of doubt, no rights can be deduced from it in favour of third States'.[52] The *pacta tertiis* principle has also been codified in the VCLT, which states in Article 34 that: 'A treaty does not create either obligations or rights for a third State without its consent.' For third parties such treaty is *res inter alio acta* (i.e., a treaty cannot adversely affect the rights of one that is not a party).

However, there are exceptions to the general rule that treaties are not binding on third parties. A treaty would be binding on a third party if its provisions have either codified customary international law or crystallised into customary international law; or if such third party assents to rights arising from the treaty or expressly accepts in writing the obligations arising from the treaty;[53] or if the treaty is a 'dispositive' treaty (e.g., treaties that deal with disposition of territory, such as delimitation of boundaries and cession of territory).[54]

States may enter into multilateral treaties with reservations. The VCLT defines a reservation as 'a unilateral statement, however phrased or named, made by a State, when signing, ratifying, accepting, approving or acceding to a treaty, whereby it purports to exclude or to modify the legal effect of certain provisions of the treaty in their application to that State'.[55] Reservations are particularly important in multilateral treaties, as they may bring about rather complex, multiple legal relationships between various parties to the same multilateral treaty. Dixon points out that it may bring about a situation whereby 'each party to a multilateral treaty is bound by a series of bilateral obligations, albeit under a general umbrella'.[56] Therefore, an understanding of the regime of reservations helps in appreciating that a party to a multilateral treaty's obligation may not exactly be the same as the black letter provisions of the treaty. Such party may by way of reservation either exclude or modify the legal effect of particular provisions of the treaty in relation to it. For instance, Article 10 of the International Covenant on Civil and Political Rights (ICCPR), an important human rights multilateral treaty, states as follows:

(1) All Persons deprived of their liberty shall be treated with humanity and with respect for the inherent dignity of the human person.
(2) (a) Accused persons shall, save in exceptional circumstances, be segregated from convicted persons and shall be subject to separate treatment appropriate to their status as unconvicted persons
(b) Accused juvenile persons shall be separated from adults and brought as speedily as possible for adjudication.
(3) The penitentiary system shall comprise treatment of prisoners the essential aim of which shall be their reformation and social rehabilitation. Juvenile offenders shall be segregated from adults and be accorded treatment appropriate to their age and legal status

Yet New Zealand filed the following reservation to the above provision:

> The Government of New Zealand reserves the right not to apply article 10(2)(b) or article 10(3) in circumstances where the shortage of suitable facilities makes the mixing of juveniles and adults unavoidable; and further reserves the right not to apply article 10(3) where the interests of other juveniles in an establishment require the removal of a particular juvenile offender or where mixing is considered to be of benefit to the persons concerned.[57]

Before the VCLT came into force what the effect would be of a reservation with respect to a state's consent to a multilateral treaty was unclear. Initially, the general view, based on the practice of the League of Nations, was that a state that made a reservation to a multilateral treaty could not be a party to such a treaty unless such reservation was unanimously accepted by all the other parties. Some states were of the view that this approach was rather rigid. The latter states took the view that a state that made a reservation to a multilateral treaty could be still be a party to such treaty, as long as such reservation was not incompatible with the object and purpose of the treaty.[58] This position was eventually endorsed by the ICJ in its Advisory Opinion in the *Genocide Convention (Reservations)* case,[59] and subsequently incorporated into the VCLT.

Under the VCLT a state can enter a reservation unless the reservation is prohibited by the treaty; or the treaty provides for only specified reservations, which does not include the reservation in question; or the reservation is incompatible with the object and purpose of the treaty.[60] The VCLT states the following rules on acceptance and objections in respect of reservations:

- A permitted reservation which is expressly authorised by the treaty does not require acceptance by the other parties unless the treaty so provides.
- If the application of the treaty in its entirety is an essential condition of consent of all the parties to be bound then any reservation must be accepted by the other parties.
- When the treaty is a constituent instrument of an international organisation such reservation must be accepted by the competent organ of the organisation unless the treaty otherwise provides.

- Acceptance of a reservation by another party makes the reserving state a party to the treaty in relation to that other party when the treaty comes into force for such state parties.
- An objection to a reservation by a state party does not preclude the entry into force of the treaty as between the objecting and reserving state, unless the former expresses a contrary intention.
- An act expressing a state's consent to be bound by the treaty which contains a reservation is effective as soon as one other party has accepted it.
- A reservation is deemed to have been accepted if a state does not raise an objection 12 months after it was notified of the reservation or by the date it expressed its consent to be bound whichever is later.[61]

The VCLT then goes on to enunciate complex rules on the legal effect of such acceptance and objections of such reservations. A reservation modifies for the reserving state and the accepting party the provisions of the treaty to which the reservation applies only to the extent of the reservation. It does not, however, modify the provisions of the treaty for the other parties to the treaty among themselves. When a state objecting to a reservation has not opposed the entry into force of the treaty between itself and the reserving state, the provisions to which the reservation relates do not apply as between the two states to the extent of the reservation. The latter rule has been criticised because if the intention of the reserving state is not merely to modify, but rather to exclude the provision of the treaty this rule in any event allows the reserving state to get its way.[62]

Some multilateral treaties, to avoid the complexities of this 'web of obligations' in the same treaty,[63] have adopted the practice of expressly prohibiting reservations. For instance, the Law of the Sea Convention 1982 in Article 309 states: 'No reservations or exceptions may be made to this Convention unless expressly permitted by other articles of this Convention.'

Treaties may be terminated in a number of ways such as by the provision in the relevant treaty on how it would be terminated, or by agreement of the parties or where there is a material breach of a provision that is essential to the accomplishment of the object and purpose of the treaty; it may be terminated in relation to the defaulting party; or where there is a supervening impossibility of performance or by reason of *clausula rebus sic stantibus*.[64] The latter way allows for termination of a treaty if there has been a fundamental change of circumstances not foreseen by the parties that radically transform the extent of the obligation still to be performed under the treaty.[65]

Customary international law

Customary international law is described in Article 38(1)(b) of the Statute of the ICJ as 'international custom, as evidence of a general practice accepted as law'. It has been pointed out that this would have been more correctly phrased as, 'international custom as evidenced by a general practice accepted as law'[66] or 'a general practice as evidence of an international custom accepted as law'.[67] According to Guzman, CIL is 'central to our understanding of international law' as one of the two main sources of international law, a primary source of universal law and also because the rules of the other main source – treaties – are based on the CIL rule of *pacta sunt servenda*.[68]

There are two basic conditions to be fulfilled for a rule to emerge as CIL; namely, the actual practice of states (state practice) and the subjective belief that such practice is 'law' (*opinio juris*). In essence, the basic formula for a rule to emerge as CIL is as follows: state practice + *opinio juris* = customary international law. According to the ICJ in the *North Sea Continental Shelf* cases:

> Not only must the acts concerned amount to a settled practice, but they must also be such, or be carried out in such a way, as to be evidence of a belief that this practice is rendered obligatory by the existence of a rule requiring it. The need for such a belief, i.e. the existence of a subjective element, is implicit in the very notion of the *opinio juris sive necessitates*. The States concerned must therefore feel that they are conforming to what amounts to a legal obligation. The frequency, or even habitual character, of the acts is not in itself enough. There are many international acts, e.g., in the field of ceremonial and protocol, which are performed almost invariably, but which are motivated only by considerations of courtesy, convenience or tradition, and not by any sense of legal duty.[69]

The twofold requirement for a rule to emerge as a rule of CIL has been affirmed in various ICJ decisions. For instance, in the *Libya* v. *Malta* case the ICJ emphasised that the substance of CIL must be identified 'primarily in actual practice and opinio juris of States'.[70]

Although the dual element for a rule to emerge as CIL is quite straightforward in theory, it is hugely problematic in practice.[71] As a result, CIL has been criticised by various scholars as being 'in trouble', 'under attack from all sides', 'incoherent', 'a fiction', 'a mess'[72] and in 'an unsatisfactory condition'.[73] Some have advocated for a more coherent theory of CIL,[74] while others go as far as calling for it to be eliminated as a source of international law.[75]

State practice (or *usus* or *diuturnitas*) is the objective element of CIL. It is a rather wide and flexible term and its exact scope is unclear. Dixon concludes that an attempt at a definition of state practice would be incomplete and, therefore, he settles for a rather open-ended explanation of what it is by stating that:

> state practice includes, but is not limited to, actual activity (acts and omissions), statements made in respect of concrete situations or disputes, statements of legal principle made in abstract (such as those preceding the adoption of a resolution in the General Assembly), national legislation and the practice of international organisations.[76]

Brownlie, in a similar vein, lists certain state actions and statements that may qualify as state practice, though he admitted that their value may vary depending on the circumstances.[77] Some scholars, like D'Amato, disapprove of a definition of state practice that lumps actual activity of states with their statements. They argue that state practice should be limited to action by states, while their statements may be used to deduce *opinio juris*.[78] Thirlway, on the other hand, though prepared to accept claims and statements of states as state practice, was prepared to do so only in respect of claims and statements concerning concrete situations and not merely those made *in abstracto*.[79] He stated that 'practice or usage consists of an accumulation of acts which are material or concrete in the sense that they are intended to have an immediate effect on the legal relationships of the State concerned'.[80] Others, notably Akehurst, have criticised the position of D'Amato and Thirlway.[81] Among other things, he points out that D'Amato's position is not supported by the generality of the decisions of the ICJ, which clearly show that the Court is prepared to accept states' claims and statements as evidence of state practice.[82] Apart from this, he acknowledged that his preference for having statements of states as evidence of state practice is, among other things, premised on the pragmatic political need to promote and strengthen the rule of law in international relations. In his view, since CIL can be changed only by the frequent breaking of such rule by states, to insist that the requisite practice must always be state action would encourage the weakening of the international rule of law. Rather, he pointed out that the rule of law would be better strengthened if CIL could be changed by the mere declaration of states that the old law no longer exists and had been replaced by new law.[83] He also criticises Thirlway's distinction (above). For instance, he argued that it is possible for states to make statements *in abstracto* and yet really have concrete situations in mind.[84] In an attempt to arrive at some generic definition of what state practice is, Akehurst submitted that 'State Practice covers any act or statement by a State from which views can be inferred about international law', and includes even omissions and silence on the part of states.[85] He points out that it also consists of declarations *in abstracto*, including General Assembly resolutions, national legislation, judgments of national courts, practice of international organisations and international courts. He was, however, rather reluctant to accept that the practice of private individuals could create CIL.[86] Be that as it may, what comes out clearly is the lack of clarity among scholars of international law on what exactly is state practice.

To meet the criteria for CIL there must be uniformity and consistency, as well as a generality of the state practice.[87] What is required is not complete uniformity, but rather substantial uniformity evidencing some level of consistency. Likewise, with generality, universality of practice is not required, though any such CIL would be binding on all states, including those who did not explicitly consent to it (these states are said to have tacitly agreed), except for states that have persistently objected to such rule as it was evolving as a rule of CIL (the persistent objector).[88] As long as the requirements of consistency and generality are satisfied, no particular duration is required. The duration of the practice may vary from subject to subject, though it must be mentioned that obviously a lengthy duration would provide useful evidence to support a case for consistency and generality. There are, however, cases where CIL develops over a short period of time, the so-called instant customs given prominence by Bin Cheng.[89] The ready example used for instant customs is that applicable to outer space, which developed fairly quickly.[90]

Nonetheless, the issue of state practice raises some problematic questions: how consistent, uniform and widespread should the practice be?; how many acts would suffice to constitute state practice that can generate CIL? Equally, what number of states is required to take part in a practice that would generate CIL? While the ICJ in the *North Sea Continental Shelf* cases insisted on 'a very widespread and representative' participation of states, including those whose interests are specially affected by the CIL rule,[91] this does not clarify certain problematic issues. In terms of numbers: is it fifty, sixty or 100 states that is required?[92] Which state practice should actually be given weight in the formation of CIL? Should this necessarily include that of the influential states in the world? Should it include an adequate representation of states from the different regions of the world? In this current multicultural world should it also include states representing the different cultures in the world?[93]

Opinio juris sive necessatatis (or *opinio juris*) is the subjective element of CIL. Article 38 of the Statute of the ICJ requires that the practice must be 'accepted as law'. Therefore, state practice must be accompanied by a belief that it is obligatory in order to distinguish CIL from other non-obligatory acts, such as acts of comity, friendship, morality, courtesy or mere social needs.[94]

The traditional approach with regard to *opinio juris* is quite problematic. It necessitates the belief by states that something is already law before it has actually become law.[95] Guzman, referring to D'Amato's criticism of the circuitousness of this approach, stated:

> It is said that CIL is only law if the *opinio juris* requirement is met. That is, it is only law if States believe it is law. But why would a State believe something to be law if it does not already have the requisite *opinio juris*? So it appears that *opinio juris* is necessary for there to be a rule of law, and a rule of law is necessary for there to be *opinio juris*.[96]

As a result of the complexities some have suggested that the need to prove *opinio juris* should either be abandoned or minimised to playing a the role of merely distinguishing CIL from other non-legal obligations.[97] However, despite the intricacies of this subjective element the ICJ insists that it is not only an essential requirement of CIL, but it is crucial in the creation of CIL.[98] For instance, the court said, 'for a new customary rule to be formed, not only must the acts concerned "amount to a settled practice", but they must be accompanied by the *opinio juris sive necessitates*'.[99] Some scholars have sought to deal with the circularity of the traditional approach by arguing that the two requirements for the formation of custom need not be both present at the outset, but rather *opinio juris* may emerge at a much later time in the life of the practice.[100]

Opinio juris as the subjective element is obviously not always clear-cut, especially since states are in reality artificial constructs. As far as Brownlie is concerned, the essential problem of *opinio juris* is actually one of proof. He points out that in the practice of the ICJ there are two methods of proof of this ingredient.[101] First, the ICJ assumes the existence of *opinio juris* from the evidence of the state practice, or based on the consensus of literature or previous decisions of the Court or other international tribunals. Second, in some cases that he identified as 'a significant minority of cases', the courts have been more rigorous and have required proof by more positive evidence that the states actually accept the practice as law.[102]

What comes out clearly is that the imprecision of the twofold requirement of CIL provides the courts with a lot of discretion and leeway in determining whether a rule is actually part of CIL or not, thereby leaving room, as has been mentioned above, for the thinking that courts may sometimes actually be engaging in law-making.

Jus cogens

Jus cogens (Latin for compelling law) refers to peremptory norms that are fundamental rules in the international order.[103] Articles 53 and 64 of the VCLT states that:

> A treaty is void if, at the time of its conclusion, it conflicts with a peremptory norm of general international law. For the purposes of the present Convention, a peremptory norm of general international law is a norm accepted and recognized by the international community of States as a whole as a norm from which no derogation is permitted and which can be modified only by a subsequent norm of general international law having the same character.
>
> If a new peremptory norm of general international law emerges, any existing treaty which is in conflict with that norm becomes void and terminates.

Some scholars identify *jus cogens* norms as part of CIL, albeit a higher form.[104] Others distinguish between the two.[105] For instance, in support of the latter view Janis argues that the 'distinctive character essence of *jus cogens* is such … as to blend the concept into traditional notions of natural law'.[106] He points out that it is 'a legal emanation which grew out of the naturalist school, from those who were uncomfortable with the positivists' elevation of the state as the sole source of international law'.[107] Lauterpacht, on the other hand, took the view that it was part of the general principles of law. As Special Rapporteur on the Law of Treaties in his report to the International Law Commission, he said: '[*Jus cogens*] may be expressive of rules of international morality so cogent that an international tribunal would consider them as forming part of those principles of law generally recognized by civilized nations which the International Court of Justice is bound to apply.'[108]

From the definition of the VCLT some points are apparent. For a norm to be *jus cogens* it must be accepted and recognised as such by the international community of states as a whole. Clearly, from this the states have the sole responsibility for creating these fundamental norms. Further, no derogation from *jus cogens* norms are permitted and rules, whether conventional or custom-based, that derogate from these fundamental norms are void.[109] Also, these *jus cogens* norms may be modified only by a subsequent norm of the same nature. What, however, is not clear is the exact scope of the substantive rules that may be classed as *jus cogens*. The generally accepted examples of *jus cogens* are: *pacta sunt servanda*; the prohibitions on the aggressive use of force;[110] genocide;[111] slavery; torture and racial discrimination.[112] Other potential candidates are: the principles of self-determination of peoples; permanent sovereignty over natural resources and the common heritage of mankind; and the prohibition on the acquisition of sovereignty over the international seabed area and outer space.[113] The idea that there are some substantive principles that are beyond state consent is a fascinating element of international law and forms part of our exploration of the evolving nature of international justice below.

Another, point of interest is the relationship between *jus cogens* and *erga omnes* rules.[114] In the *Barcelona Traction* case, the ICJ explains the latter rule as follows:

> An essential distinction should be drawn between the obligations of a State towards the international community as a whole, and those arising vis-à-vis another State in the field of diplomatic protection. By their very nature the former are the concern of all States. In view of the importance of the rights involved, all States can be held to have a legal interest in their protection; they are obligations *erga omnes*.[115]

Although the two concepts are clearly interrelated they are not necessarily coterminous. All *jus cogens* rules are necessarily *erga omnes*, but not all *erga omnes* rules are *jus cogens*. The universal, communal and hierarchical nature of *erga omnes* or *jus cogens* are the source of much controversy and we explore the political implication of such norms below.

The relationship between treaty and customary law

The relationship between the two main sources of international law – customs and treaties – has generated keen interest, among other things, because of the practical effect this may have in determining whether or not obligations arising in a treaty are binding on third party states. If provisions of a treaty are merely conventional they would bind only parties to the treaty. On the other hand, if they are not only conventional provisions, but are also simultaneously rules of customary international law they would also bind non-party states. This custom–treaty relationship has received judicial endorsement in several ICJ decisions. For instance, the ICJ in the *Nicaragua* case pointed out that the regulation of the use of force under the UN Charter exists concurrently with the regulation of this same issue under CIL.[116] The court in this case pointed out as follows:[117]

> The existence of identical rules in international treaty law and customary law has been clearly recognized by the Court in the *North Sea Continental Shelf* cases. To a large extent, those cases turned on the question whether a rule enshrined in a treaty also existed as a customary rule, either because the treaty had merely codified the custom, or caused it to 'crystallize', or because it influenced its subsequent adoption.

Baxter, in a widely cited article, points out that a multilateral treaty may be regarded as declaratory of CIL in two main senses. First, if it incorporates and gives recognition to existing CIL (i.e., codification) and, second, if the treaty provision amounts to progressive development of international law, but subsequently secures the general assent of states and becomes transformed into CIL.[118] For a rule to emerge in the latter case as CIL it must be of a fundamentally norm-creating character such as could be regarded as forming the basis of a general rule of law; enjoy a very widespread and representative participation in the treaty, including the participation of states whose interests are specially affected; enjoy extensive and general uniformity of state practice, evidencing a recognition that a legal obligation is involved and the passage of time, though on certain occasions this may actually be a short period of time.[119]

Other sources of law

Article 38(1)(c) of the Statute of the ICJ refers to 'the general principles of law recognised by civilised nations'. The phrase 'civilised nations', it has been pointed out was included because the intention was to prevent a general principle recognised by developed principal legal systems from being disqualified as such because they were not so regarded by undeveloped legal systems.[120] This phrase is, however, now obsolete. The phrase 'general principles of law' has been interpreted in divergent ways by scholars. For some scholars, it merely affirms natural law concepts. Others regard it as adding nothing new to treaties and CIL, which are the only true sources of law because they reflect the consent of states. They merely regard general principles as being ancillary to treaties and CIL. In other words, for these scholars a rule will be regarded as a general principle of law only if it is part of either a treaty or CIL. Another view, which appears to be the preferred view, is that it refers to rules and principles common to all principal municipal legal systems (e.g., fair hearing, rules of equity, concept of separate legal personality of limited liability companies, estoppel, violation of an engagement involves an obligation to make reparation, *res judicata*, good faith) and is borrowed by the international system, and applied because there is a gap in conventional and customs rules resulting in no applicable law to cover a particular situation (*non liquet*).[121]

While there is no indication of hierarchy as between treaties, customs and general principles of law under Article 38 of the Statute of the ICJ,[122] the description of judicial decisions and the writings of jurists as 'subsidiary means for the determination of rules of law', indicates that the latter are not regarded as having as much weight as the other sources of law listed.

In the international system the decisions of the courts have no binding force, except as between the particular parties and in respect of the particular case before the court. In practice, most international courts would generally follow their previous decisions to avoid arbitrariness and to achieve some level of certainty in their decision-making.

Generally, states that appear before these courts cite the previous decisions of the court to support their position. Moreover, scholars constantly cite the decisions of these courts in seeking to explain the various principles of international law.[123] Again, while technically the decisions of these courts are not intended to create international law, in reality in the exercise of their interpretative powers they exercise immense powers in determining the exact scope of international law.[124]

Article 38(1) does not make any distinction between international and municipal courts. Municipal courts also play a role in law creation in the exercise of their interpretative powers. For instance, the *Pinochet* cases decided by the then House of Lords (now the Supreme Court) of the United Kingdom has contributed immensely to the development of the law of sovereign immunity.[125] Again, such municipal decisions could be said to be part of state practice that contribute to the development of CIL in a particular area.

As noted above, while the writings of jurists may have played a crucial role in the creation of international law at the onset, it is doubtful that it currently makes any significant contribution to the creation of international law. However, again like judicial decisions, it can be said that the writings of jurist play an incidental role in law creation, since they may sometimes influence states in their decision on whether a particular rule is a rule of international law.

Wolfke identified the current role of publicists as the 'analysis of facts and opinions and in drawing conclusions on binding customary rules and on trends of their evolution'.[126] He, however, pointed out that such 'conclusions, like all generalisations of this kind, involve unrestricted supplementation by introducing elements lacking and hence, a creative factor. Further, by attracting attention to international practice and appraising it, the writers indirectly influence its further evolution, that is the development of customs.'[127]

Sometimes a position a jurist takes on a particular position of international law may also provide states with a theoretical basis to support their position on what exactly is international law. A ready example are the writings of Professor Greenwood and Professor Ruth Wedgwood, who have written several articles supporting the position of the United States that the unilateral pre-emptive use of force may be justified in certain circumstances.[128]

Sources of international law outside Article 38 (1) of the Statute of the ICJ

Some scholars have argued in favour of further sources of international law outside the framework of Article 38 of the Statute of the ICJ.[129] While there are a number of potential contenders, the following exploration of sources of international law outside Article 38 is not intended to be an exhaustive list, but is merely illustrative of ongoing debate on whether there are sources beyond the traditional sources.

An exploration of whether UN General Assembly resolutions are a source of international law is particularly important because the General Assembly as the plenary body of the United Nations, a truly global international organisation, consisting of almost universal membership of 193 states, has immense normative weight.[130] Thakur identifies the General Assembly as the 'normative centre of gravity' of the United Nations and the 'only authentic voice' of the international community.[131] Despite this, the UN Charter makes it clear that these resolutions are only recommendatory and not binding upon states.[132] An attempt to vest this plenary body with legislative competence by the Philippines delegation at the San Francisco Conference through the following proposal was roundly defeated:

> The General Assembly should be vested with the legislative authority to enact rules of international law which should become effective and binding upon the members of the Organization after such rules have been approved by a majority vote of the Security Council. Should the Security Council fail to act on any of such rules within a period of thirty (30) days after submission thereof to the Security Council the same should become effective and binding as if approved by the Security Council.[133]

Clearly, the founders intended the General Assembly to be merely a deliberative organ and not a legislative one. Its resolutions, as a general rule, would be binding only in respect of the internal workings of the UN, such as approval of the budget of the organisation and the elections of members of the various UN organs. In an effort to take advantage of the crucial role of the General Assembly as an important forum where states from various geographical regions, cultures and ideology, each having one vote based on the principle of sovereign equality, gather,[134] its resolutions, while not in themselves international legislation, may play a crucial part in discerning CIL on a particular matter. Although, there is some controversy about whether or not CIL can actually be discerned from General Assembly resolutions,[135] scholars such as Asamoah point out that though General Assembly resolutions 'are not the source of the validity of the rules, but [they] are evidence of customary international law, whose formal validity derives from subsequent practice of States'.[136]

Initially, it was clear that Security Council resolutions though binding could not be regarded as one of the sources of international law because they were not of general applicability. Rather, they were ad hoc and usually directed against specific delinquent state(s) or situations.[137] However, this appears to have changed with the growing proclivity of the Security Council, in dealing with post-9/11 terrorism, to adopt resolutions that actually have general and abstract character. Examples here include Security Council Resolution 1373 (2001), which is an anti-terrorism measure, and Resolution 1540 (2004), which seeks to control the proliferation of weapons of mass destruction.[138] It has been said that with these resolutions the Security Council has 'entered its legislative phase'.[139] However, what is clear is if the Council exercises 'legislative' or 'quasi-legislative' powers this must be done within its remit under the UN Charter of maintaining international peace and security.[140]

Another controversial 'source' of law is found in many of the instruments of public international law. The Martens clause was introduced into international relations by the Russian delegate, Fyodor Fyodorovich de Martens, during the 1899 Hague Peace Conference. It was intended to be a diplomatic ploy to arrive at a compromise between the great powers and the lesser powers represented at the conference on the issue of whether those who resisted an occupying power were to be regarded as criminals or lawful combatants.[141] The clause was inserted in the Preamble to the 1899 Hague Convention II containing the Regulations on the Laws and Customs of War on Land and reads as follows:

> Until a more complete code of the laws of war is issued, the High Contracting Parties think it right to declare that in cases not included in the Regulations adopted by them, populations and belligerents remain under the protection and empire of the principles of international law, as they result from the usages established between civilized nations, from the laws of humanity, and the requirements of the public conscience.

This clause has appeared in subsequent treaties, including the Hague Convention IV containing the Regulations on the Laws and Customs of War on Land; the Four Geneva Conventions 1949, and the Additional Protocols of 1977; and the Convention on Prohibitions or Restrictions on the Use of Certain Conventional Weapons Which May be Deemed to be Excessively Injurious or to Have Indiscriminate Effects 1980, in various permutations. Reference has also been made to this clause in various national and international court decisions.[142] The constant reference to the Martens clause in both treaties and court decisions has led to debate on its status. For some scholars the clause introduced two new sources of international law: the principles of humanity and the dictates of public conscience.[143] On the other hand, other scholars hold the view that the clause is too vague, ambiguous and indeterminate to be properly referred to as a new source of international law. Rather, it is a non-legal norm that has motivated the development of international humanitarian law and serves as a useful interpretative aid for rules of international law.[144]

There is also the notion of 'soft law' as a source of international law. There are several definitions of soft law.[145] It could be said to be normative instruments that fall short of treaties, but play a key role in shaping the behaviour of states and other non-state actors in the international system, and may sometimes evolve into hard law. Guzman and Meyer define soft law as 'non-binding rules that have legal consequences because they shape states' expectations as to what constitutes compliant behaviour'.[146] Harris explains that it consists of 'written instruments that spell out rules of conduct that are not intended to be legally binding, so that they are not subject to the law of treaties and do not generate the *opinio juris* required for them to be state practice contributing to custom'.[147] He points out that soft law instruments have a clear impact on international relations and may eventually 'harden into custom or become the basis of a treaty'.[148] Soft law may also refer to rather weak, vague or poorly drafted provisions of a binding treaty. Dixon, using the example of the Covenant on Economic, Social and Cultural Rights (CESCR) 1966, points out that this variation of soft law 'creates incremental or relative obligations'.[149] The appearance of legislative authority that we see in UN General Assembly resolutions have also been referred to as soft law.[150] In many respects the relative authority of soft law raises question concerning the precise boundaries of law and its relation to politics and ethics, and we turn now to some of the issues that are of central importance to these debates.

Normative authority and the sources of international law

If we turn once again to the politics of international law we find that the formal description of sources raises significant questions concerning the social and political foundations of law (and thus of the justice of international law). For some legal scholars the sort of questions that readers interested in the politics of international law might ask are not really relevant. Hugh Thirlway, adopting Hart's distinction between primary and secondary rules, shows that when we identify a primary rule (a specific obligation or right) we are forced to ask about the secondary rule that determines that primary rule.

> If the question is asked, 'why should I comply with this primary rule?', the answer may be, 'because it is a rule of treaty-law, laid down in a treaty to which you are a party'; but what then is the answer to the question, 'Why must I comply with treaty-law?' The classic answer is that there is a principle *pacta sunt servanda*, that what has been agreed to must be respected; this is an example of a secondary rule, one which defines treaties and agreements as formal sources of international law. Theoretically one may then ask, 'But why should I respect the principle *pacta sunt servanda*? Is there a higher principle still requiring me to respect it?'[151]

In a voluntarist system, where no absolute higher principle is recognised, the question opens up the possibility of infinite regress. If primary rules rely upon secondary rules and secondary rules rely upon tertiary rules, then what do tertiary rules rely on? The question merely repeats itself. For some this problem leads to another version of the Austinian claim that international law is not really law at all. For Thomas Hobbes, the existence of law requires a sovereign, not just to enforce the law but to create it. The sovereign (or Leviathan in Hobbes' terminology) provides the foundation for the legal order – the questioning simply stops with the answer 'because the sovereign wills it and can compel you to obey'. In the absence of an international Leviathan, however, the question remains unanswered. Yet, as Thirlway notes, the sort of questions asked of the sources are 'purely academic' as, despite the anomalies and difficulties that are evident in the doctrine, it has provided a workable system of law.[152]

For those of us interested in politics the question of whether or

```
┌─────────────────────┐
│ Issue-specific regimes │
│    e.g. GATT, NPT      │
└─────────────────────┘
           ▲
┌─────────────────────┐
│ Fundamental institutions │
│   e.g. multilateralism,  │
│     international law    │
└─────────────────────┘
           ▲
┌─────────────────────────┐
│ Constitutional structures │
│ Metavalues defining legitimate │
│ statehood and rightful state action │
└─────────────────────────┘
```

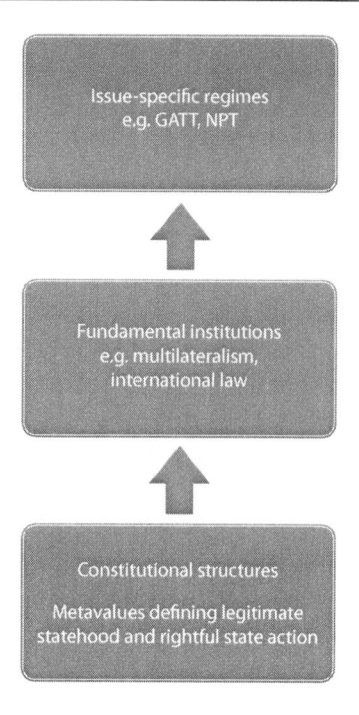

Figure 2.1 *The constitutive hierarchy of modern international institutions*[153]

not law is really law is not the prime issue. Instead of thinking purely about the determination of legal rules we need to think about the social context that makes adhering to the rule of law just or otherwise. Christian Reus-Smit draws a distinction between issue specific regimes, fundamental regimes and constitutional structures in his account of the constitutive hierarchy of international society (see Figure 2.1, above). Primary and secondary rules are found in the top two layers of the constitutive order. The foundational level, that of constitutional structures, is key to a critical grasp of questions of international justice.

For Reus-Smit this means that the question of the legitimacy of the international legal order is anterior to law rather than interior to law.[154] This is not to shift the focus away from law to politics. As we saw in Chapter One, just as lawyers need to look to processes outside the law to understand the structure of obligation,[155] so political theorists seeking 'moral accessibility' in their considerations of international justice need to engage with the processes of law. The mutually constitutive relationship between these three levels means that the interaction of agents at the level of specific regimes and fundamental institutions feeds back into the level of constitutional structures. In a legalised world order rules of law and broader political and moral claims have greater legitimacy if they can be justified in relation to the established sources of normative authority, in this case treaty and custom.[156] This plays out formally in the decisions of courts and tribunals, and less formally in the ways that states justify their actions in international politics and in the ways that other actors respond to those justifications. The further away from a coherent legal claim such statements range the more criticism and opposition they attract. The international response to claims made by the United States and the United Kingdom justifying the second Iraq War is a prominent example. This also helps us understand the role that soft law (which is law-like but not binding) plays in international law and politics.

While normative claims gain credibility from their association with treaty and custom, there are crucial moments when actors question the justice of legal rules regardless of how firm a footing they may have in terms of the formal sources of international law. At such moments the relative value of state consent is tested against the value of other principles. The core point here is that both the primary rules and fundamental institutions of multilateralism and state consent-based international law are sometimes challenged by these metavalues or constitutional structures. These metavalues are often thought to be very weak in global politics, and that weakness supports a pluralist world order where state consent is the only appropriate source of law. Indeed, the realist tradition in IR argues that the weakness of the international constitution suggests that we should not even expect law that stems from state consent to bind states to the law (see below). More recently, primary rules and the normative authority of state consent have been challenged by values that are often framed in terms of humanitarianism and human rights. The challenge may provide reasons for changing primary rules or, less frequently, changing secondary rules. An example of the former is the introduction, inspired by the international community's response to 'acts that shock the conscience of mankind' (see our discussion of the Marten's clause above), of the conventional texts of humanitarian and human rights law from the 1899 Hague Conventions to the 1998 Rome Statute establishing the International Criminal Court.[157] An example of the latter is seen in the increasing emphasis placed on the categories of *jus cogens* and *erga omnes*. The claim, advanced by the ICJ in its judgment on the jurisdiction phase of the *Armed Activities* case (*DRC v. Rwanda*), that the normative importance of the prohibition on genocide means that 'the principles underlying the [Genocide] Convention are principles which are recognized by civilized nations as binding on States, even without any conventional obligation' (at paragraph 64) is a good example. These sort of challenges arise even in the context of vitally important treaties such as the UN Charter. The Article 2(4) prohibition on the use of force is considered to be a legal rule of *jus cogens* standing. Yet in the face of ethnic cleansing and the humanitarian disaster in Kosovo in 1998 and 1999, NATO argued that it had a right to use force and did so without the UN Security Council backing. Here the justice of the rules prohibiting the use of military force by regional security actors without UN Security Council authorisation was tested against (among other concerns) the humanitarian aims of stopping war crimes and crimes against humanity. The report of the independent International Commission on Kosovo described NATO's actions as illegal yet legitimate, a conclusion that implies that there is more to international legitimacy than law (see Chapter Seven, below). What is interesting about these examples is that the challenging metavalues – humanitarian and human rights claims – have developed within the frameworks of conventional international law, have developed (in part at least) peremptory status and lead many to question the justice of an international order that privileges sovereignty over these values. The big idea at work here is that the international community has come to share metavalues associated with certain human rights claims, and that the constitutional structure of global society is such that primary and secondary rules of international law that are unresponsive to these value claims are, it is argued, unjust.

Each of the critical perspectives we examine below has a point to make about the limitations imposed by the traditional account of the normative authority of international law. In most cases the criticism stems from the claim that the sources account of the authority of legal rules is built on an inadequate account of the community to which is it said to apply. In the case of the realist critique, the international community is said to lack the necessary structure to support even this very state-centric account of law. Here, and for very different reasons in the critical legal studies approach, the myth of state equality that underpins the doctrine of sources has significant negative implications for global society. In other accounts, international society has developed beyond the statist conception of law that is formalised in Article 38. Constructivists point to the authority of legal and non-legal norms in shaping the identity and activity of agents in world affairs. While there are more and less conservative variants of constructivism (or pluralist and solidarist wings in English School jargon), the claim is that the doctrine of sources is not even wide enough to capture what goes on in judicial decision-making, let alone to characterise the dynamics of a legalised world order. As a guide to normative authority and desirability, therefore, the doctrine is compromised. Cosmopolitans, who share a political agenda with the more ambitious solidarist wing, point to the increasing centrality of human rights norms to any conception of global justice, and show how this social and legal development is an anathema to a legal order that is embedded in the doctrine of sources. We offer introductory explorations of each of these claims below. What they share, however, is a claim that the doctrine of sources is inadequate in that it fails to ground an account of normative authority in a sufficiently complex account of international society. While it may be possible to make post hoc amendments to the law of treaties or the definition of customary law to accommodate new law-making actors or more substantive accounts of peremptory norms,[158] the way the international community is portrayed masks power relations between substantively unequal actors, obscures the ways that communal norms move states and other agents to act (sometimes as a direct challenge to established legal rules) and casts in stubborn statute a 'pseudo-constitutional' moment that is the subject of radical contestation.

Realism and the sanctity of treaties

One of the earliest critiques of the post-First World War legal order offered by IR scholars was put forward by E. H. Carr in his most famous work that charted what he viewed as the twenty years crisis that was instigated by Woodrow Wilson's ambitions for a new world order. As we saw in Chapter One, Carr's critique of the utopianism of inter-war liberalism was built, in part at least, on the view that law is a function of society and that international society is primitive. Quoting Alfred Zimmern he argued that:

> Law is not an abstraction. It 'can only exist within a social framework... Where there is law, there must be a society within which it is operative'... International law is a function of the political community of nations. Its defects are due, not to any technical shortcomings, but to the embryonic character of the community in which it functions.[159]

Carr, often described as the founding father of realism in IR, offers a morally and political insightful critique of what he thought of as the undue emphasis placed on the sanctity of treaties in international law and the new found obsession with the rule *pacta sunt servanda* (agreements must be kept) which, as we have seen, is often treated as a customary norm of superior or peremptory *jus cogens* standing.[160]

Carr was not commenting directly on the work of the Advisory Committee of Jurists who were drafting the statue of the PCIJ for the League of Nations. However, his concern for the ways in which international treaty law was being presented as formal and binding and as apolitical and divorced from morality captures the heart of the concern that many realists have with the image of the role of international law put forward by the doctrine of the sources. Carr recognised that there was universal recognition that treaties are legally binding. But the way that the rule *pacta sunt servanda* was coming to be treated 'not merely as a fundamental rule of international law, but as a cornerstone of international society' was, he argued, seriously problematic. Prior to the inter-war period and the formalisation of the sanctity of treaties, states, Carr argued, treated the rule 'elastically'. In practice states did not expect treaty obligations to be absolutely binding. While it is perfectly understandable to require a contract- or consent-based system of legal obligation to rest on a strict view that contracts should be honoured, the simple fact is that legal rules are not the only concerns of international society. There are moral and political issues in play as well, and focusing solely on the legal principle distorts our perspective. Carr pointed to the repudiation of treaty obligations by France (the treaties of 1815 following the end of the Napoleonic wars), Russia (the Straits Convention of 1841 signed after the Crimean war), Great Britain (the Belgian Guarantee Treaty of 1839) and to the statements by lawyers and statesmen, including Woodrow Wilson, that confirmed the common view that there were various exceptions to the rule. Indeed,

> international lawyers had evolved the doctrine that a so-called *clausula rebus sic stantibus* was implicit in every treaty, i.e. that the obligations of a treaty were binding in international law as long as the conditions prevailing at the time of the conclusion of the treaty continued, and no longer.[161]

Even where the *clausula* was not invoked there was, observable in practice, an understanding that political or economic necessity could set aside treaty obligations. As Carr notes, 'it was not denied that breaches of such treaties are technical breaches of international law; but they were an offense against international morality'.[162] It might seem strange to find that someone who had such an influence on the tradition of realism was critical of formalism in international law because it treated as a rule of international law that which should be treated as a principle of international ethics.[163] However, Carr was deeply influenced by what he saw as the unfairness and folly of the Versailles Treaty that concluded the First World War. Treaties, he argued, are instruments of power, and treaties signed under duress with deeply inequitable provisions cannot be expected to survive a change in circumstances. For states the rule *pacta sunt servanda* is simply not as important as retrieving their standing in international society. The traditional method for achieving that goal was war, and it was simply utopian to believe that one could replace it with a moral distain for aggressive war and a legal obligation to uphold treaty obligations in a society that had not developed alternative mechanism for achieving a stable equilibrium. This utopianism, backed by the victorious allied powers that had most to gain from seeing the terms of the Versailles treaty honoured, was for Carr the principal reason why the legal order that underpinned the League of Nations crumbled in to yet another global conflict. Put simply (and in terms that Carr the realist would grasp), the attempt to ascribe determinant and absolutely binding sources of legal obligation for the international order was not normatively desirable – it was unjust.

Legalisation and the development of international society

Carr's concerns that questions of high politics (of war, sovereign self-determination and so on) could not tolerate the intrusion of hard and fast rules of law began the process of separating the study of international law from the study of international politics. This separation only hardened as neo-realism, with its strong social scientific ambitions and search for parsimony, effectively claimed that international law was merely epiphenomenal on state interests and so unworthy of study. Both forms of scepticism about the role and effectiveness of international law remain prevalent. However, as we noted in Chapter One, many scholars saw in the legalisation of world politics the development of an international society that could bear the weight of law.

The reconnection between international law and IR scholarship was not a uniform process. Over a forty-year period lawyers in the policy science and legal process schools, social scientists adopting institutionalist, liberal and constructivists approaches, English School theorists in the pluralist and solidarist schools, and cosmopolitans and communitarians in international ethics have contested the nature of international law and its role in international politics (and vice versa). Their disputes present us with differing implications for our understanding of international society and the sources of normative authority. Early legalisation scholarship reopened the lines of communication between international law and IR by recasting law as a facilitating mechanism within international regimes in a way that tracks the traditional sources of law.[164] Law was not to be seen as resting on the enforcement of rules, but as a positive social tool that generated voluntary compliance because its subjects and creators recognised its instrumental worth.[165] Later developments contested the virtue and relevance of a system of law that rest on the consent of sovereign states and even the distinction between legal and non-legal norms in a way that forces us to think creatively and critically about the authority of the traditional sources of law.

The histories of the debates between and within different traditions of scholarship can be found in many places.[166] These debates are very rich and each contribution offers a distinctive take on the core ideas. For our purposes, however, we can focus on the one issue common to all and on the issues that directly impact on our critical analysis of the sources of international law. The core issue concerns the question of whether the legal order that we find in international society is appropriate for that society. In one sense a just legal order is one that coheres with the communal norms of the society in which it operates. Several of the arguments that we examine here claim either that: (1) the legal order, in reflecting the communal norms of international society, has moved beyond formal state consent to legal rules; or that (2) the legal order *ought* to move beyond state consent to more fully reflect communal norms. An example of (1) is the claim that the international community, despite the formal prohibition on unilateral military action, accepts that unilateral humanitarian military intervention can be legitimate.[167] An example of (2) is the claim that human rights norms are now so central to the idea of just world order that giving states the option or the right to consent (or not consent) to human rights obligations gives them an unjust legitimacy veto.[168]

In all these scholarly traditions there are arguments that defend the justice of a pluralist, state-centric world order and those that defend a liberal world order. The key to these debates rests in the identification of community values (at the level of international society) and on an assessment of the extent to which the legal order reflects and supports those values. In pluralist (or institutionalist, or communitarian) accounts international community values are very limited. The pluralism of moral, religious and cultural belief around the world reinforces the need to have distinct geo-political space in which diverse peoples can live their lives. International law is, first and foremost, about protecting the sovereignty of these spaces (states) and about facilitating interaction between them in a manner consistent with that primary goal. It is also vital to note that the international community is not a single coherent society. Individual states and regional groups are divided about most constitutional values. The default position in the face of such pluralism is very conservative and suggests that greater normative ambition simply masks power politics in the guise of moral progress. The international community shares interests in peace, limiting violence, keeping promises and stable rules of property.[169] On this reading a formal account of the sources of law, one that limits the role of non-state actors, denies the applicability of norms not developed by the consent of states is appropriate. The 'pseudo-constitutional' framework of public international law found in the establishment of authoritative sources is therefore just in the sense that it coheres with core community values.

In liberal (or solidarist, or cosmopolitan) accounts the rapid development of international law under the UN system (and particularly post-Cold War) has placed many of these core assumptions under considerable pressure. Liberals point to the increasing extent to which non-state actors are subjects and creators of international law. The increasing importance of international organisations, regional organisations, multinational corporations and individual–state, individual–transnational and individual–individual relationships broadens the concern of international law.[170] They also point to the increasing disconnect between state consent and legal normativity found in the increasing use of qualified majority voting in the adoption of treaties, and in the ambitious use of peremptory norms and the language of fundamental and non-derogable rights. They also question the extent to which compliance with norms is driven by a respect for formal sources of law rather than by a commitment to community values or a conception of justice. In many accounts, the community values in question are most often cast in terms of human rights. Parallels can be drawn between the work of legal scholars such as Meron, who sees, in the incremental development of a hierarchy of norms in international law, the progressive 'humanization of international law',[171] or with Falk, who heralds a 'second Grotian moment' in the development of international law,[172] with cosmopolitan arguments such as that of Allen Buchanan, who claims that human rights norms must be systematically applied to the broader legal order if we are to live up to our most basic moral commitments.[173] In others it is the 'fairness' of a rule rather than its simple usefulness that matters.[174] Central to the liberal arguments is a claim about the dynamism of international society. The process of legalisation has not simply created new or more law. Legalisation is a constitutive process that changes the normative structure of international society. It changes the identity of the actors, their normative aspirations and behaviour, and their willingness to obey legal rules and to create new ones. Obeying the law (or transforming it) is not merely an instrumental good, but is normatively desirable.

In relation to our exploration of the normative authority of the formal sources of law there is a lot to be said here.

The institutionalists and pluralists deny the claims of the realists that international society is too 'embryonic' to sustain a proper system of law. International actors have, following Keohane, instrumentalist and normative reasons for obeying international law.[175] On the one hand, states have an interest in upholding the rule of law. In addition to this, the norms and the general idea of respect for the rule of law (even when interests are not obviously in play) themselves come to exert a 'compliance pull'. Compliance is a hallmark of legitimacy,[176] and has come to function as a non-instrumental moral constraint on state power.[177] Focusing on compliance rather than enforcement helps to overcome the Austinian challenge and the realist rejection of the relevance of international law. If actors have reasons to comply with international law that are independent of the existence or power of legislative, executive or judicial institutions, then the relative weakness of those institutions is not a crucial issue. It also helps us 'understand the conditions of justice in the emerging, but still pluralist, world order'.[178] Justice, embodied in law, presupposes a society of sovereign states where sovereignty is qualified by an obligation to respect the law that they themselves make.

Liberals acknowledge the power of the institutionalist and pluralist view, but argue that they have good reason to think that international society has evolved beyond the statist and consent-based model of law found in Article 38(1). This is evident in the ways that certain normative claims that have their origin in international law have become as important (if not more so) than sovereignty in terms of encouraging compliance. The suggestion here is that over time norms of international law that were originally designed to be subordinate to the norms establishing and protecting the sovereignty of states have developed to become equal or superior to those norms.[179] This is a part of the mutually constitutive relationship that develops over time between agents and norms. Where a sovereign state is unable or unwilling to live up to its responsibilities in respect of human rights or humanitarian norms we often find claims concerning the peremptory or *jus cogens* nature of those obligations and arguments that their dereliction is the concern of all states (that they are *erga omnes* rights or obligations). As Dinah Shelton notes, the universal and peremptory character of these norms is consequent upon the importance of the values they protect.[180] This suggests the development of a normative hierarchy in international law. But the existence of normative hierarchy poses problems for a legal order based on the sources of law as identified in Article 38(1). If states cannot opt out of certain bodies of law (either by refusing to adopt a treaty, adding reservations to treaties or by becoming a 'persistent objector' to the development of new customary law), and if we are not sure where law ends and politics begins (as in the role of soft law and broader ethical claims that challenge legal rules), is Article 38(1) really a sufficient description of public international law?

A critical note of caution

For some the idea of a politicised challenge to the doctrine of sources and the image of international society it presupposes needs more critical attention than the liberals allow. Scholars in critical legal studies or the New Stream of international law scholarship, such as David Kennedy and Martti Koskenniemi, show how reliance on the doctrine of the sources or on a universalist conception of justice obscure fundamental tensions in the international legal order. Exposing these tensions they show that the very idea of an international community rests on discourses and practices of exclusion and suppression.[181] Their fundamental contribution to the debate is their exposure of the myths of objectivity contained within both discourses. The central argument is that international law is always political, and that neither a firm adherence to the doctrine of consent or a 'flight from politics' to justice can overcome this basic fact. Famously, Koskenniemi describes international law as a constant struggle between 'apology' and 'utopia':

> To show that international law is objective – that is, independent of international politics – the legal mind fights a battle on two fronts. On the one hand, it aims to ensure the *concreteness* of the law by distancing it from theories of natural justice. On the other hand, it aims to guarantee the *normativity* of the law by creating distance between it and actual state behaviour, will or interest. Law enjoys independence from politics only if both of these conditions are simultaneously present . . . [However] the two arguments *cancel each other out*. An argument about concreteness is an argument about the closeness of a particular rule, principle or doctrine to state practice. However, the closer to state practice an argument is, the less normative and more political it seems. The more it seems just another uncritical apology for existing power. An argument about normativity, on the other hand, is an argument which intends to demonstrate the rule's distance from state will and practice. The more normative (i.e. critical) a rule, the more political it seems because the less it is possible to argue it by reference to social context. It seems utopian and – like theories of natural justice – manipulable at will.[182]

There is something very important about the claim that both the pluralist and the liberal conceptions of international law are political. Sources doctrine may have been an attempt to secure law's objectivity in distancing it from politics and ethics, and the liberal drive to extra-consensual normative principles may have been an attempt to secure law's objectivity by distancing it from the subjectivity of power politics, but neither has been or could be successful. This last point contains two elements: the first about the pattern of modernism's treatment of the subject; and the second about our inability to truly get beyond the problems that the modernist approach reifies. The first point shows how lawyers and scholars have been trapped in an endless cycle of repeating dichotomies. Naturalism versus positivism, consent versus justice, process versus rule are all versions of the apology–utopia dilemma.[183] One tradition criticises the other for being overtly political by using strategies designed to seek objectivity that ultimately come under fire for being political themselves. Not only is this intellectual strategy circular and ineffective, it is typical of the way that modernist thinking (from at least Plato onwards) aspires to the impossible.[184] The second point builds on this critique of modernist philosophy by introducing the consequences of the ways that lawyers and philosophers 'hide' the political with legal or moral objectivity. As Paulus notes, 'the vision of communitarian unity shares the vice of the ideal of the liberal community: it excludes and marginalises the outsider'.[185] Each new attempt at objectivity simply alters who or what counts as an outsider, but crucially there is always a new outsider/other against which we define the insider. As Kennedy argues, there is a dark side to every virtue, and in the contemporary international context human rights is clearly part of the problem.[186]

The critical theories of Kennedy and Koskenniemi are directed specifically at legal practitioners, but clearly their points have significant implications for the conceptions of international community that underpin the various accounts of normative authority and the justice of international law surveyed in this section. First, it must make us aware of the intellectual weaknesses inherent in treating statism–liberalism, pluralism–solidarism or communitarianism–cosmopolitanism as binary pairs, each containing the solution to the other's weaknesses. Second, it must remind us that the politics of inclusion and exclusion is at work in all justice claims. This does not mean that we must abandon the vocabulary. As Koskenniemi notes, accepting the power of this critique

> is not to say that international legal ideas would be useless. They have a considerable historical, intellectual and emotional pull. They engage citizens, diplomats and lawyers to reflect on the problems of the world in a relatively structured way. But they do not themselves resolve the problems. They give a voice to demands and interests and facilitate the articulation of controversies – and thus also their resolution – by showing how alternative acts bear on larger aspirations. They work as a critique of power and as instruments of power.[187]

It does, however, mean that we should treat this vocabulary with caution. Justice claims are not solutions to the weaknesses of international law, they are a way of continually testing the normative desirability of law. Price and Reus-Smit argue that constructivism, as an approach to social theory, is compatible with critical theory as 'its underlying ontological and epistemological assumptions are normatively predisposed to questions of change (particularly questions of moral inclusion and exclusion)'.[188] In Chapter One we examined how a political theory of international law and justice derives its platform from an active engagement with the social framework for moral and legal debate that is international society. Key to this project is the recognition that legal and moral claims are social and political claims. They are not objective claims. Rather they are intersubjective claims always subject to questions of their normative authority and desirability. A key part of this questioning is going to turn on questions of moral and political inclusivity and hegemony.

Conclusion

In practice the vast majority of international law can be seen to stem from the sources laid out in Article 38(1) of the statute of the ICJ. It seems clear, however, that the idea that the sources of international law are objective, apolitical and exclusive is problematic. Indeed, there is a real danger in immunising the sources of law from questions of justice. Asking 'is it appropriate that the issue before us is resolved by reference to treaty and custom?' may well yield a positive answer in most cases. But there are clearly also ethical and political tensions inherent in the contemporary legalised world order that require that we keep asking the question. That question, as we have developed it here, is a question about the justice, or otherwise, of the constitution of international society. The development of a normative hierarchy in international law is of particular interest in this regard. Although the extent to which the development of a normative hierarchy in international law challenges the state-centric and consent-based international order is contested, the cracks that have appeared in the doctrine have reopened significant political space for ethical reflection. As Shelton argues:

> The most significant positive aspect of this trend toward normative hierarchy is its reaffirmation of the link between law and ethics, in which law is one means to achieve the fundamental values of an international society. It remains to be determined, however, who will identify the fundamental values and by what process.[189]

It is in this political space that the challenges to the stylised account of international society that underpins the doctrine of sources takes place. The most urgent questions of international affairs emerge as the international community attempts to decide on the right response to any given challenge. International society exhibits both conservative and radical tendencies, and the clear need for rules of law to be partnered by considerations of justice is a key feature of the contemporary world.

Notes

1 Skouteris, T., 'The Force of a Doctrine: Art. 38 of the PCIJ Statute and the Sources of International Law', in F. Johns, R. Joyce and P. Sundhya (eds), *Events: The Force of International Law*, London: Routledge, 2011.
2 Hart, H. L. A., *The Concept of Law*, Oxford: Clarendon Press, 1997, ch. 5.
3 Spiermann, O., *International Legal Argument in the Permanent Court of International Justice: The Rise of the International Judiciary*, Cambridge: Cambridge University Press, 2005, pp. 14–15.
4 For a variety of different variations on this theme, see Byers, M., *Custom, Power, and the Power of Rules: International Relations and Customary International Law*, Cambridge: Cambridge University Press, 1999, p. 182; Besson, S., 'Theorising the Sources of International Law', in S. Besson and J. Tasioulas (eds), *The Philosophy of International Law*, Oxford: Oxford University Press, 2010, pp. 163–86; Kratochwil, F., 'Legal Theory and International Law', in D. Armstrong (ed.), *Routledge Handbook of International Law*, Abingdon: Routledge, 2009, pp. 55–67; Allott, P., 'The Concept of International Law', in M. Byers (ed.), *The Role of Law in International Politics*, Oxford: Oxford University Press, 2000, pp. 69–89; Shoenbaum, T., *International Relations, The Turn Not Taken: Using International Law to Promote World Peace and Security*, Cambridge: Cambridge University Press, 2006, pp. 90–2; Skouteris, 'The Force of a Doctrine, p. 76.
5 Brownlie, I., *Principles of Public International Law*, 6th edn, Oxford: Oxford University Press, 2003, pp. 3–4; Thirlway, H., 'The Sources of International Law', in M. Evans (ed.), *International Law*, 2nd edn, Oxford: Oxford University Press, 2006, p. 115, at pp. 116–17.
6 Dixon, M., *International Law*, 6th edn, Oxford: Oxford University Press, 2007, p. 25.
7 Brownlie, *Principles of Public International Law*, pp. 3–4.
8 Lowe, V., 'The Politics of Law-Making: Are the Method and Character of Norm Creation Changing?', in M. Byers (ed.), *The Role of Law in*

International Politics: Essays in International Relations and International Law, Oxford: Oxford University Press, 2000, p. 207.
9. This will be discussed in further detail in Chapter Three, dealing with subjects of international law.
10. Carr, *The Twenty Years Crisis,* p. 176.
11. Alvarez, J. E., *International Organizations as Law-makers*, Oxford: Oxford University Press, 2005, p. 61.
12. See Art. 1 of the Statute of the ILC 1947, adopted by the General Assembly in Resolution 174(II), 21 November 1947, as amended by Resolution 485(V), 12 December 1950, Resolution 984(X), 3 December 1955, Resolution 985(X), 3 December 1955 and Resolution 36/39, 18 November 1981. See ILC website at: http://www.un.org/law/ilc.
13. Higgins, R., *The Development of International Law through the Political Organs of the United Nations*, Oxford: Oxford University Press, 1963; Alvarez, *International Organizations as Law-makers,* pp. 146–83.
14. See, for instance, Szasz, P.C., 'The Security Council Starts Legislating', *American Journal of International Law*, 96(4) (2002): 901–5.
15. Alvarez, *International Organizations as Law-makers,* p. 68.
16. Hollis, D., 'Why State Consent Still Matters: Non-State Actors, Treaties and the Changing Sources of International Law', *Berkeley Journal of International Law*, 22 (2005): 137, at pp. 145–55.
17. Tinker, C., 'The Role of Non-state Actors in International Law-making during the UN Decade of International Law', *American Society of International Law Proceedings*, 89 (1995): 177–80; Charnovitz, S., 'Two Centuries of Participation: NGOs and International Governance', *Michigan Journal of International Law*, 18 (1997): 183–286.
18. See http://www.un.org/geninfo/bp/enviro.html and http://www.ohchr.org/EN/ABOUTUS/Pages/ViennaWC.aspx, accessed 27 October 2011. See Nowrot, K., 'Legal Consequences of Globalization: The Status of Non-Governmental Organizations under International Law', *Global Legal Studies Journal*, 6 (1998/9): 579–645.
19. Weissbrodt, D. and Kruger, M., 'Norms on the Responsibilities of Transnational Corporations and other Business Enterprises with Regard to Human Rights', *American Journal of International Law*, 97(4) (2003): 901–22; Hillemanns, C. F., 'UN Norms on the Responsibilities of Transnational Corporations and Other Business Enterprises with regard to Human Rights', *German Law Journal*, 4(10) (2003): 1065–80.
20. Finnemore, M. and Sikkink, K., 'International Norm Dynamics and Political Change', *International Organization*, 50(4) (1998): 887–918, at pp. 869–901.
21. Thirlway, H., *International Customary Law and Codification: An Examination of the Continuing Role of Custom in the Present Period of Codification of International Law*, Leiden: Sitjhoff, 1972.

22 Higgins, R., *Problems and Process: International Law and How we Use It*, Oxford: Clarendon Press, 1994, p. 18.
23 *The Legality of the Threat or Use of Nuclear Weapons*, Advisory Opinion [1996] ICJ Rep. 226, at para. 18, where the ICJ insisted that it merely states the existing law and does not legislate.
24 Lowe, V., *International Law*, Oxford: Oxford University Press, 2007, pp. 46–7.
25 Koskenniemi, M., 'Lauterpacht: The Victorian Tradition in International Law', *European Journal of International Law*, 8 (1997): 215, at pp. 252–7; Benvenisti, E., 'The Conception of International Law as a Legal System', *German Yearbook of International Law*, 50 (2008): 393, at pp. 396–8; Terris, D., Romano, C. and Swigart, L., *The International Judge: An Introduction to the Men and Women Who Decide the World's Cases*, Oxford: Oxford University Press, 2007, pp. 102–30.
26 Parry, C., *The Sources and Evidences of International Law*, Manchester: Manchester University Press, 1965, pp. 103–5; Thirlway, 'The Sources of International Law', p. 129.
27 Higgins, *Problems and Process*, p. 17.
28 Cassese, A., *International Law*, 2nd edn, Oxford: Oxford University Press, 2005, pp.152–3; Hollis, 'Why State Consent Still Matters', pp. 137–74.
29 Aust, A., *Modern Treaty Law and Practice*, 2nd edn, Cambridge: Cambridge University Press, 2007, p. 6.
30 See the *Reparations for Injuries Suffered in the Service of the United Nations Case* [1949] ICJ Rep. 174.
31 For more details on international organisations and treaties see Brolmann, C., 'International Organizations and Treaties: Contractual Freedom and Institutional Constraint', in J. Klabbers (ed.), *Research Handbook on International Organizations*, London, Elgar Publishers, 2011, pp. 285–312.
32 Aust, *Modern Treaty Law and Practice*, pp. 10–11.
33 Brownlie, *Principles of Public International Law*, p. 12.
34 Brownlie, *Principles of Public International Law*, p. 12.
35 Dixon, *International Law*, p. 29.
36 Dixon, *International Law*, p. 30.
37 Dixon, *International Law*, p. 30.
38 Kunz, J., 'The Meaning and the Range of the *Norm Pacta Sunt Servanda*', *American Journal of International Law*, 39(2) (1945): 180–97, at p. 181.
39 See VCLT, Art. 18, and Lukashuk, I. I., 'The Principle *Pacta Sunt Servanda* and the Nature of Obligation Under International Law', *American Journal of International Law*, 83(3) (1989): 513–18, at p. 515.
40 See VCLT, Art. 2(1)(e). It is important to note that in technical terms a

state or an international organisation is only a 'party' to a treaty if it has consented to be bound by it and such treaty has come into force. See for, e.g., VCLT, Art. 2(1)(g).
41 Aust, *Modern Treaty Law and Practice*, 2nd edn, p. 84.
42 Aust, *Modern Treaty Law and Practice*, 2nd edn, p. 84.
43 Under VCLT, Art. 18 a state that signs but has not ratified, accepted, approved or otherwise consented to a treaty is obliged to refrain from acts that would defeat the object and purpose of such treaty. This obligation on the signatory state is until it has made its intention clear not to become a party to such treaty. Also such obligation is subject to the proviso that the entry into force of the treaty is not unduly delayed.
44 See Corbett, P. E., 'The Consent of States and the Sources of the Law of Nations', *British Yearbook of International Law*, 6 (1925): 20, at p. 29.
45 Article II, s. 2 of the US Constitution. See Henkin, L., 'The Treaty Makers and the Law Makers: The Law of the Land and Foreign Relations', *University of Pennsylvania Law Review*, 107(7) (1959): 903–36; Glennon, M., 'The Constitutional Power of the United States Senate to Condition its Consent to Treaties', *Chicago-Kent Law Review*, 67 (1991): 533–70.
46 See the evidence presented by the UK Foreign and Commonwealth Office to the Royal Commission on the Reform of the House of Lords, UKMIL, *British Yearbook of International Law*, 70 (1999): 408.
47 VCLT, Arts 11–16. For more on consent to treaties see Aust, *Modern Treaty Law and Practice*, 2nd edn, pp. 94–121.
48 United Nations Treaty Series, available at: http://treaties.un.org/pages/ViewDetailsIII.aspx?&src=TREATY&mtdsg_no=XXIII~1&chapter=23&Temp=mtdsg3&lang=en.
49 Aust, *Modern Treaty Law and Practice*, 2nd edn, pp. 104, 170–1.
50 Article 308(1).
51 For a detailed exploration of this, see Fitzmaurice, M., 'Third Parties and the Law of Treaties', *Max Planck Yearbook of United Nations Law*, 6 (2002): 37–137.
52 PCIJ Ser. A, No. 7, p. 28.
53 See VCLT, Arts 35 and 36.
54 Dixon, *International Law*, pp. 75–6.
55 Article 2(1)(d). For a more detailed exploration of reservations see Aust, *Modern Treaty Law and Practice*, 2nd edn, pp. 125–61.
56 Dixon, *International Law*, p. 70.
57 See http://treaties.un.org/Pages/ViewDetails.aspx?src=TREATY&mtdsg_no=IV-4&chapter=4&lang=en.
58 Dixon, *International Law*, p. 67.
59 [1951] ICJ Rep. 15.
60 Article 19.
61 Article 20.

62 Dixon, *International Law*, p. 69.
63 Dixon, *International Law*, p. 70.
64 For more on consent to termination of treaties see Aust, *Modern Treaty Law and Practice*, 2nd edn, pp. 277–311.
65 See VCLT, Art. 62. Also see Aust, *Modern Treaty Law and Practice*, 2nd edn, pp. 297–300; Vagts, D. F., 'Rebus Revisited: Changed Circumstances in Treaty Law', *Columbia Journal of Transnational Law*, 43 (2004): 459–76.
66 Dixon, *International Law*, pp. 18–19.
67 Lowe, *International Law*, p. 36.
68 Guzman, A., 'Saving Customary International Law', *Michigan Journal of International Law*, 27 (2005/6): 115–76, at p. 116.
69 [1969] ICJ Rep. 3, at p. 44, para. 77.
70 [1985] ICJ Rep. 13, at p. 29, para. 27.
71 See Kammerhofer, J., 'Uncertainty in the Formal Sources of International Law: Customary International Law and Some of Its Problems', *European Journal of International Law*, 15(3) (2004): 523–53; Roberts, A. E., 'Traditional and Modern Approaches to Customary International Law: A Reconciliation', *American Journal of International Law*, 95 (2001): 757–91.
72 Guzman, 'Saving Customary International Law', pp. 116–17.
73 Hudson, M., *Progress in International Organization*, Oxford: Oxford University Press, 1932, p. 83.
74 Guzman, 'Saving Customary International Law', pp. 115–76.
75 Kelly, J. P., 'The Twilight of Customary International Law', *Virginia Journal of International Law*, 40 (1999/2000): 449–544.
76 Dixon, *International Law*, p. 31.
77 Brownlie, *Principles of Public International Law*, p. 6.
78 D'Amato, A., *The Concept of Custom in International Law*, New York: Cornell University Press, 1971, pp. 88–90 and 160; Roberts, 'Traditional and Modern Approaches to Customary International Law', pp. 757–8. See also the Dissenting Opinion of Lord Read in the *Anglo-Norwegian Fisheries* case [1951] ICJ Rep. 116, at p. 191.
79 Thirlway, *International Customary Law and Codification*, p. 58.
80 Thirlway, *International Customary Law and Codification*, p. 58.
81 Akehurst, M., 'Custom as a Source of International Law', *British Yearbook of International Law*, 47(1) (1974/5): 1–53.
82 Akehurst, 'Custom as a Source of International Law', pp. 1–3. Refers to ICJ cases such as the *Fisheries Jurisdiction* case [1974] ICJ Rep. 3; *North Sea Continental Shelf* cases, *supra*; *Asylum* case [1950] ICJ Rep. 66; *Rights of United States Nationals in Morocco* case [1952] ICJ Rep. 176.
83 Akehurst, 'Custom as a Source of International Law', p. 8. See also Higgins, *Problems and Process*, pp. 19–22, on violations of CIL leading

to formation of new law.
84 Akehurst, 'Custom as a Source of International Law', p. 4.
85 Akehurst, 'Custom as a Source of International Law', p. 10.
86 Akehurst, 'Custom as a Source of International Law', pp. 8–11 and 53.
87 See the *Asylum* case, *supra* at pp. 276–7.
88 Brownlie, *Principles of Public International Law*, p. 11; Charney, J., 'The Persistent Objector and the Development of Customary International Law', *British Yearbook of International Law*, 56 (1985): 1–24. However, see Casesse, *International Law*, 2nd edn, pp. 162–3, who takes the view that the possibility of the persistent objector in modern times is not tenable because of the 'current community-oriented configuration of international relations' and the lack of firm support in state practice and international case law for the persistent objector rule.
89 Cheng, B., 'United Nations Resolutions on Outer Space: "Instant" International Customary Law?', *Indian Journal of International Law*, 5 (1965): 23–112.
90 Cheng, 'United Nations Resolutions on Outer Space,' pp. 23–112.
91 [1969] ICJ Rep. 3, at pp. 42–3.
92 Baxter, writing as far back as 1960s appears to hold the view that the practice of five or ten states, which are not on its face inconsistent, may suffice. See Baxter, R. R., 'Multilateral Treaties as Evidence of Customary International Law', *British Yearbook of International Law*, 41 (1965/6): 275–300, at p. 275
93 Akehurst, 'Custom as a Source of International Law', pp. 16–31.
94 *North Sea Continental Shelf* cases, *supra*, at p. 44 and the *Nicaragua* v. *USA* case [1986] ICJ Rep. 14, at pp. 108–9, para. 207.
95 Akehurst, 'Custom as a Source of International Law', p. 32.
96 Guzman, 'Saving Customary International Law', p. 124.
97 Akerhurst, 'Custom as a Source of International Law', pp. 32–4; Elias, O., 'The Nature of the Subjective Element in Customary International Law', *International and Comparative Law Quarterly*, 44 (1995): 501–20, at pp. 503–8.
98 *Nicaragua* v. *USA*, p. 14.
99 *Nicaragua* v. *USA*, paras 108–9. See also Brownlie, *Principles of Public International Law*, p. 8, who states that *opinio juris* 'is in fact a necessary ingredient' for the formation of custom.
100 Cassese, *International Law*, 2nd edn, p. 157; Elias, 'The Nature of the Subjective Element in Customary International Law', p. 508.
101 Brownlie, *Principles of Public International Law*, p. 8.
102 Brownlie, *Principles of Public International Law*, pp. 8–10. See the *Nicaragua* case, paras 188–9; *Legality of the Threat or Use of Nuclear Weapons* case [1996] ICJ Rep. 226, paras 67 and 70 on the possibility of deducing *opinio juris* from General Assembly resolutions.
103 See *North Sea Continental Shelf* cases, p. 42, para. 72; *Nicaragua*

case, para. 100. See also Christenson, G., 'The World Court and *Jus Cogens*', *American Journal of International Law*, 81(1) (1987): 93–101; Danilenko, G., 'International *Jus Cogens*: Issues of Law-Making', *European Journal of International Law*, 2 (1991): 42–65; Shelton, D., 'Normative Hierarchy in International Law', *American Journal of International Law*, 100(2) (2006): 291–323.
104 See, for instance, Oppenheim, L., *International Law*, vol. I, London: Longmans, 1905, p. 528; D'Amato, *The Concept of Custom in International Law*, p. 132; Byers, M., 'Conceptualising the Relationship between *Jus Cogens* and *Erga Omnes* Rules', *Nordic Journal of International Law*, 66 (1997): 211–39; Kunz, 'The Meaning and the Range of the Norm *Pacta Sunt Servanda*', p. 181.
105 See, for instance, Janis, M., 'The Nature of *Jus Cogens*', *Connecticut Journal of International Law*, 3 (1987/8): 359–63.
106 Janis, 'The Nature of *Jus Cogens*', p. 361.
107 Janis, 'The Nature of *Jus Cogens*', p. 362.
108 *Yearbook of the International Law Commission*, 2, 1953, p. 90 at 93
109 This rules out the possibility of a persistent objector in the case of a *jus cogens* norm.
110 *Nicaragua* v. *USA*, para. 190.
111 See *Case Concerning Application of the Convention on the Prevention and Punishment of the Crime of Genocide* [1993] ICJ Rep. 325, at p. 440, para. 100; *Armed Activities on the Territory of the Congo* (*Democratic Republic of Congo* v. *Rwanda*), Jurisdiction and Admissibility [2006] ICJ Rep. 1, at paras 64 and 125.
112 Byers, 'Conceptualising the Relationship between *Jus Cogens* and *Erga Omnes* Rules', p. 219.
113 Cassese, *International Law*, 2nd edn, pp. 198–212; Danilenko, 'International *Jus Cogens*', pp. 57–64.
114 For more on the relationship between jus cogens and erga omnes see Byers, 'Conceptualising the Relationship between *Jus Cogens* and *Erga Omnes* Rules', pp. 229–38.
115 [1970] ICJ Rep. 3, at p. 32, paras 33–4.
116 *Nicaragua* v. *USA*, paras 176–8.
117 [1970] ICJ Rep. 95, para. 177
118 Baxter, 'Multilateral Treaties as Evidence of Customary International Law', pp. 277–80. For an example of a treaty influencing subsequent adoption of rule as customary international law, see Article 1 of the Montevideo Convention on Rights and Duties of States 1933.
119 *North Sea Continental Shelf* cases, paras 71–4.
120 Waldock, H. M., 'General Course on Public International Law', *Hague Recueil*, 106(11) (1962): 1–252, at p. 54
121 Waldock, 'General Course on Public International Law', p. 54; Shaw, *International Law*, pp. 98–105.

122 See, e.g., Shelton, 'Normative Hierarchy in International Law', pp. 291–323.
123 Shaw, *International Law*, pp. 109–12.
124 For detailed exploration of the role of the international courts in the development of international law, see Lauterpacht, H., *The Development of International Law by the International Court*, Cambridge: Cambridge University Press, 1982.
125 See *R. v. Bow Street Metropolitan Stipendiary Magistrate, ex parte Pinochet Ugarte (No. 3)*.
126 Wolfke, K., *Custom in Present International Law*, Poland: Wroclaw, 1964, quoted in Harris, D. J., *Cases and Materials on International Law*, 6th edn, London: Sweet & Maxwell, 2004, p. 54.
127 Wolfke, quoted in Harris, *Cases and Materials on International Law*, p. 54.
Wolfke, *Custom in Present International Law*, quoted in Harris, *Cases & Materials on International Law*. p.54
128 See, for instance, Greenwood, C., 'International Law and the Pre-emptive Use of Force: Afghanistan, Al-Qaida, and Iraq', *San Diego International Law Journal*, 4 (2003): 7–37; Wedgwood, R., 'Responding to Terrorism: The Strikes Against bin Laden', *Yale International Law Journal*, 24 (1999): 559–76; Wedgwood, R., 'The Fall of Saddam Hussein: Security Council Mandates and Preemptive Self-defense', *American Journal of International Law*, 97 (2003): 576–84.
129 See, for instance, Elias, T. O., 'Modern Sources of International Law', in W. Friedmann, L. Henkin, O. J. Lissitzyn and P. C. Jessup (eds), *Transnational Law in a Changing Society: Essays in Honour of Philip C. Jessup*, New York: Columbia University Press, 1972, pp. 34–69; Alvarez, J. E., 'Positivism Regained, Nihilism Postponed', *Michigan Journal of International Law*, 15 (1994): 747–84; Hollis, 'Why State Consent Still Matters', pp. 142–5.
130 See Higgins, *The Development of International Law through the Political Organs of the United Nations*, p. 2.
131 Thakur, R., 'Law, Legitimacy and United Nations', *Melbourne Journal of International Law*, 11 (2010): 1–26, at p. 5.
132 See Art. 10 of the Charter.
133 Quoted in Falk, R., 'On the Quasi-legislative Competence of the General Assembly', *American Journal of International Law*, 60 (1966): 782, at p. 783.
134 See Byers, M., 'A Decade of Forceful Measures against Iraq', *European Journal of International Law*, 13(1) (2002): 21–41, at p. 33.
135 See Higgins, *The Development of International Law Through the Political Organs of the United Nations*, pp. 22–8. For example, there were divergences on whether the various General Assembly resolutions adopted in the 1960s and 1970s on the common heritage of mankind

of the deep seabed beyond national jurisdiction are indicative of CIL. See Rembe, N., *Africa and the International Law of the Sea: A Study of the Contribution of the African States to the Third United Nations Conference on the Law of the Sea*, The Hague: Sijthoff & Noordhoff, 1980, pp. 49–57; contrast with Brown, E., *Seabed Energy and Minerals: The International Legal Regime, vol. 2: Seabed Mining*, The Hague: Martinus Nijhoff, 2001, pp. 23–44.

136 Asamoah, O., *The Legal Significance of the Declarations of the General Assembly of the United Nations*, The Hague: Martinus Nijhoff, 1967, p. 46. See also Anand, R. P., *Legal Regime of the Seabed and the Developing Countries*, The Hague: Sijthoff, 1987, p. 204.

137 Higgins, *The Development of International Law Through the Political Organs of the United Nations*, p. 28; Dixon, *International Law*, p. 49.

138 Szasz, P., 'The Security Council Starts Legislating', *American Journal of International Law*, 96(4) (2002): 901–5; Talmon, S., 'The Security Council as World Legislature', *American Journal of International Law*, 99(1) (2005): 175–93; Johnstone, I., 'Legislation and Adjudication in the UN Security Council: Bringing down the Deliberative Deficit', *American Journal of International Law*, 102(2) (2008): 275–308.

139 Talmon, 'The Security Council as World Legislature', p. 175, quoting Alvarez, J., 'Hegemonic International Law Revisited', *American Journal of International Law*, 97 (2003): 873–88, at p. 874.

140 See Article 24 of the UN Charter and Talmon, 'The Security Council as World Legislature', pp. 178–84; Johnstone, 'Legislation and Adjudication in the UN Security Council', pp. 283–94.

141 Meron, T., 'The Martens Clause, Principles of Humanity, and the Dictates of Public Conscience', *American Journal of International Law*, 94 (2000): 78–89, at p. 79.

142 Meron, 'The Martens Clause' pp. 79–82; Cassese, A., 'The Martens Clause: Half a Loaf or Simply Pie in the Sky', *European Journal of International Law*, 11(1) (2000): 187–216, at pp. 202–8.

143 Cassese, *International Law*, pp. 193–211; Roling, B. V. A., *International Law in an Expanded World*, Amsterdam: Djambatan, 1960, pp.37–8.

144 Cassese, *International Law*, pp. 189–216.

145 Shelton, 'Normative Hierarchy in International Law', pp. 319–22; Dixon, *International Law*, p. 50.

146 Guzman, A. T. and Meyer, T. L., 'International Soft Law', *Journal of Legal Analysis*, 2(1) (2010): 171–225, at p. 175.

147 Harris, *Cases and Materials on International Law*, p. 62.

148 Harris, *Cases and Materials on International Law*, p. 62.

149 Dixon, *International Law*, p. 50.

150 Hillgenberg, H., 'A Fresh Look at Soft Law', *European Journal of International Law*, 10(3) (1999): 499, at p. 514.

151 Thirlway, H., 'The Sources of International Law', in Evans, M. (ed.), *International Law*, Oxford: Oxford University Press, 2003, p. 119.
152 Thirlway, 'The Sources of International Law', pp. 119–20.
153 Reus-Smit, C., 'The Constitutional Structure of International Society and the Nature of Fundamental Institutions', *International Organization*, 51(4) (1997): 559–91.
154 Reus-Smit, *The Politics of International Law*, p. 42.
155 Byers, *Custom, Power, and the Power of Rules*, p. 9.
156 See Franck, T., *The Power of Legitimacy Among Nations*, Oxford: Oxford University Press, 1990; also Byers, *Custom, Power, and the Power of Rules*.
157 See Sutch, P., 'Normative IR Theory and the Legalization of International Politics: The Dictates of Humanity and of the Public Conscience as a Vehicle For Global Justice', *Journal of International Political Theory*, 8(1) (2012b): 1–24; Veuthey, M., 'Public Conscience in International Humanitarian Action', *Refugee Survey Quarterly*, 22 (2003): 198–201; Meron, T., 'The Humanization of Humanitarian Law', *American Journal of International Law*, 94(2) (2000): 239–78; Cassese, 'The Martens Clause in International Law, pp. 187–216.
158 Orakhelashvili, A., *Peremptory Norms in International Law*, Oxford: Oxford University Press, 2006.
159 Carr, *The Twenty Years Crisis*, pp. 164–5.
160 Carr, *The Twenty Years Crisis*, p. 168.
161 Carr, *The Twenty Years Crisis*, p. 169.
162 Carr, *The Twenty Years Crisis*, p. 172.
163 Carr, *The Twenty Years Crisis*, p. 168.
164 Slaughter Burley, A.-M., 'International Law and International Relations Theory: A Dual Agenda', *American Journal of International Law*, 87(2) (1993): 222–39.
165 Keohane, *Power and Governance*, pp. 117–31; Koh, *Why Do Nations Obey?*
166 On the early legalisation debates, especially the move from institutionalism to liberalism, see Slaughter Burley, 'International Law and International Relations Theory'; Simmons and Steinberg, *International Law and International Relations,* On constructivism, see Reus-Smit, *The Politics of International Law;* Adler 'Seizing the Middle Ground'. On the English School, see Bellamy, A. J., *International Society and its Critics*, Oxford: Oxford University Press, 2005; Linklater, A. and Suganami, H. (eds), *The English School of International Relations: A Contemporary Reassessment*, Cambridge: Cambridge University Press, 2006; Hurrell, *On Global Order*. On normative political theory, see Brown, C., *Sovereignty, Rights and Justice: International Political Theory Today*, Cambridge: Polity, 2002; Sutch, P., *Ethics, Justice and*

International Relations: Constructing an International Community, London: Routledge, 2001.
167 Wheeler, N., *Saving Strangers: Humanitarian Intervention in International Society*, Oxford: Oxford University Press, 2001.
168 See Buchanan, *Justice, Legitimacy and Self-Determination*, p. 292.
169 Bull, *The Anarchical Society*, pp. 14–19; Keohane, R., *After Hegemony: Cooperation and Discord in the World Political Economy*, Princeton, NJ: Princeton University Press, 1984, p. 246.
170 Slaughter Burley, 'International Law and International Relations Theory', p. 225.
171 Meron, 'The Humanization of Humanitarian Law', pp. 239–78.
172 Falk, 'The Grotian Quest'.
173 Buchanan, *Justice, Legitimacy and Self-Determination*.
174 Franck, *Fairness in International Law and Institutions*.
175 Keohane, *Power and Governance*, pp. 117–29.
176 Franck, T., 'Legitimacy in the International System', *American Journal of International Law*, 82(4) (1988): 702–59.
177 Nardin, 'Theorizing the International Rule of Law', p. 385.
178 Nardin 'Theorizing the International Rule of Law', p. 110.
179 Frost, M.. *Ethics in International Relations: A Constitutive Theory*, Cambridge: Cambridge University Press, 1996.
180 Shelton, 'Normative Hierarchy in International Law' p. 318.
181 Paulus, 'International Law and International Community', p. 49.
182 Koskenniemi, M., *The Politics of International Law*, Oxford: Hart, 2011, pp. 38–9. See also Crawford, J. and Koskenniemi, M., 'The Contexts of International Law', in J. Crawford and M. Koskenniemi (eds), *The Cambridge Companion to International Law*, Cambridge: Cambridge University Press, 2012, pp. 60–1; Koskenniemi, M., *The Gentle Civilizer of Nations: The Rise and Fall of International Law 1870–1960* Hersch Lauterpacht Memorial Lectures, Cambridge: Cambridge University Press, 2004.
183 Koskenniemi, *The Politics of International Law*, p. 40.
184 Rorty, R., 'Human Rights, Rationality and Sentimentality', in S. Shute and S. Hurley (eds), *On Human Rights: The Oxford Amnesty Lectures*, New York: Basic Books, 1993, pp. 175–202.
185 Paulus, 'International Law and International Community', p. 50.
186 Kennedy, D., *The Dark Sides of Virtue: Reassessing International Humanitarianism*, Princeton, NJ: Princeton University Press, 2004.
187 Crawford J. and Koskenniemi, M. (eds) *The Cambridge Companion to International Law*, p. 61.
188 Price and Reus-Smit, 'Dangerous Liaisons?', p. 30.
189 Shelton, 'Normative Hierarchy in International Law', p. 323.

CHAPTER THREE

| The Subjects of International Law | Justice in a World of States: The Moral Standing of Legal and Natural Persons |

Subjects of international law

In any society there are entities, which are subjects that enjoy rights and have obligations to carry out. The international society is no exception. The subjects of international law are said to have 'international personality'. Whether or not an entity is recognised as a person is determined by the law regulating the society of which such entity is a part. This chapter examines who or what are legal persons under international law. It examines the central role of states as the subject of International Law. Further, it explores increasing recognition of the place of non-state actors as subjects of international law. Building on this account of international legal personality we then explore the ways in which the legal account of personality maps on to broader considerations of agency in international society.

While IR is mainly interested in how and why subjects (or actors) behave the way that they do and the role they play in the anarchic international system, international law is more interested in these subjects (or actors) for the purpose of identifying entities in the international system that enjoy rights and carry out obligations under international law.[1] Wallace explains that the possession of international personality means that an entity is a subject of international law, and is 'capable of possessing international rights and duties, and has the capacity to maintain its rights by bringing international claims'.[2] Crawford also defined international personality as 'the capacity to be the bearer of rights and duties under international law'.[3] This idea has received judicial endorsement in the often cited Advisory Opinion of the International Court of Justice, the *Reparations for Injuries Suffered in the Service of the United Nations* case, where the Court alluded to the fact that a subject of international law is an entity that is capable of possessing international rights and duties, and having the capacity to maintain its rights by bringing international claims.[4] Such entities under international law have the following main capacities, some more so than others:

- enjoy rights and subject to duties under international law;
- ability to make claims before international/national tribunals in respect of rights/duties under international law;
- power to enter into valid international agreements binding under international law (i.e., treaties); and
- enjoy either absolute or partial immunities from jurisdiction of the domestic courts of States.[5]

Over the years it has been identified that subjects of international law have the above capacities on a sliding scale, depending on whether the entity is a state or a non-state actor. States have all the capacities. Some international organisations, such as the United Nations, may also possess all these capacities depending on the terms, express or implicit, of their constituent treaties, while other non-state actors may possess some capacities at varying levels. For instance, while states and some international organisations are able to enter into treaties, a number of non-state actors, such as individuals or MNCs, are unable to enter into treaties. Further, individuals and MNCs may have the right to make a claim in an international court or tribunal only if the states in entering into the relevant treaties permit such a claim. For instance, under the United Nations Charter individuals and MNCs are unable to bring contentious claims before the International Court of Justice, only states may do so.[6] On the other hand, recently individuals and MNCs have been permitted by relevant treaties to bring claims before certain international courts and tribunals, for instance, in respect of human rights violations and investment disputes.

As we saw in Chapter One, classical international law was conceived to regulate inter-state relations alone. This has since changed. Although contemporary international law regulates primarily inter-state relations, it also regulates non-state actors, such as international organisations, individuals, MNCs, indigenous peoples, NGOs, belligerent or insurgent groups, etc., that play crucial roles one way or the other in the contemporary international community. However, by reason of the initial monopoly of states over international law and its present primary role, certain scholars have declared that states have 'original personality', while non-state actors have 'derived personality' because the latter 'achieve their personality because it has been conferred, accepted or recognised by States'.[7]

States as subjects of international law

The central role of the state in international law and politics is, in the historical shorthand of the disciplines, traceable to the Peace of Westphalia which brought about the emergence of the modern sovereign state.[8] From 1648 to the present the system of global relations has been a state system or society of states. While a nuanced history of world affairs challenges the simplicity of this orthodoxy, it does capture a core element of the nature of the international affairs. In the *Reparations* case, the ICJ, alluding to the primary place of the state as the principal subject of international law, declared that: 'a State possesses the totality of international rights and duties recognised by international law'.[9]

However, although the primary position of states as subjects of international law is not in doubt, the exact number of sovereign states in the world remains a rather polemic issue because the determination of what entity is actually a state involves a complex mix of international law and politics. For instance, while some existing states in the international community regard Taiwan, Kosovo, South Ossetia or Abkhazia as states, others are very adamant that they are not. In other words, not every entity that necessarily satisfies the requirement of statehood under the rules of international law, which will be explored subsequently, is necessarily always regarded as a state by all existing state members of the international community. Some have pointed to the membership of the United Nations, presently 193, as an objective yard stick with which to determine the number of states in the world, since membership of this huge global international is open to all 'peace-loving States'.[10] However, though this may be useful as some kind of guideline, it may not always be appropriate as an all-embracing standard, since not all states are necessarily members of the United Nations. A ready example is Switzerland, which only became a member of the United Nations in 2002 due to its domestic policies, though clearly it was regarded as a state long before its UN membership.[11] Furthermore, the recommendatory powers of the Security Council, which allows the P-5 members to utilise their veto to block the admission to membership of the United Nations, may result in entities that may actually be states being refused membership of this eminent organisation.[12] Examples abound, during the Cold War, of how the bipolar powers, the United States and the then Soviet Union (USSR), used their veto powers to block, at least for some time, the membership of states that were perceived as the other power's allies. For instance, the USSR vetoed for a while the application for membership of Japan, while the United States did the same in respect of the application of the Socialist Republic of Vietnam.[13] Further, the admission of Taiwan, Kosovo and Palestine as members of the United Nations is unlikely in the near future because of the veto (or threat of use of the veto) by China, Russia and the United States, respectively. Though, it is important to note that on 29 November 2012 the General Assembly voted to grant Palestine non-member observer state status at the United Nations.[14] Moreover, the membership of the UN is not necessarily a 'set in stone' guarantee of the statehood of an entity. For instance, the admission into UN membership of Ukraine and Byelorussia, which at that time were not technically independent states but rather part of the USSR, due to Cold War diplomatic horse-trading, confirms that it may be possible for entities that are not in the strict sense states to be admitted into UN membership as long as this is acceptable to existing state members, especially the required majority in the General Assembly and Security Council, including the P-5.[15]

The usual starting point for exploring whether an entity has become a state under international law is Article 1 of the Montevideo Convention on Rights and Duties of States 1933.[16] This Convention, originally adopted on 26 December 1933 by certain states in the American continent, has since being accepted as having the status of CIL.[17] Article 1 of the Convention states: 'The state as a person of international law should possess the following qualifications: (a) a permanent population; (b) a defined territory; (c) government; and (d) capacity to enter into relations with the other states.' The Arbitration Commission of the European Conference on Yugoslavia in Opinion No. 1 also affirmed this by stating that under international law a state is 'commonly defined as a community which consists of a territory and a population subject to an organized political authority', and that 'such a State is characterized by sovereignty'.[18] Higgins points out that surprisingly in 'a rapidly changing world, the definition of "a state" has remained virtually unchanged and continues to be well described by the traditional provisions of the Montevideo Convention on the Rights and Duties of States'.[19] It is thus worth spending a little time on the detail of the Montevideo criteria.

(a) Permanent population

A state must have a permanent population. This is not to suggest that there is any real permanency in the population size, as it is clear that there would be changes in birth and death rates, as well as emigration and immigration. Neither does this suggest a fixed minimum in terms of population size, as states range from those with huge population size, such as China, India and Nigeria, to minuscule states, such as Nauru reported to have a population of about 10,000 people.[20] Dixon rightly points out that it suggests 'that there must be some population linked to a specific piece of territory on a more or less permanent basis and who can be regarded in general parlance as its inhabitants'.[21] The ICJ in the *Western Sahara Advisory* case appeared to suggest that this requirement would be satisfied even in the case of a nomadic population, as long as it can be established that they have a link to a specific territory.[22] There is, however, a lack of clarity about whether this population must be made up of a substantially indigenous population.[23] Further, would the state cease to exist if devastation makes the whole territory of the state uninhabitable? Perhaps the answer to this question would depend on whether or not the territory is permanently or temporarily uninhabitable. In the former case, arguably the state would cease to exist, while for the latter case this would not be the case. Rayfuse, discussing a situation where a state disappears due to sea level rising, points out as follows: 'Of course, disappearance is most likely to be a gradual process with the territory being rendered uninhabitable and the population having fled long before the territory's total physical disappearance. In this case . . . the criteria for statehood will cease to be met from the time of evacuation and the state will cease to exist.'[24]

(b) Defined territory

For an entity to be a state it must have an identifiable physical territory which its population occupy. This is not to suggest that the borders of all states must be absolutely certain, as in reality a number of states have border disputes with neighbouring states, some of which are settled by force of arms, while a number are taken before international courts or tribunals for peaceful settlement of these disputes. For instance, the fact that there is a debate as to the precise extent of the borders of the state of Israel does not make it any less a state. With the current possibility of certain island states losing their territory to sea level rises due to climate change, the question arises as to whether such a loss of territory due to natural causes would make a state cease to exist. Recently, it was reported that the government of the Maldives has been diverting a portion of its huge annual tourist revenue in order to buy a new homeland, possibly in Australia, India or Sri Lanka, in the event of the disappearance of the islands due to sea level rises caused by climate change.[25] While Kiribati is thinking of purchasing land at Fiji and moving its population to such land if the low-lying Pacific island state disappears due to sea level rise.[26] This raises complex issues on whether such loss of territory due to climate change would result in the extinction of the relevant states and perhaps an emergence of new states in the new location, or would it remain the same state in international law despite the loss of its territory and its relocation to a new territory? Rayfuse argues, rightly in the authors' view, that: 'As the territory of a threatened Island State disappears beneath the waves, the criteria of territory will no longer be met and the claim to statehood will fail.'[27]

(c) Government

For an entity to be a state it must have a government. Shaw points out that what is required is more 'an indication of some sort of coherent political structure and society, than the necessity for a sophisticated apparatus of executive and legislative organs'.[28] In addition, there is no requirement under international law that such government must necessarily be democratic. All that is required is some type of 'organised political authority'[29] with some level of control over the territory. In the *Aaland Islands* case the International Committee of Jurists, entrusted by the Council of the League of Nations with the task of giving an Advisory Opinion on the legal aspects of the Aaland Islands dispute between Sweden and Finland, in trying to determine when Finland actually became a state pointed out that this 'did not take place until a stable political organisation had been created, and until the public authorities had become strong enough to assert themselves throughout the territories of the State without the assistance of the foreign troops'.[30] Although the report in the *Aaland Island* case appears to indicate that the government must have control over all the territory, it would appear that the better view is that it would suffice if the government has control over either all or a significant part of the territory and is able to convince the international community that it is effectively in control and carrying out the governmental functions of a state.[31] What is clear is that an entity that has already emerged as a state does not cease to be such merely because it subsequently ceased to have an effective government. Although, such states are sometimes described as 'failed states', in reality under international law they still remain as states. Consequently, though a state, such as Somalia, which has not had an effective government for some time, may be described as a 'failed state', it is still recognised as a state under international law.[32]

(d) Capacity to enter into legal relation

This criterion has been described as connoting independence and sovereignty.[33] For an entity to emerge as a state it must not be under the control of another state, for example, as a sort of colony. Although with increasing interdependence among states, no state in reality may be said to be completely independent. What is required is that a state must have 'legal' independence or sovereignty. This criterion of capacity to enter into legal relation is satisfied if that entity has at least legally, though this may not be so in reality, the ability to chose whether or not to enter into relations with other entities in the international community, including other states and IOs.[34] For instance, Monaco is regarded as a state, though in reality it is significantly dependent on France, because technically it has the legal independence to choose whether or not to continue to be dependent on France.

Although the Montevideo Convention criteria represents the established international law requirements for statehood, over the years existing states of the international community have been known to insist on certain additional criteria before recognising an entity as a state. For instance, respect for human rights and the rights of national or ethnic groups and the provisions of the UN Charter; respect for the inviolability of existing borders; commitment to disarmament, nuclear non-proliferation and peaceful settlement of disputes have been included as criteria for recognition by the European Union of entities as states in Eastern Europe, the former Soviet Union and Yugoslavia.[35] The British and American state practices appear to support the position that additional criteria may be required for recognition. The UK Foreign and Commonwealth Office, in response to a question on non-recognition of Bopphuthatswana in Parliament in 1986. stated that:

> The normal criteria which the Government apply for recognition as a State are that it should have, and seem likely to continue to have, a clearly defined territory with a population, a Government who are able of themselves to exercise effective control of that territory, and independence in their external relations. Other factors, including some United Nations resolutions, may also be relevant.[36]

While the US State Department stated in 1976 that:

> In the view of the United States, international law does not require a State to recognize another entity as a State; it is a matter for the judgment of each State whether an entity merits recognition as a State. In reaching this judgment, the United States has traditionally looked to the establishment of certain facts. These facts include effective control over a clearly-defined territory and population; and organized governmental administration of that territory; and a capacity to act effectively to conduct foreign relations and to fulfill international obligations. The United States has also taken into account whether the entity in question has attracted recognition of the international community of States.[37]

Over the years there has been a theoretical debate between what is termed the declaratory and constitutive schools of thought on the exact role of recognition in determining whether an entity has emerged as a state.[38] The declaratory school insist that recognition is merely declaratory of a legal matter of fact, that is, the existence of an entity that meets the legal requirements of statehood under international law.[39] A German–Polish Mixed Arbitral Tribunal, exploring the emergence of Poland as a state, stated: 'the recognition of a State is not constitutive but merely declaratory. The State exists by itself and the recognition is nothing else than a declaration of this existence, recognized by the States from which it emanates.'[40] Also, the Arbitration Commission on Yugoslavia stated that 'the effects of recognition by other States are merely declaratory'.[41] On the other hand, the constitutive theory maintains that it is only through recognition by existing states that an entity may emerge as a state.[42] Oppenheim, asserting the constitutive position, points out that: 'A State is, and becomes, an International Person through recognition only and exclusively.'[43] Undoubtedly, recognition does play a role in an entity emerging as a state. In practice there are situations where an entity has emerged as a state because of widespread recognition, while another entity in similar circumstances has been unable to do so due to rather limited or non-existent recognition.[44] For example, Bangladesh, with widespread recognition by existing states, emerged as a state with India's direct help and military intervention. On the other hand, Northern Cyprus, with similar direct help and military intervention of Turkey, has not emerged as a state primarily because of the rather limited recognition. However, the challenge in accepting a constitutive approach is in respect of how to deal with the inherent difficulties arising where an entity is recognised by some states and not recognised by others. Will the entity be a state in relation to the former and not a state with regard to the latter? Ijalaye points out that to accept this would amount to what he terms a 'legal curiosity'.[45] He also raised another difficulty with regard to the problem of determining how many existing states' recognition would suffice for an entity to emerge as a state under international law. Should it be all existing states, or 50 per cent or more of such states? Should such recognitions necessarily include that of the big powers?[46] Shaw, in what appears to be an attempt to arrive at a balance between the two theories, points out as follows:

> There is an integral relationship between recognition and the criteria for statehood in the sense that the more overwhelming the scale of international recognition is in any given situation, the less may be demanded in terms of the objective demonstration of adherence to the criteria. Conversely, the more sparse international recognition is, the more attention will be focused upon proof of actual adherence to the criteria concerned.[47]

Non-state subjects of international law

Despite the centrality of states there is a variety of non-state entities (such as sub-state units, IOs and individuals) that have a degree of legal personality. Some states, such as Austria, Canada, Germany, Switzerland and Switzerland, under their internal laws allow component units to have some limited participation in the international system.[48] These sub-state units are allowed to engage at an international level with states, IOs or other sub-state entities. For instance, some actually have the capacity to enter into treaties independently of their central government. To this extent it could be said that these sub-state entities have international personality, albeit a limited one, distinct from that of the state of which they are a component unit.[49]

An international organisation, a term alleged to have been coined by a Scottish jurist called James Lorimer,[50] may be a subject of international law. Alvarez defines international organisations as 'intergovernmental entities established by treaty, usually composed of permanent secretariats, plenary assemblies involving all member states, and executive organs with more limited participation'.[51] O'Brien, making a distinction between an international organisation and a non-governmental organisation, states that the former is an 'organisation established by states under treaty as distinct from a private international union or a non-governmental organisation; the latter resulting from the initiatives of individuals or private organisations'.[52] However, since international organisation are social constructs created by states to serve different purposes there are variations of such entities and, therefore, it is perhaps rather difficult to have a comprehensive definition that would cover the diverse types of IOs. While IOs are usually created between states on the basis of a treaty as an organ with a distinct will from the state members,[53] there are exceptions to this. For instance, there are international organisations that include other IOs as part of their membership. For example, the European Community, now the European Union (EU), was actively involved in the creation of the International Seabed Authority (ISA), established by the Law of the Sea Convention (LOSC) 1982, and became a member of this organisation.[54] Also, there are organisations that are not established by treaties. An example of this is the United Nations Children's Fund (UNICEF), which was established by UN resolutions.[55] Further, not all IOs have a distinct will from the members. For instance, for a long time, prior to the Lisbon Treaty, it was not clear if the EU had a legal personality distinct from that of its members.[56]

When an international organisation has a legal personality distinct from that of its members it is regarded as being a subject of international law. Such personality may either be expressly stated in the document establishing the organisation (e.g., Article 176 of the LOSC 1982 states that 'The Authority shall have international legal personality and such legal capacity as may be necessary for the exercise of its functions and the fulfilment of its purposes') or it may sometimes be implicit. Although the UN Charter did not expressly confer personality on the United Nations, the International Court of Justice, in its Advisory Opinion in the *Reparation for Injuries Suffered in the Service of the United Nations* case,[57] after examining the provisions of the Charter found that such personality was implicit. It came to the conclusion that the UN is an international person. However, it emphasised as follows:

> That is not the same thing as saying that it is a State, which it certainly is not, or that its legal personality and rights and duties are the same as those of a State ... What it does mean is that it is a subject of international law and capable of possessing international rights and duties, and that it has capacity to maintain its rights by bringing international claims.[58]

There are a variety of international organisations that have been established to carry out different functions; some are global IOs with membership open to all states in different parts of the world (e.g., the UN), while some are regional with membership limited to states in a particular region (e.g., the African Union). Some specialise in dealing with rather limited issues, ranging from health (e.g., the WHO), trade (e.g., the WTO), finance (e.g., the World Bank), petroleum (e.g., OPEC) to security (e.g., NATO), etc., while others are multifunctional with broad powers to deal with a range of issues (e.g., the UN). With such diverse international organisations, and the variance in the structure of some of these organisations, there is sometimes debate on whether certain entities are actually IOs. A prominent example of this is the debate in respect of the EU.

Traditionally, the EU is classified as a type of regional IO.[59] However, due to its peculiar institutional structure, especially with regard to the EU Parliament, made up of directly elected members, and the cabinet-like European Commission, as well as the legal order that gives EU legislation primacy over laws of member states, there is ongoing debate as to whether the EU is actually a regional IO.[60] For instance, Börzel and Risse argue that: 'the European Union today looks like a federal system, it works in a similar manner to a federal system so why not call it an emerging federation'.[61] On the other hand, it has been pointed out that the EU is neither an IO nor a federation; rather it is in a special genre, some sort of *sui generis* entity in the international system. This peculiar supranational entity has been described by Shaw as an association of states that have established a variety of common institutions with the competence to adopt binding legal acts, which may have direct effect within the domestic legal system of the member states.[62]

Initially individuals were regarded as merely objects and not as subjects of international law. Higgins explains this distinction as follows:

> individuals [were] the objects of international law, but not subjects of that legal system. The argument, reduced to its crudest elements, runs as follows: under a legal system there exists only objects and subjects. In international law 'subjects' is the term used to describe those elements bearing, without the need for municipal intervention, rights and responsibilities. Under the existing rules of international law there is no evidence that individuals are permitted to be the bearers of duties and responsibilities. They must, therefore, be objects: that is to say, they are like 'boundaries' or 'rivers' or 'territory' or any of the other chapter headings found in the traditional textbooks.[63]

Under the object theory the individual had to depend on his or her national state to espouse a claim at the international plane. In essence, under this theory any alleged right under such claim was regarded as being that of the national state and not the individual *per se*.[64] Further, it also meant that an individual could not enforce a claim in the international plane against his or her national state.[65] The object–subject dichotomy has been criticised as not only being odd, illogical and unrealistic, but also as immoral because it treated individuals who are recognised as a person in the municipal legal system as mere objects in international law.[66] Further, it objectivises individuals, who as the real persons behind the artificial state are in reality 'the sole, the real, the indirect, or the ultimate subjects of international law'.[67] Higgins points out that this dichotomy is unhelpful, and argues that individuals should be regarded as participants in the international plane, along with states, IOs and other actors.[68]

Contemporary international law appears to have progressed beyond the rather unhelpful object–subject dichotomy, and now regards individuals as subjects of international law, albeit in a rather limited sense.[69] According to Menon:

> In spite of the traditional doctrine that States exclusively are the subjects of international law, the position of individuals in international law is becoming increasingly important in light of technological and cultural advances of society. The traditional doctrine

is being modified to the extent that an individual has become a subject of international law. States, however, are still the principal subjects of international law and international organizations are to a lesser extent subjects of that system. Nevertheless, there is no rule that individual cannot have personality for certain purposes.[70]

For instance, individuals have rights in the international plane in areas such as international human rights law. Also, individuals have clear duties at the international plane, as can be seen in the growing number of prosecutions before different international criminal tribunals and courts since the end of the Second World War, such as the Nuremberg and Tokyo War Crimes tribunals, and more recently others such as the International Tribunal for the Prosecution of Persons Responsible for Serious Violations of International Humanitarian Law Committed in Former Yugoslavia (ICTY), the International Criminal Tribunal for Rwanda (ICTR), the International Criminal Court (ICC) and the Special Court for Sierra Leone. The judgment of the Nuremberg Tribunal was emphatic that: 'Crimes against international law are committed by men, not by abstract entities, and only by punishing individuals who commit such crimes can the provisions of international law be enforced.'[71] In addition, the UN Security Council, in its important role of maintaining international peace and security, now directs its sanctions not only against states, but also against individuals (the so-called smart sanctions).[72] Further, individuals now have access to enforce claims under international law before certain international tribunals, such as the European Court of Human Rights (ECtHR) and the International Centre for Settlement of Investment Disputes (ICSID).

There are other non-state actors that are increasingly regarded as being subjects of international law. This includes NGOs,[73] MNCs,[74] belligerent and Insurgent groups, national liberation groups[75] and Indigenous persons.[76]

Justice in a world of states: the moral standing of legal and natural persons

As we have seen, the state is the central agent in public international law. Despite the acknowledgement that other entities are increasingly important bearers of rights and duties, the centrality of the concept of the sovereign equality of states is, as Brownlie notes, 'the basic constitutional doctrine' of international law.[77] Accordingly, international legal thinking is tied to the idea that the state is the foundational or fundamental actor. Theories of international ethics do not share this attachment to the sovereign state. The state, most acknowledge, is a remarkably durable social and political unit, but can we (or should we) conceive of the state has having moral worth in itself? If not is it of such instrumental importance to the realisation of other values, then we should treat it as the most important entity in global politics? Or is it the case that the reification of the state in the international legal order prevents us from remedying injustice and developing a more just global society?

The project of international political theory has been described as an attempt to construct a 'realistic utopia'.[78] International political theory is, on this reading at least, 'ideal theory'. It is an attempt to describe what ought to be as opposed to simply engaging with what is.[79] In moral terms the nation-state is a contingent fact rather than a constitutional fact. Assuming that the enduring character of the sovereign state limits our ethical horizons: that range of possible solutions to existing injustice and suffering. If, however, we think about utopian solutions to existing problems without considering the state, we introduce two major problems. The first is that we are unlikely to fully comprehend how the challenges we want to address arise. The sovereignty of states, it can be argued, is the cause of many of the injustices we see in international affairs or acts as a barrier to remedy. The second is that, having identified the problem, we have no basis for an institutional solution (or how we get to where we want to be from where we are now). In Chapter One we explored the idea of moral accessibility as developed in the theory of Andrew Hurrell, Allen Buchanan and Christian Reus-Smit. At the core of their arguments is the thought that moral reasoning must be institutional, or social, moral reasoning. The moral challenges of international politics arise in a social and institutional context. We describe justice and injustice in terms that derive from shared experiences, using ethical vocabularies that are contested in the context of international society as currently constituted. Demonstrating the ways that moral challenges arise in the social and political context of international society, often showing how existing legal structures enable or even produce normatively undesirable effects, enables us to focus on the institutionally complex questions of whether we ought to alter our practices and how to do so.

As we have seen, natural persons play a relatively minor role in public international law. But this does not mean that international law is not concerned with individuals as moral agents. It is often easier, and more effective, to deal with individuals as members of groups and as having rights and obligations by virtue of their role within collectivities. We see individuals as citizens of states (or as agents of states) or as employees of corporations, and we ascribe legal responsibility to those entities as legal persons. It is true that we do so with less and less certainty as we move away from states and international organisations to corporations and NGOs.[80] There is an observable move towards assigning responsibility to a broader range of actors than just states, including, in international criminal law, to real or natural persons. However, it is undeniably the case that the most important actor in terms of international politics is the state, and for some this means that we must conceive of the state as a moral actor in its own right. For others, however, the state gains moral authority because it represents moral agents (natural persons). In both cases, it is precisely because the state is the most important entity, in terms of its sheer range of activity and immense power, that its dominant place in the international legal order must come under critical scrutiny in terms of its ability to promote justice and prevent injustice.

At the basis of the debates between those who advocate a continued reliance upon a (modified) state system and those who advocate a cosmopolitan re-ordering of society is the question of how well, or otherwise, states 'respect, protect, promote and fulfil' the moral entitlements of relevant agents. This is a complex question and breaking it down helps us to understand the key issues. The question combines a phrase 'respect, protect, promote and fulfil' that is drawn from international human rights law with two broader categories. The increasing importance of human rights law to general public international law has reinvigorated debates about global justice. It is now increasingly plausible to claim that respect for human rights is a definitional or constitutive aspect of legitimate institutional agency.[81] If, so the argument goes, the state as a legal person is unsuited to the task of respecting, protecting, promoting and fulfilling the human rights of those within its jurisdiction, then surely we must look to other institutional forms of governance? This is an important point, but it does bring 'ideal theory' into conflict with the 'fact' of the existence of a state system. But the state system is not a straightforward fact. It is an evolving and socially constituted fact, and this conflict is vital. On the one hand, it is the driver behind the idea of the rule of law in international affairs

– an idea that suggests that we should worry more about the morality of states than human rights – and, on the other, it is the motivation behind the expansion of the range of legal persons. The phrase 'moral entitlements' leaves open the question of whether human rights law adequately responds to the full range of moral entitlements of agents. For many scholars, human beings (and the idea of justice) require more than individual human rights as a basis for moral agency. The state has developed as a bounded space within which we develop our collective, culturally rich, lives as self-determining agents. As such it is a geo-political space that underwrites freedom and must be protected. The interplay between the need to respect the state (as an historically successful defender of free societies) and to uphold the rights of individuals is the key dynamic. The final element of the phrase, 'relevant agents', opens the question of whether a world of states delivers justice for states as moral agents or whether it should aspire to deliver justice for natural persons. If the latter, does a world of states deliver justice for everyone or only for those who are lucky enough to live in states that respect such rights? If the state system cannot provide for all relevant agents, then perhaps we have to rethink the institutional structure of global society to find a new balance between the needs of self-determining groups and individuals.

In the following sections we examine the ways in which international political theory addresses the moral standing of states and of natural persons. This leads us to the many arguments that expose the fragmentation of international law and urge an unbundling of sovereignty.[82] Unbundling sovereignty means moving the locus of power and legal personality away from a singular concentration in the state and investing those qualities in sub-state and transnational organisations. Multiple legal persons/political actors can exist side by side, so this does not mean the end of the state, but it does infer a considerable move away from the Westphalian system. In these debates pluralists offer a collectivist or communitarian argument about the most desirable structure for international society. While most pluralists recognise that the power of the sovereign state has to be limited (usually through obligations to respect the human rights of those within its jurisdiction), they also think of sovereignty in a very traditional 'Westphalian' way. Here sovereignty represents political, cultural, religious and moral autonomy or freedom from the influence of those outside the self-determining unit. Strong readings of human rights are, for many, moral and cultural impositions rather than part of a global international culture. Emphasising the role of the state as the primary bearer of rights and duties thus captures the idea of international justice appropriately. Cosmopolitans, on the other hand, argue that the traditional sovereign nation-state fails internal and external tests of justice. Internally, the fall-out from the power politics between and within competing cultural, religious, ethnic and economic groups is often the exclusive concern of the most powerful of those groups and often that power is abused. Externally, the structure of a state-based legal system often hides the moral obligations we have to those outside the state. Moral boundaries and political boundaries are not the same. Here an enhanced human rights-based order offers a solution. Both pluralists and cosmopolitans recognise that the state-based legal order is continually evolving and that the sovereignty of states has become ever more permeable. What really divides them is the extent to which they believe that a more disaggregated international legal order would best articulate the moral agency of natural persons.

Moral agency: pluralism, communitarianism, solidarism and cosmopolitanism

In this section we want to demonstrate four approaches to the normative desirability of state-centrism in a legalised international order. We present a snapshot of each tradition through an introduction to the work of one of its key exponents. Beginning with a brief exploration of the pluralist position we start with the most state-centric position and work our way towards the least state-centric in liberal cosmopolitanism. None of the four approaches treats the existence of states as a simple fact. All present a consideration of the justice or injustice of state-centrism. None of the four approaches argue that the state is irrelevant to considerations of international justice, and all recognise that the state-centric nature of international society is a vital starting point for ethical reflection. Each tradition seeks to ground their alternative perspective on observable characteristics of international law as developed in a partially globalised and legalised world, rather than beginning with a set of preordained moral claims

(a) Terry Nardin: pluralism and the morality of coexistence

Terry Nardin represents the pluralist tradition of the English School or International Society approach to IR. Pluralists are often termed

'Grotians' after Hugo Grotius the father of modern international law.[83] It will come as no surprise then to find that pluralism offers a very traditional legalist approach to the idea of the role of the state in international law. Pluralists argue that while international politics has no institutional hierarchy (and is therefore anarchical) and shares only limited goals (order) it is still a *society* rather than a state of nature (see Chapter One). Their depiction of the anarchical society focuses particularly on the existence of the rule of law as a shared value. Importantly, the emphasis is not on a shared set of moral principles or desired outcomes that the law protects (Nardin refers to this as instrumental law[84]), but on the idea of legal obligation itself. Tied up with a non-instrumental attachment to the international rule of law is the existence of sovereign states as creators of law and as the primary bearers of rights and duties:

> What transforms a number of powers, contingently related in terms of shared interests, in to a society proper is not their agreement to participate in a common enterprise for as long as they desire to participate, but their participation in and implicit recognition of the practices, procedures, and other rules of international law that compose international society. The rules of international law are not merely regulatory but constitutive: they not only create normative order among separate political communities but define the status, rights and duties of these communities within this normative order. In international society 'states' are constituted as such with the practice of international law; 'statehood' is a position or role that is defined by international law and not independent of it.[85]

The centrality of the state in international society is not morally contingent because the law as the most vital constitutive element in that society is 'the source' of ethical judgement.[86] The idea is that international society would not exist at all without international law and that international law gives that society particular moral characteristics. In *Law, Morality and the Relations of States*[87] and in several later restatements Nardin, adopting Oakeshott's categorisation, describes international society as a practical rather than a purposive association. A purposive association is one that pursues shared purposes. A practical association is one that is constituted by shared rules rather than by common purposes.[88] International society is a practical association because it is inherently pluralist, there are no stable shared substantive purposes. Nevertheless, international law has developed as a shared set of rules that constitute the morality of states as a morality of coexistence.[89] In this morality it is the rule of law that binds states together, and this morality distinguishes the pluralist conception of international society from the realist power-centred state of anarchy. But it binds them together in a society that respects 'laws governing the transactions of independent, formally equal legal persons'.[90] At this point Nardin's thesis affirms the idea that the equality of sovereign states is the constitutional doctrine of international society (see above). Nardin shows that the rule of law is constitutive of international society. He goes on to argue that 'to avoid subverting the rule of law, moral criticism of a legal system must draw upon principles of justice that are already recognized, at least in part, within that system';[91] this means that justice is grounded in the authority of law itself and not on the desirability of the consequences of observing it.[92] The legalist–pluralist view may be very conservative but, argues Nardin, a respect for the rule of law is the only thing that separates international society from the unfettered power politics of a state of nature. The authoritative source of law is the will of states and, regardless of what they will, respect for the rule of law constitutes a moral relationship between states as legal persons. An attempt to subvert this relationship 'under the name of God's will, natural law, human rights, utility, or social justice – as an alternative to law is not a sign of the flourishing of law but of its decay'.[93]

(b) Michael Walzer: the moral standing of states

Communitarians privilege the state for a rather different set of reasons, and even in this philosophical tradition (often associated with tribalism and relativism) we begin to find challenges to statism. Michael Walzer offers the clearest defence of this position. For communitarians the concept of individual moral agency is something of a philosophical abstraction. Moral life is a collective experience, and the bulk of our social and political experience happens inside our communities rather than on the international plane. We generate complex, or thick, understandings of justice and injustice in the context of the various social, ethno-cultural and religious groups that give us our social identity. Those understandings are made real in the political and legal structures of our state. We develop institutions to help us mediate between competing claims and to distribute resources among groups and individuals. The fact that it is a state that gives expression to the political decisions of a particular group is historically contingent. This role could be, and has been, the role of tribes, clans, city-states or transnational organisations.[94] But in the modern period the key political unit has been the territorial state. Walzer argues that:

> Actual men and women ... claim justice, and resist tyranny, by insisting on the meaning of social goods among themselves. Justice is rooted in the distinct understanding of places, honors, jobs, things of all sorts, that constitute a shared way of life. To override those sorts of things is (always) to act unjustly.[95]

Central to the collectivist arguments is the fact that statehood has an internal and external dimension. In the preceding quotation we begin to see the external aspect of statehood. If the internal aspect of statehood is the site of complex social negotiation, the external aspect of statehood is a claim to exclusivity, to the right to be self-determining and free from external authority (from popes to progressive international law).[96] The question of a state's legitimacy is first and foremost a matter for the citizens of that state. Outsiders are not party to that set of social negotiations and so should, unless there is very clear evidence to the contrary, presume that the state is legitimate.[97] The moral fabric of the international community is very thin compared with the thick moral complexity of the domestic polity. The international community has to manage the interaction of self-determining units. Sovereignty protects the independence of states. The moral importance of sovereignty helps us to understand why the worst crime in international relations is aggressive war.[98] But the fact that sovereignty is important because it protects the ability of natural persons to be self-determining also helps us to understand why the state can sometimes be the enemy of moral agency.

The state is a hugely powerful entity. When defending the borders of a self-determining and free society this can be a good thing. It keeps the undue influence of outsiders (in military, economic and cultural terms) at bay. But the post-war international legal order is built upon the stark recognition that state power can be used against elements of its own citizenry. State power can be used to oppress as well as to defend. In urgent cases of 'extreme oppression', such as genocide or ethnic cleansing, it may be necessary, as a last resort, to use force to prevent aggressive tyranny (see our discussion of humanitarian military intervention in Chapter Seven, below). In other cases, where the self-determination of groups inside the borders of a state is threatened by religious or racial intolerance and discrimination or by poverty, we have become increasingly aware that sovereign boundaries can entrench injustice. In response to such injustice, argues Walzer, the international community has developed an account of human rights. Human rights, particularly the rights to life and liberty, are thin rights. Thin, in Walzer's terminology, does not mean weak. They are politically urgent rights, necessary to, but not sufficient for, the thick processes of self-determination. Supplementing states with international and regional institutions that are intended to protect such rights is an attempt to protect moral agency, but they cannot supplant the communal work of self-determination. Walzer rarely engages with 'ideal theory', preferring to address moral and social challenges in the context in which they arise. However, on the rare occasion that he does, Walzer recognises that international institutions are not strong enough to eliminate injustice,[99] and does advocate an unbundling of sovereignty and the distribution of power to sub-state and trans-state organisations.[100] But he is very wary of those who claim that international institutions founded on a thick, universalist account of human rights is the way forward. Moral agency requires more than universal human rights. It requires the international rule of law, but it also requires institutionalised pluralism. In the here and now institutionalised pluralism means nation-states. States may consent to the development of principles of international law that create other legal persons intended to shore up the institutions that give effect to moral and political agency. However, such institutions are weak at the international level and unevenly developed at the regional level. The reason for this, argue the pluralists, is that the injustice of imposing international political and legal rule is greater than the injustice upheld by a system of semi-sovereign states.[101]

(c) Andrew Hurrell: solidarism and normative ambition

Solidarism explores the emergence of new norms of international society. Andrew Hurrell, in *On Global Order*, offers a detailed examination of the development of broadly liberal norms and institutional structures against the background of a pluralist world order. Solidarism represents the liberal or 'revolutionist' element of the English School or International Society approach. This approach shares much with constructivist approaches to the politics of international law, and critical dialogue between the traditions has been very fruitful.[102] The liberal political ambition found in the tradition is based on the observation of normative change. Broadly, changes in the legal and social norms in international society underwrite the normative desirability of the liberalisation of global politics. Crucial to the analysis is the tension between the pluralist international order and an emerging solidarism. Despite the fact that normative change takes place within the pluralist order, solidarism emerges as a political and moral project rather than as an evolutionary process. The normative project challenges the legitimacy of the state-centric legal order.

For Hurrell solidarism is:

> A composite label for a qualitatively different kind of international society, in which four dimensions are equally important: the move to institutions and expansion of global rule-making; changes in the making, development and justification of international law; the increasing emphasis placed on the enforcement of international norms and rules; and a changed understanding of the state and of state sovereignty.[103]

The drivers of change in international society are closely entwined with the legalised nature of global politics. The principal claim is that it is the development of international law itself that leads us to question the role of the state as the primary author of law and the primary legal person or agent. For Hurrell, the coverage of international law has increased both by increasing the specificity of existing regimes (think of the development of international human rights law since the Universal Declaration of Human Rights in 1948) and the creation of new ones (e.g., on economic or environmental issues). We have witnessed a shift from narrowly bilateral treaties to multilateral and quasi-constitutional treaties (such as the UN Charter). The range of law-making entities and law-enforcing bodies has broadened, the fundamental requirement of state consent has been narrowed by the emphasis placed on general principles of law and on peremptory norms, and international law is no longer just about regulating the international acts of states, but about regulating domestic political issues.[104] These developments have implications for our understanding of states as agents. First, non-state actors have become a more significant part of the legal order. Second, states have come to be viewed not simply as persons in their own right, but as representatives of those within its jurisdiction. Here states represent, and are responsible for, national communities and their constituent sub-national communities, all the protected social and cultural groups and individuals. Third, and perhaps most importantly in this context, these developments challenge the constitutional principle of sovereign equality, and this challenge has become part of the legal and normative order.[105]

Sovereign equality is challenged in two ways. First, sovereignty becomes conditional. A legitimate state is one that respects, protects and fulfils the human rights of those within its jurisdiction or that respects the right of all peoples within its territory to self-determination. Failure to do so may bring condemnation or even sanction. The ways this impacts on domestic policy (on immigration policy, for example) and foreign and security policy (on how terrorist suspects are to be treated or how wars are fought and occupations established) is significant. Hurrell recognises that the solidarist challenge to the old order is met with severe resistance by pluralist elements of the legal order. But this is not a challenge from outside the law. It arises within the legalised world order, but the tensions are unresolved and the results of the contest uneven. The second, and related, way that the constitutional principle of international law is challenged is in the way that these legitimacy indicators lead to a differentiation of sovereign states:

> Differentiation is not simply a matter of crude power, but is reflected in the character and operation of the international legal order itself. On the one side, the capacity to opt out of what was previously a largely consent-based legal system has declined. On the other, refusal to accept either non-derogable core legal norms or those norms that are particularly valued by the powerful runs the risk of being branded 'rogue' or 'pariah'.[106]

Hurrell points to tension between solidarist and pluralist tendencies, to the multiple ways that this impacts on the power politics of the international legal order and to how these tensions play out in our understanding of legitimacy. Hurrell points to four dimensions of change. Changes in respect of the content of norms, the source of norms, the justification of norms and in the implementation of norms are all observable in the international legal order, and raise clear challenges to the positivist and 'rule of law' pluralist understandings of the inherent legitimacy of the law in itself:

> As the etymological origins of the concept suggest, this normative acceptance and the process of justification are often based on law. In many situations, legitimacy is often equated with lawfulness – lawfulness within the legal system itself, but also the lawfulness of a legally structured constitutional order within which day-to-day politics takes place. But the problem of legitimacy arises precisely because of the unstable and problematic relationship between law and morality on the one side and law and power on the other.[107]

In this complex mix moral concerns sometimes emerge as powerful claims to justice in opposition to established legal rules (once again the characterisation of the NATO intervention in Kosovo as illegal yet legitimate stands as a pertinent example). But it is not a unidirectional move towards a moralised rather than a legalised world order. Legalised politics is a series of trade-offs between all the different dimensions of legitimacy.[108] The emergence of solidarist principles in a pluralist world order provides the basis for a liberal advocacy project. Hurrell offers five reasons to engage in his project. He cites the range and seriousness of problems and challenges, the management of globalisation, massive changes in organisation of domestic society (and the transnational ideology that drives them), the ideal of common moral purposes and changes in the distribution of power. Together these issues help us to understand the challenges to the pluralist world order and provide reasons to argue for complex governance beyond the state – to a disaggregation of sovereign power and thus to a broader view of legal personality.

(d) Allen Buchanan: cosmopolitanism foundations for international law

The clearest challenge to the role of the state in moral, political and legal terms is found in the cosmopolitan tradition. Cosmopolitanism (the word derives from the ancient Greek for citizen of the world) has a venerable history in philosophical thinking. From Stoics in the third century to contemporary liberal philosophers cosmopolitans have argued that justice requires a global rather than national or international perspective. In this section we focus on contemporary liberal cosmopolitanism. With some notable exceptions cosmopolitanism has not made much of an impression on the legalisation debates.[109] In part at least this is because cosmopolitans tend to abstract from the political and legal in order to find the moral in neo-Kantian accounts of practical reason. For example, Onora O'Neill argues that moral theory requires us to abstract from the particular (from the sociological or the legal) to a formal or modal understanding of the focus and scope of practical reasoning. This is, she argues, the only way to avoid idealisation – which can be loosely cast as deriving moral boundaries by favouring contingent political borders and, in the process, denying moral access to 'outsiders'.[110] For O'Neill, then, a concern with the sociological and legal is a theoretical mistake. The reluctance to engage with questions of international law or politics as a matter of theory means that O'Neill's brand of cosmopolitan theory (which is a good example of the tradition more broadly) fails to engage with any conception of legitimacy or justice that takes respect for the rule of law or the will of self-determining peoples seriously. As critique this is important, but there are other, more socially engaged, cosmopolitan approaches that maintain the power of critique and engage the legalised world.

There are two key ways in which cosmopolitans achieve both critique and engagement. Both situate the citizen of the world in the world of states without abandoning core cosmopolitan claims. Thomas Pogge shows that:

> Three elements are shared by all cosmopolitan positions. First, *individualism*: the ultimate units of concern are human beings or persons – rather than, say, family lines, tribes, ethnic, cultural or religious communities, nations, or states. The latter may be units of concern only indirectly, in virtue of their individual members or citizens. Second, *universality*: the status of ultimate unit of concern attaches to every living human being equally ... Third, *generality*: this special status has global force. Persons are ultimate units of concern for everyone – not only for their fellow compatriots, fellow religionists, or such like.[111]

Yet, without abandoning these claims, Pogge develops what he calls an institutional (rather than an interactional) cosmopolitanism. This form of cosmopolitanism assigns responsibility for achieving just outcomes to institutional schemes, rather than to individual or collective agents. This shift of focus to shared practices both engages questions of law and politics and makes the responsibility for global justice 'a shared responsibility for the justice of any practices one supports: one ought not to participate in an unjust institutional scheme (one that violates human rights) without making reasonable efforts to aid its victims and to promote institutional reform'.[112] The clearest example of a cosmopolitan engagement with international law is Allen Buchanan's *Justice, Legitimacy and Self-Determination: Moral Foundations for International Law*. Buchanan bases his cosmopolitanism on 'institutional moral reasoning' showing that 'philosophical thinking about the ethics of international relations must take institutions seriously and that issues concerning human rights, the legitimacy of international institutions and the use of force cannot be fruitfully theorized in isolation from one another'.[113] His position here shows that philosophical reasoning about the normative desirability of institutional reform has to be supplemented by institutional (political and legal) reasoning. This understanding of the relationship between legal, social and moral normativity places cosmopolitan thinking in political context and requires it to take its chances in the legitimacy debates described by Hurrell (above). The second strategy, one that increases both the engagement and the critical potential of cosmopolitanism, is the claim that a cosmopolitan ethics is already implicit in the international legal order:

> At the dawn of the modern human-rights era, the role of human rights in the international legal order was rather minimal ... The situation is different today ... There is growing acceptance of the idea that conformity to human rights norms is a necessary condition of the legitimacy of governments and even of states ... these developments signal the transition from an international legal system whose constitutive, legitimizing aim was peace among states (and before that merely the regulation of war among states) to one that takes the protection of human rights as one of its central goals.[114]

For Buchanan (and for others like Pogge or Charles Beitz), while it is still plausible to generate a philosophical defence of cosmopolitanism, the power of the position is drawn from the legal and social 'facts' of human rights.[115] Buchanan's cosmopolitanism takes the form of a challenge to the inherent conservatism of the established legal order by issuing a demand for the systematic application of human rights principles to the idea of system legitimacy. Buchanan draws on much of the same evidence as Hurrell in describing the increasing importance of human rights claims. He goes on to pit the normative desirability of a more systemic application of human rights to international law against the 'parochialism objection' or 'the charge that human rights are expressions of either an arbitrarily limited set of values or an arbitrary ranking of values'.[116] The conservative deployment of human rights claims in the international order is not based on a fundamental rejection of human rights. Everyone shares, he argues, a modest objectivist view of human rights which, he argues, rests on three assumptions:

(1) Every person counts equally in some morally fundamental sense, and this basic equality of moral worth grounds an entitlement to

conditions needed to secure the opportunity to live a decent or dignified life (the equal regard assumption).
(2) Certain things can be done to human beings or certain deprivations they can suffer that generally undercut the opportunity for their living a decent life (the standard threat assumption).
(3) Feasible and morally acceptable social institutions and practices can significantly reduce these standard threats (the institutional response assumption).[117]

However, institutional conservatism stems from the risk that human rights justifications for institutional reform will be appropriated by the powerful or the dangerous in a way that works against the goal of respecting rights. It may also be the case that any decision about reform is hampered by moral uncertainty and disagreement about the proper goal of human rights institutions. But there is also risk in not developing a human rights-based conception of institutional legitimacy. Put simply, it is the cost of not protecting individuals against threats to their basic human rights posed by terrorists, genocidal regimes or tyrannical rulers.

Buchanan shows how great injustices are causes and exaggerated by the pluralism of the world order. Poverty is ignored, oppressive regimes act with impunity and are even given a legitimacy veto when it comes to the development of law and policy. Challenges from state failure to secession cannot be dealt with under the current legal order. We understand these as injustices because they fail to respect, protect, promote and fulfil human rights, and Buchanan shows how the legal and institutional tools we have are complicit in this failing. Reform is required, and reform means institutional change and, in particular, the development of an institutionalised global public order in which state power is qualified. Buchanan advocates the unbundling of sovereignty and the transition of legal personality to units above and below the level of the state. The full scale of the challenge to the existing legal order becomes clear as we recognise the necessity of challenging core legal doctrines. Effectivity as the condition of statehood, state consent to law-making, non-intervention, the illegality of unilateral secession, all directed at preserving the sovereign autonomy of states fail the basic tests of human rights-based justice. Institutionally Buchanan shows how reform of (or the abandonment of) the UN Security Council is also necessary to curb predation and inactivity by the powerful, and how such institutional reform can overcome the parochialism objection.[118]

Conclusion: power, the state and the fragmentation of international law

Each of these approaches challenges the existing legal order. But each position draws on a set of arguments that find real support in the normative structures of international society. In each case the role of the state as the key actor is not treated as a simple fact, but as something to be questioned. The state is the most important actor in IR and the most important bearer of legal rights and duties. But if we treat this as a simple fact or as an unchallengeable constitutional doctrine we risk obscuring obvious injustice and denying the possibility of change. Yet there is also a risk in assuming that moving away from a state-centric system will enhance justice.

Martti Koskenniemi offers several insights into the disaggregation of sovereignty that is already a part of contemporary international law. Patterns of de-formalisation and fragmentation are readily observable in the international legal order, and the contending responses of constitutionalism and pluralism are both, he maintains, inadequate.[119] Koskenniemi shows that the way the international community dealt with the challenges of the post-Cold War era fragmented the more traditional international law of states into an international law of specialised regimes:

> the new developments in the law did not point to unity. The more powerfully they dealt with international problems – problems of economics, development, human rights, environment, criminality, security – the more they began to challenge old principles and institutions. Specializations such as 'trade law', 'human rights law', 'environmental law', 'criminal law', 'security law', 'European law' and so on started to reverse established legal hierarchies in favour of the structural bias in the relevant functional expertise ... It is this change to which international lawyers have reacted by speculating on the 'dangers' of incoherence, forum shopping and, perhaps characteristically, 'loss of overall control'.[120]

Fragmentation shifts power from the legislator to the law-applier (de-formalisation). While such moves were intended to counter the political hegemony of states, they do not take politics out of the equation. They simply transfer it to a battle between different institutions, jurisdictions and regimes. Koskenniemi points to cases such as the *Tadic* case before the ICTY, *Al-Jedda* before the UK High Court of Justice and the *Nuclear Weapons* and the *Palestine Wall* Advisory Opinions of the ICJ, where the question turned on which regime (human rights or security, human rights or laws of war, etc.) was applied. Clear evidence of this political struggle can be seen in the Israeli reaction to the ICJ's application of human rights law in the *Palestine Wall* Opinion and the ECtHR's application of human rights law when the UK High Court's decision to consider the case from the perspective of security was heard (as part of the *Al-Skeini* judgment). International law is 'hegemonic technique', the articulation of political preferences in legal terms.[121] Functional institutions also compete for power. The fragmentation of international law, then, merely shifts politics away from the state. The attempted 'constitutionalisation' of international law, most evident in solidarist and cosmopolitan approaches to international law, is an attempt to counter this new politics by developing hierarchies of rules.[122] While the challenge of incompatible state interests may have been partially side-stepped by the move to functional regimes, the challenge of producing a hierarchy of values remains as these regimes and institutions compete to have their core values represented in the constitutional order:

> The undoubted increase of law in the international world ('legalization') does not translate automatically into a substantive constitution in the absence of that sense of shared 'project' or objective. If de-formalisation has set the house of international law on fire, to grasp at values is to throw gas on the flames.[123]

Koskenniemi's principal point is that both pluralism and constitutionalism are competing narrative perspectives both attempting a once-and-for-all re-description of the emerging legal order.[124] His proposal is that we should work to 'redeem' international law as a political project. Law, he argues, is a place-holder for justice. Power happens in all the fragmented institutions and we need to remain aware of this crucial fact. Koskenniemi builds on this thought, urging a new politicised approach to law:

> This would be what cosmopolitanism can be today: the ability to break out and connect, participate in the politics of regime definition by narrating regimes anew, giving voice to those not represented in the regime's institutions. To politicise govern-

ance means to rethink the activity of expert institutions not as the technical production of pre-determined decisions by some anonymous logic, but choices by well-placed men and women at various spots where power happens.[125]

In each of the traditions explored in this chapter the relationship between power, law and agency demonstrates just how deeply the politics of international law runs in the constitution of the legal order. All the tensions and challenges exist, and any simple attempt to overcome them (or for one solution to rise to the fore) is unlikely. The crucial point to note is that the political dynamism of contemporary international law requires a constant analysis of the justice or injustice of the solutions generated to any one challenge. Justice claims can be made in pluralist, solidarist and cosmopolitan terms, but justice does not transcend politics and law, it is a crucial element of legalised politics.

Notes

1 Cali, B., 'International Law for International Relations: Foundations for Interdisciplinary Study', in Cali, B. (ed.), *International Law for International Relations*, Oxford: Oxford University Press, 2010, p. 7.
2 Wallace, R. M., *International Law*, 4th edn, London: Sweet & Maxwell, 2002, p. 56.
3 Crawford, J. R., *The Creation of States in International Law*, 2nd edn, Oxford: Oxford University Press, 2006, p. 28.
4 *Reparations for Injuries Suffered in the Service of the United Nations* [1949] ICJ Rep. 174, at p. 179.
5 Dixon, *International Law*, p. 112.
6 Article 34(1) of the Statute of the International Court of Justice.
7 Dixon, *International Law*, p. 112.
8 Gross, 'The Peace of Westphalia 1648–1948', pp. 20–41; Cutler, C., 'Critical Reflections on the Westphalian Assumptions of International Law and Organization: A Crisis of Legitimacy', *Review of International Studies*, 27 (2001): 133–50.
9 The *Reparations* case, at p. 180.
10 United Nations Charter, Art. 4(1).
11 See generally on this, Watson, A., 'Hedley Bull, States Systems and International Societies', *Review of International Studies*, 13(1987): 147–53, at pp. 149–50.
12 The ICJ in its Advisory Opinion on the *Competence of the General Assembly for the Admission of a State to the United Nations*, in *International Law Reports*, 17 (1950): 326–30, pointed out that the General Assembly could not make a decision to admit a state as a

The Subjects of International Law

member of the UN under Art. 4 of the UN Charter except on the recommendation of the Security Council.

13 See Global Policy Forum, 'Changing Patterns in the Use of the Veto in the Security Council', 2008, available at: http://www.globalpolicy.org/component/content/article/102/40069.html, accessed 19 January 2011.

14 The 193-member General Assembly adopted the resolution by a vote of 138 in favour and 9 against, with 41 abstentions, UN News Centre, see at: http://www.un.org/apps/news/story.asp?NewsID=43640#.USeThmc76_w, accessed 22 February 2013.

15 See UN Charter, Arts 4(2), 18(2) and 27(3).

16 For an extensive exploration of the criteria for statehood, see Crawford, J., 'The Criteria for Statehood in International Law', *British Yearbook of International Law*, 48(1976/7): 93–182.

17 Harris, *Cases and Materials on International Law*, p. 99.

18 (1992) 31 ILM 1494, at p. 1495.

19 Higgins, *Problems and Process*, p. 39.

20 See http://www.discovernauru.com, accessed 19 January 2011.

21 Dixon, *International Law*, p. 115.

22 [1975] ICJ Rep. 12.

23 [1975] ICJ Rep. 12.

24 Rayfuse, R. 'W(h)ither Tuvalu? International Law and Disappearing States', University of New South Wales Faculty of Law Research Series, 2009, p. 1, at pp. 6-7, available at: http://law.bepress.com/unswwps/flrps09/art9, accessed 21 March 2012.

25 Ramesh, R., 'Paradise Almost Lost: Maldives Seek to Buy a New Homeland', *The Guardian*, Monday, 10 November 2008, available at: http://www.guardian.co.uk/environment/2008/nov/10/maldives-climate-change, accessed 19 January 2011.

26 BBC, 'Kiribati Mulls Land Purchase in Fiji in Battle against Sea', 8 March 2012, available at: http://www.bbc.co.uk/news/world-asia-17295862, accessed 21 March 2012.

27 Rayfuse, 'W(h)ither Tuvalu? International Law and Disappearing States', p. 6.

28 Shaw, *International Law*, 6th edn, p. 200.

29 (1992) 31 ILM 1494, at p. 1495.

30 LNOJ Sp. Supp. No. 4 (1920), pp. 8–9. See Brown, P. M., 'The Aaland Islands Question', *American Journal of International Law*, 15(2) (1921): 268–72.

31 Dixon, *International Law*, p. 116.

32 Dixon, *International Law*, p. 116; Shaw, *International Law*, pp. 201–2.

33 Dixon, *International Law*, p. 116.

34 Higgins, *Problems and Process*, p. 41.

35 'Declaration on the Guidelines on the Recognition of New States in

Eastern Europe and in the Soviet Union (16 December 1991)', *British Yearbook of International Law*, 62 (1991): 559; 'Declaration on Yugoslavia and on the Guidelines on the Recognition of New States', (1992) 31 ILM 1485.
36 British State Practice, Minister of State, Foreign and Commonwealth Office, 1986, quoted in Harris, *Cases and Materials on International Law*, p. 154.
37 US State Practice, US Department of State, 1976, quoted in Harris, *Cases and Materials on International Law*, p. 155.
38 Brownlie, I., 'Recognition in Theory and Practice', *British Yearbook of International Law*, 53 (1982): 197–201.
39 Sloane, R., 'The Changing Face of Recognition in International Law: A Case Study of Tibet', *Emory International Law Review*, 16(2002): 107–86, at pp. 115–16.
40 See *Deutsch Continental Gas Gesellschaft v. Polish State*, (1929) 5 *International Law Reports*, 5 (1929): 11, at p. 13.
41 Opinion 1, Badinter Commission, 29 November 1991, *International Law Reports*, 92 (1993): 165.
42 Sloane, 'The Changing Face of Recognition in International Law', pp. 116–18.
43 Oppenheim, L., *International Law: A Treatise*, 8th edn, New York: Longmans Green, 1955, p. 125.
44 Ijalaye, D., 'Was "Biafra" at Any Time a State in International Law?', *American Journal of International Law*, 65 (1971): 551–9.
45 Ijalaye, 'Was "Biafra" at Any Time a State in International Law?', p. 559.
46 Ijalaye, 'Was "Biafra" at Any Time a State in International Law?', p. 559.
47 Shaw, *International Law*, p. 208.
48 See, e.g., Art. 16, paras 1–2 of the Austrian Constitution; Art. 32. para. 3 of the German Basic Law; Art. 9 of the Swiss Constitution; Art. I, s. 10, cl. 3 of the US Constitution.
49 See, for instance, Rodgers, R. S., 'The Capacity of States of the Union to Conclude International Agreements: The Background and Some Recent Developments', *American Journal of International Law*, 61 (1967): 1021–8; McWhinney, E., 'Canadian Federalism and the Foreign Affairs and Treaty Making Power: The Impact of Quebec's "Quiet Revolution"', *Canadian Yearbook of International Law*, 7(1969): 3–32; Wildhaber, L., 'External Relations of the Swiss Cantons', *Canadian Yearbook of International Law*, 12(1974): 211; Schreuer, C., 'The Waning of the Sovereign State: Towards a New Paradigm for International Law?' *European Journal of International Law*, 4 (1993): 447–71, at p. 450.
50 Potter, P. B., 'Origin of the Term International Organization', *American Journal of International Law*, 39 (1945): 803–6; Klabbers, J., *An*

Introduction to *International Institutional Law*, 2nd edn, Cambridge: Cambridge University Press, 2009, p. 16.
51 Alvarez, J. E., 'International Organizations: Then and Now', *American Journal of International Law*, 100(2) (2006): 324–47.
52 O'Brien, J. *International Law*, London: Cavendish Press, 2001, p. 166.
53 Klabbers, *An Introduction to International Institutional Law*, pp. 6–12.
54 Article 156 of the Law of the Sea Convention 1982.
55 See UN General Assembly Resolution 57(I), 11 December 1946, and the Economic and Social Council Resolution 44(IV), 29 March 1947.
56 de Zwaan, J. W., 'The Legal Personality of the European Communities and the European Union', *Netherlands Yearbook of International Law*, 30 (1999): 75–113. However, see Art. 47 of the Treaty of the European Union (the Lisbon Treaty).
57 [1949] ICJ Rep. 174.
58 [1949] ICJ Rep. 179.
59 Klabbers, *An Introduction to International Institutional Law*, p. 29.
60 Wouters, J. and Duquet, S., 'The EU, EEAS and Union Delegations and International Diplomatic Law: New Horizons', Leuven Centre for Global Governance Studies, Working Paper No. 62, May 2011; Pollack, M. A., 'Theorizing the European Union: International Organization, Domestic Polity or Experiment in New Governance?', *Annual Review of Political Science*, 8(2005): 357–98; Klabbers, *An Introduction to International Institutional Law*, p. 10.
61 Börzel, T. A. and Risse, T., 'Who is Afraid of a European Federation? How to Constitutionalise a Multi-Level Governance System', NYU Jean Monnet Center for International and Regional Economic Law & Justice, Working Paper No. 7/00, available at: http://centers.law.nyu.edu/jean-monnet/archive/papers/00/00f0101.html, accessed 15 May 2012.
62 Shaw, *International Law*, p. 241.
63 Higgins, R., 'Conceptual Thinking about the Individual in International Law', *British Journal of International Studies*, 4 (1978): 1, at p. 3.
64 See the *Mavrommatis* case, PCIJ, Series A, No. 2, Judgment, 30 August 1924, p. 12.
65 Higgins, *Problems and Process*, p. 51.
66 Manner, G., 'The Object Theory of the Individual in International Law', *American Journal of International Law*, 46(3) (1952): 428–49, at pp. 430–2. See also Orakhelashvili, A., 'The Position of the Individual in International Law', *California Western International Law Journal*, 31 (2000/1): 241–76, at pp. 243–9.
67 Manner, 'The Object Theory of the Individual in International Law', p. 430.
68 Higgins, *Problems and Process*, p. 50.
69 Shaw, *International Law*, pp. 257–9.
70 Menon, P. K., 'The International Personality of Individuals in

International Law: A Broadening of the Traditional Doctrine', *Journal of Transnational Law and Policy*, 1 (1992): 151–82, at p. 154.
71 'International Criminal Law', *Encyclopaedia Britannica*, 2007, available at: http://www.britannica.com/EBchecked/topic/721820/international-criminal-law/242853/Categories-of-international-crime.
72 Wallensteen, P. and Grusell, H., 'Targeting the Right Targets? The UN Use of Individual Sanctions', *Global Governance*, 18 (2012): 207–30.
73 Charnovitz, S., 'Nongovernmental Organizations and International Law', *American Journal of International Law*, 100(2) (2006): 348–72.
74 Charnovitz, S., 'Nongovernmental Organizations and International Law'.
75 Shaw, *International Law*, pp. 245–50.
76 Barsh, R. L., 'Indigenous Peoples in the 1990s: From Object to Subject of International Law', *Harvard Human Rights Journal*, 7 (1994): 33–86.
77 Brownlie, I., *Principles of Public International Law*, Oxford: Clarendon Press, 1998, p. 289, in Warbrick, C. 'States and Recognition in International Law', in M. Evans (ed.), *International Law*, Oxford: Oxford University Press, 2003, p. 211.
78 Rawls, *The Law of Peoples*, pp. 4–6.
79 Brown, *Sovereignty, Rights and Justice*, pp. 5–21.
80 Crawford, J. and Olleson, S., 'The Nature and Forms of International Responsibility', in M. Evans (ed.), *International Law*, Oxford: Oxford University Press, 2003, p. 447. See also McCorquodale, R., 'Beyond State Sovereignty: The International Legal System and Non-State Participants', *International Law: Revista Colombiana de derecho internacional*, 8 (2006): 103–59.
81 See Buchanan, *Justice, Legitimacy and Self-Determination*. Also Buchanan, *Human Rights*.
82 See, e.g., Koskenniemi, *The Politics of International Law*; Pogge, T., 'Cosmopolitanism and Sovereignty', *Ethics*, 103(1) (1992): 48–75. Ruggie, J., *Constructing the World Polity: Essays on International Institutionalization*, London: Routledge, 2002, p. 186; Hurrell, *On Global Order*, pp. 135–6; Buchanan, *Justice, Legitimacy and Self-determination*, pp. 56–7; Caney, S., *Justice Beyond Borders: A Global Political Theory*, Oxford: Oxford University Press, 2005, pp. 150–2; Sinclair, A. and Byers, M., 'When US Scholars Speak of "Sovereignty" What Do They Mean?', *Political Studies*, 55(2) (2007): 318–40; Walzer, M., *Arguing About War*, New Haven, CT: Yale University Press, 2004, pp. 171–91.
83 Wight, M., *International Theory: The Three Traditions*, Leicester: Leicester University Press, 1994.
84 Nardin, 'Theorizing the International Rule of Law', pp. 394–5.
85 Nardin, T. (ed.), *Traditions of International Ethics*, Cambridge: Cambridge University Press, 1992, p. 23.

86 Nardin, *Traditions of International Ethics*, p. 19.
87 Nardin, T. *Law, Morality and the Relations Between States*. (Princeton, NJ: Princeton University Press, 1983).
88 Nardin, *Traditions of International Ethics*, p. 20.
89 Nardin, *Traditions of International Ethics*, p. 24.
90 Nardin, 'International Pluralism and the Rule of Law', pp. 95–6.
91 Nardin, 'International Pluralism and the Rule of Law', p. 106.
92 Nardin, *Traditions of International Ethics*, p. 21.
93 Nardin, 'International Pluralism and the Rule of Law', p. 106.
94 Walzer, M., 'Nation and Universe', *The Tanner Lectures on Human Values XI 1989*, ed. G. Peterson, Salt Lake City: University of Utah Press, 1990, p. 536.
95 Walzer, M., *Spheres of Justice: A Defence of Pluralism and Equality*, Oxford: Blackwell, 1983, p. 314.
96 Walzer, M., *On Toleration*, New Haven, CT: Yale University Press, 1997, p. 175.
97 Walzer, M., 'The Moral Standing of States: A Response to Four Critics', *Philosophy and Public Affairs*, 9(18) (1980): 209–29.
98 Walzer, M., *Just and Unjust Wars: A Moral Argument with Historical Illustrations*, New York: Basic Books, 1992, pp. 61–2, Walzer, 'The Moral Standing of States', p. 210.
99 Walzer, *Arguing About War*, p. 179.
100 Walzer, *Arguing About War*, pp. 187–8.
101 See Sutch, P., 'International Justice and the Reform of Global Governance: A Reconsideration of Michael Walzer's International Political Theory', *Review of International Studies*, 35 (2009): 513–30; Sutch, P., 'Human Rights and the Use of Force: Assertive Liberalism and Just War', *European Journal of Political Theory*, 11(2) (2012a): 172–90.
102 Reus-Smit, C., 'The Constructivist Challenge after September 11', in A. Bellamy (ed.), *International Society and its Critics*, Oxford: Oxford University Press, 2005, pp. 81–94.
103 Hurrell, *On Global Order*, p. 58.
104 Hurrell, *On Global Order*, pp. 58–60.
105 Hurrell, *On Global Order*, pp. 65–6.
106 Hurrell, *On Global Order*, p. 67.
107 Hurrell, *On Global Order*, p. 79.
108 Hurrell, *On Global Order*, p. 91.
109 Allott, 'The Concept of International Law', offers such an exception.
110 O'Neill, O., *Towards Justice and Virtue: A Constructive Account of Practical Reason*, Cambridge: Polity Press, 1996, p. 51. See also O'Neill, O., 'Abstraction, Idealization and Ideology in Ethics', in J. Evans (ed.), *Moral Philosophy and Contemporary Problems*, Cambridge: Cambridge University Press, 1987, pp. 55–69.
111 Pogge, 'Cosmopolitanism and Sovereignty', p. 48.

112 Pogge, 'Cosmopolitanism and Sovereignty', p. 50.
113 Buchanan, *Justice, Legitimacy and Self-Determination*, p. 10.
114 Buchanan, A., 'Human Rights and the Legitimacy of the International Order', *Legal Theory*, 14(1) (2008): 39–70.
115 Buchanan, *Justice, Legitimacy and Self-Determination*, p. 97.
116 Buchanan, *Human Rights*, p. 76.
117 Buchanan, *Human Rights*, p. 86.
118 See Chapter Four, below.
119 Koskenniemi, *The Politics of International Law*, pp. 345–56.
120 Koskenniemi, M., 'The Fate of Public International Law: Between Technique and Politics', *Modern Law Review*, 17(1) (2007): 4.
121 Koskenniemi, *The Gentle Civilizer of Nations*, pp. 2–3.
122 Koskenniemi, 'The Fate of Public International Law', p. 15.
123 Koskenniemi, 'The Fate of Public International Law', p. 16.
124 Koskenniemi, 'The Fate of Public International Law', p. 25.
125 Koskenniemi, 'The Fate of Public International Law', p. 29.

CHAPTER FOUR

The United Nations and International Law

The Constitution of the International Community: Justice, Power and the United Nations

The UN is of such overwhelming importance to the contemporary international legal order that most of the chapters in this book refer to it in some way. We dedicate later chapters to a full examination of what are some of the most significant and contentious issues that form the central planks of UN activity. In Chapter Five we explore the international protection of human rights. In Chapter Six we explore diplomacy and its transformation under the UN. In Chapter Seven we examine issues relating to chapter VII (non-military sanctions and use of force) of the Charter, and in Chapter Eight we explore the law of the sea as negotiated in the UN. These issues are so vital to any understanding of the evolution of post-war international society that they inevitably spill over into the consideration of other issues related to the development of the UN since 1945. This is true of the issues we have decided to explore here. In Chapter Three we began to explore the apparent 'constitutionalisation' of international law. Constitutionalist claims are those that argue that the international community has developed legal and political characteristics that transcend the anarchical society of states. There is a substantial body of work that argues that that UN provides the basis for the constitution of the international community. For some, the Charter itself is the constitutional instrument. For others, it is the UN more broadly that provides or has inspired the constitution of the global order (see below). In exploring these arguments we are once again exploring legal and political claims,

The Constitution of the International Community

and engaging in debates about justice and the normative desirability of a constitutionalised world order. Exploring the character of the UN as the foundation of the international community more broadly leads us directly to our second focus. The many factors that make it appealing to think of the UN as providing the global constitution militate against the structurally embedded power politics of the UN Security Council. The justice of the P-5 veto is directly challenged by the implications of the universality of the constitutional principles drawn from the contemporary UN framework. Calls for reform (or even the abandonment) of the UN Security Council have been a feature since Boutros Boutros-Gali convened the first summit of the Security Council in 1992. Our exploration of the call for UN Security Council reform offers a critical examination of a 'cosmopolitan institutional proposal' put forward by Robert Keohane and Allen Buchanan, and asks whether, in the absence of reform, the establishment of a 'league of democracies' that could take decisions outside the Security Council would be a justifiable and desirable.

United Nations

The establishment of the UN in 1945 could be said to be the crucial cut-off point for the transition from classical to contemporary international law, which now involves regulation of both state and non-state actors. The UN is a huge multifaceted global international organisation, which was established immediately after the Second World War with a three-pronged mandate, sometimes described as the so-called 'three pillars' of the UN: namely, maintenance of peace and security; promotion and protection of human rights; and development.[1] Historically, the UN was set up as a sort of 'reformed' international organisation intended to avoid the mistakes that led to the failure of its predecessor, the League of Nations. According to Goodrich:

> The student of international organization must recognize the United Nations for what it quite properly is, a revised League, no doubt improved in some respects, possibly weaker in others, but nonetheless a League, a voluntary association of nations, carrying on largely in the League tradition and by League methods ... Anyone desiring to understand the machinery, how it operates, the conditions of its success, must look to the experience of the

past, and particularly to the rich and varied experience of that first attempt at a general international organization, the League of Nations.[2]

Although, with the useful lessons learnt by the drafters of the Charter from the failure of the League, the UN emerged immediately after the Second World War as 'a noble experiment in human cooperation',[3] it is by no means a perfect organisation. Consequently, there have been various initiatives to reform the UN. For instance, membership of the UN Security Council and the Economic and Social Council (ECOSOC) were increased in the 1960s and 1970s.[4] However, since the collapse of the former Soviet Union and the changing power configuration from that which existed in the 1940s when the UN was established, the calls for UN reforms have been more strident. Increasingly, the query is whether the UN as originally constructed is 'fit for purpose' to face twenty-first-century challenges. Exploring the calls for reform with regard to its principal organs – the Security Council, the General Assembly, ECOSOC, Secretariat, ICJ and Trusteeship Council – is, therefore, a useful way to familiarise the reader with the nature of the UN itself.

United Nations reform

In exploring the reform initiatives of the UN, it is pertinent to point out from the outset that there are two broad types of reform initiatives: one that necessarily involves amending the constituent instrument, the UN Charter; and one that could be done without such amendment. Obviously, the former initiatives are usually more difficult to achieve because of the onerous amendment processes. Article 108 of the UN Charter states:

> Amendments to the present Charter shall come into force for all Members of the United Nations when they have been adopted by a vote of two-thirds of the members of the General Assembly and ratified in accordance with their respective constitutional processes by two-thirds of the Members of the United Nations, including all the permanent Members of the Security Council.[5]

The requirement that P-5 members concur to any amendment of the Charter makes reform of the UN involving the amendment of the

The Constitution of the International Community

Charter rather difficult to achieve. Some scholars have therefore advocated that perhaps the focus of these reforms should be with regard to areas that would not necessarily entail Charter amendment.[6] While this may be a convenient way to obtain a more speedy reform of the UN, there would be a need to amend the Charter to address the fundamental issues that affect the legitimacy of the UN.

In a report of the UN Secretary-General it was identified that 'reform is not an event; it is a process'.[7] Malloch Brown pointed out that:

> UN reform is about politics in the sense that it is a response to the frustration of governments and the UN's other stakeholders with the organization's capacity to get results. People wanted more from the UN. Unable to deliver, the managers kept on trying to fix the machine. It became an occupational obsession.[8]

Although there is nothing new about the reform agenda of the UN, the major initiatives for reform can be traced to the late 1990s when there were calls to reform the UN in order to make it more effective and relevant in order to address twenty-first-century challenges.[9] A recent initiative for UN reforms was that of the High Level Panel on Threats, Challenges and Change (HLP), established by the then UN Secretary-General, Kofi Annan, which came up in 2004 with a report titled: 'A More Secure World: Our Shared Responsibility'.[10] In this Report, the Panel proposed certain institutional reforms of the UN, including the establishment of new bodies, such as the Human Rights Council (HRC), which has since been set up, albeit in a different format to avoid the immediate need to amend the Charter.[11] This was followed by the Secretary-General's 2005 report to the General Assembly titled 'In Larger Freedom: Towards Security, Development and Human Rights for All', and the 2005 General Assembly World Summit outcome document.[12]

Security Council

The Security Council, although listed in the UN Charter as the second principal organ, is undoubtedly the most powerful of the six principal organs of the UN.[13] As far as Kofi Annan, the erstwhile Secretary-General of the UN was concerned: 'no reform of the United Nations would be complete without reform of the Security Council'.[14] Eleven states originally constituted this organ, but this has since been increased to fifteen.[15] It has the primary responsibility for the maintenance of international peace and security, with binding powers to carry out this crucial role, and may utilise non-military or military measures to do so.[16] Among its composition are five permanent members (P-5), who, by virtue of the historical incidence of being the victorious powers at the end of the Second World War, appointed themselves to this position,[17] while all other members are non-permanent members elected for a two-year term.[18] The P-5 members have immense powers to veto decisions of the Council on substantive matters. Although the Charter does not specifically designate this powers as the 'veto' power, the provision of Article 27(3) of the Charter has such practical effect. Article 27(3) states that:

> Decisions of the Security Council on all other matters [non-procedural matters] shall be made by an affirmative vote of nine Members including the concurring votes of the permanent members; provided that, in decisions under Chapter VI [Pacific Settlement of Disputes], and under paragraph 3 of Article 52 [regional arrangements for Pacific Settlement of Disputes], a party to a dispute shall abstain from voting.

The current debates on the reform of the Security Council focus mainly on the composition and decision-making process, especially the veto power of the P-5. Due to the exponential growth of the UN to the current membership of 193, there have been calls for the expansion of the Security Council from its present number. This is all the more so since some regions of the world are not currently represented in the elite P-5 membership.[19] Further, it was felt that since the 'Security Council had originally been conceived and designed as a body encapsulating, and effectively institutionalizing, the global balance of power',[20] there was a need for a reformed Security Council that would reflect the current power configuration, which has changed dramatically since 1945 when the Charter was adopted. The General Assembly as far back as 1993 set up an 'Open-Ended Working Group on the Question of Equitable Representation and Increase in the Membership of the Security Council and Other Matters Related to the Security Council'.[21] Despite meeting from January 1994, the Open-Ended Working Group has been unable to reach a consensus on the modalities of increasing the Council. This matter was further taken up by the HLP, which was unable to agree on one model and proposed two alternative models for an expanded

The Constitution of the International Community

Table 4.1 *Model A*

Regional area	Number of states	Permanent seats (continuing)	Proposed new permanent seats	Proposed total two-year seats (non-renewable)	Total
Africa	53	0	2	4	6
Asia/Pacific	56	1	2	3	6
Europe	47	3	1	2	6
Americas	35	1	1	4	6
Total Model A	191	5	6	13	24

Table 4.2 *Model B*

Regional area	Number of states	Permanent seats (continuing)	Proposed four-year renewable seats	Proposed total two-year seats (non-renewable)	Total
Africa	53	0	2	4	6
Asia/Pacific	56	1	2	3	6
Europe	47	3	2	1	6
Americas	35	1	2	3	6
Total Model B	191	5	8	11	24

twenty-four-member Council: Model A provided for six additional permanent seats without the veto power and three new two-year term non-permanent seats; while Model B provided for no new permanent seats, but created a new category of eight four-year renewable seats and one new two-year non-renewable seat (see Tables. 4.1 and 4.2).[22]

In calling for reform of the Security Council along the above lines, the HLP was keen that the reforms would be in line with the following principles:

- the need to honour Article 23 of the Charter by increasing the involvement in decision-making of those States that contribute most to the UN financially, militarily and diplomatically (specifically contributions to UN assessed budgets, participation in mandated peace operations, contributions to voluntary activities of the United Nations in the areas of security and development, and diplomatic activities in support of United Nations objectives and mandates. In addition among developed States, it included the contribution to the achieving or making of substantial progress towards the internationally agreed level of 0.7 per cent of GNP for Overseas Development Assistance);

- the need to bring into the decision-making process more States, especially developing States, to make the Security Council more representative of the broader membership of the UN;
- the need not to impair the effectiveness of the Security Council; and
- the need to increase the democratic and accountable nature of the Security Council.[23]

To allow for possible future enlargement of the Security Council, as circumstances dictate, the HLP emphasised that no change to the composition of this body should be regarded as permanent or unchallengeable in the future. It proposed that there should be a further review of the composition of the Council in the year 2020.[24] In 2005, the then UN Secretary-General in his report to the General Assembly endorsed the alternative models proposed by the HLP, however, he still left it open to the member states to also consider 'any other viable proposals in terms of size and balance that have emerged on the basis of either model'.[25] Perhaps it is unsurprising that state members of the UN have been unable to arrive at a consensus as to model, size and composition of an enlarged Security Council. According to Weiss: 'If 16 individuals [the HLP panel] cannot come up with a single way ahead, how will 191 [now 193] states and their parliaments? Even the Secretary-General by himself did not decide.'[26] The reform of the composition of the Security Council has since generated several proposals from state members of the UN. In 2005, the G4 states (India, Brazil, Japan and Germany), who are highly favoured to win permanent seats in an enlarged Council, proposed an increase to twenty-five seats by the creation of six permanent seats (intended to be for the four members of the G4 plus two African states) without veto power, and also four new non-permanent seats. The G4 proposal was opposed by another group, the Uniting for Consensus (led by Italy, Argentina, Pakistan, Mexico and South Korea; nicknamed the 'Coffee Club'), who supported the increase of the Council to twenty-five, but suggested that it be expanded by the creation of ten non-permanent seats. African states, on the other hand, under the auspices of the African Union (AU) 'Ezulwini Consensus', advocated that a full representation of Africa on the Council means that it should be allocated two permanent seats with veto power and five non-permanent seats.[27] The UN General Assembly World summit side-stepped this highly politicised issue by not taking any categorical position on which of the two models or other proposals to adopt. In a rather bland diplomatic statement, the World Summit stated:

We support early reform of the Security Council – an essential element of our overall effort to reform the United Nations – in order to make it more broadly representative, efficient and transparent and thus to further enhance its effectiveness and the legitimacy and implementation of its decisions. We commit ourselves to continuing our efforts to achieve a decision to this end and request the General Assembly to review progress on the reform set out above by the end of 2005.[28]

So far, the debate on how to enlarge the Council is still ongoing. This and other issues on Security Council reforms have since been moved to the level of intergovernmental negotiations in informal plenary meetings at the General Assembly under the leadership of Ambassador Zahir Tanin of Afghanistan.[29]

The veto power was arrived at because of a compromise between the United States, the Soviet Union and the United Kingdom at the Yalta Conference in 1945 as to how to secure the interest of the victors of the Second World War in the UN. Although during the San Francisco Conference a number of states protested at the privileged status given to the P-5 by virtue of this power, nonetheless, the veto was included as part of the provisions of the UN Charter.[30] Between 1945 and 2008, the P-5 members used the veto 261 times to block Security Council decisions on various issues, such as admission to membership of new states, and action to maintain peace and security under chapter VII.[31] The use of the veto to block chapter VII action has sometimes led to a paralysis of the Security Council and resulted in it being unable to carry out its primary responsibility of maintaining international peace and security. An example of this is in respect of the 1950 Korean War and the more recent divisive 2003 invasion of Iraq. The former led the UN General Assembly to adopt the Uniting for Peace Resolution, which allows it to act to maintain peace and security in the event of the inability of the Security Council to act due to the use of the veto by one or more of the P-5.[32]

The issue of the veto power of the P-5 members of the UN Security Council, undoubtedly a significant issue in international law and international relations, has generated a lot of debate both for and against the retention of this power.[33] Various proposals have been made to reform the veto power. For instance, as far back as the San Francisco Conference, Australia had proposed the waiving of the veto power in all proceedings arising under chapter VI of the Charter, that is, Pacific Settlement of Disputes.[34] This proposal was not accepted, however

Article 27 of the Charter requires that in decisions under chapter VI a party to the dispute shall abstain from voting. In 1998, the Non-Aligned Movement (NAM) proposed that the veto should be curtailed with a view to its elimination – as a first step it proposed that the veto power should be used only in regard to enforcement actions taken under chapter VII.[35] Others, like the African Union (AU), proposed a restriction on single P-5 member veto by suggesting that a veto should prevent the Security Council from acting only if two or more P-5 members utilise their veto to block a particular resolution before the Council.[36] However, the constraint of Article 108 of the UN Charter restricts the scope of reform of the veto power that could realistically be achieved. It is unlikely that the present holders of this power would consent to any reform of the veto that would either withdraw from them this privileged power or water it down. The HLP acknowledged this much by recognising that they see no practical way of changing the existing members' veto power, though in their view the veto power has 'anachronistic character that is unsuitable for the institution in an increasingly democratic age'.[37] In what appeared to be an indication of the Panel's sense of powerlessness in respect of this, they urged that the veto power should be limited to matters where vital interests are genuinely at stake, without a clear definition of what they mean by 'vital interests'. Further, they pleaded with each individual P-5 member, in their individual capacities, to pledge themselves to refrain from using the veto in cases of genocide and large-scale human rights abuses. They, however, recommended that under any reform the veto power should not be expanded, thereby basically advocating for inequality as between P-5 members and other permanent members to be appointed in an expanded Security Council.[38] In the view of the AU, such inequality would be contrary to 'common justice'.[39] Therefore, the AU, while opposing the veto in principle, advocated that it should be available also to new permanent members.[40]

The HLP also recommended the introduction of a system of indicative voting, whereby members of the Security Council could call for a public indication of positions on a proposed action. In this indicative vote, a 'no' vote by a P-5 member would not be regarded as a veto. Thereafter, a second formal vote would be held where the 'no' vote of such P-5 member would then be regarded as a veto. The Panel was of the view that such indicative voting system would increase the accountability of the P-5 in their use of the veto.[41] The idea appears to be that an indicative 'no' vote would leave a P-5 member open to pressure from public opinion that would embarrass them to withdraw a 'no' vote that was against public opinion. It is not clear upon what basis the Panel took the view that such indicative vote would make the veto system more accountable. If it is merely based on the pressure of public opinion, it is doubtful that this would dissuade a P-5 member from using their veto, even if such use were to be unpopular, as long as the leadership of such P-5 members were of the view that it was in their national interest to do so.

According to Blum:

> It is difficult to see the usefulness of the system of 'indicative voting' proposed unanimously by the panel ... This proposal is yet another manifestation of the panel's antipathy toward the veto and is openly intended to embarrass a permanent member contemplating use of its veto before its actual use, in the hope of deterring it from casting a formal veto. As this was the avowed motive behind this proposal, it should not have been disguised under the euphemistic cloak of 'accountability'. The intention of a permanent member to cast a veto is usually known in advance (and is often announced in the informal meetings held prior to the Council's formal meetings). The permanent member about to cast a veto also 'factors in' the public relations aspect of that vote in advance, and the panel's attempt 'to shame' it, as it were – through 'indicative voting' – into refraining from using the veto is, to say the least, somewhat puzzling.[42]

The 'In Larger Freedom' Report of the Secretary-General and the General Assembly at the 2005 World Summit deftly avoided specific reference to the veto power.[43]

The HLP Report, 'In Larger Freedom', and the 2005 World Summit were all united on the need to improve the working methods of the Security Council in order to promote transparency and accountability, a reform that may be embarked upon without the need to amend the Charter.[44] For instance, this could be done through increased involvement of states that are not members of the Council in its work. The HLP specifically mentioned as an example the need to consult with and involve troop contributing non-Council member states in deliberations with regard to the deployment of troops for Council-mandated operations as required by Article 44 of the Charter.[45]

The HLP also recommended that the Security Council establish a peace-building commission, as one of its subsidiary organs, with a peace-building support office to be located in the Secretariat to provide secretarial support to the Commission. The Panel proposed that the commission would identify states that are under stress and that risk sliding towards state collapse. Additionally, in partnership with the national governments, the commission would organise proactive assistance to prevent that process from developing further. Also, the commission should assist in the planning for transitions between conflict and post-conflict peace-building, and to marshal and sustain the efforts of the international community in post-conflict peace-building over whatever period may be necessary.[46] The 2005 'In Larger Freedom' Report and the General Assembly World Summit endorsed this proposal to establish a peace-building commission.[47] The General Assembly and Security Council, acting concurrently, established the Commission in 2005, as a subsidiary body of the Security Council.[48]

General Assembly

The General Assembly, as a plenary body composed of all UN member states, is regarded as the most democratic of all the organs of the UN.[49] Nonetheless, it has been the subject of several criticisms. For instance, it has been said that it has a democratic deficit because the representatives of the various member states are nominated by their government and not elected by the peoples of the respective states.[50] This is more so when the preamble of the UN Charter states: 'we the Peoples of the United Nations determined ... Have resolved to combine our efforts to accomplish these aims.' In contrast, its predecessor, the League of Nations, in its Covenant focused more on the states parties. In its preamble it stated that: 'The High Contracting Parties ... agree to this Covenant of the League of Nations.' Is this suggestive that the drafters of the UN Charter intended for 'the peoples' to play a direct role in the UN? Further, is this indicative of a future UN General Assembly directly elected by the 'peoples' of the world? Some, such as the World Federalists Movement, have, rather ambitiously, called for the establishment of a UN parliamentary body, modelled after the EU Parliament. They suggest it should begin first as a consultative parliamentary assembly, with its members chosen by the representative of the peoples who are elected members in existing legislatures all over the world. Thereafter, they propose that this body would evolve to become a world 'citizen-elected body with a real role in the governance of international life'.[51] This rather idealistic proposal would appear impracticable and it is unlikely that the member states of the UN would go as far as amending the Charter to have a General Assembly of so-called representatives of world citizens. In any event, the General Assembly was not conceived as a world legislative body, but rather as a deliberative and representative organ.[52] Despite the rather flowery 'we the peoples preamble', the UN, as pointed out by Schermers, is in reality an organisation of governments of states and not an organisation of peoples.[53] Moreover, the elaborate logistical demands of organising such an election for a world organisation as the UN would simply be unworkable. How, for instance, will such representatives be elected in states that are not democratic?

Another criticism of the General Assembly is that it is an 'ineffectual talking shop'.[54] Peterson points out that this phrase could be understood in two ways. First, as meaning that the General Assembly merely talks but does not take action. This he says is grossly unfair because it was never designed to be an executive body.[55] Second, it could be taken to mean that the General Assembly is unable to perform even its deliberative role because of the drastic increase in its membership, along with its rather lengthy agenda at meetings, which prevents it from engaging effectively with the various issues. Recent proposals for reform of the General Assembly have focused more on the latter criticism.[56] The HLP Report identified that for the General Assembly to perform its function as the main deliberative organ of the UN it requires a better conceptualisation and shortening of its agenda to reflect the contemporary challenges faced by the international community. It also proposed that the General Assembly should have smaller, more tightly focused committees, which would help in sharpening and improving resolutions that are brought to the whole Assembly.[57] Further, they suggested that the General Assembly should establish a better mechanism to engage with NGOs and the civil society, who provide valuable knowledge and perspectives of global issues.[58] The 2005 Report of the Secretary-General, endorsing the proposals of the HLP,[59] called on the General Assembly to take bold measures to rationalise its work and speed up the deliberative process, notably by streamlining its agenda, its committee structure and its procedures for holding plenary debates and requesting reports, and by strengthening the role and authority of its president.[60] In addition, he called on the Assembly to give focus to its substantive agenda by concentrating on addressing the major substantive issues of the day, such as international migration and the long-debated comprehensive convention on terrorism.[61] The 2005 World Summit merely welcomed the measures adopted by the

Assembly with a view to strengthening its role and authority, as well as the role and leadership of the president of the Assembly, without specifically mentioning what the measures were. It then called for the full and speedy implementation of those measures.[62] It further called for a strengthening of the relationship between the General Assembly and the other principal organs to ensure better harmonisation in respect of topical issues that require coordinated action by the UN.[63]

Economic and Social Council

The Economic and Social Council (ECOSOC), another principal organ of the UN, composed of fifty-four states, has the remit to deal with issues relating to economic and social matters and human rights.[64] One of the key initiatives to reform the ECOSOC has been in the area of human rights, where its vital subsidiary organ, the Commission on Human Rights (CHR), has played a critically role in formulating key human rights instruments, such as the Universal Declaration on Human Rights 1948 and the International Covenants and ensuring global promotion and protection of human rights.[65] The HLP identified that there was a need to reform the CHR, because, in the Panel's view, its credibility had been eroded having demonstrated double standards in addressing human rights concerns; also states sought membership of the Commission not to strengthen human rights, but rather to protect themselves from criticism or to criticise others.[66] They proposed that the CHR should have universal membership. As far as the Panel was concerned, this would underscore the fact that all members of the UN are committed by the Charter to the protection of human rights, and it could also help to shift the focus back to substantive issues rather than on who is debating and voting on them.[67] In addition, they proposed that the CHR be supported in its work by an advisory panel or council consisting of fifteen independent experts coming from the different regions of the world.[68] In the long term, they suggested that the CHR be upgraded to become a Human Rights Council (HRC) that would no longer be a subsidiary organ of the CHR, but rather would become a principal organ on a par with the ECOSOC and Security Council, and reflecting thereby the weight given to human rights, along with security and economic issues, in the preamble.[69] The UN Secretary-General, while accepting in his 2005 'In Larger Freedom' Report that the CHR had credibility problems,

The Constitution of the International Community

rejected the idea of a body with a universal membership to replace the CHR. As far as he was concerned, the 'credibility deficit' of the CHR could be cured by a smaller HRC, whose membership would be elected directly by a two-thirds majority of members of the General Assembly present and voting. He proposed that those elected would undertake to abide by the highest human rights standards. He preferred that the decision on whether the HRC should be a principal organ or a subsidiary organ of the General Assembly be left in the hands of the member states.[70] The 2005 General Assembly World Summit, pursuant to its commitment to strengthen the UN human rights machinery, resolved to create a HRC to promote universal respect for the protection of human rights.[71] The HRC has since been created as a subsidiary organ of the General Assembly to replace the CHR, which is now defunct.[72]

Trusteeship Council

The Trusteeship Council, another principal organ of the UN, completed its assignment in 1994 when the last trust territory, Palau, gained independence.[73] Since then the issue has been what to do with this organ. Should it be deleted from the UN Charter as a principal organ or should it be given another remit? As far as the HLP Panel was concerned, the provisions of the Charter dealing with the Trusteeship Council should be deleted since it had completed its assignment of decolonisation. The Panel appeared to be of the view that the deletion of the Trusteeship Council from the Charter would be an indication that the UN has turned its 'back on any attempt to return to the mentalities and forms of colonialism'.[74] They advocated, as has been shown above, that the HRC should eventually replace the Trusteeship Council as a principal organ.[75] The deletion of the Trusteeship Council from the UN Charter was endorsed by the 2005 World summit,[76] and this appears to be implicit in the 'In Larger Freedom' Report.[77]

It should be noted, however, that previously in July 1997 the UN Secretary-General had proposed in his report to the General Assembly, 'Renewing the United Nations: A Programme for Reform', that the Trusteeship Council:

> be reconstituted as the forum through which Member States exercise their collective trusteeship for the integrity of the global environment and common areas such as the oceans, atmosphere

and outer space. At the same time, it should serve to link the United Nations and civil society in addressing these areas of global concern, which require the active contribution of public, private and voluntary sectors.[78]

This proposal did not receive an enthusiastic response from the member states.[79] It is not clear how this proposal would be feasible in the case of global commons that already have an institutional framework through which states presently exercise their collective trusteeship. For instance, in respect of the seabed and ocean floor and subsoil thereof beyond the limits of national jurisdiction (the Area), which together with the resources therein, are the common heritage of mankind, there is an institutional framework. Here the International Seabed Authority (ISA) acts as a type of trustee on behalf of the states parties to the Law of the Sea Convention (LOSC) 1982.[80] It is difficult to understand how the conventional role of the ISA would be reconciled with that of the Trusteeship Council if such proposal were accepted. Will it be the Trusteeship Council or the ISA that would act in respect of the Area? This would certainly raise complex issues.

Others have suggested that the Trusteeship Council be given a new remit as a 'modern international clearing house for self-determination'.[81] This is an interesting proposal, as it would amount to a collectivisation of the whole process of recognition of entities that seek to be recognised as member states of the international community and perhaps achieve some kind of certainty in the recognition process. It is not certain what the response of states have been to this proposal. Another suggestion is that the Trusteeship Council could be used to provide support and to administer 'failed states'. However, in view of the fact that a number of such states are located in Africa, some have argued that this would amount to reintroducing 'benign colonialism' in parts of the continent.[82]

All in all, the current view among member states of the UN appears to favour the deletion of the provisions of the Trusteeship Council from the Charter.

Secretariat

The Secretariat, an international civil service, comprising the Secretary-General and such staff as the organisation may require, has also been subject to a number of reform initiatives.[83] The HLP Report pointed

The Constitution of the International Community

out that a strong Secretary-General heading a more professional and better organised Secretariat was an essential component of an effective system of collective security in the twenty-first century.[84] They proposed the establishment of a second Deputy Secretary-General, in addition to such a position that had been created in 1996. It was further proposed that one of the Deputy Secretaries-General would assist the Secretary-General in the area of economic and social development work of the UN, while the other would assist him in respect of peace and security.[85] They further recommended that the Secretary-General be provided with the resources to do his job properly and the authority to manage his staff and other resources as he deemed fit.[86] In the 2005 'In Larger Freedom' Report, while generally accepting the recommendations of the HLP, the Secretary-General opted for a cabinet-style decision-making mechanism (with stronger executive powers than his present Senior Management Group) to improve both policy and management, rather than the creation of an additional Deputy Secretary-General position. This cabinet-style decision-making mechanism, he proposed, would be supported by a small cabinet secretariat to ensure the preparation and follow-up of decision-making. His expectation was that this would ensure a more focused orderly and accountable decision-making in the Secretariat.[87] In order to improve transparency and accountability the Secretary-General undertook to establish a Management Performance Board to ensure that senior officials are held accountable for their actions and the results their units achieve. Further, to improve accountability and oversight he proposed that the General Assembly commission a comprehensive review of the Office of Internal Oversight Services with a view to strengthening its independence and authority, as well as its expertise and capacity.[88]

The 2005 World Summit endorsing reform efforts of the Secretariat, pointed out that in order to effectively comply with the principles and objectives of the Charter there is a need for an efficient, effective and accountable Secretariat, with a staff that would act in accordance with Article 100 of the Charter, in a culture of organisational accountability, transparency and integrity.[89]

International Court of Justice

The International Court of Justice (ICJ), the successor to the Permanent Court of International Justice (PCIJ), established during the time of the

League of Nations, is the principal judicial organ of the UN.[90] It is composed of fifteen judges who are elected for a term of nine years by the General Assembly and the Security Council. The Court has a dual jurisdiction: namely, a contentious jurisdiction, where it decides disputes of a legal nature submitted to it by states; and an advisory jurisdiction, where it gives advisory opinions on legal questions at the request of the organs of the United Nations or specialised agencies authorised to make such a request.[91] The ICJ has compulsory jurisdiction only if the states consent to such jurisdiction. Such consent can be discerned in four ways:[92]

- through ad hoc special agreements (or *compromis*) entered into for the particular dispute; or
- through treaties in force that have provisions for disputes arising from the interpretation of application of the treaty provisions (the so-called compromissory clauses); or
- by way of the optional clause system, where a state by way of unilateral declaration accepts the jurisdiction of the Court and such jurisdiction is triggered if the other disputing state has also similarly made such unilateral declaration accepting the jurisdiction of the Court; or
- when a state subsequently consents to the jurisdiction of the court though the case was initially filed without its consent (the so-called rule of *forum prorogatum*). In the *Genocide* case before the ICJ, Judge ad hoc Lauterpacht explained *forum prorogatum* as: 'the possibility that if State A commences proceedings against State B on a non-existent or defective jurisdictional basis, State B can remedy the situation by conduct amounting to an acceptance of the jurisdiction of the Court'.[93]

Interestingly, it was not mentioned by the HLP Report or the 'In Larger Freedom' Report in their recommendations with regard to UN institutional reforms. The 2005 World Summit Outcome document merely required states to honour their obligations to peaceful settlement of disputes in accordance with chapter VI of the Charter, including where appropriate the use of the ICJ. It also called on states 'to consider accepting the jurisdiction of the Court in accordance with its Statute and consider means of strengthening the Court's work, including by supporting the Secretary-General's Trust Fund to Assist States in the Settlement of Disputes through the International Court of Justice on a voluntary basis'.[94] It is rather surprising that the HLP Report, the 'In

The Constitution of the International Community

Larger Freedom' Report and the World Summit Outcome document did not explore the issue of the reform of the ICJ, especially since as the principal judicial organ of the UN, it plays a crucial role in achieving peaceful settlement of disputes, and in that regard contributes to peace and security. This is more so since there have been several calls by states, official bodies, including the Court itself, learned societies and individuals for reform of the Court.[95]

United Nations reform: way forward

There has certainly not been a shortage of reform initiatives with regard to the UN. Reports abound in respect of these initiatives. While some of the reforms have been adopted and implemented, a number of the reform initiatives remain 'lost' in the various report documents. The bottom line is that unless there is political will on the part of the member states of the UN it is unlikely that any reform initiatives will be far-reaching enough to move these institutions into the twenty-first century. While a number of the states intuitively recognise the need for far-reaching reforms to make these institutions 'fit for purpose' in the twenty-first century, the lack of political will, the desire to protect selfish national interests and the feeling of not wanting to 'rock the boat', will always result in state apathy regarding the implementation of any such far-reaching and radical reforms.[96] This does not dampen the desire for reform, which is itself fuelled by a vision of what the UN is or should become. The moral and political arguments for reform, to which we turn in the next sections, are built on understandings of the constitutional role of the UN (or of core UN values such as human rights) in international society. Understanding this crucial site of moral and political contention is fundamental to understanding the dynamics described above.

The United Nations and the global constitution

There are a number of ways in which we might conceive of the UN as providing the constitution of the international community. Marc Weller divides such claims into two approaches. The first he terms 'international constitutionalism', which he describes as a 'proactive, future-oriented campaign, agitating in favour of the development of an international constitutional system'. The second he labels 'the international constitutional law approach', which is, he argues, a more pragmatic approach seeking to chart the legalisation and constitutionalisation of international politics.[97] These approaches seek to separate the morally normative from the legally normative. Indeed, Joahnnes Gerald van Mulligen calls these contrasting approaches '(mere) normative' and 'positivistic' or 'direct' arguments.[98] While these contrasting approaches have the potential to offer important insights into the normative authority of constitutionalist claims, we argue that the complexity of such claims needs both sorts of argument. In Chapter One, we explored the interrelationship between the legally, socially and morally normative in establishing claims concerning the legalisation of world politics. A study of the politics of international law requires a critical analysis of all three forms of normativity if it is to fully comprehend the sort of claims in play. Throughout this book we emphasise the roles that morally normative claims play in institutionalised reasoning about justice, and the roles that legal and social norms play in enabling argument about justice (or normative desirability) to gain purchase in legal and political debates (moral accessibility). Constitutionalist claims are a specific variant of legalisation claims and, as such, the same pattern of argument is required. In Chapter One, we described this pattern of argument as institutional moral reasoning, and focused on the ways that embedding moral claims in the framework of legalised discourse enables the processes of public justification by providing a shared framework for debate. Van Mulligan offers a similar account of the approach we should take to constitutionalist claims. He shows how neither normative nor positivist lines of reasoning can shoulder the burden of the constitutionalist argument. Such claims are forced into what he terms 'indirect normative argument' (alternatively, indirect transcendental or constitutionalist argument):

> constitutionalists may argue *indirectly* that its [claims are] necessitated, *inter alia*, (i) in order to make sense of international legal argument, (ii) by explanatory desiderata regarding trends in international law-making, (iii) as a viable response to the problems posed by fragmentation and deformalization, and (iv) by international legal scepticism, that is, at the same time, grounded in international legal practice. Hence, constitutionalism may be represented as proceeding by formulating necessary conditions for making sense of international legal practice – these condi-

tions, being, paradoxically, both normative, informing international law's development if it is to be coherent, integrated, etc., and descriptive of, or grounded in, positive law ... Indirect constitutionalist arguments, however, only work in a conditional way. That is to say, only if one accepts the description of international legal practice given in the first premise will one be forced to accept the conclusion.[99]

While many of the arguments we explore in this section are not presented in quite this way, it is these combinations of normative claims that we need to be aware of if we are to explore critically the competing notions of constitutionalisation.

In order to explore the range of arguments on this topic we begin with one of the seminal arguments in the constitutionalist literature. Bardo Fassbender has argued that the UN Charter was the constitutional document not simply of the UN, but of the international community more generally.[100] This is an intentionally ambitious legal claim. Fassbender maintains that the UN Charter is not merely the constituent treaty of an international organisation, but is the constitution for all subjects of international law (see Chapter Three). He contrasts this position with the earlier positions of Alfred Verdross, Bruno Simma and Christian Tomuschat, who make similar (but not so forceful) claims, and attempts to demonstrate eight constitutional characteristics that make the Charter the founding instrument of the contemporary international order. For Fassbender the question does not focus on whether the Charter founded or gave expression to the international community (it is clearly a combination of the two), and it is both a legal claim about the nature of the Charter's provisions and an argument about the desirability of the realisation of political unity that the constitionalism has the potential to foster.[101]

Both Vendross and Tomuschat see the Charter as more than the constituent treaty of the UN. But neither scholar saw the Charter alone as the constitution of the international community. For Tomuschat, the Charter was a 'world order treaty'. A world order treaty is 'one intended to concretize, and elaborate on, principles which on their part are constituent elements of the international legal order'.[102] For Tomuschat, the UN Charter shares this status with the two 1966 human rights covenants (the ICCPR and the ICESCR), the Vienna Convention on Diplomatic Relations, the Genocide Convention and the Convention on the Law of the Sea. Such instruments concretise earlier 'unwritten law', which, Fassbender argues, begs the question of the authority of this unwritten law and suggests that the constitutional premises of the international order lie outside those world order treaties. Vendross, on the other hand, identifies the Charter as the sole constitutional instrument of the world order, but argues that general international law maintains an independent existence.[103] In essence, this means that the Charter could be amended both under the terms of Articles 108 and 109, which provide for alterations to the Charter, and also on the authority of general principles of law. Again, Fassbender argues that if this is the case then the Charter is not, in any fundamental sense, a constitutional instrument. Whatever underpins the authority of general international law is properly the constitution of international society. Emerging from these insights is Fassbender's much stronger claim that there is no room for other world order treaties or for general international law to exist beside the Charter, and that 'instead the Charter is the supporting frame of all international law and, at the same time, the highest layer in a hierarchy of norms in international law'.[104] Fassbender achieves this conclusion by arguing that the Charter 'incorporates' all secondary rules of international law and pre-1945 world order treaties, and 'upholds' primary rules of law, including those that Tomuschat identifies as other 'world order treaties', which are best seen as constitutional bylaws 'if and to the extent that they characterise in detail, or further develop, the constitutional law of the charter'.[105] This is a very strong claim for the foundational status of the Charter and leads Fassbender to present eight constitutional characteristics of the Charter. If we summarise Fassbender's argument in list form we get a sense of the overall qualities of the Charter that underwrite his position:

The Eight Constitutional Characteristics of the UN Charter

1. *A constitutional moment*: The Charter, especially the preamble and chapter I clearly indicate the will of the drafters to establish a new order.
2. *A system of governance*: The Charter establishes mechanisms for the creation, application, adjudication of law and for the execution of law.
3. *Definition of membership*: Chapter II defines rules of membership (although subsequent practice has broadened membership of the international community beyond states).
4. *Hierarchy of norms*: Article 103 establishes the primacy of the Charter's provisions in the event of conflict with the obligations of members.

5. *'Eternity' and amendment*: The Charter makes no provision for termination, but Articles 108 and 109 contain procedures for amendment and, crucially, dissenting states remain bound by the Charter in the event of such an amendment.
6. A *'Charter'*: The name itself is intended to signify the elevated nature of the treaty.
7. A *constitutional history*: Since its inception the UN has become the 'natural forum' for the discussion of all globally significant issues.
8. *Universality and sovereignty*: The UN is (almost) universal in its membership and the rule of law fostered by the Charter trumps sovereignty.[106]

We can see from this list that the UN Charter certainly has many constitution-like qualities. So should we, as Fassbender urges, view the UN Charter as the constitution of the international community as a whole?

Fassbender's claims do not meet with universal approval. Of those who agree with Klabbers that the UN Charter can be referred to as a constitution in 'more than a colloquial sense',[107] most want to significantly moderate the strong claim found in Fassbender's writing. Others still want to challenge it. For some critics of Fassbender's position, such as Erika de Wet, Anne Peters, Jean Cohen and Stephen Gardbaum, the foundations of the global constitution are implicit in post-Second World War international law (which is, of course, heavily informed by the UN), rather than explicit in the Charter itself.[108] The Charter, as de Wet puts it, is vitally important because of its linking function to other national, regional and functional communities.[109] But to subsume all the trends that point to the formation of genuine legal community at the global level law under the Charter seems artificial.[110] These scholars are happy to acknowledge the emergence of an international value system, enshrined in law, of constitutional character. But it is not found in one constituent treaty. In part, this is because membership of the international community is not co-extensive with membership of the UN. Regional organisations, such as the EU and the AU, and sectoral international organisations, such as the WTO, sit side by side with the UN. Similarly, other regional sectoral regimes (most importantly the human rights regimes) sit alongside the UN regimes to form distinct functional regimes. 'Together the different communities complement one another to constitute a larger whole in the form of the international community.'[111] It is also, Peters argues, necessary to distinguish between the hierarchical authority of Charter provision (given Article 103) and the hierarchical authority of peremptory norms of international law. Citing the Separate Opinion of Judge Lauterpacht in the *Genocide* case (1993) before the ICJ, Peters shows that 'acts privileged by Article 103 of the Charter still rank below *jus cogens* and would have to give way in case of conflict'.[112] However, both scholars show that this neither undermines the idea of constitutionalisation nor the importance of the UN to that process. Rather, it requires that we rethink what international constitutionalisation looks like and adopt a less formal view of the role of the Charter than that offered by Fassbender.

Peters argues that there is no global constitution in a formal sense, but that international legal norms do fulfil a constitutional function.[113] The analysis of Peters and de Wet pushes us to reconsider the nature of an international constitution. The international community is not characterised by a single or exclusive constitution.[114] Nevertheless, both Peters and de Wet present an image of a 'loose-knit network'[115] of constitutional orders patterned by the co-existence of national, regional, sectoral and international institutions. For both it is an 'embryonic' constitutional order that exists side by side with anti-constitutionalist tendencies, such as fragmentation and de-formalisation, the increasing softening of international law and US hegemony.[116] This network links horizontally, in the sense that it links distinct sectoral or functional regimes, and vertically, linking national, regional and international organisations. De Wet, however, does not want to underplay the role of the UN in holding together this constitutional order:

> The international value system is closely linked to the UN Charter, as the latter's connecting role is not only structural but also substantive in nature. In addition to providing a structural linkage of the different communities through universal state membership, the UN inspires those norms that articulate the fundamental values of the international community.[117]

In one sense this claim is similar to Fassbender's point that the UN, particularly the General Assembly, has become the natural forum for the great debates of international affairs. The global challenges of racism and self-determination, human rights, aggression and nuclear weapons, the seabed, outer space and environmental protection have all been the focus for sustained UN diplomacy. In addition, the multifaceted nature of the UN's role in the development of law, in particular, the increasing prominence of human rights norms and their rise to peremptory status, and the development of a legal hierarchy in which the Charter plays a significant role all add to the claim that the UN is the key to the constitutionalisation of international society. But this is not just a legal claim. It is also a claim about the political and moral desirability of constitutionalism in the face of anti-constitutionalist trends.[118] Here the morally normative claim is that, given the way that international law has developed, we have a political choice between a legal order characterised by fragmentation and one based on constitutional principles. These options have considerable legal, moral and political implications and, provided that we are prepared to live with a loose constitutional network rather than an overarching formal constitution, the critical potential of the constitutionalist route opens the door to a post-modern international society. Importantly, the constitutionalist argument seeks to keep the normative debate situated in legal and political context. It is, as Peters puts it, a defence against de-formalisation and the removal of moral argument from the social context in which contending positions exchange. Debates about the desirability of the constitutionalist approach are critical, because 'the idea of a constitution is associated with the quest for a legitimate one, the constitutionalist reconstruction *provokes the pressing question of legitimacy of global governance*'.[119] Equally crucial, however, is the fact that such debates are legalised as the terms of the debate are thus also granted a form of legitimacy.

However, some analysts are not convinced by the legal and political claims, and do not, therefore, see the appeal of the broader normative argument in favour of global constitutionalism. The pluralist position comes in a stronger and weaker form. The stronger form, found extremely clearly in the work of Robert Jackson, amounts to a full rejection of the constitutionalist claim. The weaker pluralist claim has more in common with constitutionalism than Jackson's English School pluralism.

Jackson's account of the 'Global Covenant', as the title suggests, argues that international society has a (legally) normative basis that can be described as a covenant. However,

> the global covenant is not by any means identical with the UN. It grew out of historical practices and institutions that predated the UN by several centuries. It is properly conceived as the pluralist and anti-paternalist ethics that underpins the UN: it is the underlying moral and legal standards by reference to which relations between independent states can be conducted and judged.[120]

Jackson offers a very pluralist reading of the UN Charter. Article 2(4) of the Charter, which emphasises the territorial integrity and independence of states, is emphasised, as is Article 2(7), which deals with non-intervention. Jackson argues that chapters VI and VII also reflect the global covenant. While, for example, chapter VII defines the *jus ad bellum* of the post-1945 world, the existence of the P-5 veto power also points to a crucial element of the global covenant. For Jackson, 'the basic underlying principle on which the UN Charter rests is that international responsibility must be commensurate with national power', and the veto reflects this reality.[121] Thus read, the Charter is one part of the juridical basis of the global constitution, but its constitutional elements are those reflected in the Helsinki Final Act (1975) of the Organizations of Security and Cooperation in Europe that lay heavy emphasis on state sovereignty. In particular, human rights norms, the development of which suggest to scholars such as Peters, de Wet and van Mulligen that the global constitution is beginning to transcend the Westphalian system, 'have not achieved the same standing as the procedural norms of state sovereignty'.[122]

Like Jackson, Jean Cohen is sharply critical of the constitutional monism of Fassbender's approach to the UN Charter. Its major fault is that is that it sets up an either/or dichotomy that denies the obvious continuing normative authority of state sovereignty in contemporary international affairs:

> Either there is a global legal system coupled to the global political system, based on the twin principles of sovereign equality and human rights but without the sovereign state, or there are sovereign states, and international law based on their consent but it is not an autonomous legal system. Either the UN Charter establishes a supranational political organization whose rules have acquired constitutional quality, and which, despite its origins in international treaty now subordinate the constituent units the new creation such that its decisions apply to each of them irrespective of their continuous individual consent. Or the Charter remains a treaty, the UN, a treaty organization, with legal personality but no power to eradicate its subordination to the member states or its subjection to the classical laws governing the treaty organizations. It should, however, be obvious that neither side of this either/or is compelling.[123]

The fact is that both are true and to deny one or the other risks normatively vital elements of international society. Monist constitutionalism and monist sovereignism are both false, and the more compelling approach 'empirically, pragmatically and normatively' is to think in terms of constitutional pluralism.[124] To some degree this resonates with the 'network of constitutional orders' thesis put forward by de Wet and Peters. It places more emphasis on the continuing constitutional autonomy of sovereign states and on the dangers of ignoring the normative importance of this when considering the cosmopolitan potential of constitutional moments. Constitutional pluralism acknowledges the reality of competing claims to supremacy. Internally, the UN Charter assumes authority, but from the perspective of states such authority relies on their consent. There exists, Cohen claims, a heterarchical rather than hierarchical relationship between national and international constitutional orders that drives the political, legal and moral questions of legitimacy. This heterarchy (which simply means distinct but overlapping or co-existent organisation) is the site of political dispute and debate, and it models the 'new political culture of sovereignty that has shifted from one of impunity to one of responsibility and accountability'.[125] This does not mean that the pluralist order has ceased to exist. Rather, it exists alongside the global order with each serving to temper the other. A proper understanding of the constitutional character of the UN Charter recognises this dualism and the aspirational nature of constitutionalist claims.

Understanding the place of the UN in international affairs is more complex than understanding the multifaceted organisational structures and the vitally important work of the various organs and agencies. The debate about constitutionalism is a debate about normative authority and normative desirability, of legitimacy and justice. Its contours provide the critical context for all the substantive debates of contemporary world politics. In later chapters we examine how the relatively abstract concern with the constitutional standing of the UN plays out in debates concerning human rights and the use of force. In the next section we pick up on one of the key tensions that emerge in the debate over the character of the UN and its role in international society. Jackson's scepticism regarding the constitutionalist argument is founded, as we noted, in the manner in which the UN Charter embeds power politics within one of its principal organs. The UN Security Council is a hugely powerful organ. Jackson argues that its power to maintain international peace and security is so sensitive that the establishment of the P-5 veto reflects 'the reality that if great powers cannot agree on action it probably should not be taken because it might provoke a conflict between then which could be dangerous if not disastrous'.[126] Here, of course, Jackson has a point. But the effects of the veto have come under severe criticism from those who see inaction in the face of humanitarian suffering as a betrayal of the fundamental values or constitutional principles of the UN.

The UN Security Council and the normative desirability of reform

The call for a League of Democracies (sometimes a Concert of Democracies) has been the subject of articles in many key newspapers,[127] journals,[128] conferences and reports[129] and books.[130] We have chosen to explore this rather bold claim because it highlights some of the core tensions at work in the pluralist versus constitutionalist debates about the legitimacy of UN governance. While there is significant consensus that the UN Security Council needs to be radically reformed if it is to become 'fit for purpose', there is also general acknowledgement that the UN system has limited resources for reform and that there is little appetite among members (especially the veto-holding P-5) for the significant reforms necessary.[131] In general terms the very existence of an effective veto power in the UN Security Council breeds a lack of efficiency and accountability. The fact that this power is concentrated in the hands of the P-5 (Britain, Russia, China, America and France) reflects the situation in 1946 rather than 2013, and calls for the abolition of the veto and an expansion of permanent membership to include states such as Germany, Japan, Brazil and India have garnered widespread support in liberal theory since it was proposed by the UN High Level Panel on Threats, Challenges and Change.[132] Nevertheless, many analysts have significant reservations, arguing that whether you think in terms of a 'coalition of the willing', a 'coalition of the just' or a league of democracies that it would 'aggravate rather than alleviate global sensitivities over U.S. democracy promotion and the U.S. global security agenda' and, more generally, that it would not reflect the true basis of the global covenant.

The case in favour of UN Security Council reform, or where that is impossible for a league of democracies, is made most completely by Allen Buchanan and Robert Keohane. Their 'cosmopolitan institutional proposal' is, they argue, premised on many of the same core values as the UN system of international politics. Buchanan and Keohane make the thesis most explicit when they claim that cosmopolitan liberalism, which on their reading advocates the establishment of a concert of democracies, and the UN system (what they call the legal *status quo*) share a moral foundation in their basic commitment to human rights.[133] If this argument is granted, then the inability of the UN to effectively reform itself in line with the principle that where states cannot protect their citizens from gross violations of their most basic rights then the obligation to do so passes to the international community (the principle called responsibility to protect or R2P) does suggest that the institutions of the UN lack legitimacy.

The use of force is the crunch issue that drives reformers towards a new league of democracies. This, put simply, is because nowhere is the tension between the human rights agenda of the post-Cold War UN in such direct conflict with the structures of the 1945 Charter. The failure of the UN Security Council to act to ease the suffering of those in Eastern Europe, Rwanda, Timor and Darfur is exacerbated by the claims, eagerly pointed out by the UN's liberal critics, by the Independent International Commission on Kosovo (the Kosovo Report) that the NATO intervention, while unauthorised by the UN Security Council (and thus illegal), was legitimate.[134] If the use of force outside the UN Charter can be legitimate, then the question that immediately arises is 'what sort of institutional framework can best govern the legitimate use of force?' The liberal–cosmopolitan case, then, is that the structural failures of the UN and its inability to reform itself have cost the UN Security Council its legitimacy and the trust that it needs to act effectively in relation to the governance of force.[135]

In developing a moral theory of international law Buchanan links his grasp of public international law with the critical power of cosmopolitan political theory. His claim is that such a moral theory would not be particularly grandiose, but would set about systematically examining the principles at work in the international legal order.[136] Buchanan strengthens his case here by insisting on what he terms 'institutional moral reasoning' (see Chapter One, above). He argues that a defensible moral theory of international law must take into account the fact that moral principles of international law are institutional principles that need to be developed *in situ*, as it were, with a proper respect for the existing world order.[137] Buchanan's acknowledgement that, in reality, the international system has limited resources for change, that the institutionalisation of principle has a moral impact in itself, and that therefore our approach to reform of international law must be a key part of cosmopolitan theory has the potential to add much to cosmopolitanism and to our understanding of the case for a league of democracies.

Buchanan realises that the reason why a case for a league of democracies is controversial is that its foundation relies upon a commitment to a human rights-based conception of justice. No one denies that human rights law (and the moral concepts that underpin human rights claims) are a key element of the international legal order or that the global system has undergone dramatic changes in the name of human rights. However, the legal order also has as its goal the maintenance of international peace and security, and the preservation of the sovereign independence of the states that are the primary subjects of international law. Buchanan is not denying that this is the case, but, given that human rights norms have come to bestow an extraordinary level of legitimacy upon international institutions and actions, he suggests that a human rights-based conception of justice should become the primary goal of the global community.

Institutional moral reasoning does not constitute the whole of Buchanan's moral theory of international law. Running alongside it we have the central or foundational argument that underpins Buchanan's account of human rights. He refers to this as the 'Natural Duty of Justice' argument. Put simply, the natural duty of justice insists that:

> Each of us – independently of the institutions we find ourselves in and the special commitments that we have undertaken – has a limited obligation to help ensure that all persons have access to institutions that protect their basic rights.[138]

Buchanan refuses to engage in any debate about the moral equality principle. This is partly because he is adamant that something like the moral equality principle is fundamental to any conception of morality worth thinking about, and partly because his is a theory of international law and not a treatise on the foundations of ethics. Buchanan is quite clear. He writes:

> I wish to emphasize that much of what I say in the remainder of this volume does *not* depend upon the argument there is a Natural Duty of Justice. My main concern is to develop a moral theory of international law that takes justice – understood as a respect for basic human rights – seriously. All that is required is the assumption that there are basic human rights.[139]

In defence of each reform proposal he suggests that he is only asking for what he terms a 'systematic moral view' of the implications of basic human rights.

The basic structure of the argument starts from the recognition that the UN is failing to institutionalise one of its core values and that it has limited resources to affect any reform. Institutional moral reasoning requires that we add a reflective understanding of that process of institutionalising any such reform and so think critically about 'the morality of transition'. An important subset of the morality of transition is what Buchanan has called 'the morality of illegal international legal reform'.[140] Sometimes actions that fall outside the law as it currently stands are required to instigate, or enable, system reform. Any league of democracies would, of course, be constituted outside the UN system of law and, initially at least, be in conflict with it, and our analysis must examine the moral and political cost and benefits of contentious change. Charter provision allowing the international community to intervene forcefully in the domestic affairs of a sovereign state that is abusing its citizens is deeply contentious. While the normative climate in which discussions of humanitarian intervention has become more receptive to the claim that such action is necessary and lawful,[141] and while the accepted interpretation of the phrase 'international peace and security' in the Charter has been broadened to include domestic or civil conflict,[142] the central elements of the Charter that protect sovereign independence contrive to frustrate any attempt to institutionalise humanitarian military action. As Buchanan, citing Kofi Annan, demonstrates, the clash between the legitimacy and the legality of humanitarian military intervention shows 'a disturbing tension between two core values of the international legal system itself'. Buchanan goes on to argue:

> More precisely, the perception is growing that the requirement of Security Council authorization is an obstacle to the protection of basic human rights in internal conflicts. Since the majority of violent conflicts are now within states rather than between them, the time is ripe to consider changing or abandoning a rule of humanitarian intervention that was created for a quite different world.[143]

The institutional reforms necessary here are laid out in detail in an article by Buchanan and Keohane on preventive force, and usefully supplemented by sections of Buchanan's *Justice, Legitimacy and*

Self-Determination.[144] The first proposed model Buchanan writes, 'relies exclusively on the Security Council but creates mechanisms for *ex ante* and *ex post* accountability and removes decisions about [preventative] force from the scope of the Council's permanent member veto'.[145] The accountability mechanisms would include the need for a supermajority of nine council members and an impartial *ex-post* review. Where there is no time for *ex ante* discussion due to the pressing need for action, there would still be an *ex -post* review backed up (as in the first case) by sanctions. A treaty-based system of sanctions would apply to those who acted where there was no clear mandate or *ex post* justification and to those who voted against action where there was clear justification.[146] All the mechanisms – from dropping the veto to imposing sanctions on recalcitrant members – are designed to reduce inertia and promote fair-dealing and the use of information in matters concerning the governance of force. Dropping the veto has the additional benefit of removing a morally suspect relic from the early days of the post-war UN.[147] Indeed, it is the key to this reform proposal, but it is also the reason why Buchanan believes this to be the least feasible proposal as

> States that now possess the veto are unlikely to relinquish it and no one else can make the proposed change. Moreover it is especially unlikely that they would relinquish the veto over something as important and controversial as the [preventive] use of force.[148]

The second proposal, dubbed 'accountability despite the veto', offers the same measures, but leaves the veto intact. Buchanan's hope is that this would reduce the likelihood that vetoes would be used during the process, but, ultimately, is not convinced that it would prevent the arbitrary and self-interested use of the veto that breeds inaction.[149]

The principal reason that Buchanan begins by exploring the reform option from within the existing structures of the UN is that this is the route that most fully adheres to his ideal of institutional moral reasoning. This is the case because there are legally developed routes to such reform (even if there are doubts about the political will required to travel them). Buchanan argues that:

> there appear to be three main types of strategies for reforming the international law of intervention: (1) developing new customary law, (2) modifying the UN charter based law of intervention, and (3) creating an alternative treaty-based intervention regime outside the UN framework.[150]

Yet, despite the fact that the first two options are the only available options under current international law, Buchanan argues that: '(3) offers the best prospect for morally defensible, effective reform within a reasonable time-span'.[151] It is clear that treaty reform is a limited prospect and that significant change to customary international law is also unlikely in highly contested areas. For Buchanan, the inability of the UN to reform itself is born of the principle, deeply seated in the structure of both customary and treaty law, that international law must be based on state consent. Buchanan argues forcefully that the requirement of state consent is both the cause of legal and institutional stagnation and is itself a 'legitimacy veto' that stands in opposition to the moral equality principle that underpins any account of human rights.

This last argument raises the stakes considerably. While we might agree that the way the P-5 protected their interests at the origin of the Charter, and the way that now inhibits Charter reform, is inconsistent with contemporary international values, here Buchanan is going further. The claim is that the state consent model of international law and the more basic principle of sovereignty are themselves morally dubious and politically and legally unnecessary.[152] At this point the pursuit of a human rights-based conception of justice parts company with state consent, sovereign equality and global democratic governance and clears the way for Buchanan to argue for the development of a coalition of democratic rights respecting states that, under a treaty made outside the UN system, would govern the use of force in respect of preventive war and humanitarian intervention. It clears the way in the sense that Buchanan now begins to show that in the face of the moral and logistical problems that reform within the UN system exhibits, the third option becomes the most satisfactory in relation to the principles laid out in his account of institutional moral reasoning. Despite being illegal, despite challenging what most commentators see as the fundamental norms of international society, Buchanan believes that the transition to a coalition of the just most adequately institutionalises the virtues of feasibility, accessibility and moral progressivity. Here, at last, we get to the theoretical heart of the liberal case for a league of democracies.

Buchanan and Keohane write:

> Our proposal is to begin with a core group of states whose democratic credentials are uncontroversial, such as the members of the European Union plus such states as Australia, Canada, Chile,

Costa Rica, Japan, South Africa and South Korea. Unlike NATO, the coalition that intervened in Kosovo in 1999, such a coalition would be open to states from all regions of the world.[153]

Buchanan is wary of giving the USA a lead role in the coalition, indeed he thinks non-US leadership would enhance the coalitions legitimacy.[154] There is, of course, considerable doubt about the ability of such a coalition to get off the ground without US support and military muscle but the organisation would benefit from the 'comparative moral reliability', not in the sense that we can expect them to act always on principles of cosmopolitan morality, but in the sense that they will be comparatively more likely to do so and that they will be subject to criticism by their citizens when they do not.[155] Buchanan and Keohane conclude that:

> The most obvious advantage of model 3 is that it provides the possibility of responsible decisions to use force when the security council fails to do so. But another equally important advantage is that the possibility that a decision will go to the democratic coalition provides an incentive for the security council to act more responsibly... The third institutional model creates healthy competition with the UN system without bypassing it all together. More specifically the democratic coalition provides the incentive for the permanent members to use the veto more responsibly and for all members of the council to realize that they no longer enjoy an absolute monopoly on the legitimate authorization of the [preventive] use of force.[156]

Buchanan's position, therefore, is that there are such significant moral and political impediments to reform within current legal and political structures that an illegal transition to a coalition of democratic states that would then authorise the illegal (under the Charter) use of military force is the option most consistent with cosmopolitan principles, and that this proposal is the most feasible and morally accessible option for anyone that takes human rights seriously. We are now in a position to critically analyse this bold claim.

The first two criteria of institutional moral reasoning are feasibility and accessibility. We can grant the claims that the creation of a league of democracies is both physically and practically possible. Buchanan and Keohane argue that:

The third model is feasible, since formal UN action would not be necessary to implement it. Indeed, if a large and diverse cluster of democracies proposed it, no single state could easily block it. The democratic coalition would be based on agreements among its members – not necessarily a formal treaty. Over time, its practices could become part of customary international law. Furthermore, recent experience with respect to the Anglo-American war against Iraq suggests that democratic countries are capable of making independent judgements about the proposals of a superpower, even when faced with the prospect of bilateral sanctions.[157]

Of course, it is equally feasible that states such as China and Russia (who have the most to lose under these proposals) will react strongly against these moves. Equally plausibly, many democratic states, asked to permanently limit or give up their sovereign rights in favour of a system that privileges human rights norms in this manner, will not wish to sign up to such a coalition. Given Buchanan's earlier critique of the possibility of reform through the development of new customary law, we would have to say that it is also unlikely that those who object to these radical changes will demure to the point where we might be able to honestly argue that a new norm has developed to the effect that human rights rather than state consent provides the basis of international law. Finally, the prospect of sanctions becomes far more serious if we are looking at the prospect of great power conflict or another Cold War.

The next criterion is moral accessibility. This requirement must include a shared (but not uniform) sense of moral direction and a shared sense of the need to transcend multilateralism, state consent and non-intervention as cardinal rules. Buchanan is absolutely correct to claim that any sensible account of international justice will have a significant human rights element. But in claiming that any sensible account of international justice has to follow him if it is to use its account of human rights systematically he goes too far. Recall Kofi Annan's argument that debates over humanitarian intervention highlight the tension between the two core values of the international system (above). Buchanan's line of argument suggests that these two values (sovereignty and human rights) are not only in tension, but in absolute conflict. Indeed, his reform agenda anticipates the triumph of human rights over sovereign rights. But this seems far too strong a claim to be based on any real consensus about human rights or the future of the international system. Here we need to return to the idea of the global constitution investigated above. If we explore the trends in the development of the continually evolving world community, we gain critical insight into the ways that Buchanan and Keohane present the normative desirability of the placing of human rights principles at the heart of their argument. The core claim – that a just world order would privilege human rights – has two potential bases in Buchanan's work. The first is his philosophical 'natural duty of justice' argument. The second can be read as the claim that human rights are a key part of the constitution of the global order, and that that value is not being adequately institutionalised. Buchanan, while not abandoning the force of the philosophical argument, makes a compelling case for the virtues of relying on the force of the political and legal norms already embedded in global discourse. The treatment of human rights that underpins the case for moving outside the UN to a coalition of democratic states is, when we compare it with the arguments we have explored, very demanding. Buchanan's core claim clearly goes beyond the constitutionalist arguments that associate the constitutionalisation of world politics with the UN and its Charter. The Charter certainly underpins the rapid development of human rights principles, their codification in international law and their rise to peremptory status. But if we think of the Charter as having constitutional standing, then its own provisions for amendment are essential to the legitimacy of any reform. We might, of course, think of the Charter as being one among several world order treaties, or as being part of a loose network or heterarchical order of constitutional regimes and institutions. In such a scheme we are bound to acknowledge the significance of human rights instruments, and there is strong evidence to suggest that human rights principles are gaining constitutional significance in themselves. Bypassing the Charter provisions for reform could be considered a legitimate option. But to ignore all other elements of such a network is to present a human rights-based constitutional monism that seems just as artificial as a sovereigntist monism. Yet Buchanan and Keohane are correct to challenge the UN Security Council on human rights grounds. Failure to protect those suffering gross abuses of their human rights is, uncontroversially, seen as a moral, political and legal failure. Here again we see the critical potential of constitutionalist discourse and the space in which the politics of international law is to be conducted.

There is much more to say about the power of the position adopted by Buchanan and Keohane. Much rests on issues that we deal with in subsequent chapters on international human rights law (Chapter Five), and in our exploration of issues relating to preventative self-defence and humanitarian intervention (Chapter Seven). Both chapters offer new insights into the power of specific aspects of the case for the abandonment of the UN Security Council, and we will return to the question at the appropriate time. Here, however, we note that the case for a coalition of rights-respecting states is premised on a very strong constitutionalist reading of the current basis of justice and legitimacy in the international community, and that as a basis for institutionalised reform it requires significant additional support from a close analysis of the ethics and politics of human rights and of the use of force.

Notes

1 See Art. 1 of the United Nations Charter and the UN Secretary-General, In Larger Freedom Report, 2005, para. 12, available, respectively, at: http://www.un.org/en/documents/charter/index.shtml and http://www.un.org/largerfreedom/contents.htm.
2 Goodrich, L. M., 'From League of Nations to United Nations', *International Organization*, 1(1) (1947): 3, at p. 21.
3 'Renewing the United Nations: A Programme for Reform'. Report of the Secretary-General, A/51/950, 14 July 1997, p. 9.
4 In 1965, the membership UN Security Council and the ECOSOC were increased from eleven to fifteen and eighteen to twenty-seven, respectively. In 1973, the membership of the ECOSOC was again increased from twenty-seven to fifty-four.
5 See also Art. 109.
6 See Sohn, L., 'Important Improvements in the Functioning of the Principal Organs of the United Nations that can be made without Charter Revision', *American Journal of International Law*, 91 (1997): 652–62; Reisman, M., 'Amending the UN Charter: The Art of the Feasible', *American Society of International Law Proceedings*, 88 (1994): 108–15.
7 UN, 'Renewing the United Nations', para. 25.
8 Brown, M. M., 'Can the UN Be Reformed?', The John W. Holmes Lecture, *Global Governance*, 14(1) (2008): 1–12.
9 Morris, J., 'UN Security Council Reform: A Counsel for the 21st Century', *Security Dialogue*, 31 (2000): 265–77. See, for instance, the UN Secretary-General, 'Renewing the United Nations'; UN Secretary-General, 'Strengthening the United Nations: An Agenda for Further Change', A/57/387, 9 September 2002.
10 Available at: http://www.un.org/secureworld. The HLP members were: Anand Panyarachun (Thailand), Robert Badinter (France), Joao Clemente Baena Soares (Brazil), Gro Harlem Brundtland (Norway), Mary Chinery-Hesse (Ghana), Gareth Evans (Australia), David Hannay

(United Kingdom), Enrique Iglesias (Uruguay), Amre Moussa (Egypt), Satish Nambiar (India), Sadako Ogata (Japan), Yevgeny Primakov (Russia), Qian Qichen (China), Nafis Sadik (Pakistan), Salim Ahmed Salim (Tanzania) and Brent Scowcroft (United States).
11 The Human Rights Council and Peace Building Commission have been set up as subsidiary organs of the General Assembly and Security Council, respectively.
12 A/59/2005, 21 March 2005, available at: http://www.un.org/larger-freedom; 2005 World Summit Outcome, A/RES/60/1, 24 October 2005, available at: http://daccess-dds-ny.un.org/doc/UNDOC/GEN/N05/487/60/PDF/N0548760.pdf?OpenElement.
13 Article 7 of the Charter lists the principal organs in the following order: General Assembly, Security Council, Economic and Social Council, Trusteeship Council, International Court of Justice and Secretariat.
14 UN, 'In Larger Freedom', para. 169.
15 Article 23 of the Charter.
16 See Arts 24, 25 and chapter VII of the Charter.
17 The five permanent members are China, France, Russia (successor to the USSR), the United Kingdom and the United States.
18 Article 23 of the Charter.
19 The African and Latin America and Caribbean Grouping are not represented among the P-5.
20 See Morris, 'UN Security Council Reform', p. 266.
21 General Assembly Resolution, 48/26, 3 December 1993.
22 HLP Report 2004, paras 251–3.
23 HLP Report, paras 247–8.
24 HLP Report, para. 255.
25 UN, 'In Larger Freedom', para. 170. See generally Blum, Y. Z., 'Proposals for UN Security Council Reform', *American Journal of International Law*, 99(3) (2005): 632–49.
26 Weiss, T. G., 'An Unchanged Security Council: The Sky Ain't Falling', *Security Dialogue*, 36 (2005): 367, at pp. 368–9.
27 The Common African Position on the Proposed Reform of the United Nations, the 'Ezulwini Consensus', Ext/EX.CL/2, 2005. See also the previous Harare Declaration of the Assembly of Heads of State and Government of the Organization of African Unity on the Reform of the United Nations Security Council, AHG/Decl.3(XXXIII), June 1997.
28 UN, 2005 World Summit Outcome, para. 153.
29 See speech of President of the General Assembly to the 63rd Session of the General Assembly, 14 September 2009, available at: http://www.un.org/ga/president/63/statements/finalsession140909.shtml and see World Federalist Movement, Institute of Global Policy(WFM-IGP) ReformtheUN.org Project, available at: http://www.reformtheun.org/index.php/eupdate/3086.

The Constitution of the International Community

30 Wouters, J. and Ruys, T., 'Security Council Reform: A New Veto for a New Century', Egmont Paper No. 9, Royal Institute for International Relations (IRRI-KIIB), Brussels, August 2005, p. 5, available at: http://www.egmontinstitute.be/paperegm/ep9.pdf.

31 Global Policy Forum, 'Changing Patterns in the Use of the Veto in the Security Council', 2008, available at: http://globalpolicy.org/security-council/tables-and-charts-on-the-security-council-0-82/use-of-the-veto.html.

32 GA Resolution 377(V), 3 November 1950.

33 See generally Fassbender, B., *UN Security Council Reform and the Right of Veto: A Constitutional Perspective*, The Hague, Kluwer Law, 1998.

34 Wouters and Ruys, 'Security Council Reform', p. 21.

35 Wouters and Ruys, 'Security Council Reform', p. 21. See also Report of the Open-ended Working Group on the Question of Equitable Representation on and Increase in the Membership of the Security Council and Other Matters related to the Security Council, General Assembly, Official Records, 53rd Session, Supplement No .47, A/53/47, p. 34, available at: http://www.undemocracy.com/A-53-47.pdf.

36 Wouters and Ruys, 'Security Council Reform', p. 22.

37 HLP Report, para. 256.

38 HLP Report, para. 256.

39 'Ezulwini Consensus', Ext/EX.CL/2 of 2005, para. C(e)(3), available at: http://www.responsibilitytoprotect.org/files/AU_Ezulwini%20Consensus.pdf, accessed 29 October 2012.

40 'Ezulwini Consensus', para. C(e)(2).

41 HLP Report, para. 257.

42 Blum, 'Proposals for UN Security Council Reform', pp. 643–4.

43 UN, 'In Larger Freedom', paras 167–70 and UN, 2005 World Summit Outcome, paras 152–4.

44 Secretary-General's Report, 'Strengthening the United Nations', para. 21.

45 HLP Report, para. 258; In Larger Freedom Report, para. 168; World Summit outcome document, para. 154.

46 HLP Report, paras 261–9.

47 In Larger Freedom Report, paras 114–17; World Summit outcome document, paras 97–105.

48 See GA Resolution 60/180 and Security Council Resolution 1645(2005), 20 December 2005.

49 Article 9 of the UN Charter states: '(1) The General Assembly shall consist of all members of the United Nations. (2) Each Member shall have not more than five representatives in the General Assembly'; Article 18(1) states: 'Each Member of the General Assembly shall have one vote.' The 1997 Report of the Secretary-General states: 'The General Assembly is the organ of the United Nations which most fully embodies

the universal and democratic character of the world organization', in 'Renewing the United Nations', para. 97, and the 2002 Report of the Secretary-General pointed out that the 'General Assembly is the only universal forum in which all States have an equal voice', 'Strengthening the United Nations', para. 15. See generally Peterson, M. J., *The UN General Assembly*, London: Routledge, 2006.
50 See, e.g., Peterson, *The UN General Assembly*, pp. 132–6.
51 Heinrich, D., 'The Case for a United Nations Parliamentary Assembly', unaltered edition of the first printing by the World Federalist Movement, October 1992, made available by the German Committee for a Democratic UN, June 2003, available at: http://www.wfm-igp.org/site/files/UNPA1992-Heinrich.pdf.
52 Paragraph 30, General Assembly, United Nations Millennium Declaration, A/RES/55/2, 18 September 2000, states as follows: 'We resolve therefore: To reaffirm the central position of the General Assembly as the chief deliberative, policy-making and representative organ of the United Nations and to enable it to play that role effectively,' available at: http://www.un.org/millennium/declaration/ares552e.pdf. See also UN, 'In Larger Freedom', para. 158 and UN, 2005 World Summit Outcome, para. 149.
53 Schermers, H. G., 'We the Peoples of the United Nations', *Max Planck Yearbook of United Nations Law*, 1 (1997): 111, at p. 112.
54 See, e.g., Peterson, *The UN General Assembly*, pp. 125–30.
55 Peterson, *The UN General Assembly*, pp. 125–30.
56 See UN, 'Renewing the United Nations', paras 97–100; UN, 'Strengthening the United Nations', para. 16.
57 UN, 'Renewing the United Nations', para. 242.
58 UN, 'Renewing the United Nations', para. 243.
59 'In Larger Freedom' Report, paras 162 and 163.
60 'In Larger Freedom' Report, para. 160.
61 'In Larger Freedom' Report, para. 161.
62 World Summit Outcome document, para. 150.
63 World Summit Outcome document, para. 151.
64 Article 62 of the UN Charter. See generally Rosenthal, G., 'Economic and Social Council', in T. G. Weiss and S. Daws (eds), *The Oxford Handbook on the United Nations*, Oxford: Oxford University Press, 2007, pp. 136–48.
65 Other initiatives for reform were proposed in respect of the ECOSOC. For instance, the HLP also proposed that the ECOSOC be used to provide normative and analytical leadership about the linkages between economic and social issues and security. In this regard it suggested the establishment of a Committee on the Social and Economic Aspects of Security Threats. It also proposed that the ECOSOC should be an arena in which states could measure their commitments to achieving

key development objectives and, further, that the ECOSOC should be a sort of 'development cooperation forum' for engaging the development community, including the Bretton Woods organisations, at the highest level. See HLP Report, paras 276–8.
66 HLP Report, para. 283.
67 HLP Report, para. 285.
68 HLP Report, para. 287.
69 HLP Report, para. 291.
70 HLP Report, para. 183.
71 World Summit Outcome document, paras 157 and 158.
72 See GA Resolution A/RES/60/251, 3 April 2006. For more on the HRC see: http://www2.ohchr.org/english/bodies/hrcouncil.
73 Trusteeship Council, Resolution 2199 (LXI), 25 May 1994. On the Trusteeship Council, see chapter XIII of the UN Charter and Wilde, R., 'Trusteeship Council', in T. G. Weiss and S. Daws (eds), *The Oxford Handbook on the United Nations*, Oxford: Oxford University Press, 2007, pp. 149–59.
74 HLP Report, para. 299.
75 HLP Report, para. 291.
76 World Summit Outcome document, para. 176.
77 'In Larger Freedom' Report, paras 165 and 166.
78 UN, 'Renewing the United Nations', para. 85.
79 Wilde, 'Trusteeship Council', p. 156.
80 LOSC 1982, Arts 1(1), 136 and 137(2).
81 Wilson, C. L., 'Changing the Charter: The United Nations Prepares for the Twenty-first Century', *American Journal of International Law*, 90(1) (1996): 115, at p. 122.
82 Wilde, 'Trusteeship Council', pp. 155–6.
83 See chapter XV of the UN Charter, and on the Secretariat and Secretary-General, see Jonah, J. O. C., 'Secretariat Independence and Reform' and 'Secretary-General', in T. G. Weiss and S. Daws (eds), *The Oxford Handbook on the United Nations*, Oxford: Oxford University Press, 2007, pp. 160–74 and 175–92, respectively.
84 HLP Report, para. 292.
85 HLP Report, paras 293–4.
86 HLP Report, para. 296.
87 'In Larger Freedom' Report, para. 191.
88 'In Larger Freedom' Report, para. 192.
89 World Summit Outcome document, para. 161.
90 See Chapter XIV of the UN Charter and the Statute of the ICJ. Also see Crawford, J. and Grant, T., 'International Court of Justice', in T. G. Weiss and S. Daws (eds), *The Oxford Handbook on the United Nations*, Oxford: Oxford University Press, 2007, pp. 193–213.
91 The specialised agencies are as follows: International Labour

Organization (ILO), Food and Agriculture Organization of the United Nations (FAO). United Nations Educational, Scientific and Cultural Organization (UNESCO). World Health Organization (WHO). International Bank for Reconstruction and Development (IBRD). International Finance Corporation (IFC); International Development Association (IDA), International Monetary Fund (IMF), International Civil Aviation Organization (ICAO), International Telecommunication Union (ITU), International Fund for Agricultural Development (IFAD), World Meteorological Organization (WMO), International Maritime Organization (IMO), World Intellectual Property Organization (WIPO), United Nations Industrial Development Organization (UNIDO) and International Atomic Energy Agency (IAEA).

92 Articles 34–6 of the Statute of the International Court of Justice. See also Thirlway, H., 'The International Court of Justice', in M. Evans (ed.), *International Law*, 2nd edn, Oxford: Oxford University Press, 2006, p. 561, at pp. 567–75.

93 International Court of Justice, *Application of the Convention on the Prevention and Punishment of the Crime of Genocide* (*Bosnia and Herzegovina v. Serbia and Montenegro*), Order, 13 September 1993 (*Further Requests for the Indication of Provisional Measures*), Separate Opinion of Judge ad hoc Lauterpacht, para. 24, p. 416, available at: http://www.icj-cij.org/docket/index.php?p1=3&p2=3&k=f4&case=91&code=bhy&p3=3, accessed 5 December 2012.

94 2005 World Summit Outcome document, paras 73 and 134(f).

95 For various proposals on the reform of the ICJ, see Yee, S., 'Notes on the International Court of Justice, Part 2: Reform Proposals Regarding the International Court of Justice – A Preliminary Report for the International Law Association Study Group on United Nations Reform', *Chinese Journal of International Law*, 8(1) (2009): 181–9.

96 Luck, E. C., 'How Not to Reform the United Nations', *Global Governance*, 11 (2005): 407–14.

97 Weller, M., 'The Struggle for an International Constitutional Order', in D. Armstrong (ed.), *Routledge Handbook of International Law*, Abingdon: Routledge, 2009, pp. 180–1.

98 Mulligen, J. van, 'Global Constitutionalism and the Objective Purport of the International Legal Order', *Leiden Journal of International Law*, 24 (2011): 279.

99 van Mulligen, 'Global Constitutionalism', p. 290.

100 Fassbender, B., 'The United Nations Charter as Constitution of the International Community', *Colombia Journal of Transnational Law*, 36 (1998): 529.

101 Fassbender, 'The United Nations Charter', p. 562.

102 In Fassbender, 'The United Nations Charter', p. 550.

103 In Fassbender, 'The United Nations Charter', p. 550.

104 Fassbender, 'The United Nations Charter', p. 585.
105 Fassbender, 'The United Nations Charter', p. 588.
106 Fassbender, 'The United Nations Charter', pp. 573–82.
107 Klabbers, J., 'Constitutionalism Lite', *International Organizations Law Review*, 1 (2004): 32.
108 de Wet, E., 'The International Constitutional Order', *International and Comparative Law Quarterly*, 55 (2006): 51–76; Peters, A., 'Compensatory Constitutionalism: The Function and Potential of Fundamental International Norms and Structures', *Leiden Journal of International Law*, 19 (2006): 579–610; Cohen, J., 'Sovereignty in the Context of Globalization: A Constitutional Pluralist Perspective', in S. Besson and J. Tasioulas (eds), *The Philosophy of International Law*, Oxford: Oxford University Press, 2010, pp. 261–80; Gardbaum, S., 'Human Rights as International Constitutional Rights', *European Journal of International Law*, 19(4) (2008): 749–68.
109 de Wet, 'The International Constitutional Order', pp. 54 and 56.
110 Peters, 'Compensatory Constitutionalism', p. 598.
111 de Wet, 'The International Constitutional Order', p. 56.
112 Peters, 'Compensatory Constitutionalism', p. 598.
113 Peters, 'Compensatory Constitutionalism', p. 579.
114 de Wet, 'The International Constitutional Order', p. 75.
115 Peters, 'Compensatory Constitutionalism', p. 601.
116 Peters, 'Compensatory Constitutionalism', pp. 601–5.
117 de Wet, 'The International Constitutional Order', p. 57.
118 Peters, 'Compensatory Constitutionalism', p. 605; van Mulligen, 'Global Constitutionalism', p. 304.
119 Peters, 'Compensatory Constitutionalism', p. 610 (added emphasis).
120 Jackson, *The Global Covenant*, p. 19.
121 Jackson, *The Global Covenant*, p. 18.
122 Jackson, *The Global Covenant*, p. 17.
123 Cohen, 'Sovereignty in the Context of Globalization', pp. 271–2.
124 Cohen, 'Sovereignty in the Context of Globalization', pp. 274–5.
125 Cohen, 'Sovereignty in the Context of Globalization', p. 277.
126 Jackson, *The Global Covenant*, p. 18.
127 See, e.g., R. Kagan, 'The Case for a League of Democracies', *Financial Times*, 13 May 2008; A.-M. Slaughter, 'Plugging the Democracy Gap', *International Herald Tribune*, 30 July 2007; J. Diehl, 'A "League" By Other Names', *Washington Post*, 19 May 2008; S. Tharoor, 'This Mini-League of Nations Would Cause only Division', *The Guardian*, 27 May 2008.
128 See, e.g., Buchanan, A. and Keohane, R., 'The Preventive Use of Force: A Cosmopolitan Institutional Proposal', *Ethics and International Affairs*, 18(1) (2004): 1–22; McCain, J., 'An Enduring Peace Built on Freedom: Securing America's Future', *Foreign Affairs*, November/December 2007,

available at: http://www.foreignaffairs.org/20071101faessay86602/john-mccain/an-enduring-peace-built-on-freedom.html, accessed 4 June 2008; Daadler, I. and Lindsay, J., 'Democracies of the World Unite', *Public Policy Research*, 14(1) (2007): 47–58, see also *The American Interest*, (2) (2007): 3; Allesandri, E., 'World Order Re-Founded: The Idea of a Concert of Democracies', *International Spectator*, 43(1) (2008): 73–90.

129 See particularly Ikenberry, G. J. and Slaughter, A.-M., 'Forging a World of Liberty Under Law: US National Security in the Twenty-First Century', Final Report of the Princeton Project on National Security, 2006, available at: http://www.princeton.edu/~ppns/report/FinalReport.pdf, accessed 4 June 2008; Carothers, T., 'Is a League of Democracies a Good Idea?', Carnegie Endowment for International Peace, Policy Brief No. 59 2008, available at: http://www.carnegieendowment.org/events/index.cfm?fa=eventDetail&id=1137.

130 See Kagan, R., *The Return of History and the End of Dreams*, London: Atlantic Books, 2008; Buchanan, *Justice, Legitimacy and Self-Determination*; Holzgrefe, J. L. and Keohane, R. O. (eds), *Humanitarian Intervention: Ethical Legal and Political Dilemmas*, Cambridge: Cambridge university Press. 2003.

131 Luck, E., 'Prospects for Reform: Principal Organs', in T. Weiss and S. Daws (eds), *The Oxford Handbook on the United Nations*, Oxford: Oxford University Press, pp. 654–5.

132 Report of the UN High Level Panel, 'A More Secure World: Our Shared Responsibility', New York: United Nations, 2004. See also Ikenberry and Slaughter, 'Forging a World of Liberty Under Law', p. 24.

133 Buchanan and Keohane, 'The Preventative Use of Force', p. 2.

134 Independent International Commission on Kosovo, *The Kosovo Report: Conflict, International Response, Lessons Learned*, Oxford: Oxford University Press, 2000, ch. 6. See Ikenberry and Slaughter, 'Forging a World of Liberty Under Law', p. 24; Buchanan and Keohane, 'The Preventative Use of Force', p. 9.

135 For a broader discussion of this argument, see Buchanan, A and Keohane R. O., 'The Legitimacy of Global Governance Institutions', *Ethics and International Affairs*, 20(4) (2006): 405–37.

136 Buchanan, *Justice, Legitimacy and Self-Determination*, p. 10.

137 Buchanan, *Justice, Legitimacy and Self-Determination*, p. 23.

138 Buchanan, *Justice, Legitimacy and Self-Determination*, p. 27.

139 Buchanan, *Justice, Legitimacy and Self-Determination*, p. 97.

140 Buchanan, A., 'From Nuremburg to Kosovo: The Morality of Illegal International Legal Reform', *Ethics*, 111(4) (2001): 673–705, also available in edited form as Buchanan, A., 'Reforming the International Law of Humanitarian Intervention' in J. L. Holzgrefe and R. O. Keohane (eds), *Humanitarian Intervention: Ethical Legal and Political Dilemmas*, Cambridge: Cambridge university Press, pp. 130–73.

141 See Wheeler, *Saving Strangers*.
142 Cassese, A., *International Law*, Oxford: Oxford University Press, 2001, p. 344; Wellens, K., 'The UN Security Council and New Threats to Peace: Back to the Future', *Journal of Conflict and Security Law*, 8(1) (2003): 15–70.
143 Buchanan, 'From Nuremburg to Kosovo', p. 131.
144 Buchanan recognises that the institutional structures that govern the use of force in respect of preventative war will be the same as those tasked with governing humanitarian intervention and that the arguments share enough to be interchangeable. See Buchanan and Keohane, 'The Preventive Use of Force', p. 1 and Buchanan, *Justice, Legitimacy and Self-Determination*, p. 443.
145 Buchanan and Keohane, 'The Preventive Use of Force', p. 16 (parentheses added).
146 Buchanan and Keohane, 'The Preventive Use of Force', p. 15.
147 Buchanan and Keohane, 'The Preventive Use of Force', p. 16; also Buchanan, *Justice, Legitimacy and Self-Determination*, Pt 4.
148 Buchanan and Keohane, 'The Preventive Use of Force', p. 17.
149 Buchanan and Keohane, 'The Preventive Use of Force', p. 18.
150 Buchanan, *Justice, Legitimacy and Self-Determination*, p. 446.
151 Buchanan, *Justice, Legitimacy and Self-Determination*, p. 446.
152 Buchanan, *Justice, Legitimacy and Self-Determination*, ch. 7.
153 Buchanan and Keohane, 'The Preventive Use of Force', pp. 18–19.
154 Buchanan, *Justice, Legitimacy and Self-Determination*, pp. 452–4.
155 Buchanan and Keohane, 'The Preventive Use of Force', p. 19.
156 Buchanan and Keohane, 'The Preventive Use of Force', p. 20.
157 Buchanan and Keohane, 'The Preventive Use of Force', p. 19.

CHAPTER FIVE

The Protection of Human Rights and International Law

Justice and Injustice in the Age of Human Rights

International human rights law (IHRL) is the iconic achievement of post-war legalisation. The many universal and specialised international treaties, the plethora of Charter- and treaty-based human rights institutions, the regional instruments and institutions, the gradual judicialisation of human rights law and the incorporation of human rights into the domestic legal orders of so many states suggest that it is by this measure that contemporary international actors, indeed all of humanity, can gauge their success. A 'richer view'[1] of human rights legalisation appears to confirm this view. The normative force of human rights has enabled the work of non-coercive institutions, driven the development of new customary law, as well as a subset of non-derogable and peremptory human rights norms, and, most strikingly perhaps, has altered the essence of political debate. Countless declaratory resolutions and reports from international governmental and non-governmental organisations 'recall' or 'reaffirm' the core human rights principles or describe an increasing range of human activity in terms of human rights failure creating a raft of soft law. Theodore Meron refers to these phenomena as the 'humanization of international law'.[2] The process began a long time before the Universal Declaration of Human Rights (UDHR) in the bid to protect persons from slavery, from the fall-out of war, from apartheid and from genocide, but since 1948 human rights has accelerated the process, broken new ground and drawn other forms of protection under its mantle. It is no wonder, then, that some point to the 'International Bill of Rights' (the UDHR and the two covenants of 1966) as the constitution of international society (see Chapter Four). Human rights reasoning operates interstitially filling in gaps in legal and political argument, providing compelling reasons to adopt one set of norms or policy prescriptions over others and enabling the recognition of an ever greater range of human suffering as injustice or political failure.[3]

There are some, however, who view the very success of the legalisation of human rights as lacking in several respects. Michael Freeman and Jack Donnelly both voice concerns about the extent to which human rights discourse has moved to a singularly legalised mode. Law, argues Donnelly (noting that the fight for justice would be impoverished without it) falls short of justice.[4] This is compounded by the fact that,

> In order to achieve universal credibility in a philosophically diverse world, the Universal Declaration said very little about its own philosophical foundations ... The cost of this attempt to universalize the concept of human rights was to alienate it from Western philosophy and social science.[5]

The idea of the rights of man (as it was then styled) was an extraordinarily strong current in enlightenment political thought. The debates about the moral foundations of individual rights that burned bright in the European (later American) revolutions of the sixteenth–eighteenth centuries were the critical motor of the rights movement. While the critical apparatus of the European enlightenment might not be suitable for the appraisal of the contemporary human rights movement some critical apparatus is required. The key problem, for social scientists like Freeman and Donnelly and for critical or New Stream lawyers like Kennedy, is that the very success of the legalisation of human rights has stifled that critical edge. This leads to two potential problems. The first is that we forget that law is a place-holder for justice and we pursue human rights for their own sake without regard for the goods they are intended to achieve.[6] The second is that even if we keep this crucial point in mind we find the projects of political theory and law doing virtually separate things or unable to engage with each other.[7] The fact that agreement on the UDHR was made possible only by avoidance of moral questions is symbolic of the tense politics of human rights. However, the rapid development of human rights continually forces us to confront tough moral questions that the law often has no resources to answer. This is at once both the success and the failure of legalised human rights. The normative authority of human rights is such that the reach of IHRL is constantly either being extended or facing demands for extension or tighter enforcement. Like the rights of man in the Early Modern period, human rights have enabled us to uncover more ways in which societies fail to live up to the requirements of justice. But the fact that the legalised human rights regime has been thought of as being resistant to moral claims means that rights-based understandings of injustice often lack the normative vocabulary to secure political support for legal change.

While this pattern is clearly observable in the literature, we have argued that the disciplines of political theory, law and IR are showing signs of an interdisciplinarity that helps us to confront the big questions of justice and the politics of international law. The issues surrounding the ethics, law and politics of human rights have been a central part of this overdue reunion. In many ways, the overwhelming success of the introduction and development of IHRL and its normative impact on the international community has forced this re-engagement. The loudest voice in the moral and political theory of IR is very closely tied to the idea of human rights. Cosmopolitans seized on the power of human rights discourse to articulate their moral commitment to the idea of individual autonomy. But in many cases the value of individual autonomy was given *a priori* and considered independently of IHRL. Cosmopolitanism has been tremendously important in criticising the resistance of international theory to debates concerning justice and in uncovering the scope of injustice obscured by IR's resistance to normative or moral concerns. Yet the cosmopolitan approach to moral authority minimises (as a matter of moral theory) the relevance of the sociological or the legal.[8] One concern with such approaches is that it removes moral thinking from the context in which questions of justice arise and in which solutions are negotiated, and entrenches the separation of moral and legal thinking identified above. Such was the resistance of law and IR to moral theory that the debates continued in isolation from each other, but as this antipathy to argument about moral normativity receded some cosmopolitan theorists found considerable merit in forging links between the discourses of law, politics and morality. In this chapter we offer an exploration of two of the most powerful cosmopolitan arguments concerning human rights and global justice. These scholars seek a 'political conception of justice', an idea that found seminal expression in Rawls' *Political Liberalism*.[9] A political conception of justice is free-standing (not drawn from any comprehensive ethical doctrine), and gains its content from ideas implicit (or explicit) in public political culture. In presenting their thesis this way they are not endorsing Rawls' specific version of a political conception of justice (Justice as Fairness) or his theory of international justice. Indeed, they are often rather hostile to Rawls' *The Law of Peoples*. On our reading, forms of institutional moral reasoning across all the theoretical traditions we have explored are intended to provide the basis for a political conception of justice. The contending claims about the normative authority of key principles is central to the debates concerning the proper content of a political conception of justice or of institutional moral reasoning. In both cases the argument draws on existing commitments to human rights principles and draws radical conclusions about the requirements of justice in a world where human rights have normative force. Before we turn to these questions, however, it is important to gain an understanding of the nature of international human rights law.

The protection of Human Rights in international law

The idea of human rights is not a recent conception. Medieval philosophers had engaged with the notion, mostly in the form of natural rights, and also it had been engrained in certain significant historical domestic landmark documents, such as the Magna Carta 1215, the Petition of Rights 1628, the US Declaration of Independence 1776, the US Constitution 1787, the French Declaration of the Rights of Man and the Citizen 1789, and pre-1945 there were limited attempts to deal with certain human rights issues, such as slavery and self-determination, at the international level.[10] However, since the end of the Second World War, with the atrocities committed during the war, the concept of human rights has assumed greater prominence. After the Second World War, with the United Nations playing a leading role, the promotion and protection of human rights has become internationalised, and from this has emerged international human rights law – a crucial and continually developing area of international law. This is one of the areas of international law that provides for individuals to possess rights directly under international law and, in certain instances, to have direct access to international tribunals to protect these rights against their national governments.[11]

An exploration of various perspectives on what exactly human rights are is necessary to have an understanding of various debates arising in international human rights law. Bilder rightly points out that examining the various definitions of human rights is not inconsequential, because whatsoever definition is adopted would determine value judgements on not only the 'types of claims to recognize as human rights, but also [the] expectations and programs for implementation and compliance with these standards'.[12] Over the years, the question of the definition of human rights has been the subject of much philosophical debate, especially between the naturalist and positivist conception of human rights.

The naturalists, at the risk of simplifying this rather wide-ranging school of thought, generally believe that human rights are natural rights given by God or nature to every human being by reason of their being human beings. According to Higgins:

> Human Rights are rights held simply by virtue of being a human being. They are part and parcel of the integrity and dignity of the human being. They are thus rights that cannot be given or withdrawn at will by any domestic legal system. And although they may most effectively be implemented by the domestic legal system, that system is not the source of the right.[13]

Forsythe points out that these rights are fundamental moral rights of the person that are necessary for a life with human dignity.[14] D'Amato, however, emphasises that human rights is not just a political and moral concept, but also a legal one.[15] An understanding of the definition of human rights from a naturalist conception immediately helps us to appreciate why those who belong to this school of thought are more inclined to insist on the universality and inalienability of human rights. If human rights are rights applicable to all human beings, it follows that all individuals are entitled to have their human rights respected and protected notwithstanding their identity, location or circumstances. Higgins puts it this way:

> The non-universal, relativist view of human rights is in fact a very state-centred view and loses sight of the fact that human rights are human rights and not dependent on the fact that states, or groupings of states, may behave differently from each other so far as their politics, economic policy, and culture are concerned. I believe, profoundly, in the universality of the human spirit. Individuals everywhere want the same essential things: to have sufficient food and shelter; to be able to be able to speak freely; to

practise their own religion or to abstain from religious belief; to feel that their person is not threatened by the state; to know that they will not be tortured, or detained without charge, and that, if charged, they will have a fair trial. I believe there is nothing in these aspirations that is dependent upon culture, or religion, or stage of development. They are as keenly felt by the African tribesman as by the European city-dweller, by the inhabitant of a Latin American shanty-town as by the resident of a Manhattan apartment.[16]

On the other hand, the positivists, again at the risk of simplifying this rather expansive school of thought, generally challenge *a priori* rights and believe that human rights derives its authority from what the state or society prescribes. Bentham, an early nineteenth-century jurist belonging to the positivist school, opposed the idea of natural law and natural rights, which he stated were 'nonsense upon stilts'. He said that 'there are no such things as rights anterior to the establishment of government: for natural, as applied to rights, if it means anything, is meant to stand in opposition to legal – to such rights as are acknowledged to owe their existence to government and are consequently posterior in their date to the establishment of government'.[17] Such a positivist position is inclined to a more relativist conception of human rights, which takes into consideration variations, such as culture, religion and stage of development, in seeking to determine the applicable human rights regime in a given state or society. Non-Western states and scholars that take a relativist position on human rights argue that a universalist approach to human rights, without taking into consideration cultural and other differences, is merely an attempt by the West to impose their values on other sections of the international community – a sort of Western imperialism.[18] On the other hand, there is the concern that authoritarian regimes may use cultural relativism as an excuse to abuse the rights of individuals within their jurisdiction.[19]

The universalism–relativism debate is rather complex and not always clear-cut. Both sides of the debate do make important claims. On the one hand, there is no doubt that for human rights to be effective it needs to be universal. However, it is difficult to imagine a human rights regime in a multicultural world that is completely devoid of culture, provided, of course, it is not used as an excuse by authoritarian regimes to abuse the rights of their nationals. The real tension in this debate arises mainly because of the extreme positions taken by those on both sides of the fence. Donnelly argues against what he terms 'radical universalism', which maintains that culture is completely irrelevant in human rights, and 'radical culture relativism', which contends that culture is the sole affirming authority of the validity or otherwise of human rights.[20] He points out that in between the two extreme positions there are 'varying mixes of relativism and universalism', which could be roughly divided into 'strong and weak cultural relativism'.[21] Across the continuum of strong and weak relativism, he identifies three levels of relativity; namely, cultural relativity in the substance of the list of human rights, in the interpretation of such rights and in the form in which particular rights are to be implemented.[22] He then asserts a weak relativist position that permits limited deviations from universal human rights, mainly at the level of form and interpretation, as representing the international consensus.[23] The practice of states supports the idea of universalism of human rights with certain variations. For instance, the Bangkok Declaration 1993, putting forward Asian values, recognises that 'while human rights are universal in nature, they must be considered in the context of a dynamic and evolving process of international norm-setting, bearing in mind the significance of national and regional particularities and various historical, cultural and religious backgrounds'.[24] In addition, the African Charter on Human and Peoples' Rights (African Charter), although taking into consideration African historical tradition and values in the conception of human rights, asserts, 'that civil and political rights cannot be dissociated from economic, social and cultural rights in their conception as well as universality'.[25] Further, the Vienna Declaration 1993 declares as follows:

> All human rights are universal, indivisible and interdependent and interrelated. The international community must treat human rights globally in a fair and equal manner, on the same footing, and with the same emphasis. While the significance of national and regional particularities and various historical, cultural and religious backgrounds must be borne in mind, it is the duty of States, regardless of their political, economic and cultural systems, to promote and protect all human rights and fundamental freedoms.[26]

Despite the general agreement on the universality of human rights with certain deviations due to cultural differences, the universalism–cultural relativism debate still rages on because it is difficult for states to arrive at a consensus as to what core human rights are actually universal. A determination of this is usually a value judgement that may be influenced by the cultural experience of whoever is arriving at such conclusion. For instance, it could be argued that some of the rights that have been included by Higgins, as quoted above, could be said to be influenced by her background as a Western scholar.[27] While an African tribesman, European city-dweller, the inhabitant of a Latin American shanty-town or the resident of a Manhattan apartment may share the common aspiration of human rights, it is doubtful that they would be able to reach a full consensus on what rights are actually core rights.[28] As pointed out by Tharoor, many from other cultures are sceptical about certain rights that they feel merely reflect a Western notion, such as the so-called right to a paid holiday under the UDHR, and, therefore, the universality of such rights is disputed.[29] Even if there were a consensus on what are actually core rights, there may be variance in the interpretation of such rights, sometimes based on cultural or religious differences. For instance, does the right to life, undoubtedly a core right, include or exclude the death penalty imposed by a court of law? Is there a violation of this right if the death penalty is imposed by a duly constituted religious court in an Islamic state for an alleged offence that would probably be regarded as a moral indiscretion in some other parts of the world? These and other comparable questions, one way or the other, tend to fuel the universalism–cultural relativism debate, even though clearly the two extremes – 'radical' universalism and 'radical' cultural relativism – are not the favoured positions in the debate.

Karel Vasak, a French jurist, put forward the idea of dividing human rights into the so-called three generations of human rights, based on the French Revolution principles of liberté, egalite and fraternité. Burns, however, rightly warns that this is merely 'a simplified version of an extremely complex historical record; it is not intended as a literal representation of life in which one generation gives birth to the next and then dies away'.[30] The first generation of civil and political rights demonstrates liberty. It includes right to life, liberty and the security of persons; freedom from torture and cruel, inhuman or degrading treatment; freedom from arbitrary arrest or detention; freedom of movement and residence; freedom of thought, conscience and religion; freedom of expression; freedom of association; right to a fair and public trial. The rights listed in Articles 2–21 of the UDHR and a number of those in the International Covenant for Civil and Political Rights (ICCPR) portray the first generation rights. It conceives of human rights more in terms of liberal individualism and negative rights that grant individuals freedom from certain actions by the state. Although generally negative, there are, however, aspects of these rights that may require positive government action. For instance, while the right to a fair trial requires that the government refrain from any action that would preclude individuals within its jurisdiction from enjoying such rights; it also has to take positive actions to ensure that the facilities are available for such right to be enjoyed. For example, court buildings have to be built, provision of legal aid for less privileged individuals of the society and the independence of the judiciary guaranteed through positive actions, such as the appointment of qualified and able judges.[31]

The second-generation rights, economic, social and cultural rights, relate to equality and derive their origins mainly from the socialist tradition. They include rights such as the right to work; the right to join and form trade unions; the right to education; the right to rest and leisure, including reasonable limitation of periodic holidays with pay; the right to a standard of living adequate for the health and well-being of self and family; the right to food; and the right to the protection of one's scientific, literary and artistic production. These rights are shown in Articles 22–27 of the Universal Declaration and the International Covenant of Economic, Social and Cultural Rights (ICESCR). Generally, these rights are positive rights requiring governments to take affirmative action. Thus, the realisation of these rights usually requires resource-intensive measures. Again, it must be emphasised that though these are generally positive rights, there are examples of such rights that could also be designated as negative rights, which require the government to refrain from actions that would affect the realisation of such rights. For instance, with the right to join and form trade unions, apart from affirmative actions to encourage workers to exercise this right, the government is required to refrain from actions that would prevent persons from exercising this right.[32]

Third-generation rights, or group or solidarity rights, on the other hand, depict fraternity or communal values. These include the right to self-determination; the right to development; the right to participate in the mining of, and benefit from, the common heritage of resources of global commons, such as the seabed area, outer space and moon; the right to a clean and healthy environment; the and right to peace. The idea of group or solidarity rights is relatively recent, emerging in the 1960s and 1970s, and supported mainly by developing states.[33] The most common of third-generation rights, the right to self-determination, is contained in common Article 1 of the two International Covenants on human rights. Additional group rights may be found in other international instruments. For instance, the African Charter on Human and Peoples' Rights (the African Charter) provides for 'peoples' the right to development and the right to equal enjoyment of the common heritage of mankind (Article 22), the right to peace (Article 23) and the right to a generally satisfactory environment (Article 24).

There has been controversy about whether the second- and third-generation rights are human rights. For instance, the United States has consistently opposed the idea of second-generation rights as human rights. Rather, it believes that they are merely 'societal goals'[34] that are not justiciable. Consequently, although the United States signed the International Covenant of Economic, Social and Cultural Rights, it is yet to ratify it.[35] For group rights, certain Western states and scholars are reluctant to accept these rights as human rights because of the perception that the concept of human rights applies only to individuals and not groups. For instance, Sieghart points out with regard to the so-called group rights as follows:

> What these rights have in common is that it is sometimes difficult to see how they can be vested in, or exercised by, individuals. According to the classical theory, only the rights of human individuals can be 'human' rights; any rights belonging to entities of some other kind (such as states, churches, corporations, trade unions, and so forth) may be highly desirable, accepted, valid, and even enforceable – but, whatever else they may be, they cannot be human rights.[36]

Perhaps this merely points to the cultural difference between the West, where there is more of an emphasis on individual rights, and other cultures, especially in Africa and Asia, where prominence is given to the communal rights. There are also concerns on the justiciability of these group rights and whether they end up devaluing human rights.[37] How and against whom, for instance, would the right to development be enforced?

In addition, there is discourse on the priority that the implementation of the different generations of rights should be given. Western states generally give primacy to first-generation rights and are sceptical about the human rights nature of the other generations. On the other hand, socialist states and developing states are more inclined to give priority to social, economic and cultural rights. These states have argued that, due to their stage of development, certain economic, social and cultural rights have to be given priority in implementation, sometimes to the detriment of certain civil and political rights. For instance, the Singapore School argues that the phenomenal economic success of Singapore may be attributed to the fact that they have given more attention to second-generation rights, sometimes to the detriment of the first-generation ones.[38] Further, developing states are seeking to give prominence to the implementation of certain group rights, such as the rights to self-determination and development.

The United Nations, the main driver of the promotion and protection of human rights in contemporary international law, takes the view that human rights are universal and all human rights should be given equal priority. After a major human rights conference in Vienna under the auspices of the UN, the Declaration issued stated that: 'Human Rights and fundamental freedoms are the birth right of all human beings; their protection is the first responsibility of Governments', (Article 1); and that 'All human rights are universal, indivisible and interdependent and interrelated. The international community must treat human rights globally in a fair and equal manner, on the same footing, and with the same emphasis' (Article 5). It further reiterated 'the importance of ensuring the universality, objectivity and non-selectivity of the consideration of human rights issues' (Article 32).[39] The UN's conviction that human rights are universal is notably demonstrated by its stance on the discourse on whether terrorists should enjoy human rights. For instance, the former UN Secretary-General Kofi Annan, had emphasised as follows: 'Our responses to terrorism, as well as our efforts to thwart it and prevent it, should uphold the human rights that terrorists aim to destroy. Respect for human rights, fundamental freedoms and the rule of law are essential tools in the effort to combat terrorism – not privileges to be sacrificed at a time of tension.'[40]

The role of the United Nations in protection of human rights

Although human rights predate the United Nations, this organisation has played a crucial role in what Sohn has termed the 'human rights revolution', which occurred in the aftermath of the Second World War.[41] The provisions of the UN Charter point to the significance the UN attaches to human rights. Its preamble re-affirms the organisation's 'faith in fundamental human rights, in the dignity and worth of the human person, in the equal rights of men and women and of nations large and small'. In Article 1 the UN Charter identifies, as one of the fundamental pillars of the organisation, the promotion and encouragement of 'respect for human rights and for fundamental freedoms for all without distinction as to race, sex, language, or religion'. Further, Articles 55 and 56 emphasise that the UN shall promote 'universal respect for, and observance of, human rights and fundamental freedoms for all without distinction as to race, sex, language, or religion', and enjoin all members to take joint and separate action in cooperation with the organisation to achieve this purpose. Although the provisions of the Charter are a far cry from the comprehensive chapter on human rights that certain smaller states sort to incorporate into the UN Charter during the San Francisco Conference that preceded the establishment of the UN,[42] they have served as a vital launch pad for the subsequent adoption, under the auspices of the UN, of key human rights instruments and treaties, such as the Universal Declaration, the International Covenants (together often referred to as the International Bill of Rights), as well as various other human rights treaties and instruments covering a diversity of areas.

In 1948, three years after the establishment of the UN, the General Assembly adopted the UDHR as 'a common standard of achievement for all peoples and all nations' in promoting respect for human rights and securing universal recognition and observance of these rights. It contains reference to both civil and political rights (Articles 3–21) and economic, social and cultural rights (Articles 22–27). The Declaration, which has been described as 'the primary source of global human rights standards',[43] though not binding as it is a General Assembly resolution, is certainly not devoid of legal value. It has been argued that a significant part of the Declaration has over the years become part of customary international law as a result of widespread evidence of the requisite state practice and *opinio juris*.[44]

Almost eighteen years after, in 1966, the other parts of the International Bill of Rights, namely, the International Covenant on Civil and Political Rights (ICCPR) and the International Covenant of Economic, Social and Cultural Rights (ICESCR), as well as a first Optional Protocol to the International Covenant on Civil and Political Rights, all binding treaties, were adopted and came into force ten years later in 1976. Buergenthal attributes this delay to the fact that for a time governments, though ready to embrace a non-binding instrument such as the Universal

Declaration, were reluctant to assume specific and binding international legal obligations on human rights.[45] Two covenants, rather than a single one, were eventually adopted because of the difficulty in reconciling the positions in respect of the perception of the import of human rights by the two ideological poles during the Cold War. In 1989, a second Optional Protocol to the International Covenant on Civil and Political Rights, aimed at the abolition of the death penalty, was adopted and came into force in 1991. The ICCPR and ICESCR appear to spell out and expand on the civil and political rights, as well as the economic, social and cultural rights, contained in the Declaration.[46]

However, while parties to the ICCPR have an immediate legal obligation to comply with its provisions, the ICESCR provides for progressive compliance depending on the available resources. Article 2(1) of the ICESCR states:

> Each State Party to the present Covenant undertakes to take steps, individually and through international assistance and co-operation, especially economic and technical, to the maximum of its available resources, with a view to achieving progressively the full realization of the rights recognized in the present Covenant by all appropriate means, including particularly the adoption of legislative measures.

The two International Covenants have enjoyed widespread ratification by states: the ICCPR having, as at 17 April 2013, up to 167 parties (with the notable absence of China as a party); and the ICESCR having as at the same date, 160 parties (with the notable absence of the United States as a party).[47]

The first Optional Protocol of the ICCPR allows for the Human Rights Committee to receive petitions from individuals within the jurisdiction of a state party who allege a violation of his or her rights guaranteed under the ICCPR by such a state party. The second Optional Protocol, on the other hand, requires a state party to desist from executing any individual within its jurisdiction and to take necessary measures to abolish the death penalty.

Apart from the above treaties, the UN has also adopted a significant number of binding human rights treaties dealing with specific wrongs, such as the Convention on the Prevention and Punishment of the Crime of Genocide, the Convention against Torture and Other Cruel, Inhuman or Degrading Treatment or Punishment and the International Convention on the Elimination of All Forms of Racial Discrimination;

and Conventions protecting the human rights of particular categories of people, such as the Convention on the Elimination of All Forms of Discrimination against Women, the Convention on the Rights of the Child, the International Convention on the Protection of the Rights of All Migrant Workers and Members of Their Families and the Convention on the Rights of Persons with Disabilities.[48]

Human rights: customary international law, *jus cogens* or general principles of law?

Although human rights law has been developed mainly through the use of treaties and other instruments, some scholars have argued that all human rights, especially those contained in the Universal Declaration, are actually part of customary international law.[49] For others, only certain core human rights have emerged as CIL. Additionally, some scholars maintain that certain core human rights, such as the right to life, self-determination, prohibition of torture, prohibition of genocide and prohibition of racial discrimination, have attained the status of *jus cogens*.[50] Judge Tanaka, as far back as 1966, in his Dissenting Opinion in the *South West Africa* cases (*Ethiopia* v. *South Africa*; *Liberia* v. *South Africa*), Second Phase Judgment, appears to support the latter view, when he stated:

> If we can introduce in the international field a category of law, namely *jus cogens*, recently examined by the International Law Commission, a kind of imperative which constitutes the contrast to *jus dispositivum*, capable of being changed by way of agreement between States, surely the law concerning the protection of human rights may be considered to belong to the *jus cogens*.[51]

Even more recently, Bianchi points to 'an almost intrinsic relationship between peremptory norms and human rights'.[52]

Further, some scholars have taken the position that human rights are general principles of law.[53] For instance, the ICJ, in its Advisory Opinion on *Reservations to the Genocide Convention*, stated in respect of genocide, which is generally acknowledged to be a *jus cogens* norm, that: 'the principles underlying the Convention are principles which are recognized by civilized nations as binding on States, even without any conventional obligation'.[54]

UN human rights enforcement mechanisms

The effective enforcement of human rights largely depends on the domestic machinery, through judicial, executive and legislative action.[55] In addition, some regions of the world have established regional human rights courts to deal with human rights violations, a notable example being the European Court of Human Rights. However, at a global level there is no human rights court, though recently there have been calls for such a court to be established.[56] Rather, the enforcement of human rights depends on the mostly flexible machinery that rests mainly on naming and shaming offending states. As a legal tool for enforcement, such machinery may be regarded as rather weak, but as political device, it may lead to social pressure that may push states to conform in order to avoid the stigma of being identified as a pariah state. The UN human rights enforcement machinery includes: the UN ECOSOC subsidiary body, the Commission on Human Rights, which was subsequently replaced in 2006 by the Human Rights Council; and also Human Rights Treaty bodies, established by some of the core human rights treaties, which utilise procedures, such as States Periodic Reports, inter-state complaints, individual or group complaints and, in some cases, the system of country or thematic special rapporteurs, to seek to persuade states to improve their human rights records. Other UN bodies, such as the UN General Assembly, Office of the High Commission on Human Rights and the Security Council are also involved in seeking to ensure that states to desist from human rights violations. It must be pointed out that the Security Council, if able to overcome the political constraint of the veto is actually able to take binding enforcement powers to stop human rights violations by states, as long as this is somehow tied up with its remit to maintain peace and security (Articles 24 and 25 of the UN Charter).[57]

Regional human rights treaties

There are various regional human rights treaties, such as the European Convention on Human Rights and Fundamental Freedoms 1950, which came into force in 1953; the American Convention on Human Rights (Pact of San Jose) 1969, which came into force in 1978; and the African Charter on Human and Peoples' Rights 1981, which came into force in 1986. The aforementioned conventions have established various mechanisms, including regional commissions and courts (i.e., the European Commission of Human Rights and European Court of Human Rights; the Inter-American Commission on Human Rights and the Inter-American Court of Human Rights; the African Commission on Human and Peoples' Rights and the African Court on Human and Peoples' Rights),[58] to seek to promote and protect human rights within the respective regions.

In addition, there is the Arab Charter on Human Rights, adopted by the League of Arab States in 1994, and revised in 2004, which came into force in 2008. Although the Association of Southeast Asian Nations (ASEAN) does not presently have a region-wide comprehensive human rights treaty, Articles 2(2)(i) and 14 of the ASEAN Charter provide for respect for fundamental freedoms, the promotion and protection of human rights and for the establishment of an ASEAN human rights body. However, the latter two regional treaties, unlike the former treaties mentioned above, have comparatively weak enforcement provisions. The Arab Charter currently has a seven-member expert committee to receive reports from state members,[59] and does not presently have a regional court. Similarly, the ASEAN does not have a regional court, but in 2009 it established the ASEAN Intergovernmental Commission on Human Rights (AICHR), which is required to pursue 'a constructive and non-confrontational approach and cooperation to enhance promotion and protection of human rights'.[60]

Justice and injustice in the age of human rights

Justice claims are not separate from the realm of law and politics, but integral to it. Human rights-based justice claims are relatively common because they can draw on a sustained and dynamic legal, political and moral source. In the contemporary international system it is extremely difficult to sustain an argument about justice that ignores, still less transgresses, human rights principles. Yet drawing on the authority of human rights creates as many challenges as it resolves. One of the key challenges in human rights theory and practice concerns the question of the relative value of all the different rights found under the heading human rights. This question has dogged the idea of human rights from its initial framing in the UDHR to the present day. As we have seen, the drafting of the UDHR and the two subsequent covenants that make up the International Bill of Rights was heavily influenced by the failure of UN member states to agree on the relative merits of political and civil rights, on the one hand, and social, economic and cultural rights, on the other. Over the sixty years since the UDHR some human rights proponents have been at pains to demonstrate the fundamental indivisibility of all human rights in order to show that human rights as a category represent a unified normative standard. At the same time, there have been proposals for the emergence of new human rights (the so-called third generation of solidarity rights championed by Karel Vasak in ECOSOC) and claims that certain 'fundamental' or 'basic rights' have achieved a higher legal status. Both claims are powerful voices in the moral and legal debate. Getting to grips with these core arguments offers much to an exploration of the normative authority of human rights and to a critical grasp of the policy prescription developed in the name of justice and human rights. In what follows we explore two arguments that offer human rights-based challenges to the existing social and legal order. The first is an argument about the pervasive injustice of a system that entrenches (indeed, causes) poverty on a global scale. One of the leading figures in this debate is Thomas Pogge, who argues that poverty must be viewed as human rights violation and that the obligation to eradicate poverty is the responsibility of the international community.[61] The broad features of this argument are important and controversial. They are important because they demonstrate both the affront to human dignity that poverty represents and show that global distributive justice obligations are a necessary and feasible response to this challenge. In showing how failures in respect of economic and social rights cause human suffering in tragic measure, Pogge is insisting that the international community recognise the fundamental indivisibility of all human rights and demanding action. As well as being compelling and important, such claims are controversial because they cast global distributive justice in human rights terms (rather than in terms of the more usual charity/poverty eradication/social justice or development agendas) and because they assign responsibility not only to the state, but to the international community. The second section of this chapter explores a series of arguments that sees the emergence of 'basic' human rights as demanding significant changes in global governance. In the development of a hierarchy of human rights,[62] many see the emergence of principles of global justice that underwrite a greater cosmopolitanism. Here we explore the potential of a human rights-based conception of justice to demand greater international action in respect of secession and state breakdown, humanitarian intervention, environmental and intergenerational justice and democratic governance. Both sets of arguments provide reasons for robust international action where a state is unable or unwilling to fulfil its extended obligations under their conception of justice.

Pogge, human rights and global distributive justice

Thomas Pogge grounds his cosmopolitan political theory in a rejection of Rawls' *Law of Peoples*. In political theory Rawls was the target for much critical work. As the author of *A Theory of Justice* (1971) and later *Political Liberalism* (1993), Rawls is credited with the re-invigoration of normative liberal theory. His work was the model for many in the Anglo-American analytic tradition. Yet his *Law of Peoples* (first published as an Amnesty Lecture in 1993 and re-presented in a revised and elongated form in 1999) appeared to betray the promise of normative liberalism at the turn of the millennium. His 'ideal theory' developed a relatively conservative account of international justice. It reflected the post-war consensus in that it was premised on the equality of states ('peoples' who were non-aggressive and guaranteed their citizens basic human rights) and emphasised the principle of non-intervention. Even more disappointing for liberals was the fact that Rawls, who had re-invigorated discussion about the essential inclusion of a principle of economic distributive justice in any liberal theory, included no international redistributive justice requirement save, in the later book, a duty to assist those suffering from the absence of a state that can provide a basic standard of decency.[63] Rawls' conservative nationalism[64] reinforced two related ideas that are quite common. The first is that provided a state upholds (or at least does not severely violate) the key civil and political rights of its citizens (taken to be Articles 3–18 of the UDHR), then that state is legitimate and enjoys the sovereign rights of non-intervention and self-determination. The second is that poverty is not a pressing human rights issue. For Rawls poverty is an internal rather than international issue: 'The crucial element in how a country fares is its political culture . . . and not the level of its resources.'[65] The focus is very much on civil and political rights, and this reinforces the tendency to categorise civil and political rights as prior to social economic and cultural rights. This prioritisation of civil and political rights has a number of sources. In part it represents a continuation of the ideological struggle between liberal capitalist societies and socialist states that saw the project of creating a binding bill of rights transformed into a declaration and the later drafting of two separate covenants (see above). It is also said to be a consequence of the nature of the rights contained in each covenant. Commonly, civil rights are said to be negative rights. They require a state to stop doing things (detention without trial, torture). Economic and social rights, on the other hand, are often regarded as positive rights. Fulfilling the right to healthcare or education is costly and requires significant action on behalf of the state. For these reasons, and others associated with the rhetoric of those such as Karel Vasak who proposed a third emerging category of solidarity rights,[66] many refer to civil and political rights as first-generation rights, and to economic and social rights as second-generation rights. Often proponents of this division point to the differing constructions of Article 2 in the ICCPR and the ICESCR. While the ICCPR obliges states 'to respect and to ensure to all individuals within its territory and subject to its jurisdiction the rights recognized in the present covenant' and to 'adopt such laws or other measures as may be necessary to give effect to' those rights, the ICESCR exhorts parties to

> take steps, individually, and through international assistance and cooperation ... to the maximum of its available resources, with a view to achieving progressively the full realization of the rights recognized in the present Covenant.

There has been significant effort in the Committee for Economic, Social and Cultural Rights,[67] by the International Commission of Jurists[68] and by the General Assembly[69] to underscore both the indivisibility of all human rights and the obligation to respect, protect and fulfil all obligations immediately. In the United Nations High Commissioner for Human Rights (UNHCHR) Handbook on Economic, Social and Cultural Rights we find the following:

> The progressive realization component of the Covenant is often mistakenly taken to imply that economic, social and cultural rights can be realized only when a country reaches a certain level of economic development. This is neither the intent nor the legal interpretation of this provision. Rather, this duty obliges all States parties, notwithstanding the level of national wealth, to

move as quickly as possible towards the realization of economic, social and cultural rights. The Covenant requires the effective and equitable use of resources immediately.

Nevertheless, there is still a reluctance to engage with economic rights generally or to treat poverty as an urgent class of human rights.

Pogge consciously sets out to offer a morally normative account of human rights that can open our eyes to the suffering of the global poor, and challenge the statist reading of human rights obligations found in Rawls and associated with the post-war *status quo*. He proposes 'modest and feasible, but significant, global institutional reforms that would better align our international order with our moral values'.[70] He presents his proposal in human rights form because this provides his argument with a valuable context that can appeal to his audience. Human rights are a part of the discourse of global ethics. Agents accept them as being 'political not metaphysical', as not burdened with the ontological baggage of a concept like natural rights, but nevertheless as being morally weighty.[71] The discourse assumes that all human beings matter equally, and that governments have both the obligation to protect such rights and the potential to violate them in a morally relevant way. Yet Pogge wants to generate a moral rather than legal argument. This is partly because he wants us to focus on the ends to be achieved rather than on the specific ways of institutionalising their protection, but also because he has concerns about the ability of the international legal order to protect those ends. Indeed, he is concerned that the existing legal order is complicit in the continued violation of moral human rights.

> Various human rights are widely recognised in codified and customary international law. These human rights promise all human beings protection against specific severe harms that might be inflicted on them domestically or by foreigners. Yet, international law also establishes and maintains institutional structures that greatly contribute to violations of these same human rights: central components of international law systematically obstruct the aspirations of poor populations for democratic self-government, civil rights and minimal economic sufficiency. And central international organizations, like the World Trade Organization (WTO), the International Monetary Fund (IMF) and the World Bank, are designed in ways that systematically contribute to the persistence of severe poverty.[72]

His account of human rights, as we saw in Chapter Three, is an institutional rather than an interactional account of rights. To recap, this form of cosmopolitanism assigns responsibility for achieving just outcomes to institutional schemes. This focus on shared practices makes the responsibility for global justice 'a shared responsibility for the justice of any practices one supports: one ought not to participate in an unjust institutional scheme (one that violates human rights) without making reasonable efforts to aid its victims and to promote institutional reform'.[73] Note the rather clever negative rendering of the moral obligation. We have obligations to others insofar as we participate in institutions that cause foreseeable and avoidable harm. The case for a moral and interactional account of human rights is a strong one. It makes room for moral critique of existing law, but works with values essential to the law and frames its claims as negative rather than as positive duties that require us to stop causing harm rather than to simply help the needy. Does this translate, however, into a strong cosmopolitan argument in favour of global distributive justice?

Pogge begins much of his work with the facts of poverty. One-third of all human deaths are the consequence of poverty. In raw numbers that is 18 million premature deaths annually or 50,000 poverty-related deaths daily, 35,000 of which are children under the age of five. If we then move on to issues other than mortality – malnutrition, lack of drinking water, illiteracy, lack of shelter or power or healthcare – the picture of grinding poverty is overwhelming.[74] Over 1,200 million people live below the World Bank's poverty line, which now stands at US$1.25 per day. We can put this in global context by referring to the 1998 UN *Human Development Report* which estimated that:

> The cost of achieving and maintaining universal access to basic education for all, basic health care for all, reproductive health care for all women, adequate food for all and safe water and sanitation for all is roughly $40 billion a year. This is less than 4% of the combined wealth of the richest 225 people in the world.[75]

Given the declaratory and conventional aspirations of human rights, these facts immediately pose the questions that drive Pogge's argument. How can severe poverty continue despite economic and technical progress? The world has the wealth and the technology to eradicate poverty, so why is there a reluctance to treat poverty as a human rights violation? While Pogge explores, and rejects, several reasons that are commonly presented to defend our acquiescence to the facts of poverty, the crucial issue turns on the word violation. Typically, we do not associate global poverty with moral wrongdoing. Either poverty is a natural, if regrettable, phenomenon or it is the product of the underdevelopment of the political culture of those states in which it is widespread. In either case the international community is not responsible and surely it would be unfair to tax them for the plight of unconnected strangers. Some cosmopolitans, such as Peter Singer, reject this claim. What, he asks, is the moral difference between causing poverty and failing to do something about it when that act would be relatively costless?[76] Pogge does not take this line. Instead, he attacks the 'explanatory nationalism' that isolates the international community from moral blame and keeps the stunning indignities of poverty off the human rights agenda. Placing responsibility for the global inequalities that perpetuate poverty on the poorest states seems rather short-sighted. The international legal order is a social construct. That construction, forged in empire-building and war, needs to be viewed, argues Pogge, in the light of our moral commitments:

> Everyone has the right to a standard of living, adequate for the health and well-being of himself and of his family, including food, clothing, housing and medical care.
> Everyone is entitled to a social and international order in which the rights and freedoms set forth in this Declaration can be fully realized.[77]

Citing Articles 25 and 28 of the UDHR is not intended to be an appeal to legal obligation. The ways that these Articles have been codified or transformed into customary international law is inadequate. But the moral sense of the declaration is clear. Pogge goes on to show that institutions such as the WTO are shaped by richer developed nations and imposed on the less developed nations. Where we have the drugs to treat the biggest killers, in low-income societies should Trade-Related Aspects of Intellectual Property Rights (TRIPS) rules deny millions access to essential medicines? Similarly, international rules recognising the legitimacy of tyrannical and corrupt rules and granting them international borrowing rights impose enormous debt on struggling societies with little or no benefit to the poorest. Traditionally the international economy is seen as the archetypical free market, an ungoverned space where supply and demand between sovereign equals can proceed unhampered. But Pogge asks us to think about how the rich nations, so advantaged in an industrialised capitalist market system, gained their wealth:

> The affluent Western states are no longer practising slavery, colonialism or genocide. But still they enjoy crushing economic, political and military dominance over the rest of the world.[78]

We are not morally obligated to end poverty because our ancestors engaged in activities that we have now acknowledged as immoral and illegal. Rather, we are obligated because we still benefit hugely from the institutional structures that were established on the back of these practices and cause and sustain avoidable harm that we can recognise as human rights deprivations and as abuses.

Pogge's claim is that the suffering caused by poverty is an avoidable harm, and is produced and reproduced by the very institutions that we inhabit. We may be geographically divorced from much of the world's poverty, but we are institutionally connected to it and that morally relevant fact triggers obligations to reform the system or to compensate victims of that system. Reform would have to be significant. Like many cosmopolitans, Pogge calls for the remodelling of international society and the dispersal of sovereignty on vertical (global to sub-state) lines.[79] Compensation would require, Pogge argues, about US$300 billion annually in the first phases of any serious offensive against poverty (0.5 per cent of the global product or 0.7 per cent of the GNP of the most affluent countries) and could be raised fairly simply via a Tobin tax, a global resources dividend or a health impact fund.[80] Poverty, then, is a violation of our institutionally embedded negative duties not to cause avoidable harm. Thus, poverty ought to be viewed as a human rights violation and our obligations under the ICESCR read in the light of this factor. On this reading, the way the international community has condoned or tolerated the treatment of economic, social and cultural rights as subordinate or as second-generation rights is severely remiss and the power of thinking about such rights as essential to a clear grasp of the human rights necessary for securing human dignity is clear.

Positive hierarchies of human rights

Pressure on the idea of the indivisibility of human rights is not simply a product of human rights failings. It also appears to be a product of the remarkable success of human rights. There are many plausible arguments that point to the increasing importance of some (but not all) human rights norms. The explorations of non-derogable human rights, the gradual attainment of *jus cogens* status for some IHRL norms or the generation of *erga omnes* obligations by a similar subset of IHRL norms have been of considerable interest to lawyers and of even more interest to political theorists. In this section we explore some of these claims and the political and moral arguments they offer to underwrite. For some commentators the emergence of binding and legally superior human rights norms adds an intriguing cachet to the developing significance of IHRL to the politics of international law. On the face of it this development can only augment the moral authority of human rights claims. The concepts suggest that human rights norms have attained the same status as sovereignty or state consent, or even transcended that status, downgrading or severely qualifying sovereignty in their rise to prominence. Allied to the moral and political arguments that infer the desirability of this state of affairs it appears to license bold cosmopolitan prescriptions.

While there have been intriguing developments around these ideas, we need to understand how they are developed in a human rights context and what that implies for an argument about justice. Having done this, we need to think about whether the evolution of a higher tier of human rights norms pushes us to transcend the sovereign state-based world order to establish a hierarchical system. Alternatively, we need to ask whether the legal argument is weaker than it might at first appear and if the relationship between IHRL and sovereignty needs a more subtle gloss. We have come across many of the strands of the arguments in earlier chapters. In particular, we have seen how some claims about the growing importance of human rights norms plays a role in the development of the constitution of international society (see Chapter Four, above), and how the superior nature of human rights claims may underscore new sources of legal normativity (see Chapter Two, above). These are very strong claims and suggest that human rights principles are best thought of as a challenge to the authority of sovereignty. Painting human rights as the core normative principles of the international legal order is said to provide an antidote to the system of sovereignty that gets in the way of effectively protecting human rights. As Allen Buchanan presents it, a human rights-based conception of justice

> represents a real challenge not only to some central features of the existing legal order, but also to the dominant ways that theorists

conceive of international law and international relations. I offer a sustained, principled argument for rejecting the almost universally accepted assumption that the international legal order not only is but ought to be a society of equal sovereign states, governed by laws grounded in the consent of states.[81]

As we have seen, Buchanan's argument is intended to offer a political conception of justice. His account of institutional moral reasoning, in substituting moral theory for a 'systematic moral view', draws on existing norms to claim that the moral foundation of his argument is the '(limited) obligation to help ensure that all persons have access to institutions that protect those basic human rights'.[82] This, of course, is the phrase drawn from Article 28 of the UDHR and cited by Pogge (above). The implications of this limited obligation are, in Buchanan's work, far from minimal. He challenges the criteria for statehood found in the Montevideo Convention. He rejects the principle of sovereign equality that Brownlie described as the basic constitutional doctrine of international law (Chapter Three, above).

He argues that state consent is neither representative of how laws arise nor a desirable ideal. These core ideas lead him to support a much more assertive policy on the use of force, including advocating humanitarian military intervention and defending preventative self-defence (see Chapter Seven, below), to offer an alternative framework for unilateral secession (a remedial right overseen by the international community) and, as we saw in Chapter Four, to insist on the reform or the bypassing of the UN Security Council. Crucial to the success of Buchanan's argument is the claim that his account of international justice shares a moral foundation with human rights norms, a foundation that challenges sovereignty. Our first question, therefore, concerns whether or not we should really see human rights as antagonistic to norms of sovereignty.

In order to explore this we can gain real insights from Theodore Meron's exploration of the 'Humanization of International Law'. Central to this idea is the claim that the progressive development of much international law (particularly humanitarian law) is now guided by human rights standards.[83] This has been a vital element in the expansion of robust legal and institutional responses to gross violations of human rights, which are often characterised as crimes against humanity and war crimes. In particular, it has served as the basis for the justification for humanitarian military action and the establishment of *ad hoc* and permanent international criminal tribunals. A second vital claim is that the gradual legal development of 'principles of humanity and of the public conscience' (a version of the Martens Clause (see Chapter Two, above) that is found in all human rights conventions from the UDHR to the Rome Statute) is creating new normative hierarchies in public international law.[84] The Martens Clause may be taken to be part of customary international law and is, therefore, of universal scope. It serves to remind all actors that there are some standards that are binding regardless of whether a state has become party to a particular treaty or has reservations against some elements of treaty law.[85]

The interpretation given to the 'dictates of public conscience' is even more interesting because there is some dispute over the source of 'public conscience'. For some, it has its roots in *opinio juris*, for others, it is broader and can be found in the *vox populi* or public opinion more generally.[86] *Opinio juris*, as we have seen, is the subjective element of customary law: the belief that an act is required by international law. If the public conscience were to be determined by the (admittedly rather tricky) exploration of *opinio juris*, it would not really add anything to existing customary international law, but it would demonstrate that states believe that they have obligations as a result of the dictates of humanity. At the other end of the scale is the thought that public conscience reflects natural law,[87] and as such represents universally binding moral rules. The displacement of natural law by legal positivism has meant that contemporary public international law is quite hostile to the idea of natural law, nevertheless, some scholars maintain that the Martens Clause has preserved its influence. A third view here (and one that co-exists with the first interpretation) is that public opinion influences the development of international law (including customary law) 'when governments are moved by public opinion to regard certain developing norms as already declaratory of customary law or as *jus nascendi*'. According to Meron, 'this was precisely how the Rome Conference on the Establishment of an International Criminal Court formulated certain crimes in its proposed statute'.[88]

The influence of human rights has been central to this process. As early as 1950 human rights principles were being used to flesh out the meaning of the Martens Clause.[89] Now, however, human rights principles are being used to assert the peremptory nature of norms closely associated with 'acts that shock' in a way that has started 'a limited transition from bilateral legal relations to a system based on community interests and objective normative relationships'.[90] It is the development of this hierarchy of norms that suggests to some the subversion of the state consent model of international law and its replacement with a hierarchy of universally binding, human rights-based norms.[91]

While the categories of norms *erga omnes* and *jus cogens* have been recognised in courts, treaties, the declaratory statements of key actors and in much scholarly work, the idea that we have an uncontroversial hierarchy of norms is still hotly disputed. The way these categories respond to 'community interests' and issues of global public policy based on 'basic human rights' is fascinating. However, while it is clear that *erga omnes* obligations are associated with 'the basic rights of the human person' (*Barcelona Traction* case), we are not sure what that means. It might refer to the different lists of non-derogable rights found in the ICCPR or the ICESCR, or it may be wider, but states have shown a real reluctance to test the extent of this concept. While *jus cogens* have clear peremptory status this is a matter of treaty law (limiting a state's right to contract in opposition to such norms), and states do not contract to violate human rights.[92] This gets us to the crux of the matter. While the existence of these categories is certain, the question of what follows from this in law does not really suggest that these categories fundamentally challenge the norms protecting sovereignty.

There is clear evidence to suggest that human rights norms have become increasingly important to the development of the international legal order. But the bolder claim, that human rights have come to challenge sovereign norms directly, does not have much credibility in legal or social terms. It is certainly not the case that the progressive development of international law leads inexorably to cosmopolitan conclusions. We do see some striking examples of superior norms in action. The overruling (in *Armed Activities: Rwanda* v. *DRC*) of Rwandan reservations to the Racial Discrimination Convention and the Genocide Convention on the grounds that the rights and obligations contained in those conventions were *erga omnes* is a case in point.[93] We also see some important Dissenting Opinions, which, while not influencing the judgment of the World Court, have an important impact on the development of law. Here the views of Judges Weeramantry and Shahabuddeen (in the *Nuclear Weapons* Advisory Opinion) that the threat or use of nuclear weapons could not satisfy the requirements of the Martens Clause are especially important.[94] But this does not license too bold a conclusion, as neither legal position ultimately triumphed over more traditional, statist principles. The ruling in *Armed Activities* did not mean that the ICJ had jurisdiction to hear the case, as the right of Rwanda to refuse or to accept jurisdiction remained intact despite the fact that breaches of the rights in question gave rise to *erga omnes* obligations. The majority opinion in *Nuclear Weapons* was that their use did not conflict with any law. We also see the persistent abuse of human rights that are readily acknowledged as *jus cogens*, such as the prohibition of torture and *refoulement*, the ongoing controversy concerning humanitarian military intervention in the UN and passivity in the face of gross human suffering. This does not mean that the international community does not see these things as great wrongs. The issue is not really about the status of human rights, it is about the appropriate way to deal with violations and there is no evidence that cosmopolitan remedial structures (such as compulsory jurisdiction of courts, unilateral rights of military intervention or secession, etc.) have any significant support.

The fact is, then, that the superior quality of a norm does not overrule other norms that support sovereignty. The acknowledgement that the violation of basic human rights is wrong does not imply that remedies should automatically override norms governing non-use of force, non-intervention or consent to jurisdiction of courts. The evidence suggests that a great deal of care has been taken to ensure that such considerations of humanity are compatible with pluralist rather than cosmopolitan institutional structures. The scholarly consensus seems to be that we must manage the development of this element of international law to avoid 'foisting'[95] these substantive and systemic changes on reluctant parties. The cosmopolitan version of institutional moral reasoning likens the increasing role of human rights norms in international society to the development of a clear hierarchy of superior norms. However, this seems to be an over-ambitious interpretation and one that threatens the realisation of the human rights project. Meron argues that:

> Caution should therefore be exercised in resorting to hierarchical terminology. Too liberal an invocation of superior rights such as 'fundamental rights' and 'basic rights', as well as *jus cogens*, may adversely affect the credibility of human rights as a legal discipline.[96]

The incremental changes (noted above) have given us the tools to act to prevent or react to gross violations of human rights, to hold individuals criminally liable, whatever their political position, and this is both to be welcomed and supported as an as yet unfinished project. This is not so much because the legitimacy of community values is not apparent to the moral conscience of the international community, but because the institutional processes by which the ideals are developed, specified and institutionalised are not settled. The legal and political interpretation of these crucial norms does not take place in a political vacuum. As Buchanan argues forcefully, the relative strength of institutions to deal fairly with hegemonic influence (Buchanan calls this the parochialism objection) is crucial. Actors adopt pluralist approaches to institutional reform to create political defences against the imposition of parochial interpretations of communal norms. Where these developments threaten this pluralism we find the greatest controversy, the most objections and the general refusal to engage with the processes that might institutionalise the superiority of human rights as an independent source of law or as a matter of global public policy.

Human rights, sovereignty and international justice

Pogge and Buchanan are correct to assert that human rights norms are very important to the international community. Pogge's argument that we have duties to the poorest and Buchanan's claims that we have duties to those suffering human rights abuses at the hands of their own governments are well grounded in international law. This, however, does not establish the case that cosmopolitan structures are the most suitable remedy for failures in the protection of human rights. It is possible to make further instrumental arguments about the efficiency of cosmopolitan institutions in this endeavour (and both theorists do so), but it may be the case that norms that protect sovereignty also protect key values and that those values are not (despite appearances) in conflict with human rights. Where protecting the values that are furthered by sovereignty threatens values protected by human rights we do see changes in law and in practice. But cosmopolitan remedies threaten to throw the baby out with bath water. In large part, this is because the analysis neglects other values embedded in the international legal order that derive in significant ways from constitutional principles of sovereignty, multilateralism and state consent (see our discussion of Reus-Smit's account of constitutional structures in Chapter Two). Human rights arose in the context of a state-based system. They serve to qualify the sovereignty of states in an attempt to protect individuals, but they are only fully comprehended in the context in which they have been developed as a social institution. Mervyn Frost usefully describes this context as the modern state domain of discourse.⁹⁷ Even when the international community is challenging sovereignty in the name of human rights it is always in the context of how these norms might function in international society that has a range of settled norms or values in addition to human rights.⁹⁸ The state is not a brute fact getting in the way of the application of moral principles. Sovereignty is one of the principal 'settled norms' of the modern world, and human rights have been developed within this normative framework. Frost lists the settled norms of international society, noting the ways in which so many derive from sovereignty. He writes:

> It is settled that the following are goods:
>
> S1. The preservation of the society of states.
> S2. State sovereignty.
> S3. Anti-imperialism.
> S4. The balance of power.
> S5. Patriotism.
> S6. Protecting the interests of a state's citizens.
> S7. Non-intervention.
> S8. Self-determination.
> L1. International law.
> L2. *Ius ad bellum*.
> L3. *Ius in bello*.
> L4. Collective security.
> L5. Economic sanctions (under specified circumstances).
> L6. The diplomatic system.
> M1. Modernization.
> M2. Economic cooperation.
> D1. Democratic institutions within states.
> D2. Human rights.⁹⁹

These norms, drawn in compelling fashion from analysis of the sort of questions that dominate the global agenda, all need to be taken into consideration if we are to make an understanding of human rights accessible to actors in international society. As Hurrell notes, moral claims that seek to privilege human rights over sovereignty miss the fact that states 'are the source of the system, the locus of responsibility, and the focus for pressure'.¹⁰⁰ This recognition is not altogether absent from the neo-Kantian tradition. Indeed, Rawls' political conception of justice found in the *Law of Peoples* begins with the recognition that it is a law of *peoples* or modern states. Rawls is clear that:

Peoples as corporate bodies organized by their governments exist in some form all over the world. Historically speaking, all principles and standards proposed for the law of peoples must, to be feasible, prove acceptable to the considered and reflective public opinion of peoples and their governments.[101]

Rawls assumes that there is, as Philip Pettit puts it, 'a certain geography to justice'.[102] But Rawls emphasised the centrality of human rights principles to state legitimacy by insisting that we think in terms of 'Peoples' rather than 'States' as traditionally conceived. His *Law of Peoples* is grounded in the structure of international society as it has developed since the Second World War. Human rights are a key part of the post-1945 political culture of international society, but so are the many other values that foster non-intervention and self-determination. Respect for human rights, on Rawls' reading, is one of the key indicators of a legitimate society (along with non-aggression and having a 'decent' constitution or legal order). In his words, the insistence that peoples respect human rights is the claim that rights-respecting institutions are a minimal standard of well-ordered political institutions for all peoples who belong as members in good standing to a just political society.[103] Human rights, then, are key values in international society, but the primary responsibility for upholding them belongs necessarily to the state. If a state fails (dramatically) in this responsibility, Rawls argues that international society has obligations to assist.[104] But this must happen in ways that are compatible with the systemic logic of a law of peoples. It is this thought that underpins the core debates concerning dispute resolution that we examine in Chapter Seven, below.

Notes

1 Finnemore and Toope, 'Alternatives to "Legalization"'.
2 Meron, T., *The Humanization of International Law*, The Hague: Martinus Nijhoff, 2006.
3 Lowe, 'The Politics of Law-Making', ch. 10. Also Reus-Smit, *The Politics of International Law*, p. 26.
4 Donnelly, J., 'The Virtues of Legalization', in S. Meckled-García. and B. Cali (eds), *The Legalization of Human Rights: Multidisciplinary Perspectives on Human Rights and Human Rights Law*, London: Routledge, 2006, p. 71.
5 Freeman, M., 'Putting Law in its Place: An interdisciplinary Evaluation of National Amnesty Laws', in S. Meckled-García and B Cali (eds), *The Legalization of Human Rights: Multidisciplinary Perspectives on*

Human Rights and Human Rights Law, London: Routledge, 2006, p. 51.
6 Freeman, 'Putting Law in Its Place', p. 54; Kennedy, *The Dark Sides of Virtue*, passim.
7 S. Meckled-García and B. Cali (eds), 'Lost in Translation: The Human Rights Ideal and international Human Rights Law', in *The Legalization of Human Rights: Multidisciplinary Perspectives on Human Rights and Human Rights Law*, London: Routledge, 2006, p. 12.
8 O'Neill, 'Abstraction, Idealization and Ideology in Ethics'.
9 Rawls, J., *Political Liberalism*, New York: Columbia University Press, 1993.
10 Weston, B., 'Human Rights', *Human Rights Quarterly*, 6 (1984): 257–83, at pp. 257–71; Brownlie, *Principles of Public International Law*, pp. 530–1.
11 Higgins, *Problems and Process*, p. 95.
12 Bilder, R., 'Rethinking International Human Rights: Some Basic Questions', *Wisconsin Law Review*, 171(1) (1969): 171–217, at p. 174.
13 Higgins, *Problems and Process*, p. 96.
14 Forsythe, D. P., *Human Rights in International Relations*, 2nd edn, Cambridge: Cambridge University Press, 2005, p. 3.
15 D'Amato, A., 'The Concept of Human Rights in International Law', *Columbus Law Review*, 82(6) (1982): 1110–59, at p. 1110.
16 Higgins, *Problems and Process*, pp. 96–7.
17 Waldron, J., *Nonsense upon Stilts: Bentham, Burke and Marx on the Rights of Man*, London: Taylor & Francis, 1987, p. 52.
18 Cerna, C., 'Universality of Human Rights and Cultural Diversity: Implementation of Human Rights in Different Socio-Cultural Contexts,, *Human Rights Quarterly*, 16 (1994): 740–52; Mutua, M., 'Savages, Victims and Saviors: The Metaphor of Human Rights', *Harvard International Law Journal*, 42 (2001): 201–45, at pp. 202 and 204.
19 Zechenter, E., 'In the Name of Culture: Cultural Relativism and the Abuse of the Individual', *Journal of Anthropological Research*, 53(3) (1997): 319–47.
20 Donnelly, J., 'Cultural Relativism and Universal Human Rights', *Human Rights Quarterly*, 6(4) (1984): 400–19, at p. 400.
21 Donnelly, 'Cultural Relativism and Universal Human Rights', p. 401.
22 Donnelly, 'Cultural Relativism and Universal Human Rights', p. 401.
23 Donnelly, 'Cultural Relativism and Universal Human Rights', pp. 401–2; Donnelly, J., 'The Relative Universality of Human Rights', *Human Rights Quarterly*, 29(2) (2007): 281–306.
24 Bangkok Declaration 1993, para. 8.
25 Preamble of African Charter 1981.
26 African Charter, para. 5.
27 Higgins, *Problems and Process*, p. 105.

28 Meron, T., 'On a Hierarchy of International Human Rights,, *American Journal of International Law*, 80(1) (1986): 1–23, at p. 11.
29 See Tharoor, S., 'Are Human Rights Universal?', *New Internationalist Magazine*, March 2001 and Art. 24 of the UDHR.
30 Weston, 'Human Rights', p. 264.
31 Weston, 'Human Rights', pp. 264–5.
32 Weston, 'Human Rights', pp. 265–6.
33 Weston, 'Human Rights', pp. 266–7. Also see Sohn, L., 'The New International Law: Protection of the Rights of Individuals Rather than States', *American University Law Review*, 32(1) (1982): 1–64, at pp. 48–62.
34 See US statement before the UN, UN Doc. A/40/C.3/36, p. 5.
35 Available at: http://treaties.un.org/Pages/ViewDetails.aspx?src=TREATY&mtdsg_no=IV-3&chapter=4&lang=en.
36 Sieghart, P., *The Lawful Rights of Mankind: An Introduction to the International Legal Code of Human Rights*, Oxford: Oxford University Press, 1986, p. 161.
37 Alston, P., 'A Third Generation of Solidarity Rights: Progressive Development or Obfuscation of International Human Rights Law?', *Netherlands International Law Review*, 29 (1982): 307–22.
38 Tay, S., 'Human Rights, Culture, and the Singapore Example', *McGill Law Journal*, 41 (1996): 743–80.
39 Vienna Declaration and Programme of Action, World Conference of Human Rights, 1993.
40 Statement made at a special meeting of the Security Council's Counter-Terrorism Committee with International, Regional, and Sub-Regional Organizations, 6 March 2003, available at: http://www2.ohchr.org/english/issues/terrorism/index.htm, accessed 6 August 2012.
41 Sohn, 'The New International Law', pp. 9–48.
42 Buergenthal, T., 'International Human Rights Law and Institutions: Accomplishments and Prospects', *Washington Law Review*, 63(1) (1988): 1–19, at p. 5; Månsson, K., 'Reviving the "Spirit of San Francisco": The Lost Proposals on Human Rights, Justice and International Law to the UN Charter', *Nordic Journal of International Law*, 76 (2007): 217–39.
43 Hannum, H., 'The Status of the Universal Declaration of Human Rights in National and International Law', *Georgia Journal of International and Comparative Law*, 25 (1995/6): 287–395, at p. 290.
44 Hannum, 'The Status of the Universal Declaration of Human Rights in National and International Law', pp. 287–354. Also see Cerna, 'Universality of Human Rights and Cultural Diversity', pp. 745–9.
45 Buergenthal, 'International Human Rights Law and Institutions', pp. 5–6.
46 Buergenthal, 'International Human Rights Law and Institutions', pp. 9–13; Sohn, 'The New International Law', pp. 17–48.

47 See http://treaties.un.org/Pages/Treaties.aspx?id=4&subid=A&lang=en, accessed 31 July 2012.
48 For a comprehensive list of all the human rights treaties and other instruments, see Office of the United Nations High Commissioner for Human Rights (OHCHR) website at: http://www2.ohchr.org/english/law, accessed 31 July 2012.
49 Sohn, L., 'The Human Rights Law of the Charter', *Texas International Law Journal*, 12 (1977): 129–40, at p. 133.
50 Parker, K., '*Jus Cogens*: Compelling the Law of Human Rights', *Hastings International and Comparative Law Review*, 12 (1988/9): 411–65; Simma, B. and Alston, P., 'The Sources of Human Rights Law: Custom, *Jus Cogens* and General Principles', *Australian Yearbook of International Law*, 12 (1988/9): 82–108; Lillich, R., 'The Growing Importance of Customary International Human Rights Law', *Georgia Journal of International and Comparative Law*, 25 (1995/6): 1–30; Bianchi, A., 'Human Rights and the Magic of *Jus Cogens*', *European Journal of International Law*, 19(3) (2008): 491–508.
51 [1966] ICJ Rep. 6, at p. 298.
52 Bianchi, 'Human Rights and the Magic of *Jus Cogens*', p. 491.
53 Simma and Alston, 'The Sources of Human Rights Law', pp. 102–6; Hannum, 'The Status of the Universal Declaration of Human Rights in National and International Law', pp. 351–2.
54 [1951] ICJ Rep. 15, at p. 23.
55 Koh, H., 'How is International Human Rights Law Enforced?', *Indiana Law Journal*, 74 (1998/9): 1397–417; Weston, 'Human Rights', pp. 277–80.
56 Nowak, M., 'The Need for a World Court of Human Rights', *Human Rights Law Review*, 7(1) (2007): 251–9; Ulfstein, G., 'Do We Need a World Court of Human Rights?', in O. Engdahl and P. Wrange (eds), *Law at War: The Law as it Was and the Law as it Should, Liber Amicorum Ove Bring*, The Hague: Martinus Nijhoff, 2008, pp. 261–72.
57 For details on UN enforcement machinery, see Mertus, J., *The United Nations and Human Rights: A Guide for a New Era*, 2nd edn, New York: Routledge, 2009.
58 Weston, 'Human Rights', pp. 277–80. See also the Protocol Establishing the African Court of Human and Peoples' Rights 1998; Mohamed, A. A., 'Individual and NGO Participation in Human Rights Litigation before the African Court of Human and Peoples' Rights: Lessons from the European and Inter-American Courts of Human Rights', *Journal of African Law*, 43(2) (1999): 201–13; Mutua, M., 'The African Human Rights Court: A Two-Legged Stool?', *Human Rights Quarterly*, 21 (1999): 342–63.
59 See Art. 48. However, note that under Art. 52 the Charter does allow state members to adopt an additional optional protocol, which could, if

the example of Africa is anything to go by, create hope for a future Arab human rights court.
60 Article 2(4) of the Terms of Reference of the ASEAN Commission, available at: http://www.aseansec.org/22769.htm, accessed 6 August 2012.
61 Pogge, T., *World Poverty and Human Rights*, Oxford: Polity Press, 2002; Pogge, T., 'Divided Against Itself: Aspiration and Reality of International Law', in J. Crawford and M. Koskenniemi (eds), *The Cambridge Companion to International Law*, Cambridge: Cambridge University Press, 2012, pp. 373–97.
62 Meron, 'On a Hierarchy of Human Rights', pp. 1–23.
63 Rawls, *The Law of Peoples*, pp. 106–20.
64 Ackerman, B., 'Political Liberalisms', *Journal of Philosophy*, 41(7) (1994): 364–86.
65 Rawls, *The Law of Peoples*, p. 117.
66 Wellman, C., 'Solidarity, the Individual and Human Rights', *Human Rights Quarterly*, 22(2000): 639–57; Alston, 'A Third Generation of Solidarity Rights,' pp. 307–22.
67 See General Comment 3, 1990.
68 See the Limburg Principles 1987 E/CN.4/1987/17 and the Maastricht Guidelines 1997.
69 Vienna Convention and Programme of Action, A/CONF.157/23, 1993.
70 Pogge, *World Poverty and Human Rights*, pp. 1–2.
71 Pogge, *World Poverty and Human Rights*, p. 56 (quoting Rawls).
72 Pogge, 'Divided Against Itself', p. 373.
73 Pogge, 'Cosmopolitanism and Sovereignty', p. 50.
74 Pogge, *World Poverty and Human Rights*, pp. 2, 97–100; Pogge, 'Divided Against Itself', p. 373.
75 UN, *Human Development Report*, 1998, p. 30.
76 Singer, P., 'Famine, Affluence, and Morality', *Philosophy and Public Affairs*, 1(3) (1972): 229–43.
77 Pogge, *World Poverty and Human Rights*, p. 1, citing UNDHR, Arts 25 and 28.
78 Pogge, *World Poverty and Human Rights*, p. 6.
79 Pogge, *World Poverty and Human Rights*, pp. 168–95.
80 Pogge, 'Divided Against Itself', pp. 394–5; Pogge, *World Poverty and Human Rights*, pp. 111, 196–216.
81 Buchanan, *Justice, Legitimacy and Self-Determination*, pp. 5–6.
82 Buchanan, *Justice, Legitimacy and Self-Determination*, p. 4.
83 Chetail, V., 'The Contribution of the International Court of Justice to International Humanitarian Law', *International Review of the Red Cross*, 85 (2003): 235–69, at p. 241; Meron, *The Humanization of International Law*, p. 9.
84 Meron, 'On a Hierarchy of Human Rights'; Thirlway, 'The Sources of International Law', p. 142; Pustogarov, V. V., 'The Martens Clause

in International Law', *Journal of the History of International Law*, 1 (1999): 125–35, at p. 134; Chetail, 'The Contribution of the International Court of Justice', p. 338.
85 Cassese, 'The Martens Clause in International Law', p. 192. See also Ticehurst, R., 'The Marten's Clause and the Laws of Armed Conflict', *International Review of the Red Cross*, 37 (1997): 125–34, at pp. 128–9. On the impact of this on case law, see Meron, 'The Humanization of Humanitarian Law', pp. 82–3.
86 Meron, *The Humanization of Humanitarian Law*, p. 83.
87 Ticehurst, 'The Marten's Clause', p. 133.
88 Meron, *The Humanization of Humanitarian Law*, p. 83.
89 Cassese, 'The Martens Clause in International Law', p. 207.
90 Meron, *The Humanization of International Law*, pp. 187 and 256.
91 Sutch, 'Normative IR Theory and the Legalization of International Politics'.
92 Meron, 'On a Hierarchy of Human Rights', p. 14.
93 Shelton, 'Normative Hierarchy in International Law', pp. 306–7.
94 See Meron, *The Humanization of Humanitarian Law*, p. 86; Cassese, 'The Martens Clause in International Law', p. 192; Chetail, 'The Contribution of the International Court of Justice', pp. 239–41; Ticehurst, 'The Marten's Clause', pp. 126–33; Gardam, J., 'The Contribution of the International Court of Justice to International Humanitarian Law', *Leiden Journal of International Law*, 14 (2001): 349–65, at pp. 351–2.
95 Shaw, M., *International Law*, Cambridge: Cambridge University Press, 2003, pp. 115–20.
96 Meron, 'On a Hierarchy of Human Rights', p. 22. See also Meron, *The Humanization of International Law*, p. 396; Shelton, 'Normative Hierarchy in International Law', p. 292.
97 Frost, *Ethics in International Relations*, p. 78.
98 Frost, *Ethics in International Relations*, pp. 77–9.
99 Frost, *Ethics in International Relations*, pp. 111–12.
100 Hurrell, *On Global Order*, p. 149.
101 Rawls, *Political Liberalism*, p. 50.
102 Pettit, P., 'Rawls' Peoples', in R. Martin and D. Reidy (eds), *Rawls's Law of Peoples: A Realistic Utopia?*, Oxford: Blackwell, 2006, p. 49.
103 Rawls, *The Law of Peoples*, pp. 79–80.
104 Rawls, *The Law of Peoples*, pp. 106–12.

CHAPTER SIX

| Diplomatic Communications | Diplomacy and Justice |

Diplomacy is one of the fundamental institutions of international society. It is emblematic of the type of politics we expect to find on the international plane, but there is far more to glean from a critical examination of diplomacy as a fundamental institution than as an understanding of the formal means of communication and negotiation between states. In what follows we argue that modern diplomacy is 'new' and distinct from the diplomacy of earlier iterations of international society. We can understand the distinctive character of modern diplomacy in a number of ways, but it is useful to think of contemporary diplomacy as highly legalised. Here the legalisation of diplomacy refers both to the way that diplomacy is regulated by international law (and to specific tensions in the relationship between diplomacy and law visible, for example, in the competing claims to sovereign immunity and criminal accountability for international crimes), to the portion of diplomatic practice now dedicated to the production of new or newly codified law and to the multilateralism of that process. In the period after the Second World War the rapid development of international law was, in significant part, enabled by the establishment of a permanent multilateral diplomatic forum in the shape of the UN. The preamble to the UN Charter is clear that the road to social progress relies upon the establishment of 'conditions under which justice and respect for the obligations arising from treaties and other sources of international law can be maintained'. What we refer to as the legalisation of diplomacy is a feature of modern international society, yet diplomacy also has a rather ambiguous relationship to international law. Gerry Simpson points to three images of this crucial relationship. In the first image law appears 'virtuous yet marginal . . . a mostly frustrated project to civilise war, tame anarchy, restrain the Great Powers and ensure fairer re-distributive outcomes'. In the second image international law is constitutive of diplomacy and as such has 'facilitated and established the conditions for many of the practices that are thought to be the impediments for a just world order'. Finally, international law may be seen as combination of norm and aspiration as both declaratory of power politics and prescriptive about a more just future order.[1] Trying to understand the place of diplomacy in IR and its relationship with international law is essential if we are to understand the challenges of the contemporary world order. On the one hand, we can agree with Adam Watson that the post-war boom in international legal rules and institutions 'is one of the greatest constructive achievements of diplomacy'.[2] On the other hand, it is difficult to shake the image presented by Thomas Pogge of the diplomatic processes that led to the establishment of the WTO and other grand international institutions of the post-war order as being the work of 'hunger's willing executioners'.[3] On the face of it this last claim might seem rather exaggerated. However, as we saw in Chapter Five, poverty and the misery and death it brings can be seen to be, in part at least, a product of the post-war economic order. Pogge's claim is that the diplomats of the victorious powers negotiated an institutional framework that benefited the states that they represented. While this is clearly what diplomats are intended to do, Pogge's moral criticism stems from the harm that this settlement has caused the world's poorest. In Pogge's terms, this is a significant human rights failing and raises a question that is central to this chapter. The question, framed most starkly, asks whether the practices of diplomacy tend to produce just or unjust outcomes. In diplomatic practice the tensions between the modern desire to establish universal standards of international conduct and the traditional desire to advance the national interest yet maintain peace are clear. As a general rule of thumb we should be wary of any answer to the question of the justice of contemporary diplomacy that does not acknowledge these tensions. As we shall see, these tensions are not a puzzle to be solved or a problem to be overcome. Rather, it is itself an important part of the normative framework of the practice and of international society more generally. An understanding of this framework should have critical and praxeological (practice-oriented) impact. In other words, it should help us to understand the practice at a deeper level and provide us with some tools for making judgements about the claims to justice and injustice that we find throughout the practice. All eras of diplomacy have a particular normative basis that describes or underpins legitimate diplomatic practice. Central to the standards of legitimacy and justice are specific, historically bound understandings of who should make international rules of conduct (and what they should look like) and how actors should be held accountable to them. Where we are able to see evident disjuncture between these background norms or constitutive principles and action we are in a position to consider the merits of normative claims that urge resistance of unjust action within a practice or reform of the system. The English School tradition (in its traditional and contemporary variants) captures the centrality of diplomacy to international affairs and its central tensions in its analysis of the international pursuit of order and justice. This pressure is manifest both in the very nature of diplomacy as a fundamental element of international society (in the relation of diplomacy to international law) and in the specific challenges of contemporary diplomatic practice (such as environmental issues or humanitarian intervention). After a brief exploration of contemporary, legalised diplomacy we turn to the English School for insights into the moral and political questions that arise from the normative conflict at the heart of diplomatic practice.

The legalisation of diplomacy

The legalisation of diplomacy can be seen in the institutional developments in international politics between The Hague conferences of 1899 and 1907 and the present day. Legalisation describes the characteristics of 'new' diplomacy found in the novel, multilateral, later omnilateral, fora for diplomatic dialogue developed at The Hague conferences and made permanent in the aftermath of the world wars *and* post-Cold War innovations in diplomacy. These later innovations include the increasing participation of new actors, such as NGOs, in multilateral negotiation (as witnessed in the Ottawa negotiations leading up to the Convention on the Prohibition of the Use, Stockpiling, Production and Transfer of Anti-Personnel Landmines and their Production (1997); the negotiation of the Rome Statute of the International Criminal Court (1998); and the many negotiations on environmental regimes), as well as the increasing focus on the rule of law. The hallmarks of these developments are increasing commit-

Diplomacy and Justice

ment to inclusivity and universality or the ideas that all should participate in the creation of rules of international conduct and all should be accountable to them. The virtue of inclusivity moved contemporary diplomatic practice first to convene conferences of all important (and later simply all) sovereign states and, more recently, to include a greater range of relevant agents in negotiations. The relationship between the commitment to accountability and traditional diplomacy is at its most stark in the growing institutionalisation and pursuit of international criminal responsibility, including, crucially, the erosion of head of state immunity. This new diplomacy contrasts with traditional diplomacy, and it is in this contrast that we find fertile ground for the questions of justice and injustice with which we are concerned. The most prominent institutional development is the establishment of the UN, and since 1946 the UN focus on the development of international law has underpinned the practice of multilateral diplomacy in a way that structures the contemporary diplomatic tradition. There is not a complete break between old and new diplomacy. Bilateral, private negotiations are a constant feature of all diplomacy and even of multilateral conferences. The relationship is one of co-existence and continuity rather than radical difference. Nevertheless, what was begun at The Hague was to have far-reaching effects. The first Hague conference was an extraordinarily ambitious undertaking. An international conference (surrounded by civil society groups and the world's media) is a commonplace in contemporary diplomacy, but was new in 1899.[4] The subject of the conference was also groundbreaking. The agenda included the revision of the laws of war, the establishment of an international court of arbitration aimed at avoiding armed conflict between states and disarmament. In its form and its focus the first Hague conference set the direction of travel for international affairs in the modern period. The establishment of the League of Nations by the covenant of 1919 and later (and with remarkably few alterations) of the UN in 1945, both with commitments to multilateral diplomacy and to the civilising influence of law and the benefits of international judicial procedures, gave permanent institutional presence to the values of 'open' diplomacy that were seen in the international conferences that followed The Hague conferences. The characteristics of new diplomacy were then, multilateralism, openness (as opposed to secrecy) and faith in the rule of law.

If the basic features of new or legalised diplomacy are the subject of broad agreement, the merits of the contemporary practice are hotly disputed. There are at least three basic positions: the critical, the pluralist and the transformationalist. For critics the increasing use of public and parliamentary-style multilateral or omnilateral negotiation fora threatens the very essence of diplomatic relations. This is clearest in Morgenthau's critique of the decline of diplomacy since the First World War. Such scepticism is also present, albeit in tempered form, in the analysis of English School pluralists who emphasise the need to focus on the continuity of traditional forms of diplomatic discourse among distinct agents, rather than any sense of universal solidarity that may appear to emerge through the contemporary institutionalisation of international politics. The transformationalists, on the other hand, see the emergence of a distinctively post-Wesphalian politics and the urgent need for a greater cosmopolitanism in diplomatic affairs.

For Morgenthau, the approach to diplomacy found in special conferences and later in the permanent institutions of the League of Nations and the UN amounted to a disastrous decline in diplomacy. While modern communications have enabled 'shuttle diplomacy' and led to the devaluing of permanent diplomatic representatives, the crucial failing was normative. Morgenthau referred to the normative change as 'the depreciation of diplomacy' or the belief that traditional diplomatic methods 'not only contribute nothing to the cause of peace, but actually endanger it'.[5] Morgenthau's distain for 'diplomacy by parliamentary procedures', and for UN diplomacy in particular, rests on criticisms of openness, majority decision-making and the claim that such practices entail the fragmentation of international issues, as well as his well-documented criticisms of international law in general (see Chapter One). The first criticism rests on the argument that publicity and openness in negotiation leads to the degeneration of diplomacy into a propaganda match.[6] Openness, he argues, far from leading diplomats to be more honest, undercuts the nature of negotiation. There are, he writes, 'more edifying spectacles than the bluffing, blustering, haggling, and deceiving, the real weakness and pretend strength, that go with horse-trading and the drive for a bargain'.[7] Publicity undercuts the government's position because they cannot afford to give up publicly what they claimed to be just and necessary at the outset of a negotiation. This failure is compounded by 'the vice of majority decision-making' in the General Assembly and, with the addition of the veto, in the UN Security Council. International society has none of the constitutional safeguards (a bill of rights or judicial review) that a state might have to guard against the tyranny of the majority. Morgenthau also argues that majority voting in the context of a society of states has the potential to undermine peace:

> To outvote habitually a powerful minority in a deliberative international agency ... does not contribute to the preservation of peace. For the minority cannot accept the decision of the majority, and the majority cannot enforce its decision short of war. At best, parliamentary procedures transferred to the international scene leave things as they are; they leave problems unsolved and issues unsettled. At worst, however, these procedures poison the international climate and aggravate the conflicts that carry the seed of war ... In the form of the veto ... these procedures provide the minority with a weapon with which to obstruct the will of the majority and to prevent the international agency functioning at all.[8]

Both of these failings relate to the third, the tendency to view individual challenges as separate from the broader issues of global power politics. Whether the issues (such as the 'Middle East') are treated as a legal case or as a political matter to be disposed of by a vote the process deals only with surface issues, rather than with fundamental ones leading to 'the fragmentation of the conduct of foreign affairs'.[9] Unsurprisingly, Morgenthau viewed the normative critique of traditional diplomacy as utopian. While his critical account of 'new' diplomacy is particularly stark, it remains central to a world view that finds the 'reality' of power politics only vaguely masked by the institutional structures of contemporary open diplomacy. There are, however, alternative perspectives on the evolution of diplomacy that view the move to multilateral institutions and omnilateral negotiations as normatively desirable, if not entirely effective or even as the beginning of something more radical.

If we turn to consider the more transformationalist agenda that the emergence of 'new' diplomacy throws up we can see that two general features of contemporary diplomacy are the offspring of the normative basis of the push to open diplomacy. The first is the democratising (Falk) or civilising (Watson) tendency of omnilateralism. Omnilateralism, a word found in Watson's analysis of modern diplomacy to suggest a more comprehensive multilateralism, refers to the attempt to include all relevant parties in negotiation.[10] Increasingly, this has come to include not just the representatives of states, but also of civil society groups and technical or specialist organisations. This development was particularly prominent during and after the 1990s, and has been described as a post-Westphalian form of diplomacy. In Richard Falk's analysis:

The defining novel feature of this new internationalism was active and very effective coalitions between clusters of nongovernmental actors and governments of state. This innovative diplomacy was able to overcome concerted geopolitical objections of the most powerful nations, notably the United States itself, but also China and Russia, to produce new authoritative norms, procedures and institutions for international society.[11]

For Falk this feature of contemporary diplomacy is one of the core structural and attitudinal ideas that challenge the existing structure of international society in what he describes as a second Grotian moment or tectonic shift in the world order.[12] Falk recognises that states still have the power to derail or undermine these developments, but also sees even the most ardent objectors to institutions such as the ICC as getting bound up in its practices.[13] For Falk the move to omnilateralism suggests a move to global democracy, 'a mode of democratic representation . . . independent of governmental representation'. Others view this development less as fundamental change and more as a development in the communicative framework for diplomatic dialogue. This development warrants critical attention. The increasing inclusion of NGOs, whose commitment may be to universal values (such as human rights or humanitarianism) rather than to any particular state, has been significant in new diplomacy. Yet critics also point to the ways that such developments move control from the accountable representatives of peoples to technocratic elites.[14] Pluralists, however, offer a tentative optimism when exploring this development. Watson, for example, recognises that privacy is necessary for diplomatic bargaining, but argues that private bilateralism continues alongside multilateralism both at the UN and in the specialised conferences.

The permanent institutions of the UN are only one part of the contemporary diplomatic tradition. Indeed, Watson argues that most of the productive multilateral work is done outside the UN in international conferences on technical issues and in regional organisations. But he also sees value added by the permanent institutions of new diplomacy. The UN may be 'inadequate and corrupt' in many respects, but 'the collective diplomacy that issues from it does reflect the changing conscience of mankind, and is not committed to the *status quo*'.[15] The symbolic value of the UN and the civilising influence of collective diplomacy exists alongside a more traditional diplomatic dialogue outside the UN, meaning that 'it functions more often as a counterpoint to the distribution of power than as an expression of it'.[16] Watson captures something of the tension between pluralism and solidarism that is at the heart of contemporary diplomacy and we will return to an analysis of his position below.

The tensions that exist in a world where diplomacy appears to encompass both pluralist and cosmopolitan tendencies do not just stem from a normative clash between a commitment to national self-interest and universal values. Increasingly advocates of new diplomacy point to the global challenges that seem unmanageable by traditional means. Nowhere is this more apparent than in the diplomatic dialogue on environmental protection. For cosmopolitans such as Paul Harris,[17] as well as solidarists,[18] the challenges of the twenty-first century, typified by the rise to prominence of global environmental issues, underscores the need to move beyond statist diplomacy and law. Repeated failures to address urgent questions of climate change, resource depletion, pollution and the manifestly global impact of regional and local environmental challenges such as deforestation suggests that retreat to the classic techniques of Westphalian diplomacy will not be sufficient. Harris argues that 'the doctrine of international environmental justice that has emanated from Westphalian norms, discourse and thinking has taken the world politics of climate change in a direction that has been characterised by diplomatic delay [and] minimal (or no) action'.[19] His alternative approach urges a global rather than an international perspective on justice. His 'cosmopolitan corollary' is intended as 'a bridge across the divide between the nation-state system and the imperative of climate protection'.[20] Harris adopts a similar pattern of argument to Thomas Pogge to urge an ambitious cosmopolitan diplomacy that both takes account of the human rights of those suffering from the effects of climate change, the responsibility of the wealthy polluters and of the inability of traditional diplomacy to manage the problems associated with climate change. States represent both rich and poor and it is the rich, wherever they are found, that bear the responsibility for the vast majority of the pollution that leads to environmental degradation and the poor, even those in the most advanced societies, that are the innocent victims. Diplomacy, he argues, has to change to become sensitive to the cosmopolitan aims and objectives of climate change policy. In short, we need a diplomacy that can take account of individuals as bearers of rights and obligations rather than merely as citizens of states.[21] Treating climate change as a human rights issue is not just academic utopia. Olivier de Schutter, the UN Special Rapporteur on the right to food, has recently made a similar argument urging 'human rights courts and non-judicial human rights bodies to treat climate change as the immediate threat to human rights that it is'.[22] Here, then, universal values and global challenges underpin the normative desirability of a radical new diplomacy and the restraint of diplomatic freedom by the law. The pressures that led to omnilateralism urge us on to cosmopolitanism.

The second normative ideal inherent in the move to new diplomacy is particularly bound up with the legalisation of international politics. The growing emphasis on the normative importance of the rule of law has underpinned increasingly ambitious attempts to bring core elements of the Westphalian system to account. De Schutter's claim (above) is one example of the sort of demands being made. In effect, his claim seeks to bypass diplomatic efforts and constrain states through the application of human rights law. This tendency to will the replacement of diplomatic dialogue with judicial process is a highly controversial part of new diplomacy. The most ambitious example impinges on a quintessentially diplomatic endeavour: the cessation of violence and post-conflict peace-making. Since the international military tribunals at Nuremburg and Tokyo after the Second World War the desire to hold individuals (usually leading members of a regime) criminally accountable for atrocities committed in war has driven a challenge to the very idea of sovereign immunity and the ability of diplomats to negotiate impunity or amnesty in order to facilitate the cessation of violence or handover of power. This practice has matured from individual extradition hearings for former heads of state (Pinochet) to *ad hoc* military tribunals (Rwanda and the Former Yugoslavia), to the establishment of a permanent court with the ability to bring criminal charges (independent of the diplomatic processes of the UN) against an incumbent head of state (such as al-Bashir of Darfur) as well as to those who have negotiated exile (Taylor). Falk views the tension inherent in this process as one of the principal contemporary dramas in the pursuit of global justice. He is intuitively in support of putting an end to impunity, as acts such as genocide, war crimes or crimes against humanity cannot possibly be an official function of a head of state. Yet practical questions remain:

> The dynamics of global justice would benefit from expanded opportunities for prosecution and the denial of claims to immunity. But would the dynamics of peace be obstructed by undermining the reliability of impunity bargains struck in the past?

Would dictators hesitate to relinquish the reins of power knowing that they may be vulnerable to future prosecutions?[23]

These practical questions led diplomats such as Henry Kissinger (himself the subject of judicial and activist interest for his actions while in office) to warn of the risks of judicial tyranny and the use of the principle of universal jurisdiction as a means of settling political scores.[24] Yet, as we write, the Special Court for Sierra Leone has just delivered the first judgment on criminal allegations against a former head of state since Nuremburg and the momentum appears to be with the transformationalists (at least in this aspect of new diplomacy).

In order to gain purchase on these debates it is important that we first grasp the principal elements of the law relating to diplomatic immunities. One of the essential attributes of the sovereignty of a state is its power and authority over all persons, properties and events occurring within its territory. However, over the years states, on the basis of reciprocity, have recognised the need to grant immunity to certain persons and properties in their jurisdiction in order to facilitate diplomatic communications between states and international organisations. A crucial part of such immunities are sovereign (or state), diplomatic and consular immunities. The ICJ in the *Case Concerning the Arrest Warrant of 11 April 2000 (Democratic Republic of Congo v. Belgium)*, pointed out that 'in international law it is firmly established that, as also diplomatic and consular agents, certain holders of high-ranking office in a State, such as the Head of State, Head of Government and Minister for Foreign Affairs, enjoy immunities from jurisdiction in other States, both civil and criminal'.[25] Dixon explains the difference between these two types of immunities as follows:

> state or sovereign immunity . . . concerns the rights and privileges accorded to a state, its government, representatives and property within a national legal system . . . diplomatic and consular immunity . . . deals with the immunities enjoyed by official envoys of the foreign sovereign state and the duties owed to them by the 'host' state.[26]

To this end we now turn to an examination of the applicable rules of international law for sovereign and diplomatic immunities, as well as the immunities of international organisations.

Sovereign (or state) immunity

Sovereign immunity arose basically out of a tension between two important norms, namely, sovereign equality and the exclusive territorial jurisdiction of states.[27] It is a concept of international law whereby a court declines to adjudicate in both criminal and civil cases because a foreign sovereign, state or its agent is the defendant, or the subject matter of the proceedings (e.g., a ship) is linked to the exercise of sovereign or state governmental power.[28] It also includes immunity from enforcement of a judgment in a foreign court. Lord Browne-Wilkinson in the *R. v. Bow Street Magistrates, ex parte Pinochet (No. 3)* case pointed out that sovereign immunity:

> is a basic principle of international law that one sovereign state (the forum state) does not adjudicate on the conduct of a foreign state. The foreign state is entitled to procedural immunity from the processes of the forum state. This immunity extends to both criminal and civil liability.[29]

Initially, sovereign immunity was attached to a particular individual – a king, queen, sultan, emir – or his or her representatives. However, in the present day it attaches to an abstract entity – the state – and its representatives and government departments.[30] The international law on sovereign immunity has been developed mainly through customary international law by means of domestic case law and national legislation, such as the United States of America Foreign Sovereign Immunities Act 1976 and the United Kingdom State Immunity Act 1978. In addition, certain treaties have been adopted in this regard. Examples of such treaties include the Brussels Convention for the Unification of Certain Rules concerning the Immunities of Government Vessels 1926, and its subsequent Protocol adopted in 1934; the European Convention on State Immunity 1972; the Law of the Sea Convention (LOSC) 1982 (Article 32); and the United Nations Convention on Jurisdictional Immunities of States and their Property 2004, which is yet to come into force.

Immunity may be of two types: *ratione personae* (personal or status immunity), that which is attached to the person by reason of his or her office as an agent of the state; and *ratione materiae* (functional or official act immunity), that which is afforded to the nature of the act.[31]

Sovereign immunity must be distinguished from two other almost similar, but distinct, restraints on the exercise of jurisdiction of the national courts of states, namely, act of state and non-justiciability.[32] For doctrine of 'act of state', the national courts would decline to adjudicate on the acts of a foreign state in its own territory. In the nineteenth century, in the US case of *Underhill* v. *Hernandez*[33] the US Supreme Court, in the often quoted statement of Fuller CJ, explained the doctrine as follows:

> Every sovereign is bound to respect the independence of every other sovereign state, and the courts of one country will not sit in judgment on the acts of another done within its own territory. Redress of grievances by reason of such acts must be obtained through the means open to be availed of by sovereign powers as between themselves.[34]

In the English case of *Luther* v. *Sagor*,[35] the court declined, based on the act of state doctrine, the invitation by the plaintiff to declare as invalid and ignore an expropriatory decree relating to its assets by the newly established Soviet government. As far as the court was concerned to do so would be a serious breach of international comity. Warrington LJ, in this case, stated that it 'is well settled that the validity of the acts of an independent sovereign government in relation to property and persons within its jurisdiction cannot be questioned in the Courts of this country'.[36] However, it has since been established by the English courts that an exception to this doctrine is permitted if the act of state is contrary to public policy. For instance, in the cases of *Oppenheimer* v. *Cattermole*[37] and *Kuwait Airways Corp.* v. *Iraqi Airways Co. (No. 2)*,[38] the English courts made it clear that the act of state doctrine would not apply, on grounds of public policy, if it involves a contravention of fundamental human rights or is contrary to a fundamental and well-established rule of international law.

Non-justiciability, on the other hand, has been described as 'a doctrine of uncertain scope'.[39] It is a doctrine whereby the national courts decline to adjudicate on a matter because either it involves sensitive political questions, which the courts are of the view falls within the discretionary powers of either the executive or legislative arm of a foreign state, or it is a matter that should appropriately be settled in another forum, such as international settlement. Lord Wilberforce, referring to the doctrine of non-justiciability, declared in the English case of *Buttes Gas and Oil Co.* v. *Hammer (No. 3)* as follows:[40]

there exists in English law a general principle that the courts will not adjudicate upon the transactions of foreign sovereign States. Though I would prefer to avoid argument on terminology, it seems desirable to consider this principle, if existing, not as a variety of 'act of state' but one for judicial restraint or abstention.

The English courts have, for instance, held that they would not, based on non-justiciability, enquire into the making of war and peace and the disposition of the armed forces, which falls within the discretionary powers of the Crown (*R. v. Jones*),[41] whether a state has breached the terms of a treaty (*British Airways Board* v. *Laker Airways Ltd*),[42] and the creation of an international organisation via an unincorporated treaty by a group of states at the international plane (*Maclaine Watson* v. *Department of Trade and Industry*).[43] Similarly, the US courts, on grounds of non-justiciability. have declined to adjudicate on the US deployment of Cruise missiles to a base in the United Kingdom (*Greenham Women Against Cruise Missiles* v. *Reagan*).[44]

The maxim usually invoked as the rationale for sovereign immunity is *par in parem non habet imperium* (an equal has no authority over an equal). It has been argued that to make one sovereign entity subject to the legal process of another sovereign would be contrary to the horizontal nature of the international order, which has as an intrinsic part of it the principle of equality of states.[45] Apart from equality, sovereign immunity has also been justified based on the dignity and comity of states, as well as on the functionality of the agents of states when acting in a foreign state. In the early US Supreme Court case, *The Schooner Exchange* v. *McFaddon*,[46] where the plaintiff sought to take possession of a French naval ship, which in reality was the *Schooner Exchange*, an American ship owned by the plaintiff that had previously been seized by the French Government, the Supreme Court refused to exercise jurisdiction based on sovereign immunity. Marshall CJ, delivering the judgment of the Court, said:

> [The] full and absolute territorial jurisdiction being alike the attribute of every sovereign, and being incapable of conferring extra-territorial power, would not seem to contemplate foreign sovereigns nor their sovereign rights as its objects. One sovereign being in no respect amenable to another, and being bound by obligations of the highest character not to degrade the dignity of his nation, by placing himself or its sovereign rights within the jurisdiction of another, can be supposed to enter a foreign

territory only under an express license, or in the confidence that the immunities belonging to his independent sovereign station, though not expressly stipulated, are reserved by implication, and will be extended to him. This perfect equality and absolute independence of sovereigns, and this common interest impelling them to mutual intercourse, and an interchange of good offices with each other, have given rise to a class of cases in which every sovereign is understood to waive the exercise of a part of that compete exclusive territorial jurisdiction . . .

In the *Arrest Warrant* case (*Democratic Republic of Congo v. Belgium*), the ICJ emphasised the functional necessity basis of sovereign immunity. The Court in this case pointed out that:

the functions of a Minister for Foreign Affairs are such that, throughout the duration of his or her office, he or she when abroad enjoys full immunity from criminal jurisdiction and inviolability. That immunity and that inviolability protect the individual concerned against any act of authority of another State which would hinder him or her in the performance of his or her duties.[47]

The doctrine of sovereign immunity has also been justified on the basis of comity of nations.[48]

Some of the bases for jurisdiction have been discredited. For instance, Lauterpacht has notably argued that since domestic sovereigns are increasingly subject to the jurisdiction of their own courts (e.g., the UK Crown Proceedings Act 1947, which allows civil proceedings to be taken against the Crown), it should follow, if the basis of equality is relied upon, that foreign sovereigns should similarly be subject to the jurisdiction of such courts and not be entitled to immunity.[49] He pointed out further that 'the strained emanations of the notion of dignity are an archaic survival and that they cannot continue as a rational basis of immunity'.[50] With regard to the basis of comity, it is generally accepted that sovereign immunity is based on international law rather than on comity. In a recent decision the ICJ noted that 'both Parties agree that immunity is governed by international law and is not a mere matter of comity'.[51] On the other hand, with the decision of the ICJ in the *Arrest Warrant* case, it would appear that functional necessity still appears to be accepted as a tenable and cogent basis for sovereign immunity.[52] Fox points out that the idea of sovereign immunity is to enable the necessary officials of a state 'to carry out their public functions effectively and . . . to secure the orderly conduct of international relations'.[53]

At the outset the immunity a state and its agents enjoyed was absolute. Absolute immunity meant that the state, recognised by the forum government, and its officials would enjoy immunity from the jurisdiction of the domestic courts in all cases regardless of the circumstances. National cases such as *The Prins Frederik*,[54] *Mighel v. Sultan of Johore*,[55] *The Parlement Belge*,[56] *Porto Alexandre*,[57] *The Christina*[58] and *Krajina v. Tass Agency*[59] applied absolute immunity.

However, from the early twentieth century, with states increasingly engaging in trading and other commercial activities, especially with the emergence of socialist and developing states, many jurisdictions, with some notable exceptions such as China and Nigeria,[60] began to adopt the restrictive immunity approach. Cases such as *Philippine Admiral*,[61] *Trendtex v. Central Bank of Nigeria*[62] and *I Congreso del Partido*[63] have adopted this approach. Under this approach a distinction is made between governmental or sovereign acts (*acta jure imperii*) and commercial or sovereign acts (*acta jure gestionis*), with immunity enjoyed by the former, but not by the latter. Lord Wilberforce, in the *I Congreso del Partido* case,[64] explained the reason for the restrictive approach as follows:

> The relevant exception, or limitation, which has been engrafted on the principle of immunity of States, under the so-called restrictive theory, arises from the willingness of States to enter into commercial, or other private law, transaction with individuals. It appears to have two main foundations: (a) it is necessary in the interests of justice to individuals having transactions with States to allow them to bring such transactions before the courts; (b) to require a State to answer a claim based on such transactions does not involve a challenge or inquiry into any act of sovereignty or governmental act of that State. It is, in accepted phrases, neither a threat to the dignity of the State nor any interference with its sovereign functions.

This approach, however, raises contentious issues on how to make the distinction between *acta jure imperii* (governmental act) and *acta jure gestionis* (commercial act) in practice. Some have advocated the nature of the act test to make this distinction. Under this test an act that could be performed only by a government would by its nature be a governmental act that would enjoy immunity, while an act that could also be performed by a private citizen would be regarded as a commercial act that would not be entitled to immunity. For instance, a transaction involving the supply of goods would by its nature be a commercial act and, therefore, would not be able to enjoy immunity, while the enactment of legislation would be a governmental act and would be entitled to immunity. However, this is not always clear-cut. Would a commercial contract entered into by a sovereign for a public purpose be classified as a governmental act or a commercial one? For instance, will a contract for the supply of cement to a sovereign to build military barracks be regarded as a governmental or a commercial act? Consequently, others have argued that the appropriate test to determine whether or not an act is entitled to immunity should be the purpose test. This test advocates that if the purpose of the transaction is a sovereign public one, it would be entitled to immunity, but if the purpose is a private one, it would not. Thus, a transaction whether or not it is a commercial one for the purpose of building a military barracks would be governmental act entitled to immunity, while one for the purpose of building a new office block would arguably be a commercial act because an office block can also be put up by a private builder.[65] The purpose test distinction has been criticised because the so-called commercial transactions by states for whatever purpose are similarly intended to benefit the whole community, a public purpose.[66]

In some cases both the nature and purpose tests have been utilised simultaneously to make the distinction between *acta jure imperii* and *acta jure gestionis*. For instance, Article 2(2) of the UN Convention on Jurisdictional Immunities of States and their Property 2004 states:

> In determining whether a contract or transaction is a 'commercial transaction' . . . reference should be made primarily to the nature of the contract or transaction, but its purpose should also be taken into account if the parties to the contract or transaction have so agreed, or if, in the practice of the state of the forum, that purpose is relevant to determining the non-commercial character of the contract or transaction.

Some states, in trying to avoid the complexities of having to distinguish between *acta jure imperii* and *acta jure gestionis*, have resorted to listing in legislation which acts would not enjoy immunity. For instance, the UK State Immunity Act 1978, in section 3(3) lists a commercial transaction that would not enjoy immunity as follows:

any contract for the supply of goods or services, any loan or other transaction for the provision of finance and any guarantee or indemnity in respect of any such transaction or of any other financial obligation, and other transaction or activity (whether of a commercial, industrial, financial, professional or other similar character) into which a State enters or in which it engages otherwise than in the exercise of sovereign authority.

Sovereign immunity and violation of human rights

In recent times there has been interest in whether a sovereign would still enjoy immunity in respect of acts that are violations of human rights, especially those that could be regarded as *jus cogens* norms. The UK House of Lords in the *ex Parte Pinochet (No. 3)* case,[67] where a former head of state of Chile, Augusto Pinochet, sought to raise the procedural plea of sovereign immunity in respect of an application for his extradition for certain human rights violations that were gross crimes under international law, notably torture, which he committed during his tenure as head of state, held that he was not entitled to such immunity with respect to the acts of torture committed after the Torture Convention was transformed into UK domestic law.[68] Bianchi points out that the frequent references in the Pinochet case to the 'notions as *jus cogens*, obligations *erga omnes* and crimes of international law attests to the fact that the emerging notion of an international public order based on the primacy of certain values and common interests is making its way into the legal culture and common practice of municipal courts'.[69] This has led to a debate on whether the prohibition of torture and other gross human rights violations of a *jus cogens* character, which are in a superior position in the hierarchy of international law, should prevail over the norm of sovereign immunity, which is not *jus cogens* – the so-called normative hierarchy theory.[70] In the *Al-Adsani* v. *United Kingdom* case,[71] the majority decision of the European Court of Human Rights (ECtHR) held that while the prohibition of torture was clearly a norm of a *jus cogens* character there was no evidence that under international law a State was prevented from claiming immunity in respect of civil claims for alleged torture committed outside the forum state.[72] On the other hand, the minority Dissenting Opinion of this case upheld the normative hierarchy theory and held that the 'acceptance therefore of the *jus cogens* nature of the prohibition of torture entails that a State allegedly violating it cannot invoke hierarchically lower rules (in this case, those on State immunity) to avoid the consequences of the illegality of its actions'.[73] The majority decision of the ECtHR in the *Al-Adsani* case was followed by the UK House of Lords in *Jones v. Saudi Arabia*,[74] which held that the state of Saudi Arabia was immune from the jurisdiction of the court in respect of alleged acts of torture, and that such immunity was not affected by the normative hierarchy.[75] Lord Hoffmann in his decision in the *Jones* case pointed out that, '[t]o produce a conflict with state immunity, it is therefore necessary to show that the prohibition on torture [a *jus cogens* norm] has generated an ancillary procedural rule which, by way of exception to state immunity, entitles or perhaps requires states to assume civil jurisdiction over other states in cases in which torture is alleged'.[76] The ICJ in the *Arrest Warrant*[77] and *Jurisdictional Immunities of the State*[78] cases also refused to uphold the normative hierarchy argument. The Court in the *Arrest Warrant* case held that there was no rule of customary international law that recognised an exception to the immunity of incumbent foreign ministers because they are suspected of committing international crimes having a *jus cogens* character.[79] The Court, however, accepted that there were the following other exceptions to state immunity in respect of foreign ministers:

- they would not enjoy criminal immunity in their own states and therefore may be tried by their home courts;
- they cease to enjoy such immunity if their home state waives that immunity;
- if they cease to hold the office they would no longer enjoy immunity in respect of acts committed prior or subsequent to their period in office, as well as in respect of acts committed during that period of office in a private capacity;
- current or former foreign ministers would not enjoy immunity when they are brought before certain international criminal courts, for instance the ICTY, ICTR and ICC, which have jurisdiction over the crimes they are alleged to have committed.[80]

In the *Jurisdictional Immunities of the State* case, the ICJ took the view that there was no conflict between *jus cogens* norms and rule of state immunity, since they address different matters. The rule of state immunity was procedural and was merely to determine whether a forum court could exercise jurisdiction over a foreign state, while *jus cogens* rules deal with substantive matters.[81]

Diplomatic immunity

Diplomatic immunity may be traced back to ancient times when different societies in their diplomatic interaction with each other adopted the practice of granting certain immunities to representatives acting on behalf of their sovereign in a foreign territory.[82] With time states began to set up permanent missions to help to promote diplomatic relations with the host state, and customary international law rules then developed in respect of immunities that host states were to grant to diplomatic agents of the sending state, their diplomatic premises and diplomatic bags and other materials. According to the ICJ in the *Case concerning US Diplomatic and Consular Staff in Tehran (USA v. Iran)*, Merits:

> The rules of diplomatic law, in short, constitute a self-contained regime which, on the one hand, lays down the receiving State's obligations regarding the facilities, privileges and immunities to be accorded to diplomatic missions and, on the other foresees their possible abuse by members of the mission and specifies the means at the disposal of the receiving State to counter any such abuse.[83]

The ICJ in this case described the 'whole corpus of the international rules' of diplomatic and consular law as being of a 'fundamental character'.[84] However, it has been argued that though the Court tags the rules of diplomatic and consular laws as being of fundamental character there is no suggestion that these are *jus cogens* norms.[85] In the UK case of *Empson* v. *Smith*, Diplock LJ pointed out that it 'is not immunity from legal liability but immunity from suit'.[86]

The customary international law rules on diplomatic immunities and privileges have been generally codified by the Vienna Convention on Diplomatic Relations (VCDR) 1961, which entered into force on 24 April 1964 and as at 17 April 2013 had 188 parties.[87] In addition to codification, the VCDR is also progressive development of the law on diplomatic immunity.[88] This section will therefore rely mainly on this treaty in its discourse of diplomatic immunities.

The concept of diplomatic immunity is said to be based on three theories, namely, extraterritoriality, representational and functional necessity. Extraterritoriality argues that the embassy and the ambassador's residence in the receiving state should be considered as an extension of the territory of the sending state. Therefore, the diplomatic agents within such extraterritorial spaces in the receiving state should enjoy immunity and privileges on that basis. This theory has been discredited. For instance, Akehurst points out that the 'diplomatic premises are not extraterritorial; acts occurring there are regarded as taking place on the territory of the receiving State, not on that of the sending State'.[89] Representational theory, on the other hand, argues that diplomatic agents are the personal representatives of the sending state, and therefore should enjoy the immunities and privileges as representatives of a foreign state. While the functional necessity theory argues that such immunities and privileges are enjoyed by diplomats to enable them to perform their official functions efficiently and without interference by the host state. The VCDR endorses this theory in its preamble by stating, 'that the purpose of such privileges and immunities is not to benefit individuals but to ensure the efficient performance of the functions of diplomatic missions as representing States'.

The VCDR provides that the premises of the mission shall be inviolable and no agent of the receiving state may enter such premises without the permission of the head of mission. The mission premises, its furnishings and other properties thereon and the means of transportation of the mission are immune from search, requisition, attachment or execution (Article 22(1) and (3) VCDR). The premises of the mission are buildings or parts of buildings, as well as land ancillary to such buildings, irrespective of ownership, that are being used for the purposes of the mission, and this includes the residence of the head of mission (the ambassador, high commissioner, etc.). (Article 1 VCDR). Apart from the residence of the head of mission, the private residences of other diplomats are also inviolable (Article 30 VCDR). The VCDR imposes an obligation on the receiving state to protect the mission premises, the residence of the head of mission and other diplomats.[90] In the *Armed Activities on the Territory of the Congo (Democratic Republic of the Congo v. Uganda)*,[91] the ICJ held that the attacks on the Ugandan Embassy in Kinshasa, the capital of the DRC, by Congolese armed forces was a violation of the duty of the DRC under Article 22 of the VCDR.[92]

Recently, Julian Assange, the Wikileaks founder, seeking asylum took refuge in the Ecuadorian Embassy in London.[93] The issue had arisen as to whether the UK Government could strip the Ecuadorian Embassy of its immunity under the UK Diplomatic and Consular Premises Act 1987,[94] which states that a premises ceases to be diplomatic or consular premises if a state stops using it for the purposes of its mission or exclusively for the purposes of a consular post; or if the Secretary of State withdraws his or her acceptance or consent in relation to the premises (Article 1(3)). The debate here focuses on whether the UK Government could employ the provisions of the legislation to strip the Ecuadorian Embassy of its immunity so as to allow the police go in to arrest Assange. It must be noted that the legislation requires the Secretary of State to give or withdraw consent or withdraw acceptance of the premises as a diplomatic or consular premise only 'if he is satisfied that to do so is permissible under international law' (Article 1(4)). It is difficult to accept that the withdrawal of the immunity of the Ecuadorian Embassy because it granted asylum to Assange would be permissible under international law. Although the United Kingdom and most other states, unlike some Latin American states such as Ecuador, do not accept that customary international law permits an embassy to grant asylum,[95] the best the UK Government may do in this case is to refuse to allow Assange safe passage to leave the country and to arrest him immediately he leaves the Ecuadorian Embassy.[96]

The person of a diplomatic agent is inviolable and he or she is not liable to any form of arrest or detention. The receiving state has a duty to treat diplomatic agents with respect, and to take all appropriate steps to prevent any attack on the person, freedom or dignity of diplomatic agents (Article 29 VCDR).[97] Diplomatic agents have absolute immunity from criminal jurisdiction, and immunity from civil and administrative jurisdiction except actions in his or her private capacity in respect of private immovable property, succession and any professional or commercial activity (Article 31 VCDR). The members of the family of a diplomatic agent forming part of his or her household also enjoy the same privileges and immunities as the diplomatic agent if they are not nationals of the receiving state (Article 37 VCDR). Members of the administrative and technical staff, as well as members of their household, who are not nationals or permanent residents of the receiving state also enjoy the same privileges and immunities as the diplomatic agents. However, their immunity in respect of civil and administrative jurisdiction shall not extend to acts performed outside the course of their duties. Members of the service staff of the mission, on the other hand, who are not nationals of or permanently resident in the receiving state shall enjoy immunity in respect of acts performed in the course of their duties, and exemption from dues and taxes on the emoluments they receive by reason of their employment. Private servants of members of the mission, if they are not nationals of or permanently resident in the receiving state, shall be exempt from dues and taxes on the emoluments they receive by reason of their employment. In other respects, they may enjoy privileges and immunities only to the extent permitted by the receiving state. However, the VCDR requires the receiving state to exercise its jurisdiction over these persons only in such a manner as not to interfere unduly with the performance of the functions of the mission (Article 37). All these immunities and privileges are actually that of the sending state, which may waiver such if it chooses. Any such waiver must be express. The waiver of immunity from jurisdiction in the case of civil and administrative cases would necessarily amount to a waiver in respect of execution of judgment, except when a separate waiver is given for this (Article 32).

The VCDR provides that the receiving state shall permit and protect free communication on behalf of the diplomatic mission for all official purposes. Its official communication is inviolable, and the mission may use all appropriate means to communicate with the government, other missions and consulate of the sending state, including diplomatic couriers and messages in code or cipher. However, to install and use a wireless transmitter it has to obtain the consent of the receiving state (Article 27(1) and (2)). For correspondence using a diplomatic bag, the VCDR provides that the bag shall not be opened or detained and should contain only diplomatic documents or articles intended for official use. Packages constituting the diplomatic bag must bear visible external marks of their character (Article 27(3)). In the Umaru Dikko incident in 1984 a minister in the deposed Nigerian Government, who was wanted on charges of embezzlement of government funds by the military regime that took over power, was kidnapped, drugged and put in a large crate. The crate was accompanied to the airport by diplomats from the Nigerian High Commission in London to be loaded on an aircraft en route to Nigeria. However, due to suspicion about the contents of the crate custom officials at the airport opened it. The UK Government justified this on the ground that though the sender was the Nigerian High Commission, the crate was not a diplomatic bag as required by Article 27(3) of the VCDR because it lacked 'visible external marks of their character'. Further, the UK Foreign Secretary was of the view that even if the crate was a diplomatic bag the overriding duty to protect and preserve human life justified the opening of the crate.[98] Recently there have been concerns about diplomatic bags being used for non-diplomatic activities, such as drug trafficking, and whether a receiving state that has reasonable suspicion about the contents of a diplomatic bag could open it. The International Law Commission (ILC) of the General Assembly in its Draft Articles on

Status of the Diplomatic Courier and the Diplomatic Bag, which it adopted in 1989, proposed that if the competent authorities of receiving or transit state have strong reasons to believe that a diplomatic bag contains non-diplomatic items, then they may request the bag to be opened in their presence by an authorised representative of the sending state. If such request is refused by the sending state, the bag should be returned to its place of origin.[99] Further, in response to debates on whether the use of scanning equipment violates Article 27 of the VCDR, the ILC proposed in the Draft Articles that diplomatic bags should 'be exempt from examination directly or through electronic or other technical device'.[100] It is not clear if the use of sniffer dogs would be contrary to Article 27. It is argued that if examination using electronic or other technical devices is regarded as prohibited by Article 27, in the same vein the use of sniffer dogs should be regarded as a breach of the relevant Article.[101]

Although, there are various examples where there have been abuses of diplomatic immunity by states, generally most states actually comply with the provisions of this widely ratified treaty.[102]

The VCDR points out that all persons enjoying the immunities and privileges in the Convention are not exempt from obeying the laws of the receiving state, and therefore must respect the laws and regulations of the receiving state. They also have a duty not to interfere in the internal affairs of that state. The premises of the mission are not be used in any manner incompatible with the functions of the mission as laid down in the present Convention and other rules of international law (Article 41). What, then, is the remedy available to the receiving state if persons enjoying these immunities and privileges do not respect its laws and regulations? The VCDR allows the receiving state to declare any diplomatic agent as *persona non grata* or any other staff of the mission as unacceptable by notifying the sending state. It may do this at any time without providing any explanation for its action (Article 9).

Immunity of international organisations

According to Shaw the position of customary international law rules in relation to immunities of international organisations is not very clear.[103] With international organisations now playing an important role in international society, and most of them having international legal personality, generally their constituent treaties provides that they shall enjoy those privileges and immunities that are necessary for the fulfilment of their purposes or functions. For instance, the UN Charter provides that the: 'Organization shall enjoy in the territory of each of its Members such privileges and immunities as are necessary for the fulfilment of its purposes' (Article 105(1)). Also, the Charter provides that 'the representatives of the members of the UN and officials of the organisation shall also enjoy such privileges and immunities that are necessary for the independent exercise of their functions in connexion with the Organisation' (Article 105(2)). The General Convention on the Privileges and Immunities of the United Nations 1946, usually referred to as the 'General Convention', was adopted again by the General Assembly and came into force on 17 September 1946. It provides the various privileges and immunities to be enjoyed by the UN and its personnel. Similarly, the Convention on the Privileges and Immunities of the Specialized Agencies 1947 was adopted again by the General Assembly and entered into force on 2 December 1948. The latter Convention provides for the different privileges and immunities to be enjoyed by the UN specialised agencies and their personnel, and its provisions are generally the same as those in the General Convention.

The ICJ in its Advisory Opinion on the *Applicability of Article VI, Section 22, of the Convention on the Privileges and Immunities of the United Nations*,[104] pointed out that privileges and immunities under this Convention could be enjoyed by special rapporteurs of UN Sub-Commission. It stated as follows:

> [this] Convention is applicable to persons (other than United Nations officials) to whom a mission has been entrusted by the Organization and who are therefore entitled to enjoy the privileges and immunities provided for in this Section with a view to the independent exercise of their functions. During the whole period of such missions, experts enjoy these functional privileges and immunities whether or not they travel. They may be invoked as against the State of nationality or of residence unless a reservation to Section 22 of the General Convention has been validly made by that State.[105]

Similarly, in the *Difference Relating to Immunity from Legal Process of a Special Rapporteur of the Commission on Human Rights*,[106] the ICJ was of the view that the immunities and privileges of the

General Convention was applicable to the Special Rapporteur of the Commission on Human Rights on the Independence of Judges and Lawyers.

Generally, most international organisations enter into bilateral agreements with states where their headquarters are located (the so-called Headquarters Agreement), and these agreements usually also provide for the state to afford various privileges and immunities for the organisation and its personnel. For instance, the UN Headquarters Agreement makes provision for persons who are resident representatives of member states and of specialised agencies to enjoy privileges and immunities (Article 15).[107]

Diplomacy and justice

Understanding these broad contours of new diplomacy brings us back to the concern raised by Simpson that a legalised diplomacy has an uneasy relationship with international law. The law at once wishes to restrain the diplomatic dialogue by describing the boundaries of acceptable state behaviour and enables states to stand apart from innovations such as the ICC or sanctions outcomes that fail to address key injustices (such as poverty or the harm that follows from environmental degradation). Simpson's conclusion captures this perfectly:

> International diplomacy is unimaginable without international law. The principles that structure international politics (sovereignty, immunity, territory), the institutional arrangements that facilitate it (the United Nations, international treaty conferences, regional organisation) and the norms that regulate it (prohibiting force, humanising war, organising trade) have become an indispensable part of diplomacy's repertoire. It is not clear whether the gains (a common tradition of argument, a language of critique and transformation, an association with fairness or openness in decision-making) outweigh the losses (a technocratic detachment from the conditions of life, the occlusion of redistributive outcomes, the finessing of hegemonic desire, a culture of expertise).[108]

The lack of clarity that Simpson finds in new diplomacy and the reason why sceptics, pluralists and transformationalists find evidential support for their viewpoint is that the juxtaposition of new and traditional diplomacy appears to rest on a clash of values. There is some truth to this, but if we begin to explore the normative basis of diplomacy and think critically about the relative authority of these competing claims it is possible to gain some purchase on the questions of justice and diplomacy.

New diplomacy, the English School and global justice

New diplomacy both exists side by side with traditional diplomacy and challenges it at a normative level. How, then, do we engage with the fundamental normative issues at the heart of contemporary diplomacy? The English School tradition has dedicated more time than most to the study of diplomacy. It is also a school of thought that is driven by the ever-present tensions between tradition and transformation or between pluralism and solidarism. There is an observable shift in the focus of many English School theorists from analysis of the relationship between realist and rationalist approaches to international relations to the debates between rationalists and revolutionists (in Wight's terminology), or from realist and pluralist to pluralist and solidarist positions. While this shift signals progress (or at least change) in diplomatic practice, there is no urgent drive to overcome this normative tension at the heart of global politics. Rather, the project is to capture something of the explanatory force that understanding of this normative tension lends to the study of international affairs. *Diplomatic Investigations* (1966), edited by Herbert Butterfield and Martin Wight, represents the beginning of this tradition of IR thinking, and it is a preoccupation that continued in English School classics, such as Adam Watson's *Diplomacy: The Dialogue Between States* (1989), and in the work of contemporary contributors, such as Christian Reus-Smit (*The Moral Purpose of the State*, 1999) or Paul Sharp (*Diplomatic Theory of International Relations*, 2009).[109] The work in this tradition is not simply an historical overview of diplomatic practice from the ancient world to the present. Rather, it began as a conscious attempt to understand diplomacy from the perspective of the practitioner. Wight argued that, unlike political theory with its established canon of great texts, there was no international theory. This was the case because, while political theory with its focus on politics within the state may have been an appropriate context in which to think about justice, international relations was the realm of 'recurrence and repetition' and as such had not produced a classic literature.[110] The raw material for the scholars of the English School was thus 'the speeches, dispatches, memoirs and essays of statesman and diplomats'.[111] Wight's own project was to show how the underlying rationalism of diplomacy captured the nature of international society more fully than the realists allowed. However, his position, the focus on the recurrence and repetition of diplomatic practice, the claim that there is no tradition of reflection on international affairs and the associated idea that justice is therefore absent from the analysis has been challenged both from within and from outside the English School.[112] Nevertheless, the English School approach to the historical evolution of diplomacy in the context of the development of international society enables us to understand the nature of the relationship between contemporary international law and much contemporary diplomacy, and between the diplomatic pursuit of order and of justice.[113] Diplomacy is the art of the possible, a practical and political dialogue where compromise for the sake of consensus or peace is highly valued. It is also, like law, a professional discourse. The choice to focus on the reflection of diplomats has obvious merits. It also has challenges. Practitioners find themselves bound by the rules of a practice and internalise its objectives in a way observers (scholars or social critics) do not. This does not mean that the perspective of those outside the practice is any more or any less problematic. Marti Koskenniemi suggests that any perspective (the judge, the lawyer-diplomat, the activist or the academic) is fraught with tensions between commitment and cynicism, between engagement and critical distance, between responsibility to the practice or to sociological or scientific objectivity.[114]

Nevertheless, arguing that we must restrict ourselves to the perspective of practitioners can commit us to problem-solving rather than to critical theory (see above). Wight's position has also been challenged by those who deny that there is no tradition of reflection on international affairs (equivalent to the canonical literature of political thought that we can trace from the ancient world).[115] Not only is there an historically and philosophically rich literature, but within that literature normative questions are central. More recent additions to the English School literature, particularly those that chart the rise of solidarist or cosmopolitan principles in the aftermath of the Cold War, cross the traditional English School approach with contemporary social and political theory and offer us a way into the normative questions that arise in the context of diplomatic affairs. These questions confront the perspective of the diplomat arguing that the normative development of international society, embodied in law and responding to contemporary political challenges, requires that traditional diplomacy cedes ground to, or comes to accommodate, universal principles of justice. Many studies of diplomacy downplay the role of normative claims. If we search for the reason behind this fact we quickly arrive at the key issue. Diplomatic theory and practice emphasises fundamental separateness of actors. Pluralism and separateness sit particularly uneasily with questions of justice and morality, and exploring the relationship between these ideas and the constitutive structures of international society is important if we are to gain some purchase on the critical questions of justice and injustice that revolve around diplomatic practice in the twenty-first century. If Wight and others in the earlier iterations of English School scholarship were concerned with the tensions between the pluralist and the realist understandings of the anarchical society, then contemporary scholars in this tradition are drawn to the tensions between pluralist and solidarist readings. This later concern, typified in Nicholas Wheeler's work on humanitarian intervention (see Chapter Seven) and Reus-Smit's work on international law and international society, draws on the evolution of humanitarian and human rights concerns within international society that sit uneasily with traditional understandings of the role of diplomacy.

The instrumental importance of information gathering and exchange and unfettered negotiation means that diplomacy appears as a constant throughout the history of international relations. But the means of diplomacy and the agents that are represented have evolved over time so that the diplomacy of the ancient world bears only a superficial resemblance to that of the contemporary era. This is not to suggest that there is no connecting thread between the envoys of the Pharaohs to the Hittites in the fourth century BC and the arts of contemporary diplomacy.[116] However, while it is important to focus on the concept of diplomacy as relations of separateness,[117] it is also important to historicise the idea of international society in which diplomatic relations take place. Indeed, we want to suggest that the abiding feature of diplomatic exchange (the dialogue between separate agents) exhibits significant normative change throughout history. For students of the diplomatic tradition the essential condition of diplomacy is a dialogue between independent states.[118] This basic fact can be viewed in a number of ways. For Sharp, the existence of conditions of separateness takes a particular form in the consciousness of diplomats:

> The common terms of reference for how diplomats – as diplomats – see the world are the mutually constitutive ideas of conditions and relations of separateness ... they encounter a plural world in which people and peoples believe themselves to be living in conditions of separateness. They encounter this world from the positions they occupy between these people and peoples ... it is the conditions of separateness that provide the distinctive site or space from which diplomats see the world, and from which a diplomatic tradition of international thought emerges to make its own distinctive sense of the resulting relations.[119]

For Sharp, this separateness, the reality of the daily lives of diplomats, is an uncomfortable feature of international politics for those outside the profession. This is particularly true of Europeans in the post-war world, who tend to see 'other Europeans, and possibly all foreigners seen as humanity as a whole' as 'less strange and less separate' than before.[120] It is also true of IR scholars, who view separateness as a problem,[121] viewing the consequences of separateness in highly moralised terms such as 'oppressing, dominating, enslaving and exterminating' the other.[122] For Sharp, this accounts for the uneasiness that IR theory has with diplomacy, but, he insists, diplomacy is about keeping relations going regardless. The form that relations of separateness take are therefore interesting only insofar as it gives rise to different kinds of relations that need to be managed, and this is what gives his diplomatic theory of international relations its distinctive (pluralist) tenor. Sharp is interested in the approach to international relations that stems from adopting this specific perspective. In this he is keeping faith with Wight's account of the proper subject matter of international theory. However, when we think about the way that separateness has come to be viewed as a problem from outside the diplomatic profession, it seems relevant to ask more questions. Who, for example, counts as outside the profession? Many diplomats are lawyers, others have legal training and all are advised by lawyers. Both Simpson and Koskenniemi are clear that the professional logic of the international lawyer is itself uneasy with the tension between order and justice that characterises legalised diplomatic practice in the contemporary period.[123] We also need to consider the nature of the fundamental institutions of contemporary international society. Is it not the case that the institutions created to mediate the specific relations of separateness in the modern period have at their heart constitutional structures that generate precisely that sense of uneasiness that Sharp describes?

Relations of separateness change over time. This is true over the vast sweep of historical development each scholar addresses, but the crucial change, for our purposes, can be thought of as the globalisation of diplomacy in the twentieth century. It was not until the twentieth century that the modern European state system became a truly global order. Until this point the Ottoman caliphate, the Chinese empire, Imperial Japan and the Russia empire were largely independent. Successive military defeats, the growing economic power of the newly industrialised West, colonialism and (ironically perhaps) anti-colonial nationalism led to the development of a global international system ordered along Wesphalian (European) lines.[124] The universalisation of the Westphalian system has both pluralist and solidarist connotations. Watson (whose work forms an important inspiration for Sharp) argues that the nature of contemporary (universal) diplomacy means that the cultural and historical identity of the society of states that provided the European diplomatic system with the background context for the social practice as a whole has been eroded. Having expanded beyond its 'cultural cradle' the system had to adopt new conventions and rules.[125] The development of the UN as an omnilateral organisation is, of course, a core innovation but, Watson claims, while the organisation has been successful in fostering diplomatic dialogue on technical issues, cooperation becomes more problematic when matters turn to more political or normative issues.[126] Because global institutions are a response to cultural pluralism (a feature of international society that grows stronger as newer members of the system gain confidence and power within it – or as Western influence on the organisation diminishes) Watson argues that problems of justice are intractable and subject to the pervasive pluralism of diplomacy. Justice must wait on consensus or else become an enemy of peace. While standards of justice, such as human rights, are important, they are 'inadequate for the resolution of international conflict'. Here diplomacy indicates the limits of the possible (for law and justice). We need to understand that 'diplomatic activity does not merely operate in favour of securing the observance of new standards of justice. States are also usually concerned with peace, and always with independence.'[127] Watson finds a deep normative pluralism between and within states. While states have mechanisms to overcome or at least manage such pluralism, the international community does not. Its tools are dialogue, war and peer pressure, and diplomacy is, in Nardin's terms, a practical rather than a purposive association (see above, p. 115). Nevertheless, when exploring the character of multilateral diplomacy at the UN, Watson acknowledges that 'the moral authority of international society has some effect'. In particular, he describes the vehicle for this effect as the diplomacy of judgement before the conscience of mankind, and gives the fall of the Apartheid regime in South Africa as well as anti-colonialism and the suppression of the slave trade as examples.[128] The claim that 'ideas of justice gradually affect and modify *international legitimacy*'[129] does not fit particularly well with a starkly pluralist account of international society as a practical association. Although his insight that new ideas of justice usually fare poorly against established conceptions of international legitimacy is important, the thought that ideas of justice shape the prevailing understanding of legitimacy and that this changes over time also suggests an important line of enquiry.

The set of questions identified by Watson and Sharp are taken up fully by Reus-Smit. Reus-Smit is critical of the ways in which pluralists treat multilateralism in the contemporary era. In *The Moral Purpose of the State*, Reus-Smit enhances the English School account of the evolution of international society by applying aspects of constructivist social theory. The results add much to both traditions.[130] Against the English School pluralists he argues that international society is a purposive rather than practical association that demonstrates significant change over time. In response to constructivist accounts of the constitutive basis of this association he draws upon the richer historical and moral sensitivity of the English School.[131] In arguing that the English School should take the social ontology of international society more seriously, Reus-Smit is really pushing scholars like Sharp and Watson to ask deeper questions about the ideas of justice that sanction certain forms of diplomacy and lead to the different responses to international challenges over time. In urging the constructivists to adopt a more detailed or nuanced approach to history he is asking that they recognise that sovereignty, while recognisable in international societies across time, is itself informed by constitutional structures (ensembles of metavalues) that differ significantly across time.[132] This approach recognises that contemporary international society is a hybrid society, being both the product of European hegemony and post-war multiculturalism, but argues that if we focus on the constitutional structures we come to a better understanding of the fundamental institutions and the higher order values that give them meaning and prescribe action.[133]

In Chapter Two we introduced Reus-Smit's account of the constitutive structure of international society (see p. 74, above). Building on this, Reus-Smit argues that changes to constitutional structures help us to understand changes in fundamental institutions over time.

Constitutional structures incorporate three normative components. Reus-Smit offers the following analysis, which he demonstrates with a broad historical analysis of societies of states from Ancient Greece, Renaissance Italy, absolutist Europe and the modern universal state system:

> Hegemonic beliefs about the moral purpose of the state represent the core of this normative complex, providing the justificatory foundations for the organizing principle of sovereignty, and a systemic norm of procedural justice ... the prevailing norm of procedural justice shapes institutional design and action, defining institutional rationality in a distinctive way leading states to adopt certain institutional practices and not others.[134]

Constitutional structures define sovereign meta-narratives, so that while sovereignty (as a claim to legitimate separateness) is found throughout the period, the practice of diplomacy is culturally and historically distinct. In fact, it is these differences more than the pervasive fact of separateness that help us to understand diplomacy. Throughout history changes in the dominant or hegemonic conception of the moral purpose of the state underwrites changes to the organising principle of sovereignty, the systemic norms of procedural justice and, therefore, the fundamental institutions of international society. Reus-Smit traces these patterns from the *poleis* of Ancient Greece to the modern society of states. Here we focus on the move from old diplomacy to multilateralism that defines the contemporary period.

One of the founding myths of IR is that the modern state system began in 1648 after the Peace of Westphalia. While there is some merit to this claim,[135] it gets certain key normative features of international affairs out of focus. The states that emerged from the Thirty Years War were not modern states. They were absolutist and relied on a 'pre-modern set of Christian and dynastic constitutional values', including the preservation of a divinely ordered social order.[136] These values shape the development of natural law and 'old diplomacy', and find expression in the norms of dynastic sovereignty and authoritative procedural justice. In this period of history standards of right and wrong were determined by God or kings who ruled by divine right.[137] The condition of separateness, or the character of sovereignty, in this period is very distinctive. The Early Modern period saw the spread of social and political revolution throughout Europe and in the New World. The Reformation, the English Civil War and the French and

245

American revolutions all represent fundamental challenges to the norms that structure both domestic and international affairs in absolutist Europe. The challenge to the idea of the divine right of kings or to the hierarchical relationship between citizens, the clergy and God was underwritten by a new commitment to individualism, and over time these fundamental challenges were to alter the nature of politics and international affairs.[138] The revolutions of the seventeenth and eighteenth centuries bred 'a radically different social ontology' that, by the end of the nineteenth century, provided the normative basis for truly modern or new diplomacy. Reus-Smit characterises the fundamental normative shift as the move from holism to individualism arguing that:

> The moral purpose of the modern state lies in the cultivation of a social, economic and political order that enables individuals to engage in the self-directed pursuit of their 'interests'.[139]

With the source of sovereignty now invested in the people, the authoritative norm of procedural justice that characterised early modernity developed into a legislative norm of procedural justice. Here the core values are (like 'new' diplomacy) inclusivity and accountability: that those subject to the rules have a right to define them and must be accountable to them rather than to the absolute authority of a divinely appointed sovereign. This hallmark of modern political thought provides the constitutional metavalues that lead to the development of the fundamental institutions of international society. Here natural law is replaced by contractual law (and an emerging system of international courts) and old diplomacy is supplemented by multilateralism.[140] Yet, as Watson noted, this development was largely European. The institutions of new diplomacy may have been universalised, but how far can we argue that the underlying metavalues have also gone global in a hybrid multicultural world? Here we need to bear in mind the hegemonic nature of social values. Citing Bull's and Watson's account of *The Expansion of International Society*, Reus-Smit shows that:

> The practical imperatives of coexistence under conditions of high interdependence have nevertheless encouraged [all] states to employ, and even further, existing 'Western' institutional practices . . . 'a striking feature of the global international society of today is the extent to which the states of Asia and Africa have

embraced such basic elements of European international society as the sovereign state, the rule of international law, the procedures and conventions of diplomacy and international organization'. In one sense, therefore, modern international society is indeed a practical association, but in an equally important sense, a deep structural sense, it is informed by the institutional and organizational values of the constitutively prior European (now Western) gemeinschaft society.[141]

There is, of course, something quite ironic about recognising the hegemonic influence of a value system that abhors hegemony. But this is where the sense of unease that Sharp describes and where the tension between the notion of the civilising influence of omnilateralism and the enduring will to independence that Watson articulates stem from. However, this tension is not a clash of systemic ideas between a Westphalian and post-Westphalian world order. We must, Reus-Smit argues, distinguish between purposive change and configurative change (or the end of sovereignty). The questions that new diplomacy pose are not about the end of sovereignty or the reconfiguration of international society, they are about normative or ideational change. Therefore, the maintenance of relations of separateness does not deny the emergence of universal values and nor should the emergence of cosmopolitan or solidarist policy programmes necessarily undermine sovereignty or diplomacy.

Reus-Smit's sociology of the moral community is intended as a contribution to critical theory.[142] It has no *a priori* commitment to any particular conception of the good life, but seeks the normative authority of socially sanctioned understandings of legitimate agency and behaviour. It recognises that pluralist and solidarist claims are both attempts to solve cooperation problems in the context of the normative structure of international society. It nevertheless enables a critical perspective on several sets of normative claims. In particular, it helps us to think about the shortcomings of Morganthau's claims that new diplomacy represents a utopian rejection of the permanent nature of international politics. There is, after all, no sense to the thought that states have natural and permanent interests and, read sixty-four years on from publication, Morgenthau's nostalgia for a world of aristocratic and plenipotentiary diplomats answerable only to their sovereign and not to international community values such as human rights, seems unjustifiable. At the other extreme, it leads Reus-Smit to challenge Buchanan's claim that human rights concerns should legitimately lead to the bypassing of the UN and to the establishment of a league of democracies (see Chapter Four). Human rights claims ought not to be divorced from the multilateral fora and consent-based legislative principles that are the fundamental institutions of contemporary international society.[143] This is a strong normative claim. Both Buchanan and Reus-Smit pick up on what Reus-Smit calls 'the progressive cosmopolitanisation of international law'.[144] Yet in the face of Great Power intransigence Buchanan urges the creation of a league of democracies that would take decisions on, among other things, the use of force as a response to gross humanitarian atrocities. Buchanan's rejection of what Reus-Smit calls the equalitarian regime that gives institutional expression to the constitutional value of multilateralism, bypasses the diplomatic process that is the only way to grant legitimacy to something as radical as overcoming the general prohibition on the use of force to further humanitarian or human rights causes. The same is likely to be true of any demand to use human rights courts and institutions to police poverty or environmental challenges. In both cases the emergent normative claims are challenging core constitutive ideas. Buchanan's argument privileges the role of human rights over multilateralism and the prohibition on the use of force. While Reus-Smit only describes multilateralism as a constitutional structure, the *jus cogens* nature of Article 2(4) of the UN Charter is a central element of multilateralism as constituted in the post-war world. The claims of Pogge or de Schutter also challenge constitutional structures. Pogge's account of poverty as a gross violation of human rights relies on his institutional cosmopolitanism (see Chapter Five). His argument, which has significant critical impact, relies at heart on the moral claim that human rights (conceived of in moral terms) are more important than any other aspect of international law, including multilateral institutions: that they are the ultimate test of the justice or injustice of institutions. This is captured in the provocative image of diplomats as 'hunger's willing executioners', but Pogge admits that 'it will never be taken seriously in the developed world'.[145] Similarly, the radical claims of the environmental cosmopolitans challenge the dominant norms of economic, scientific, industrial and technological progress that underpin the global economy.[146]

If poverty and environmental degradation are significant moral and social problems (and we think they are), and if they can be usefully thought of in terms of (moral) human rights failings (and we think they can), is this not a rather pessimistic position? In fact, it does not mean that the purposive change that is clearly an essential part of contemporary practice has no effect. Watson's depiction of the UN as symbolic of the conscience of mankind or as a counterpoint to the power of states has been strengthened by the unprecedented period of political ambition and institution-building that took place after the fall of the Berlin Wall. Questions of humanitarian intervention, poverty reduction and environmental policy are now clearly questions of justice framed in universalist normative terms and competing (quite successfully) in institutional terms with other aspects of the multilateral project. Normative debates are intrinsically related to the social, political and institutional framework in which they arise and through which shared solutions must be found. The critical power of the claims of the cosmopolitans is drawn, in part, from the authority of the virtues of humanitarianism, human rights and universalism within contemporary international society. But the institutional solutions demanded are often significantly divorced from the social fabric of international society. It is just as problematic to prescribe the sort of hierarchical solutions that the league of democracies represents as it is to deny the moral import of poverty or humanitarian atrocity, or the importance of acting to excise such injustice. Watson articulates the moral responsibility of actors in terms of *raison de système*. This does not amount to a reification of the diplomatic process (although the commitments to its constitutive values are crucial). The power of the cosmopolitan or solidarist argument has to link back to the requirement that justice claims are put before the 'conscience of mankind' and negotiated through diplomatic dialogue that is now linked with the purposive power of international law. Legalised diplomacy, however, is more favourable ground for the ideas of justice and the criticisms of injustice that underpin the cosmopolitan position, but there is a very delicate relationship between law as an enabler of power and law as a restraint on power. That is why critical and diplomatic dialogue have to remain a constant feature of the contemporary international legal order.

Notes

1 Simpson, G., 'International Law in Diplomatic History', in J. Crawford and M. Koskenniemi (eds), *The Cambridge Companion to International Law*, Cambridge: Cambridge University Press, 2012, pp. 26–9.
2 Watson, A., *Diplomacy: The Dialogue Between States*, London: Routledge, 1982, p. 42.
3 Pogge, T., '"Assisting" the Global Poor', in T. Pogge and K. Horton

(eds), *Global Ethics: Seminal Essays*, St Paul, MN: Paragon, 2008, p. 551.
4 Best, G., 'Peace Conferences and the Century Of Total War: The 1899 Hague Conference and What Came After', *International Affairs*, 75(3) (1999): 619–34, at p. 623.
5 Morgenthau, *Politics Among Nations*, p. 546.
6 Morgenthau, *Politics Among Nations*, p. 553.
7 Morgenthau, *Politics Among Nations*, p. 552.
8 Morgenthau, *Politics Among Nations*, p. 556.
9 Morgenthau, *Politics Among Nations*, p. 558.
10 Watson, *Diplomacy*, p. 7.
11 Falk, R., 'What Comes after Westphalia: The Democratic Challenge', *Widener Law Review*, 13 (2007): 243–54, at p. 251.
12 Falk, 'What Comes after Westphalia', p. 244.
13 Falk, 'What Comes after Westphalia', p. 251.
14 Anderson, K., 'The Ottawa Convention Banning Landmines, the Role of International Non-governmental Organizations and the Idea of International Civil Society', *European Journal of International Law*, 11(1) (2000): 91–120.
15 Watson, *Diplomacy*, p. 155.
16 Watson, *Diplomacy*, p. 156.
17 Harris, P.. *World Ethics and Climate Change: From International to Global Justice*, Edinburgh: Edinburgh University Press, 2010.
18 Falk, R., 'The Global Environment and International Law: Challenge and Response', *University of Kansas Law Review*, 23 (1974): 385; Falk, R., *Human Rights Horizons: The Pursuit of Justice in a Globalizing World*, London: Routledge, 2000; Hurrell, A. and Kingbury, B. (eds), *The International Politics of the Environment*, Oxford: Oxford University Press, 1992; Hurrell, *On Global Order*.
19 Harris, *World Ethics and Climate Change*, p. 5.
20 Harris, *World Ethics and Climate Change*, p. 164.
21 Harris, *World Ethics and Climate Change*, ch. 7.
22 Schutter, O. de, 'Human Rights and the Post-Carbon Economy', Oxford Amnesty lecture, 2012.
23 Falk, *Human Rights Horizons*, p. 26.
24 Kissinger, H., 'The Pitfalls of Universal Jurisdiction', *Foreign Affairs*, 80(4) (2001): 86–96.
25 [2002] ICJ Rep. 3, para. 51.
26 Dixon, *International Law*, p. 174.
27 Caplan, L., 'State Immunity, Human Rights and *Jus Cogens*: A Critique of the Normative Hierarchy Theory', *American Journal of International Law*, 97(4) (2003): 741–81, at p. 745.
28 Fox, H., *The Law of State Immunity*, Oxford: Oxford University Press, 2002, p. 14.

29 [2000] 1 A.C. 147, at p. 201.
30 Shaw, *International Law*, 6th edn, pp. 697–8.
31 Akande, D. and Shah, S., 'Immunities of State Officials, International Crimes and Foreign Domestic Courts', *European Journal of International Law*, 21(4) (2010): 815–52; Akande, D. and Shah, S., 'Immunities of State Officials, International Crimes and Foreign Domestic Courts: A Rejoinder to Alexander Orakhelashvili', *European Journal of International Law*, 22(3) (2011): 857–61.
32 Fox, H., 'International Law and Restraints on the Exercise of Jurisdiction by National Courts of States', in M. Evans (ed.), *International Law*, 2nd edn, Oxford: Oxford University Press, 2006, pp. 361–92.
33 168 US 250 (1897). See Burley, A. M., 'Law among Liberal States: Liberal Internationalism and the Act of State Doctrine', *Columbia Law Review*, 92 (1992): 1907–96; Patterson, A., 'Act of State Doctrine is Alive and Well: Why Critics of the Doctrine are Wrong', *University of California Davis Journal of International Law and Policy*, 15 (2008): 111–55.
34 168 US 250 at 252 (1897).
35 [1921] 3 K.B. 532 (CA).
36 [1921] 3 K.B. 532, at p. 549 (CA).
37 [1976] A.C. 249.
38 [1995] 1 W.L.R. 1147.
39 Fox, 'International Law and Restraints on the Exercise of Jurisdiction by National Courts of States', p. 384.
40 [1982] A.C. 888, at p. 931.
41 [2006] U.K.H.L. 116, at para. 65.
42 [1985] A.C. 58, at pp. 85–6.
43 [1989] 3 All E.R. 523, at p. 544.
44 [1984] 99 I.L.R. 44.
45 Sornarajah, M., 'Problems in Applying the Restrictive Theory of Sovereign Immunity', *International and Comparative Law Quarterly*, 31(4) (1982): 661–85, at p. 664.
46 7 Cranch 116 (1812) US Supreme Court.
47 [2002] ICJ Rep. 3, para. 54.
48 Damrosch, L., 'Changing the International Law of Sovereign Immunity through National Decisions', *Vanderbilt Journal of Transnational Law*, 44 (2011): 1185–200, at pp. 1184–9.
49 Lauterpacht, H., *International Law: Collected Papers*, vol. 3, Cambridge: Cambridge University Press, 1977, pp. 331–6.
50 Lauterpacht, *International Law: Collected Papers*, p. 327.
51 See *Jurisdictional Immunities of the State (Germany v. Italy, Greece Intervening)*, para. 53, available at: http://www.icj-cij.org/docket/index.php?p1=3&p2=3. See review of this case by Orakhelashvili, A., 'Jurisdictional Immunities of the State (Germany v. Italy, Greece

Intervening),' *American Journal of International Law*, 106(3) (2012): 609–16. See also Damrosch, 'Changing the International Law of Sovereign Immunity through National Decisions', pp. 1184–9,
52 [2002] ICJ Rep. 3, para. 54.
53 Fox, *The Law of State Immunity*, p. 1.
54 (1820) 2 Dods. 451.
55 (1894) 1 Q.B. 149.
56 (1879–90)5 Prob. Div. 197 (CA).
57 (1920) P. 30.
58 [1938] A.C. 485.
59 [1949] 2 All E.R. 274.
60 See Qi, D., 'State Immunity, China and its Shifting Position', *Chinese Journal of International Law*, 7(2) (2008): 307–37; Egede, E., 'The Nigerian Territorial Waters and the 1982 Law of the Sea Convention', *International Journal of Marine and Coastal Law*, 19(2) (2004): 151, at pp. 174–5.
61 [1976] 2 W.L.R. 214.
62 [1977] Q.B. 529.
63 [1983] 1 A.C. 244.
64 [1983] 1 A.C. 244, at p. 260.
65 Dixon, *International Law*, 6th edn, pp. 180–2.
66 Sornarajah, 'Problems in Applying the Restrictive Theory of Sovereign Immunity', p. 669.
67 (1999) 2 All E.R. 97.
68 Fox, H., 'The Pinochet Case (No. 3)', *International and Comparative Law Quarterly*, 48(3) (1999): 687–702; Byers, M., 'The Law and Politics of the Pinochet Case', *Duke Journal of Comparative & International Law*, 10 (1999/2000): 415–41.
69 Bianchi, A., 'Immunity versus Human Rights: The Pinochet Case', *European Journal of International Law*, 10(2) (1999): 237, at p. 248.
70 Akande and Shah, 'Immunities of State Officials', pp. 832–8; Caplan, 'State Immunity, Human Rights, and *Jus Cogens*', pp. 741–81.
71 (2001) 34 E.H.R.R. 273 (ECtHR).
72 (2001) 34 E.H.R.R. 273, paras 61 and 66.
73 Joint Dissenting Opinion of Judges Rozakis, Caflisch, Wildhaber, Costa, Cabral Barreto and Vajic, para. 3.
74 [2006] U.K.H.L. 16.
75 See Orakhelashvili, A., 'State Immunity and Hierarchy of Norms: Why the House of Lords Got It Wrong', *European Journal of International Law*, 18(5) (2008): 955–70.
76 [2006] U.K.H.L. 16, para. 45.
77 [2002] ICJ Rep. 3.
78 *Jurisdictional Immunities of the State*, paras 92–7, available at: http://www.icj-cij.org/docket/index.php?p1=3&p2=3.

79 [2002] ICJ Rep. 3, para. 58.
80 [2002] ICJ Rep. 3, para. 61.
81 *Jurisdictional Immunities of the State*, para. 93.
82 Bederman, D., *International Law in Antiquity*, Cambridge: Cambridge University Press, 2001, pp. 106–20.
83 [1979] ICJ Rep. 3, at p. 40, para. 86.
84 [1979] ICJ Rep. 3, at para. 91.
85 Hoof, G. J. H. van, 'Rethinking the Sources of International Law', Deventer: Kluwer Law, 1983, p. 157.
86 [1966] 1 Q.B. 426, at p. 438.
87 United Nations Treaty Series.
88 Brown, J., 'Diplomatic Immunity: State Practice Under the Vienna Convention on Diplomatic Relations', *International and Comparative Law Quarterly*, 37(1) (1988): 53–88.
89 Akehurst, M., *A Modern Introduction to International Law*, 4th edn (London: George Allen & Unwin, 1982), p. 115.
90 *Case concerning US Diplomatic and Consular Staff in Tehran*, Merits, [1979] ICJ Rep. 7, paras 69, 77 and 78.
91 [2005] ICJ Rep. 168.
92 [2005] ICJ Rep. 168, at pp. 277–8, paras 337–8 and 340.
93 BBC News, 'Julian Assange: Ecuador Grants Wikileaks Founder Asylum', available at: http://www.bbc.co.uk/news/uk-19281492.
94 Available at: http://www.legislation.gov.uk/ukpga/1987/46.
95 Rossitto, A., 'Diplomatic Asylum in the United States and Latin America: A Comparative Analysis', *Brooklyn Journal of International Law*, 13 (1987): 111–35.
96 *Asylum* case (*Columbia* v. *Peru*) [1950] ICJ Rep. 266.
97 See *Congo* v. *Uganda* [2005] ICJ Rep. 168, paras 338–40.
98 Cameron, I., 'First Report of the Foreign Affairs Committee of the House of Commons', *International and Comparative Law Quarterly*, 34 (1985): 610–20, at pp. 614–15; Harris, *Cases and Materials on International Law*, pp. 368–9.
99 See *Yearbook of the International Law Commission*, 1989, vol. II, Pt 2, pp. 42–3.
100 *Yearbook of the International Law Commission*, 1989, vol. II, Pt 2, pp. 42–3.
101 Harris, *Cases and Materials on International Law*, p. 369.
102 Harris, *Cases and Materials on International Law*, pp. 361–70.
103 Shaw, *International Law*, 6th edn, p. 776.
104 Advisory Opinion [1989] ICJ Rep. 177.
105 Advisory Opinion [1989] ICJ Rep. 195–6, para. 52.
106 Advisory Opinion [1999] ICJ Rep. 62.
107 See at: http://avalon.law.yale.edu/20th_century/decad036.asp.
108 Simpson, 'International Law in Diplomatic History', p. 45.

109 For a useful overview of the English School contribution, see Neumann, I., 'The English School on Diplomacy: Scholarly Promise Unfulfilled', *International Relations*, 17(3) (2003): 341–69.
110 Wight, M., 'Why is There No International Theory', in H. Butterfield and M. Wight (eds), *Diplomatic Investigations: Essays in the Theory of International Politics*, London: Allen & Unwin, 1966, p. 26.
111 Wight, 'Why is There No International Theory', p. 20.
112 Brown, C., *International Relations Theory: New Normative Approaches*, London: Harvester Wheatsheaf, 1993, pp. 4–7; Boucher, D., *The Limits of Ethics in International Relations: Natural Law, Natural Rights and Human Rights in Transition*, Oxford: Oxford University Press, 2009, pp. 4–6. See also our discussion of Watson and Reus-Smit, below.
113 Wight, M., *Power Politics*, Leicester: Leicester University Press, 1979, p. 113; Reus-Smit, *The Moral Purpose of the State*, p. 7.
114 Koskenniemi, *The Politics of International Law*, ch. 11.
115 Boucher, *The Limits of Ethics*, pp. 4–7.
116 Watson, *Diplomacy*, p. 85.
117 Sharp, *Diplomatic Theory of International Relations*, p. 81.
118 Watson, *Diplomacy*, p. 15.
119 Sharp, *Diplomatic Theory of International Relations*, p. 81.
120 Sharp, *Diplomatic Theory of International Relations*, p. 86.
121 Sharp, *Diplomatic Theory of International Relations*, p. 88.
122 Sharp, *Diplomatic Theory of International Relations*, p. 87.
123 Crawford and Koskenniemi (eds), *The Camridge Companion to International Law*, chs 1 and 2.
124 Watson, *Diplomacy*, pp. 18–20; Watson, A., *The Evolution of International Society: A Comparative Historical Analysis*, London: Routledge, 1992, p. 169.
125 Watson, *Diplomacy*, p. 19.
126 Watson, *Diplomacy*, p. 28.
127 Watson, *Diplomacy*, pp. 48–50.
128 Watson, *Diplomacy*, pp. 47–50.
129 Watson, *Diplomacy*, p. 48 (original emphasis).
130 Neumann, 'The English School on Diplomacy', p. 23; Reus-Smit, *The Moral Purpose of the State*, p. 26.
131 Reus-Smit, *The Moral Purpose of the State*, pp. 24, 37–9.
132 Reus-Smit, *The Moral Purpose of the State*, p. 6.
133 Reus-Smit, *The Moral Purpose of the State*, p. 37.
134 Reus-Smit, *The Moral Purpose of the State*, p. 6.
135 Osiander, A., 'Sovereignty, International Relations and the Westphalian Myth', *International Organization*, 55(2) (2001): 251–87, at p. 266.
136 Reus-Smit, *The Moral Purpose of the State*, p. 8.
137 Reus-Smit, *The Moral Purpose of the State*, p. 109.

138 Roberts, P. and Sutch, P., *An Introduction to Political Thought*, Edinburgh: Edinburgh University Press, 2004, chs 3 and 4.
139 Reus-Smit, *The Moral Purpose of the State*, p. 122.
140 Reus-Smit, *The Moral Purpose of the State*, pp. 131–4.
141 Reus-Smit, *The Moral Purpose of the State*, p. 38.
142 Price and Reus-Smit, 'Dangerous Liaisons?'.
143 Reus-Smit, *The Politics of International Law*.
144 Reus-Smit, *The Politics of International Law*, p. 29.
145 Pogge, '"Assisting" the Global Poor', p. 551.
146 Reus-Smit, *The Moral Purpose of the State*, ch. 5.

CHAPTER SEVEN

The Ethics of Coercion Sanctions and the Use of Force in Contemporary International Affairs

Coercion has always been a part of international relations. One longstanding and influential perspective on this fact describes it as a feature of the anarchical, pre-political nature of the international 'state of nature'. Thomas Hobbes famously described this state of nature as a war of everyman against everyman arguing that in this condition:

> Nothing can be unjust. The notions of right and wrong, justice and injustice, have no place. Where there is no common power, there is no law; where no law, no injustice. Force and Fraud are in war the two cardinal virtues.[1]

In Chapter One we saw why the argument that there can be no international law without a global government or international leviathan was inadequate. The claim that in war nothing can be unjust also makes little sense of our experience of international politics. In fact, war has always been the subject of forms of social regulation. Religious, moral and legal rules have always provided a framework for the use of force. One particularly strong strand of moral and legal reflection on conflict is found in the just war tradition that can be traced from the works of early Roman philosophers and Christian theologians (from Cicero 106–43 BCE, St Augustine 354–430 and St Thomas Aquinas 1225–74) to the reflections of scholars, lawyers, soldiers and statesmen in the present day. In the contemporary period the core principles of just war theory find institutional expression in laws of war. While conflict is a seemingly permanent feature of international politics, the way we conceive of the morality of war changes as the tools of war and the normative context of international society develop. Indeed, the legal, political and moral debates surrounding the use of force since the end of Cold War show the dynamism of the legalised politics of coercion.[2] To claim that the politics of coercion has been legalised is far more complex than claiming that war is governed by legal rules. As politics becomes legalised, so the law becomes politicised and 'the distinctions between politics and law and between peace and war become unglued'.[3] David Kennedy's account of the legalisation of the laws of war shows how political an act it has become to say that wars themselves or the acts of warriors are or are not legal:

> Law has become more than the sum of its rules; it has become a vocabulary for judgement, for communication. Most importantly it has become the mark of legitimacy – and legitimacy has become the currency of power.[4]

Throughout this book we have explored the politics of international law and suggested that the law has become a vital site of social and political contestation. Claims to legitimacy are often tied to claims about the lawfulness of a particular action, but often such claims are tied not to strict, technical claims about the legal validity of an act, but to a broader series of claims about the normative legitimacy or moral desirability of an act. 'Lawfare', as Kennedy styles it, presents contemporary international affairs with opportunities and costs, and demonstrates the extent to which legalisation is a central characteristic of contemporary world politics. There may be no authoritative determiner of the validity of legal norms (to this extent Hobbes is correct), but 'the court of public opinion' invests the persuasiveness of legal claims with rhetorical and legitimating authority, and such claims have had a significant impact on the development of the way we enable and constrain violence and killing.[5]

In this chapter we are examining a moral and legal framework that works from the assumption that the use of force or other coercive tools that can endanger the lives and well-being of human beings (sometimes on an enormous scale) can be morally and legally legitimate. Traditionally, when we think about this topic we think almost exclusively in terms of war. In this chapter we explore a number of crucial ways in which warfare has developed in the contemporary period and the moral challenges this throws up. In particular, we

The Ethics of Coercion

explore heightened interest in the justice of armed conflict within states (rather than between states) and the arguments surrounding the merits of humanitarian military intervention. We also explore responses to the rise of international terrorism and the relative merits of the new doctrine of preventative self-defence found most clearly in the 'Bush Doctrine' that underpinned a core element of US foreign and security policy in the wake of the attacks on the World Trade Center and the Pentagon on 11 September 2001 (or 9/11). But war is not the only permissible coercive act that threatens the lives and well-being of individuals. The use of non-military sanctions, both unilaterally and through the UN Security Council, has become an increasing feature of international affairs since the end of the Cold War. Both comprehensive sanctions regimes (economic embargoes on exports, boycotts of imports, disruption of financial flows) and 'smart' or targeted sanctions (asset freezing or travel bans on government leadership or targeting corporations associated with the leadership) have human costs. Here we include an exploration of the ethics of non-military sanctions alongside our examination of the justice and the use of force.

The legal regimes applied to non-military sanctions are much less developed than laws of war. However, there has been significant institutional development at the UN (in part, as a response to the humanitarian costs of sanction regimes imposed on Iraq and Haiti in the 1990s) and considerable debate over how the law of countermeasures as well as humanitarian law and human rights law should be developed and applied in this context. In large part, these debates are inspired by the same moral concerns that underpin debates on the use of force. Taken together these concerns examine the circumstances under which we can apply measures that intend to cause harm to others. They ask what sort of acts or omissions can make an actor liable to become a target of coercion, how far actors can go to ensure that the target complies with their demands and, crucially, what sort of 'collateral damage' is tolerable. The answers to these questions change over time. Some pressures for change stem from the development of new military technology. Nuclear weapons, laser-guided smart bombs and dirty bombs deliverable by suicide bombers all generate new security challenges and require constant reflection on the justice of their use or of defensive techniques developed to prevent their use. Other pressures are normative. The growing importance of human rights norms and an increasing determination to police humanitarian norms have raised significant challenges to existing law and practice. The moral debates that we have explored in other areas of international law loom large here too, but, as we shall see, viewed through the prism of the ethics of coercion they gain an uncomfortable nuance and a sense of urgency. These features stem from the basic thought that killing and causing severe harm are sometimes legitimate – an idea that sits uneasily, or if we agree with Kennedy's analysis, too easily, with the idea of universal human rights.

Maintenance of peace and use of force

The use of force has assumed prominence in contemporary international law and politics. Since this relates to high politics there are a number of difficult questions that arise in this area of international law. In particular, the 9/11 'attack' by terrorists on the United States, the 2003 Iraqi War led by the so-called 'coalition of the willing' that ousted the Saddam Hussein regime and the growing impact of internal conflicts in international relations have generated debate on place of the use of force in international law.

International law and use of force: pre-1945

Originally, the use of force was permitted for a 'just cause'. Kelsen explained that such war was permitted 'only as a reaction against an illegal act, a delict and only when directed against the State responsible for this delict'.[6] Although international law has since progressed from the idea of just war towards a general prohibition of the use of force, recently certain states have revived the notion in their rhetoric (see below for a fuller discussion of just war). For instance, the United States in its 2002 National Security Strategy, putting forward a case for pre-emptive self-defence, stated: 'The purpose of our actions will always be to eliminate a specific threat to the United States or our allies and friends. The reasons for our actions will be clear, the force measured, and the cause just.'[7] It has also been resuscitated in the whole debate on military humanitarian intervention.

By the nineteenth century, international law had developed to the viewpoint that states have the sovereign right to resort to war. At this time it was felt that a state could resort to war as an inherent right of its sovereignty for 'a good reason, a bad reason or no reason at all'.[8] Since there was no general prohibition of the use of force the focus of international law was more on the conduct of war, or *jus in bello*,

The Ethics of Coercion

rather than on the right to wage war, or *jus ad bellum*. The maintenance of peace at this time was based primarily on balance of power. An example of this was the Concert of Europe established in the nineteenth century by European great powers. However, this failed to prevent the First World War, and it was therefore felt that there was a need to have a more formal institution to maintain peace and security. This led to the establishment of the League of Nations in 1920.

The Covenant of the League of Nations, still in line with the sovereign right to resort to war, did not prohibit states from going to war, but rather provided a procedural restriction. Under this procedure, member states were required first to submit their disputes to arbitration, or judicial settlement or the Council for peaceful settlement of such disputes and not to resort to war until three months after the arbitral award, or judicial decision or Council report (the so-called three-month cooling off period – Article 12). Outside the League of Nations, the General Treaty for the Renunciation of War 1928 (also known as the Kellogg–Briand Pact or the Pact of Paris) was adopted, which condemned recourse to war and renounced it as an instrument of state policy.[9] However, the latter treaty, which interestingly is still in force, does not provide any enforcement mechanism. Notwithstanding the League and the Pact of Paris, the Second World War could not be averted. This led to the establishment of the United Nations in 1945.

International law and use of force: post-1945

The establishment of the United Nations moved the law on the use of force to another phase. From a mere procedural restriction on the use of force during the League of Nations era, the UN provided for a general prohibition of the use of force, with certain exceptions. This general prohibition does not exclude countermeasures (unilateral and proportional non-forcible measure) taken by an injured state in response to another state's unlawful wrongful act in order to induce the latter state(s) to desist from such wrongful act and in appropriate cases to make reparations. Examples of countermeasures include the freezing of the assets of the offending state(s) located within the territory of the injured state and the suspension by the injured state of its treaty obligations towards the offending state(s).[10]

It must be noted that as a corollary to the general prohibition of the use of force the UN Charter provides that member states should settle their disputes by peaceful means through negotiation, enquiry, mediation, conciliation, arbitration, judicial settlement, resort to regional agencies or arrangements, or other peaceful means of their own choice (Articles 2(3)and 33(1)).

General prohibition of the use of force: an examination of the UN Charter

The UN Charter in Article 2(4) states: 'All members shall refrain in their international relations from the threat or use of force against the territorial integrity or political independence of any State, or in any other manner inconsistent with the purposes of the United Nations.'

The general prohibition on the use of force under Article 2(4) has been accepted by the ICJ in case of the *Military and Paramilitary Activities in and Against Nicaragua (Nicaragua v. USA)*, Merits, as reflecting not merely a conventional rule, but also a norm of customary international law, which has achieved the status of *jus cogens*.[11] Article 2(4) prohibits not only the actual use of force, but also the threat of force. Clearly not all threats of force would be regarded as violating Article 2(4). The ICJ in the Advisory Opinion on the *Legality of the Use of Nuclear Weapons* sought to explain what threat would contravene this provision as follows:

> Whether a signalled intention to use force if certain events occur is or is not a 'threat' within Article 2, paragraph 4, of the Charter depends upon various factors. If the envisaged use of force is itself unlawful, the stated readiness to use it would be a threat prohibited under Article 2, paragraph 4 . . . if it is to be lawful, the declared readiness of a State to use force must be a use of force that is in conformity with the Charter.[12]

The scope of the meaning of force under Article 2(4) has been the subject of some debate. While the provision clearly covers military force, it is not clear if it extends beyond this. For instance, for a while a number of developing states had argued that this provision extended to economic and political coercion.[13] Although the Declaration on Principles of International Law concerning Friendly Relations and Co-operation among States in accordance with the Charter of the United Nations 1970 and the Declaration on the Enhancement of the effectiveness of the Principle of Refraining from the Threat or Use of Force in International Relations 1987[14] alike state that: 'No State may use or encourage the use of economic, political or any other type of measures to coerce another State in order to obtain from it the subordination of the exercise of its sovereign rights and to secure from it advantages', the issue of whether or not Article 2(4) extended beyond military force was polemic.[15] It must be noted that the 1987 Declaration made it clear that nothing in the Declaration should be construed as enlarging or diminishing in any way the scope of the provisions of the Charter concerning cases in which the use of force is lawful.[16] The preferred view has over the years been that the scope of force under Article 2(4) does not include economic or political coercion. In support of this reference is usually made to an attempt by Brazil at the San Francisco Conference, before the UN was established, to introduce an amendment to include the threat or use of economic force as part of Article 2(4), which was rejected.[17] It is argued that though the threat or use of economic or political coercion may be regarded as unfriendly acts, it is doubtful that such threat or the use of such forms of coercion would fall within the remit of Article 2(4).[18]

Further, over the years the nature of conflicts has dramatically changed, and therefore Article 2(4) has had to be interpreted in the light of new conflict situations not envisaged by the drafters of the Charter. The radical change in the nature of conflicts led Franck, as far back as the 1970s, to bewail the death of Article 2(4).[19] However, in contrast, Henkin was of the view that in spite of the challenges faced by Article 2(4) due to new forms of conflicts such lament was rather exaggerated.[20] The adaptability of the Charter does allow for Article 2(4) to be interpreted in such a way as to cover certain new threats and conflicts. Lately, with examples of cyber-attacks during the 2008 Georgia–Russia conflict over South Ossetia and the 2009–2010 Stuxnet (a computer worm) attack on computers used for the Iranian nuclear programme, there have been debates on whether cyber-attack should be regarded as falling within the scope of Article 2(4).[21] Undoubtedly, not all cyber-attacks would fall within the scope of Article 2(4); nonetheless, such attacks not falling within the remit of this provision may certainly be regarded as unfriendly acts that may warrant countermeasures by the targeted state.[22] Still it is argued that cyber-attacks may, in certain limited circumstances, actually be regarded as force under Article 2(4).[23] For instance, a cyber-attack would be regarded as 'use of force' under Article 2(4) if it is directed at strategic military targets, with a view to weakening the targeted state's national defence as a prelude to an actual armed attack; or if the cyber-attack is of such a gravity that it results in large-scale damage or paralysis to the military operations of the targeted state; or there is evidence of a direct link between the cyber-attack and large-scale death or personal injury to the civilian population and destruction of physical property in the targeted state.[24] The United States in its International Strategy for Cyberspace 2011, obviously takes the view that cyber-attacks may in certain instances be regarded as the use of force. The document states:

> the United States will respond to hostile acts in cyberspace as we would to any other threat to our country. All States possess an inherent right to self-defense, and we recognize that certain hostile acts conducted through cyberspace could compel actions under commitments we have with our military treaty partners. We reserve the right to use all necessary means – diplomatic, informational, military, and economic – as appropriate and consistent with applicable international law, in order to defend our Nation, our allies, our partners, and our interests.[25]

There is also the debate about whether the threat or use of force, which is not against the territorial integrity or political independence of any state, or in any other manner inconsistent with the purposes of the United Nations, should be regarded as a violation of Article 2(4). This has become more prominent in the discourse on the legality of unilateral humanitarian intervention, an issue which would be explored further below.[26]

Exceptions to the general prohibition

The UN Charter permits the use of military force by states in self-defence. Article 51 states:

> Nothing in the present Charter shall impair the inherent right of individual or collective self-defence if an armed attack occurs against a Member of the United Nations, until the Security Council has taken measures necessary to maintain international peace and security. Measures taken by Members in the exercise of this right of self-defence shall be immediately reported to the Security Council and shall not in any way affect the authority and responsibility of the Security Council under the present Charter to take at any time such action as it deems necessary in order to maintain or restore international peace and security.

The ICJ in the *Nicaragua* case, Merits, decided that the reference in Article 51 to 'the inherent right' of self-defence meant that the customary international law rules on self-defence were not subsumed, but rather existed side by side with the conventional provisions in the Charter.[27] The customary international law rule on self-defence is traceable to the statement of Daniel Webster, the US Secretary of State, in the *Caroline* incident in 1837. Here certain British officers attacked and destroyed a steamboat, the *Caroline*, located in an American port, which had been used for conveying troops and arms during the Canadian insurrection. The US Secretary of State, protesting this action in his correspondence with his British counterpart, argued that to establish self-defence the British had to demonstrate the 'necessity of self-defence, instant, overwhelming, leaving no choice of means and no moment for deliberation'.[28] States have since accepted that under CIL a state must establish requirements of necessity and a proportional response to the attack to exercise a valid right of self-defence. Although these requirements are not explicitly stated in Article 51, it accepted that these prerequisites are still operative.[29]

Although it is clear that the Article 51 provision may be triggered when there is an actual armed attack, there is some debate on whether in certain cases the right to self-defence could be activated before such armed attack. These debates often lead to some confusion in respect of terminologies, such as anticipatory and pre-emptive self-defence. Greenwood rightly points out that:

> there is no agreement regarding the use of terminology in this field. As a result, some commentators distinguish between 'anticipatory' military action (which they generally use to describe military action against an imminent attack) and 'pre-emptive' force (normally employed to describe the use of force against a threat that is more remote in time). Although this approach offers the appearance of precision, the appearance is deceptive because so many others use the two terms interchangeably. Statements about 'pre-emptive' or 'anticipatory' action need, therefore, to be treated with some caution.[30]

A noteworthy example of such confusion is reflected in the 2004 High Panel Report on Threats, Challenges and Change, where the Panel appeared to regard both pre-emptive and preventive self-defence as an anticipatory exercise of this right, with pre-emptive being one against 'imminent or proximate' threats, and preventive being against 'non-imminent or non-proximate' threats.[31] It is therefore important at the outset to be clear on how these terminologies are used in this book. For the purposes of developing arguments in this regard, we will use the term 'anticipatory or pre-emptive self-defence' as applying to self-defence against imminent threats; while 'preventative self-defence' refers to that used in response to non-imminent threats. Anticipatory self-defence is generally accepted as valid under international law.[32] On the other hand, preventative self-defence is more controversial. This controversy has been stimulated by the 2002 US National Security Strategy (NSS) Report.[33] The report, while acknowledging that international law recognised that a state may defend itself against an imminent threat, went on to maintain that the United States had to 'adapt the concept of imminent threat to the capabilities and objectives of today's adversaries', and could take actions to defend itself even against non-imminent threats.[34] This position was reaffirmed in the 2006 NSS Report, which emphasised that the place of pre-emption in the American security strategy remained the same.[35] Franck points out that this polemical doctrine 'seeks to forestall a danger before it materializes – rather than just to anticipate or prevent it after it has risen to the level of an actual threat'.[36] He criticises it as not based on law, but rather on power which 'abandons [the] multilateral process in favour of action at the sole behest' of the United States, a situation that is exemplified by the unilateral invasion of Iraq in 2003 by the United States and its allies when they failed to obtain UN Security Council authorisation.[37]

Another issue that arises from Article 51 is whether the relevant armed attack necessarily has to be by a state. In the *Nicaragua* case, the ICJ held that armed attack includes not only actions by states' regular armed forces, but also 'the sending by or on behalf of a State of armed bands, groups, irregulars or mercenaries, which carry out acts of armed force against another State of such gravity as to amount to an actual armed attack conducted by regular forces'.[38] Prior to the terrorist attacks on 9 September 2001 the requisite armed attack was either by or on behalf of a state. However, with the 9/11 attack the scope of armed attack was expanded to include attacks by non-state actors who were not necessarily acting on behalf of a state.[39] In Resolutions 1368 and 1373, which condemned the terrorist attacks, the UN Security Council affirmed the right of the United States to self-defence. Also, NATO invoked Article 5 of its constitutive treaty – an attack on one is an attack on all – to act together with the United States in collective self-defence after the 9/11 terrorist attacks.

Further, there is also the debate on whether self-defence extends to the use of force by a state to protect its nationals abroad. For instance, in 1976 Israel claimed the right to self-defence when it used force to free its nationals who were held as hostages in Entebbe, Uganda. While a number of states sympathised with Israel's actions, they were unwilling to accept this as a valid extension of the Article 51 provision.[40]

It must be noted that the right to self-defence under Article 51 is meant to be a temporary right to be exercised until the Security Council is able to act. It may either be individual (when the attacked state responds alone), or collective (when the attacked state invites other states to assist it in defending itself against such an attack).[41] Article 5 of the NATO Treaty is an example of collective self-defence.

Use of force under the authority of the Security Council

Another exception to the prohibition of the use of force is the collective use of force under chapter VII of the Charter by the UN Security Council, which has the primary responsibility to maintain international peace and security (Article 24, UN Charter). This immense power given to the Security Council under the Charter has, however, been hindered by the frequent use of the veto by the P-5 members, which has on several occasions prevented the Council from acting even in appropriate cases. As a result, there have been calls for the reform of the Council to make it more effective (see Chapter Four).[42] Examples of the Security Council's inability to act under chapter VII as a result of the veto of one or more of the P-5 abound. A recent example is the failure of the Security Council to take action in respect of the crisis in Syria because of the veto of Russia and China.[43] The inability of the Security Council to continue to take enforcement measures in the 1950 Korean War due to the veto of the former USSR led the General Assembly to adopt the 1950 'Uniting for Peace' Resolution. This Resolution empowers the General Assembly, in the case of the paralysis of the Security Council due to the use of the veto, to consider the matter immediately and adopt appropriate recommendations to seek to restore peace and security.[44]

Under Article 39, the Security Council first has to 'determine the existence of a threat to the peace, breach of the peace or act of aggression' to trigger its chapter VII powers. The phrases – 'threat to the peace', 'breach of peace' and 'act of aggression' – are nowhere defined in the Charter. However, in 1974 the General Assembly adopted a

Resolution that sought to define an 'act of aggression' by listing seven acts.[45] This includes armed invasions or attacks, bombardments, blockades, armed violations of territory by one state against another and the employment by a state of armed irregulars or mercenaries to carry out acts of aggression in another state.[46] Even at that the Resolution still emphasises that the acts listed are not exhaustive and that 'the Security Council may determine that other acts constitute aggression under the provisions of the Charter'.[47] Consequently, the Security Council has wide discretion in making a determination under Article 39. Over the years, a wide range of situations, such as disputes between states, apartheid, invasion of one state by another, the overthrow of a freely elected government, internal conflicts, proliferation of nuclear, chemical and biological weapons, terrorism, massive abuse of human rights such as genocide, war crimes and crimes against humanity, and piracy have been determined by the Security Council as a threat to international peace and security. Recently, the Security Council has engaged in debates on whether to regard climate change as a threat to international peace.[48] It has also been suggested that 'serious cyber-attacks' against a state's security may fall within the remit of the Security Council.[49]

When the Security Council makes an Article 39 determination it may adopt either non-military and military measures, if it is of the view that the former is inadequate, to maintain or restore peace and security.

Under Article 41 of the Charter the Security Council is able to undertake non-military measures. This is usually done by way of sanctions, which may be imposed against a state, a group of states, an organisation or group (e.g., the Al Qaeda terrorist group and the RUF rebel group in Sierra Leone) or an individual. Such sanctions may be in the form of comprehensive economic and trade sanctions, arms embargoes, travel bans, financial or diplomatic restrictions.[50] More recently, the Security Council has begun to adopt the so-called targeted or smart sanctions. These sanctions are targeted at designated individuals or entities who, in the view of the Security Council, are directly involved in the situation which is regarded as a threat to international peace and security.[51] Bothe explains the rationale for targeted sanctions as follows:

> Traditional non-military enforcement measures pursuant to Article 41 of the Charter are value deprivations imposed upon states as collectivities ... This type of measure has rightly been

criticized as both ineffective and unjust. It is unjust because it mainly hits the innocent population. It is ineffective because it does not or only rarely reaches those who are personally responsible for a threat to the peace or a breach of the peace. In the light of this experience, a system of 'targeted' sanctions has been developed which is directed specifically against these persons.[52]

He points out that these sanctions are usually in the form of travel and financial restrictions, as well as criminal responsibility.[53] Targeted sanctions are increasingly being challenged on human rights grounds that the targeted persons and entities were not given a fair hearing by being told the specific reason why they have been listed in the resolution. It is contended that the Security Council may not impose obligations that would breach fundamental principles of human rights, which is a key pillar of the United Nations (Article 1(1)).[54] Further, the Security Council in its counterterrorism actions since the 9/11 terrorist attacks, has imposed certain non-military measures that have a general and abstract character. This has led certain scholars to argue that the Council is now acting in a legislative capacity (see Chapter Two).

In addition, the Security Council has utilised its Article 41 power to establish *ad hoc* international criminal tribunals, the International Criminal Tribunal for Former Yugoslavia (ICTY) and the International Criminal Tribunal for Rwanda (ICTR), in respect of internal conflicts in the former Yugoslavia and Rwanda, respectively.[55]

Article 42 of the Charter allows the Security Council to use military force, if necessary, to maintain international peace and security. The Charter originally envisioned a situation where a sort of 'standing army' would be made available to the Security Council through special agreements between states and the Council (Article 43) with a military staff committee to advise and assist with military planning (Articles 45–47). However, though the military staff committee was established, due to the politics by the two super powers during the Cold War no such special agreements were entered into. This situation has not changed post-Cold War. Consequently, the Security Council has had to adopt a rather pragmatic method of authorising coalitions of willing and able states or regional organisations to carry out military measures on its behalf.[56] Notable examples of its use are: the 1950 Korean War 1950–1953,[57] where it was used for the first time when the former USSR boycotted the Council in protest at the occupation of the Council seat by the Republic of China, rather than the Communist Peoples' Republic; the Iraq invasion of Kuwait in 1990;[58] and more recently the Libyan crisis.⁵⁹ Such resolutions of the Council authorising military measures usually use the phrase 'all necessary means', as a euphemism for the authorisation of the use of force.⁶⁰

The ambiguity of some resolutions of the Security Council sometimes raises issues on whether a particular resolution actually authorises the use of force. A noteworthy example of this is UN Security Council Resolution 1441 (2002).⁶¹ During the First Gulf War the Security Council adopted Resolution 678 (1990), which authorised the use of force to repel Iraq from Kuwait. Thereafter, the Council adopted another Resolution, 687 (1991), which set out ceasefire conditions, including an obligation on Iraq to eliminate its weapons of mass destruction. After Iraq had violated the conditions of several weapons inspection programmes, the Council unanimously adopted Resolution 1441 in 2002, which condemned the failure of Iraq to comply with Resolution 687 and declared it to be in 'material breach' of the 1991 resolution. Following the failure by the United States and the United Kingdom to obtain the authorisation of the Security Council, due to the threat of veto by China, France and Russia, they put together a coalition of willing states and invaded Iraq in 2003. One of the arguments raised by them in support of the invasion was that since Iraq was in material breach of Resolution 687, the authority to use force under Resolution 678 was revived.⁶² This so-called revival argument is controversial, and has been disputed by a number of states and scholars who have opined that the 2003 invasion of Iraq was done without the authority of the Council and was therefore illegal.⁶³ With the end of the Cold War, internal conflicts now appear to dominate the Security Council chapter VII agenda.⁶⁴

In addition to using non-military and military measures (e.g., authorising humanitarian military intervention) as described above, the Security Council has had to utilise peacekeeping operations to maintain international peace and security in certain cases, including internal conflicts.⁶⁵ Although there are no explicit provisions in the Charter for peacekeeping the flexibility in interpreting the Charter has provided the basis for this. Dag Hammarskjöld, the second UN Secretary-General, referred to peacekeeping as belonging to 'Chapter Six and a Half' of the Charter because it could be placed at an imaginary middle point between chapter VI (dealing with Pacific Settlement of Disputes) and chapter VII (dealing with the Security Council's enforcement powers).⁶⁶ Although, some peacekeeping operations seek to maintain peace between states (e.g., in the first peacekeeping operation in 1948 the United Nations Truce Supervision Organisation

(UNTSO) was to monitor the Armistice Agreement between Israel and its Arab neighbouring states), over the years such operations have increasingly been employed for the maintenance of peace in respect of internal conflicts (e.g., the United Nations Mission in the Republic of South Sudan (UNMISS); the African Union–UN Hybrid Operation in Darfur (UNAMID); the UN Operation in Côte d'Ivoire (UNOCI); and UN Interim Administration Mission in Kosovo (UNMIK)).[67]

Generally, the Security Council determines when and where a peacekeeping operation should be deployed. If the Council fails to act as a result of the veto of the P-5, the General Assembly under the Uniting for Peace Resolution may also make recommendations for a peacekeeping operation to be deployed (e.g., in 1956 the General Assembly established the First UN Emergency Force (UNEF I) in the Middle East). A significant constrain faced in deploying a peacekeeping operation is the unwillingness of member states to contribute troops, which sometimes results in a rather slow deployment in crisis situations – some involving serious humanitarian catastrophe. Consequently, some have called for the setting up of a permanent peacekeeping standing force, while others have even gone as far as calling for such operations to be privatised by using private military companies.[68]

Peacekeeping operations are deployed based on three key principles: the consent of the parties; impartiality; and non-use of force by the peacekeepers except in self-defence and defence of the mandate. In addition, post-Cold War peacekeeping operations have become more flexible, having different configurations, namely, the traditional peacekeeping, peace enforcement and peace-building. [69]

Humanitarian military intervention

Humanitarian military intervention has been defined by Holzgrefe as 'the threat or use of force across State borders by a State (or group of States) aimed at preventing or ending widespread and grave violations of the fundamental human rights of individuals other than its own citizens, without the permission of the State within whose territory force is applied'.[70] A distinction must be made between humanitarian military intervention under the authority of the Security Council and unilateral humanitarian military intervention (UHMI).

Under the Charter and the practice of states over the years, it is accepted that the Council has wide powers under chapter VII to authorise military humanitarian intervention. Article 2(7) of the Charter states:

> Nothing contained in the present Charter shall authorize the United Nations to intervene in matters which are essentially within the domestic jurisdiction of any state or shall require the Members to submit such matters to settlement under the present Charter; *but this principle shall not prejudice the application of enforcement measures under Chapter VII.* (emphasis added)

The United Nations High Level Panel 2004 endorsed the power of the Security Council to authorise humanitarian military intervention as a last resort in cases of massive human rights abuses within the territory of states.[71] Also, the International Commission on Intervention and State Sovereignty (ICISS) Report, putting forward arguments for a shift in the language of the debate from humanitarian intervention to responsibility to protect (R2P), also endorsed the Security Council as the 'right authority' to authorise such intervention.[72]

The UHMI is, however, more controversial. There is great debate on whether such intervention is legal or not. Supporters of UHMI insist that Article 2(4) of the Charter permits unilateral humanitarian intervention because it merely prohibits 'the threat or use of force against the territorial integrity or political independence of any state, or in any other manner inconsistent with the Purposes of the United Nations'. They maintain that UHMI is not against the territorial integrity or political independence of the target state. Also, since it is intended to prevent human rights violations it certainly is not inconsistent with the purposes of the United Nations.[73] Some scholars have contended that UHMI is permitted under customary international law and they rely on certain Cold War state practice, such as India's intervention in Bangladesh to prevent repression by Pakistan (1971), Tanzania's intervention in Uganda that overthrew the oppressive regime of Idi Amin and Vietnam's intervention in Cambodia to put an end to Pol Pot's brutal rule (1978).[74] Opponents of UHMI, on the other hand, insist that the provisions of Article 2(4) relied upon by its supporters was not intended to support UHMI, but rather to emphasise the general prohibition of the use of force.[75] They maintain that there are only two exceptions to the general prohibition of the use of force, namely, self-defence and action with the authorisation of the Security Council. They further argue that the Cold War state practice relied upon by its supporters does not actually support UHMI, since the states did not invoke UHMI but rather preferred to rely on self-defence.[76] In any event, the opponents argue that the divergent views of states on the legality of the NATO unilateral military intervention in 1999 indicate that state practice on this is conflicting and therefore cannot validly support the contention that UHMI is now part of customary international law (see below for further discussion).[77]

Role of regional organisations

The UN Charter allows for regional arrangements or agencies, such as NATO, the AU, the Organisation of American States (OAS), the Economic Community of West African States (ECOWAS) and the Arab League, to deal with such matters relating to the maintenance of international peace and security within their respective regions, provided that such arrangements or agencies and their activities are consistent with the Purposes and Principles of the United Nations (Article 52).[78] Any enforcement action by these regional arrangements or agencies, however, has to be authorised by the Security Council (Article 53). Over the years, the Practice of the Security Council allows not only for prior approval by the Security Council, but also retroactive approval of enforcement action by regional arrangements or agencies. The latter is commonly referred to as the notion of *ex post facto* authorisation.[79]

Just war theory

The highly sensitive and political nature of security and defence issues means that the ways that actors relate to the legal framework concerning the use of force foregrounds the political and ethical dilemmas in play. Actors do not deny that there are legal rules, but in this field, more than any other, non-legal considerations are often weighed up against existing norms in a very explicit way. Throughout history actors have linked instrumental and practical considerations to ethical decision-making using the framework of just war theory. We begin with an overview of just war theory, as the core principles of that tradition are broadly applicable to each of the issues we examine below. Just war theory was developed to apply to classic instances of war between separate communities, but has proven to be remarkably adaptable to different forms of international society (with distinct political structures and normative priorities) and different types of coercive act. Just war theory divides questions of war into two main categories. The first is called *jus ad bellum* and concerns the question of when it is right to resort to war. The second is termed *jus in bello* and concerns the rules that regulate the conduct of war (such as what type of weapons can be used or who can be a legitimate target). There is renewed interest in relatively neglected, but increasingly relevant, ideas such as *jus post bellum* (or the justice of post-conflict peace-building[80]), but here we focus on the traditional elements of the theory.

Michael Walzer's *Just and Unjust Wars* is a classic contemporary redrafting of the tradition that updates the two categories to suit a contemporary examination of conflict. *Jus ad bellum* becomes the 'legalist paradigm' referring to the fact that rules concerning the right of a state to go to war have been deeply embedded in the public international law of the UN system. The rules relating to the right to use force are amended with a series of exceptions or revisions that deal with pressing questions of contemporary conflict from legitimate anticipation (or preventive self-defence) to humanitarian intervention (or the duty/right to save civilians from the horrors of genocidal regimes and lawless failed states). *Jus in bello* is presented as the 'War Convention' and explores both traditional questions of non-combatant immunity and contemporary questions of the legitimacy, or otherwise, of weapons of mass destruction (WMD) and terror tactics.

Walzer's account of the legalist paradigm rests on an account of the danger of aggression to international politics, a danger that Walzer refers to as a crime and one that contemporary international society (at Nuremburg after the Second World War and at Kampala in 2010) has labelled the greatest crime in international relations:

> Aggression is the name we give to the crime of war. We know the crime because of our knowledge of the peace it interrupts – not the mere absence of fighting, but peace-with-rights, a condition of liberty and security that can exist only in the absence of aggression ... Aggression is remarkable because it is the only crime that states can commit against other states ... the rights in question are territorial integrity and political sovereignty. The two belong to states, but they derive ultimately from the rights of individuals, and from them they take their force.[81]

This account of aggression makes sense of many of our core commitments at the international level. Indeed, Walzer's starting point is very conventional in that it appears to map on to existing international law as the starting point for moral and legal reflection. If, however, the legalist paradigm is to have any practical application, it must be able to help us think about the hard cases. War has a habit of creating new normative challenges that require more than the simple application of the rules of just war. Developments in weapons technology that create new ways to kill, the emergence of new threats such as that posed by international terrorism, an increase in genocidal and nationalist wars in the aftermath of colonialism and the Cold War all require that we revisit the rules and their moral foundation to develop our responses to these developments. Contemporary world politics has seen the development of new claims about the justice of preventative self-defence and humanitarian intervention in response to precisely these challenges. Such claims pose a direct challenge to the non-intervention/non-aggression principle. Yet surely it seems right to acknowledge both that states have the right to defend their citizens against terrorists and the right (and duty) to intervene to stop genocide. The question we face is: how do instances of pre-emptive self-defence or humanitarian military intervention 'fit' with the rules of non-intervention? In order to answer this question we need to dig a little deeper into the political theory that underpins Walzer's approach to war and to explore some of the challenges to just war theory that stress the moral and legal primacy of human rights.

Once conflict has started we turn to a distinctive set of rules that enable us to think about who may or may not be a legitimate target and how they may or may not be treated. As was the case with *jus ad bellum*, the rules of *jus in bello* or the war convention are quite straightforward in the ordinary run of things. When war begins we are told that it does not matter whether the combatants fight for the 'just side' or the 'unjust side'. What matters is how the combatants conduct themselves. This is referred to as 'the moral equality of combatants'.[82] It is important because it allows us to acknowledge that there are rules that govern combatants regardless of whether the state they serve has just cause or not. In war we tend to accept that soldiers on both sides may have to kill enemy soldiers in the course of their duty. There is also a long-standing view that non-combatants are not to be targeted. This includes civilians, wounded soldiers and prisoners of war. But the issues quickly become morally complex. What if the enemy soldier poses no threat (Walzer uses the example of a soldier coming across an enemy soldier bathing 'the naked soldier')?[83] What if the force we are fighting wears no uniform or insignia, or mixes freely with a civilian population? What if our enemy is using terror tactics? What if our objective can best be achieved with the use of weapons that pose a threat to non-combatants (from landmines to high-level bombing campaigns or even nuclear weapons)? How do we balance the need to achieve our objective (bearing in mind the means necessary to do so) with the need to observe the war convention? The war convention applies what Walzer calls 'the sliding scale of utilitarianism'. If the highest priority is the very survival of the state (as the basis of security, community and liberty), then the closer we get to the extreme possibility of national destruction the further away from the norms of the war convention we may stray. The moral/theoretical challenge here is to find the principle that overrides the commitment to the non-targeting of civilians.

In both elements of just war theory the moral/theoretical challenges require that we seek out the principle that makes non-aggression or non-combatant immunity valuable, so that we can weigh the value of non-intervention against the hard cases that conflict throws up. Some of these hard cases are questions of *jus ad bellum*. Is it morally permissible to declare war on a regime that is ethnically cleansing part of its population? When does anticipatory self-defence become aggression? Others are questions of *jus in bello*. Is it appropriate to use unmanned drones or high-level bombing tactics when we know it increases the risk of civilian casualties? Is torture justified if it helps to avoid a terrorist attack? These questions are deeply serious and complex, and like any moral and political theory the borderline between a just and an unjust war has been contested throughout history. Just war theory traditionally simplifies these complex questions by setting a series of threshold tests that action has to pass before it can be considered legitimate. The list of tests varies in order and content throughout just war theory, but generally covers the following questions:

- Is there a *just cause*?
- Is going to war the *last resort*?
- Has the war been declared by the *legitimate authority*? This is a tricky and very legalistic question. The United States and many other states argue that the provisions of the UN Charter concerning the use of force supplement rather than supplant the rights of sovereign states.
- Is there *right intention*? Is the war fought solely for the just cause or are there other, less legitimate, ends?
- Will the war pass the test of *proportionality*? Do the benefits of fighting this war outweigh the harms it is likely to cause (including as a separate consideration the potential risk to innocents (*discrimination*)?

- Is there a *reasonable chance of success*? Given the means at our disposal, and deploying them with the principle of proportionality in mind, can this strategy deliver the war aims (e.g., can the military strategy in Afghanistan deliver security from international terrorism)?

Underpinning these tests is the core idea that aggression undermines all the core rights protected by international law. We therefore ought to operate a policy of non-aggression and this, of course, is the principle that underpins Article 2(4) of the UN Charter. The most obvious exception to this rule is that 'states may use military force in the face of threats of war, whenever failure to do so would seriously risk their territorial integrity or political independence'.[84] However, increasing emphasis on human rights has placed considerable stress on the idea that the integrity of the sovereign state (and thus a doctrine of non-intervention) is the best way to protect the core rights at stake. This brings us up against the real challenge of contemporary just war thinking. Turning to the challenges of humanitarian military intervention and anticipatory self-defence that have dominated post-Cold War discussion of the topic gets us to the core of this challenge.

Use of force: humanitarian intervention and anticipatory war

The end of the Cold War brought with it an unprecedented level of UN Security Council activity in response to threats to international peace and security under chapter VII of the Charter. Indeed, the first decade after the fall of the Berlin Wall saw chapter VII invoked in UN Security Council resolutions over 160 times, in contrast to the twenty-four citations between 1948 and 1989. The UN Security Council responded to traditional threats to peace (such as the Iraqi invasion of Kuwait), and expanded its understanding of such threats by responding to those that emanated from within states rather than from aggression between states.[85] The normative basis of this last development also led to increasing, but always controversial, support (particularly from NATO members) for the use of military force to meet humanitarian objectives without chapter VII authorisation where P-5 members were divided. The period between the fall of the Berlin Wall and the attacks on the World Trade Center were the high water mark of humanitarian intervention. Interventions in Iraq, Somalia, East Timor and in response to the break-up of the FYR were amplified by the regret expressed at the failure to act to prevent the Rwandan genocide of 1994. Diplomatic moves to achieve consensus on a new doctrine of humanitarian intervention (the Responsibility to Protect or R2P) suggest the emergence of a legitimate exception to the settled rules of non-intervention. Indeed, many respected commentators argue that the emergence of R2P as a global doctrine of humanitarian response is well advanced.[86] Nevertheless, the political and legal challenges presented by claims concerning the legitimacy of humanitarian military intervention are still significant. After 9/11 attention shifted to the 'War on Terror' as states focused on how to combat the new security threat posed by international terrorism. The intervention debates continued in the background, maintained in part by the policies of UN Secretary-General Kofi Annan and later Secretary-General Ban Ki-Moon and returned to structure the debates surrounding the appropriate response to crises generated by popular uprisings in the Middle East in 2011 and 2012 (especially those in Libya and Syria). Understanding both debates requires that we focus on the changing normative framework of international society. In both cases the heightened importance of humanitarian and human rights norms challenged the *status quo*.

The legalist paradigm places high value on self-determination and therefore on non-intervention. Walzer puts forward what we can refer to as a theory of 'presumptive legitimacy'. He writes:

> By democratic standards most states throughout human history have been oppressive (and illegitimate) but this is not necessarily or usually the standards by which they are judged by their own people. On the other hand, we can always assume that murder, slavery, and mass expulsion are condemned, at least by their victims.[87]

For Walzer non-intervention is a positive thing. It recognises that self-determination is about building your political future in partnership with your fellow citizens, 'to have a history of one's own'. Walzer argues that we need to respect the self-determination of peoples as far as possible. We do not have the right to intervene in cases of what he calls 'ordinary oppression'. Rather, the difficult moral judgement we need to make is when ordinary oppression becomes extreme oppression – where there is an obvious and 'radical lack of fit' between a people and the government. Walzer, and anyone who thinks that humanitarian military intervention is a good idea, is trying to draw a distinction between social injustices, which are rightly to be sorted out without the intervention of outsiders, and social injustices, which are so extreme that outsiders have a duty to intervene. Walzer adopts an evocative phrase that we find repeatedly in international law and tells us that it is only 'acts that shock the conscience of mankind' that can warrant forceful intervention. This, of course, begs a further question about what acts fall into this category.

Walzer argues that we should consider intervening only where self-determination is impossible. A people being ethnically cleansed (a broad-brush term for acts such as forcible deportation, genocide and crimes against humanity) are never going to be in a position to do so, where peoples suffering from a lack of democratic rights or from severe gender discrimination (such as women and girls under the Taliban) may one day find the strength and non-military means to achieve freedom. The first is an example of extreme oppression, the latter 'ordinary' oppression. Both are unjust, but only the former warrants military intervention because military force, as a tool, has devastating human costs and must be used only *in extremis*. Walzer's claim is that self-determination is the freedom of people to become free by their own efforts and according to their own standards. For Walzer 'given what liberty is [intervention] necessarily fails'.[88] This claim underwrites the traditionally conservative or restrictionist approach to the use of force that is the core of just war thinking. Nevertheless, under extreme circumstances we may be obliged to intervene. Recalling what we are intervening for, we must strive to act in a way that preserves the potential of a people to create their own future. This implies that any intervention should be a quick as possible, followed by complete military withdrawal.

The logic of Walzer's position is clear and makes sense of many of the core commitments of the international community. However, the theory of intervention draws criticism from those who see it as too interventionist *and* from those who think it not interventionist enough. Those who think Walzer's position is too permissive point to the difficulty of judging the motive of the intervening power (if they have an economic or strategic interest in the area can we say they have right intention?), to the difficulty in drawing the line between a national government dealing with the illegal use of force by secessionist groups and one acting unjustly, and to the medium- to long-term consequences of interventions. If we have learned anything from interventions in the Balkans and the Middle East, surely it is that military intervention is rarely a surgical 'in and out' affair. Rather, the interveners end up playing a full and long-term role in the development of the post-conflict polity. Additional *in bello* considerations, particularly the humanitarian costs of conducting military operations for humanitarian reasons – the oxymoron of humanitarian war,[89] combine with these considerations to reiterate the value of non-intervention. On the other side of the debate many solidarists and cosmopolitans argue that Walzer's position (often prioritising communal integrity over the human rights of citizens) makes no sense. The cosmopolitan argument has two basic steps. The first is to point out that Walzer himself acknowledges that the rights of states are based on the rights of individuals within those states (above). The second is to suggest that, given this position, Walzer sets the bar to intervention too high. David Luban (an important contributor to the contemporary debates) argues forcefully that waiting for an observable and radical lack of fit between a people and their government requires inaction in the face of some horrific abuses of power. Truly oppressive regimes are such that 'the government fits the people the way a sole of a boot fits the human face: after a while the patterns of indentation match with uncanny precision'.[90] The argument is simple: if we have a list of rights that every human being has then why should the international community adopt rules that mean there can be an intervention only in the most horrific of cases, often after much damage has been done and that may even encourage non-intervention in the face of genocide (as was the case in Rwanda in 1994). We shall return to the cosmopolitan case below.

Nicholas Wheeler's *Saving Strangers: Humanitarian Intervention in International Society* offers the seminal solidarist exploration of the development of humanitarian intervention in the period up until 2001. He argues, drawing explicitly on Walzer's just war theory, that the overriding normative importance of protecting peoples from supreme humanitarian emergencies (or acts that shock the conscience of mankind) has altered the way we answer the questions that the just war tradition poses. This has not altered the existing legal prohibition on the use of force (there is neither customary nor treaty law to this effect). Nevertheless, as Byers and Chesterman demonstrate, it has led to a broad recognition that, on its own, the legal debate is 'sterile and unhelpful'.[91] For Wheeler, this is an empirical–normative claim. Humanitarian concerns in the form of moral arguments about the justice of humanitarian intervention as a response to major atrocities have carried the debate even where the law explicitly rules out the sort of actions undertaken by NATO or the UN Security Council. For Wheeler, this evidence suggests that the governance regime is evolving towards a solidarist and counter-restrictionist approach to the use of force. He argues that the 'key solidarist claim to be raised in any such dialogue is that it is not acceptable for permanent members to exercise the veto in situations where states request Council authorization, and where there is significant international support for intervention to prevent or stop gross human rights abuses'.[92] This, he suggests, helps us to understand the international reaction to the NATO intervention in Kosovo and to the failure to act in Rwanda, and gives clear direction to claims concerning the normative desirability of changing the established rules regarding the use of force.

Wheeler shows how humanitarian catastrophe in East Pakistan (modern-day Bangladesh), Uganda and Vietnam (all during the Cold War period) were treated very differently by the international community than relevantly similar disasters after 1989. Equally importantly, he shows how a concern for those suffering from genocide, crimes against humanity and war crimes either by government design or through state failure significantly alters the appeal of traditional notions of the appropriate threshold criteria that provide for the justice of war. The most obvious challenge is to the traditional account of just cause. The defence of others (the victims of severe human rights abuses or humanitarian atrocity) now carries significant weight as a claim to just cause. The concerns that challenge the traditional account of just cause also challenge the questions of legitimate authority and last resort. Like questions of just cause, the question of right authority appeared to be settled by the UN Charter. States are permitted to act in self-defence until the UN Security Council takes measures (Article 51). Beyond this provision the UN Security Council has sole responsibility (Article 41). Yet the need to protect innocents from gross violations and continuing ideological disagreement in the UN Security Council has prompted states to act without UN authorisation. The responses to the NATO-led intervention in Kosovo in 1999, to the US–UK-led war in Iraq in 2003 and to NATO's expansive interpretation of UN authorisation in Libya in 2011, all paint a similar picture. In each case it was explicitly recognised that UN authorisation is the basis of the legality of the use of force. In each case the intervening powers claimed the authority of the UN, pointing to resolutions determining threats to peace even where they may not have explicitly authorised 'all necessary means' (the phrase that permits the use of military means). The difficulty in achieving a resolution explicitly authorising military force, combined with the urgency of the humanitarian threat, it was argued, legitimated unilateral responses. There is no universal view on the legitimacy of such actions. Russia, in particular, has repeatedly accused NATO of violating international law in the case of Kosovo and in Libya. Such accusations, however well founded, do not appear to generate the response Russia desired. In the former case, Wheeler shows significant support for NATO action resulted in the defeat of a Russian attempt to gain a UN Security Council resolution condemning the intervention.[93] Wheeler's summary notes:

> The vote in the Security Council was historic because, for the first time, since the founding of the Charter, seven members legitimated or acquiesced in the use of force justified on humanitarian grounds where there was no express Council authorization.[94]

Yet despite the willingness to retrospectively legitimate the NATO action, there is broad consensus that unilateral intervention undermined international law and the UN as an institution, and concern that attempts to bring the Kosovo experience into the framework of international law would legitimate the exceptionalism of the powerful rather than create universally desired rules.[95] One of the core *ad bellum* concerns is the lack of institutional capacity to control and regulate humanitarian intervention. This is most apparent in the case of unilateral action. Yet the UN Security Council is often paralysed by division between the permanent members, where such divisions are sustained by strategic issues (the maintenance of alliances or trading partnerships) or domestic issues (both relating to public opinion in the member states' civil society and to the human rights record of would-be interveners). This means that even in the face of extreme humanitarian suffering a resolution may not be attainable.

Wheeler's analysis suggests that there is considerable support behind the solidarist claim that the restrictionist or pluralist position that privileges P-5 unanimity over the lives of victims of humanitarian atrocity is morally questionable. However, concerns over a lack of regulatory and governance capacity have led many experienced lawyers to argue that institutionalising a right of humanitarian military intervention, whether by changing the charter or reforming the UN Security Council, is problematic. Hans Correll, Under-Secretary General for legal affairs and the UN Legal Counsel from 1994 to 2004, has argued that humanitarian intervention should not be codified, but should be treated under the category of necessity because the institutional and moral challenges will simply 'not go away' regardless of the reforms that are put in place.[96] The ILC articles on state responsibility excuse conduct which 'is the only means for a state to safeguard an essential interest against a grave and immanent peril'.[97] Correll recognises the normative importance of humanitarian claims and therefore sees intervention as falling naturally under this category. In similar fashion, Franck and Rodley, deeply concerned with the potential of any new legal rule to be abused, argue that the issue belongs in the realm of morality rather than law. These positions, argues Wheeler, represent the new *status quo* in which humanitarian motives are now accepted as mitigating arguments where such action is taken in defiance of existing law. Wheeler, however, sides with Wil Verwy who argues that this solution undermines the law as it amounts to a recognition that 'international law is incapable of ensuring respect for socially indispensable standards of morality', and urges states to take the moral and institutional risks necessary to live up to their solidarist obligations.[98]

The solidarist argument is a powerful one and, as we have seen, Walzer's just war theory and many of the opinions of numerous legal scholars and practitioners are also influenced by the normative desirability of protecting victims of humanitarian atrocity. This normative change, however, challenges the traditional core of both just war theory and the UN Charter. Both are designed to limit the occurrence of war. Yet the shift in the normative basis of moral judgement towards the idea that states and the international community have a responsibility to protect individuals from serious violations of their human rights leads to a far more permissive regime concerning the use of force. This is evident in the treatment of the criterion of 'last resort' that we see extend from debates concerning humanitarian intervention to more recent claims about an expanded right of self-defence. On the face of it, humanitarian justifications for the use of force and self-defence claims appear distinct. Yet as the normative basis of the use of force develops, so the distinctive nature of these claims diminishes. The experiences of the international community in humanitarian operations undermined the belief in the efficacy of the criterion of last resort. The NATO intervention in Kosovo was unique in that it was a preventative intervention (a decision based in part on the desire to avoid another massacre like the one witnessed by a helpless UN Protection Force (UNPROFOR) in Srebrenica in 1995). But, as Wheeler notes, with this exception all other interventions have come 'too late to protect civilians from their killers'.[99] If saving strangers is a key normative commitment, then timely action is essential. The problem is that preventative action is by definition not supported by the evidence of mass atrocities. The case is, therefore, less compelling and a more restrictionist approach to the use of force tends to dominate in these circumstances. Nevertheless, preventative action does appear to be called for by the normative commitment to human rights. The normative concerns that drive the debate on humanitarian military intervention are clear. The moral dilemma posed by the need to protect individuals from gross violations of their human rights challenges the restrictionist international legal order. These tensions also play a key role in the debate concerning preventative self-defence where the primary responsibility of states to protect their citizens from violations of their human rights is invoked to justify anticipatory military action in the face of the threat posed by international terrorism. Here a combination of a new security threat and a new normative framework combine to challenge the restriction on the use of force in self-defence.

Self-defence is the traditional exception to the prohibition on the use of force. International law has long acknowledged that self-defence can sometimes be pre-emptive. The classical legal position is often referred to as the Webster formula (see above). While the Webster formula is often held up as the standard position many commentators argue that there is in fact a broader spectrum of permissible anticipatory action. Walzer begins by acknowledging that 'there are threats with which no nation can be expected to live and that acknowledgement is an important part of our understanding of aggression'.[100] When dealing with something as catastrophic as war it has long been acknowledged that a moral or legal rule that required states to wait until the first blow had been struck to resort to force in self-defence would be unrealistic and morally problematic. Walzer asks us to imagine a spectrum of anticipatory defensive actions, from a typical pre-emptive act (akin to throwing up your arms when you see a blow coming, and defined traditionally by the 'Webster formula' to preventative war.[101] The clearest contemporary example of preventative war in the contemporary period is the 'Bush Doctrine'. The Bush Doctrine was formulated in response to the terrorist attacks on the United States which culminated most vividly with the attack now known simply as 9/11. The 2002 National Security Strategy stated:

> The United States has long maintained the option of preemptive actions to counter a sufficient threat to our national security. The greater the threat, the greater is the risk of inaction – and

the more compelling the case for taking anticipatory action to defend ourselves, even if uncertainty remains as to the time and the place of the enemy's attack. To forestall or prevent such hostile acts by our adversaries, the United States will, if necessary act preemptively.

What the NSS calls pre-emption extends the doctrine of pre-emptive self-defence to the point where we need to distinguish between pre-emptive and preventative self-defence. Both are anticipatory, but they are distinct. The former reacts to 'instant and overwhelming danger'. The latter, however, responds to what President Bush called a 'grave and gathering danger'. The difficulties in identifying the threat from terrorist cells is a significant factor here (it is not like having the army of a neighbouring state massing on the border). The devastating effect of WMD (nuclear, chemical or biological weapons that are easily transported and deployed) is another key factor. It would be unreasonable to deny a state the right to defend itself from terrorist attack. However, both international law and just war principles have difficulty accommodating the US view. The Bush Doctrine reserves the right for the United States to defend itself against future threats. We know only that a group 'whose avowed tactics are wanton destruction and the targeting of innocents' want to harm those they identify as their enemy. We know also that they have, or are seeking, the means to do so. Lacking certainty of where the attack is coming from, the United States was aware that 'the overlap between states that sponsor terrorism and those that pursue WMD' was significant and that the 'most potent protection' of the terrorists was their statelessness. With this in mind, the Bush Doctrine sought to take the war to those states it saw as providing a haven for terrorists, either because of sympathy with their cause or because the state had no effective control over its territory. The strategy is one that tries to deal with terrorism at its root, but this requires military action in the territory of states that have not committed acts of aggression against the United States and before any actual threat becomes imminent. It is also the case that many of the victims of such a war are innocent civilians killed by direct attack (such as those killed in drone attacks in Pakistan) or indirectly through the humanitarian and societal chaos brought about by war. Here, then, we have *in bello* and *ad bellum* considerations to weigh up against the need for the United States to defend itself from further unjust attacks. The rules have to be applied carefully in light of detailed consideration of key claims. To what degree is the state in which we are thinking of conducting the War on Terror colluding in terrorism? If, as Walzer has suggested in the case of Afghanistan, the state was in league with the terrorists,[102] then the case for war becomes stronger. We must then ask what means we have of achieving the goal of preventing terrorist attacks. If we do not have a reasonable chance of success, then war is futile. If we do have the means, but they would impose such a heavy cost on non-combatants, then the case against war is strengthened. If we (or the weapons we use) cannot discriminate clearly between just targets and innocents or if the war is likely to bring devastation to the region, then we have cause to think that war is not the appropriate response. The crux of the issue concerns the way we balance the need to defend the rights of the innocent victims of terrorism and the rights of the innocent victims of a war on terror.

Alan Buchanan and Robert Keohane argue that just war theory (and the existing legal regime) is unduly conservative. They argue for a more permissive regime governing the use of force that places the protection of human rights at the centre of the normative order.[103] We have explored the basis of Buchanan's cosmopolitanism in earlier chapters. The central elements that are relevant here are the claims that conformity to human rights standards is now a central element of the legitimacy of states and international organisations, and that there has been a 'transition from an international legal system whose constitutive, legitimizing aim was peace among states (and before that the regulation of war among states) to one that takes the protection of human rights as one of its central goals'.[104] One of the key reasons for the just war/legalist conservative approach to the use of force is that the legitimacy (and efficacy) of military action to protect human rights is hotly disputed. Buchanan acknowledges this key concern. Such initiatives can be self-interested or based on biased or parochial, rather than universally shared, accounts of what human rights require or justify.[105] Our commitment to human rights may, indeed, urge us towards relaxing the constraints on the use of force. However, the international community is reluctant to accept the argument that our commitment to human rights implies this policy shift because the institutions that govern force do not appear to have the power to prevent self-interested or biased abuses of any relaxing of these constraints. Buchanan's point, however, is that we must consider these normative risks in light of the supposition that we can always reform institutions, should the risk–reward analysis require it. The biggest risk is what Buchanan terms the parochialism objection: 'the charge that human rights are expressions of either an arbitrarily limited set of values or an arbitrary ranking of values'.[106] But there is also risk in not developing a human rights-based conception of institutional legitimacy. Put simply, it is the cost of not protecting individuals against threats to their basic human rights posed by terrorists, genocidal regimes or tyrannical rulers. Buchanan argues that his institutional approach reduces the risk of abuse and the risk of factual or moral uncertainty in a way that alters the risk–reward analysis, and that it is this possibility that has been overlooked by those who object to his liberal proposition.

The argument in favour of rejecting the constraint on the use of force typically found in the contemporary just war/legalist position rests on the cost in terms of human rights violations versus the cost in terms of the risk of abuse and uncertainty concerning the moral outcomes of preventative war. Buchanan (and other liberal commentators) acknowledge that risks posed by abuse–parochialism and uncertainty are indeed significant, but argue that some feasible reforms to the governance institutions serve to mitigate such risks.[107] We explored the structure of Buchanan's proposed UN Security Council reforms and the argument in favour of a coalition of rights-respecting states in Chapter Four. To recap, the recommended reforms (new customary law, Charter and UN Security Council reform or the creation of a coalition of democracies) are intended to provide the oversight and accountability necessary to enable us to institutionalise the normative desire to protect rights. With such reforms (and Buchanan argues that the third option is the most realistic) we can have more confidence in policies of humanitarian intervention, preventive self-defence and (for Buchanan at least) forcible democratisation because each of these policies suffers from the same risks, and seeks to respond to the same challenges (massive violations of human rights). Risks of self-interested action are to be mitigated either by removal of the P-5 veto and the establishment of *ex post* and *ex* ante accountability mechanisms or (if such reforms cannot be effected) by shifting decision-making to a coalition of rights-respecting states. Such reforms are intended to alter the *ad bellum* assessment of the risk–reward of using force to protect human right. The *in bello* challenges (the cost to innocent civilians in the target state, the likelihood of restoring or establishing a genuinely self-determining polity while negating the terrorist threat, the costs (both human and economic) incurred by the intervening states measured against the goals achieved) remain significant. Nevertheless, removing the 'just war blanket prohibition' on war in the name of human rights significantly alters the *ad bellum* assessment of the justice of warfare.

Despite acknowledging the increasing importance of human rights norms, English School scholars, critical theorists and just war theorists remain wary of the permissive liberal approach. Reus-Smit sharply criticises the liberal argument in favour of a 'formal rehierachisation' of international politics 'whereby democratic states would gain special governance rights – particularly with regard to the legitimate use of force – and other states would have their categorical rights to self-determination and non-intervention qualified'.[108] Reus-Smit's account of legitimacy is close enough to Buchanan's that he too argues that human rights are a central constitutive norm in modern international politics, and therefore understands the attractiveness of the way that Buchanan and others attempt to resolve the trade off between order and justice in international society.[109] But the crucial point is that the overriding importance of human rights norms is not settled in the manner Buchanan suggests. If it were, then UN Security Council or Charter reform would not be the obstacle that it is. Humanitarian and human rights concerns are high on the agenda of states. It is entirely plausible to argue that these concerns have qualified the idea of sovereignty. However, the idea that the commitment to human rights principles would lead members of international society to abandon what Reus-Smit refers to as the 'equalitarian' regime based on sovereign equality in favour of a formal re-hierachisation overlooks the centrality of the norms of procedural justice tied up with multilateralism in contemporary international politics. The increasing normative weight of human rights concerns does not, in itself, insist on the reconstitution of the international legal order. It does offer that possibility, but the debate is one that asks all actors to choose between an equalitarian conservative approach to the use of force or an assertive hierarchical approach. If, as the evidence suggests, there is still a significant North–South and West–East division on the extent to which human rights concerns provide legitimate grounds for an expanded right to use force then, as Reus-Smit puts it, the judgement of liberal philosophers to the contrary is moot.

Reus-Smit continues his attack on 'the liberal license to use force' by pointing to the practical problems in identifying democratic states that appear to live up to the minimal moral acceptability criterion that befits them for superior status in international decision-making.[110] Buchanan recognises that the record of the United States in recent world affairs may mean that any coalition of democratic states might benefit from the absence of a superpower 'widely regarded – and not without reason – as an international scoff-law'.[111] Add to this the reaction of powerful but excluded states such as China and Russia, and it is hard to avoid the conclusion that the assertive liberal position threatens the primary goal of the just war tradition, which is the avoidance of great power conflict. Similarly, for Walzer, morality is a social object, and recognition of that fact encourages a respect for the political processes through which people create and contest those vital social objects.[112] Agents may not choose to give up multilateralism for a human rights-based and hierarchical international order. In fact, Walzer goes further to argue that there are good reasons (stemming from the reiterative nature of universal moral principles) for endorsing a pluralist and multilateralist institutional structure. Walzer's exploration of institutional reform found in the final chapter of *Arguing About War* sets out to answer the question 'what constitutional goals should we set ourselves in an age of globalization?'.[113] Giving himself the theoretical option of seven different constitutional arrangements ranging from an imaginary Kantian 'world republic' to international anarchy, Walzer opts for a constitutional model that aspires to overcome the problems of the 'decentralization of sovereign states' through a series of institutional reforms, but chooses, as an ideal, a pluralist model that has, as one of its acknowledged potential shortcomings, a limited capacity for peacekeeping and human rights enforcement.[114] Walzer does recognise the importance of human rights in contemporary international society, but argues (following his account of human rights developed elsewhere) that:

> Difference as a value exists alongside peace, equality, and autonomy, it does not supersede them. My argument is that they are best pursued in circumstances where there are many avenues of pursuit. The dream of a single agent – the enlightened despot, the civilising imperium, the communist vanguard, the global state – is a delusion.[115]

This is not just an argument about the degree to which human rights have become important to international society. It is a disagreement about the nature of human rights and the socially determined understanding of what a proper respect for human rights requires. Walzer's account of the reiterative, inherently social development of human rights leads him to argue that 'we can (and should) defend some minimal understanding of human rights and seek its universal enforcement, but enforcement in the third degree of pluralism would necessarily involve many agents, hence many arguments and decisions, and the results are bound to be uneven'.[116] This is considered preferable because it protects 'the equality for groups and individuals across the globe', and in doing so it preserves the social freedom to shape our human rights culture, which is a key feature of its current and continued legitimacy.[117] Similarly, Kennedy's account of the legalisation of war casts doubt on the moral desirability of emphasising human rights by showing that human rights and humanitarian standards are themselves the site of moral and political contest rather than an appeal to clear moral and legal standards. Kennedy acknowledges that the legalisation of war appears to be an attractive strategy for human rights activists and others outside the military, but shows how law has been weaponised – or that lawfare has blurred the boundaries between war and peace to the point where the military and humanitarians speak the same language and have created a context where we think of war as a civilised activity.[118] Because contemporary developments in the nature and means of war have 'made it unrealistic to build a law of war on the fantasy of a demarcated battlefield of uniformed soldiers' humanitarians have successfully sought to blur the line between human rights and the law of war.[119] But the legitimating power of human rights has made force something to be proud of and the new vocabulary of war 'beats ploughshares into swords as often as the reverse'.[120]

Human rights claims have extraordinary legitimating power in the contemporary legalised world order, but they have become as much a strategic tool for licensing or privileging new forms of coercion as for limiting old ones. It seems to make sense to push states to employ the standard of human rights law in security situations that seem divorced from the battlefields of a bygone age (whether in Basra or Gaza). But is it normatively desirable that concern for the human rights of the victims of 9/11 should support torture or the development of a category of 'illegal combatants' without rights or the ready invocation of a responsibility to protect that puts regime change beyond moral question? The way that law has become politicised has uneven results and appears to divorce actors (political, military, humanitarian) from a sense of responsibility. The contemporary law of war, then, encourages the interplay of multiple perspectives on what law requires as a strategic communicative act. In terms of law is there a difference between the International Committee of the Red Cross reformulating the customary law of war so that it advances the Red Cross agenda and the US claims that terrorists are a new form of unlawful combatant in a way that suited the security agenda?[121] It also enables an avoidance of responsibility where a broad interpretation of the law leads to violence being seen not as a decision, but as the operation or implementation of a rule. Kennedy's solution is to argue that the legalisation of war makes law a strategic tool (just as it is in commerce), a patchwork of contested general standards on a shifting political terrain. This, at least, he argues, should make us wary of trusting too much in virtues of humanitarian violence.

The moral and legal debates concerning the just use of force are urgent and continue to play out both inside the UN and in the foreign and security policies of member states. Inside the UN, as Secretary-General Ban Ki-Moon continues efforts to implement R2P, furious debates rage within the UN Security Council concerning the appropriate response to humanitarian crises in Libya and Syria. Outside we see the development of the US Atrocity Prevention Board against the backdrop of criticism of the United States' interventionist overstretch and diplomatic concerns about the collateral damage of the War on Terror, increasing European calls for NATO intervention in Syria and the continuing human costs of conflicts in Africa. Despite all these developments, the international community remains appropriately wary of unleashing the scourge of war that the UN was intended to eradicate. Nevertheless, there are clear normative drivers that point to the need to reform the law and that give rise to exceptions to the application of legal rules prohibiting the use of force. Lessons continue to be learned about the costs that intervening states should bear in order to affect humanitarian rescue, about the cost of non-intervention and about the ways that conflicts, both humanitarian and defensive, escalate into long and drawn out military and political battles. In the face of these extremely challenging situations moral clarity and consensus has been difficult to achieve, yet the urgency of humanitarian protection has been a constant theme in contemporary debates. Nevertheless, there is also an understandable scepticism towards the moral and practical benefits of the use of force, and international society has attempted to implement alternative strategies intended to force delinquent states to abide by their international obligations.

Non-military sanctions

Because of the moral and legal crisis concerning the legitimate use of force the international community has increasingly turned to non-military forms of coercion. Recent practice, however, raises the question of whether non-military coercion should also be judged by just war criteria (and what this means for existing law). As we have seen, there are several types of non-military but still coercive acts. Armed force is regulated by laws designed to distinguish between combatant and non-combatant and to demand just cause and proportionality. As Michael Reisman and Douglas Stevick note:

> The same type of examination is not transposed, *mutatis mutandis*, for prospective assessment of [other instruments]. The apparent reason for this persistent blind spot in international legal analysis has been the incorrect assumption that only the military instrument is destructive.[122]

Unilateral countermeasures and collective sanctions are permissible methods of forcing the 'target' state to comply with its international obligations. The system of unilateral countermeasures is the product of a 'self-help' system. Even after the UN Charter appeared to invest the UN Security Council with the primary authority to pursue enforcement action (Articles 41 and 53(1)), the continuing legality of unilateral countermeasures was outlined first in the *Air Services Arbitration*, confirmed by the ICJ in *Gabĉíkovo-Nagymaros* and codified by the ILC in the 2001 Articles on state responsibility (Article 22). The law governing unilateral countermeasures sits uneasily with the more centralised UN system and in both cases the law is comparatively underdeveloped.[123] In both cases the 'sender' is permitted to pursue proportionate measures in response to the failure by the 'target' in the fulfilment of its obligations. Such responses might be trade embargoes (limiting imports, exports or credit flows), arms embargoes, diplomatic sanctions or (more recently) international criminal prosecution.[124] Countermeasures and sanctions must be proportionate to the breach and aim at forcing the target to comply with their obligation (as opposed to being a punitive reprisal). They should also respect basic obligations under international law, including humanitarian and human rights obligations.[125] Collective sanctions are mandatory if authorised by the UN Security Council under chapter VII, meaning that all member states are obliged to observe the imposition of measures. UN Security Council mandated sanctions are instituted after the Council has determined the existence of a breach of international law as a key element of a threat to peace and security. Council practice has increased the role of the UN Security Council as a law-enforcing body and has gone some way to defining a conception of community interest or public policy.[126] Finally, some states act in response to what Cassese terms 'aggravated responsibility', where the offending state breaches community norms and the 'sender', while not directly harmed, acts on behalf of the community.[127] Beyond countermeasures and sanctions some states use economic measures to attempt to alter the policy of a third party in the absence of a breach (retorsion). Retorsive acts are said to be lawful insofar as a state is free to choose its trading and diplomatic partners, but this must be balanced against the principle of non-intervention. In what follows we confine our comments to countermeasures and sanctions.

In this brief summary it is possible to see some of the core concerns of just war theory. Just cause, right intention, proportionality and discrimination are all clear issues. Yet the law regulating countermeasures and sanctions is underdeveloped compared with the law of war, as is the tradition of ethical reflection that accompanies its application. It is also the case that the use of non-military coercive measures has increased since 1945 as sanctions are often seen as more restrained and more legitimate than the use of force. The United States is by far the most prolific unilateral 'sender' of sanctions, with the United Kingdom, the European Union and Russia following behind.[128] There has also been a marked increase in UN authorised action. Prior to the end of the Cold War the UN imposed sanctions on two occasions (Rhodesia and South Africa), but since 1989 has applied sanctions against Iraq, Yugoslavia, Libya, Cambodia, Somalia, Liberia, Rwanda, Haiti, Angola, Sudan, Afghanistan, Ethiopia-Eritrea, Somalia, DR Congo, Côte D'Ivoire, Sudan, DR Korea and Iran (in some cases on multiple occasions), as well as on terrorist organisations such as Al Qaeda. The policy has not been without controversy. As Mary O'Connell demonstrates, the sanctions 'debates' have centred on several issues. The first debate concerned the authority of the Security Council to impose sanctions on states that did not act in ways that obviously threatened *international* peace and security (the *ultra vires* debate). In the cases of Rhodesia (now Zimbabwe) and South Africa the object of the sanctions was a white minority regime that was, by definition, internally oppressive rather than externally aggressive. In deciding to act in these cases the history of the UN Security Council use of sanctions took a clear path. As Vera Gowlland-Debbas argues:

> Beginning with the case of Southern Rhodesia in 1966, the Council has singled out breaches of those norms that are now considered to be fundamental. The concept of international

peace and security has thus acquired a meaning that extends far beyond that of collective security . . . one in which ethnic cleansing, genocide and other gross violations of human rights, including the right to self-determination, as well as grave breaches of humanitarian law, including those encompassed within a state's own borders, are considered part of the security fabric.[129]

The second debate concerned the relative effectiveness of sanctions, but the third debate both added to these concerns and overwhelmed them. This third debate concerned the humanitarian impact of such measures. The question of the justice of a particular act that causes civilian casualties is amplified if the likelihood of success is limited. The standard figure referred to in the literature suggests a success rate, of all types of sanctions and policy goals, of just 34 per cent.[130] When this figure is broken down and placed next to the human cost for the target state, the argument for the justice of sanctions, especially as a policy option for dealing with non-democratic states, appears weak. What O'Connell refers to as the second debate (on effectiveness) merged into the third debate (on humanitarian impact) as the toll that the comprehensive sanctions regimes imposed on Iraq after the invasion of Kuwait in 1990 and on Haiti after the coup against President Aristide in 1991 became clear. In both cases a sanctions committee was established to oversee compliance and to permit limited exports so that medical and food supplies essential to humanitarian needs could be purchased. In both cases, however, the human cost was significant. These 'sanctions of mass destruction'[131] attracted the interest of human rights and humanitarian activists and lawyers as the toll became clear. In Iraq inflation reached 6,000 per cent and unemployment soared, while UNICEF reported that 3.5 million Iraqi's were exposed to significant health risks. In Haiti the pattern was similar with 1,000 extra child deaths per month reported as a consequence.[132] The Centre for Economic and Social Rights commissioned research that concluded that the 'case of Iraq illustrates why sanctions are not always the humane alternative to war'.[133] The institutional response to the humanitarian cost of comprehensive sanction regimes was to develop smart sanctions as 'the precision guided munitions of economic statecraft'.[134] The idea was to use measures such as restrictions on private lending, asset freezes or travel bans 'that could be aimed at specific officials or government functions without damaging the overall economy and imposing exceptional hardship on the general public'.[135] However, while smart sanctions do appear to reduce the humanitarian cost, they also appear less effective at achieving the goals of the sender states and organisations.[136] This has meant that even smart sanctions have been 'imposed in combination with selective export restriction or aid suspensions' or are used merely as a signalling device.[137]

Although just war theory does not apply in any straightforward way to countermeasures and sanctions, it seems clear from this brief discussion that we could and should apply its basic tenets. There are clear *ad bellum* concerns relating especially to just cause and right authority and urgent *in bello* issues of proportionality and discrimination. Turning first to just cause, it seems appropriate to distinguish, following Cassese, between cases of ordinary and aggravated responsibility. Both forms of responsibility follow from a wrongful act. However, aggravated responsibility is distinct from ordinary responsibility in that it follows a breach of fundamental community values owed to all other members of the international community or to all parties to a multilateral treaty, such as the ICCPR or the Geneva Conventions (an obligation *erga omnes/erga omnes partes*). Furthermore, the breach must be gross or systematic.[138] In the case of ordinary responsibility, providing the countermeasures are proportionate and do not conflict with human rights or humanitarian principles, then unilateral action is just and lawful. There may, nevertheless, be a case for requiring sender states to refer the issue to the UN Security Council and for the establishment of a sanctions committee or to an alternative multilateral body such as the Committee on Economic, Social and Cultural Rights (CECSR).

In the case of aggravated responsibility the challenges are greater. Gross and systematic abuses of fundamental community norms take the form of genocide, crimes against humanity, war crimes and crime against peace. Under these circumstances even proportionate sanctions are likely to be severe. It is now established practice that the UN Security Council has authority to act under these circumstances and it has developed an impressive array of techniques to achieve its goals. The significance of this post-Cold War development to our present understanding of just cause is considerable. The role of the UN Security Council (an inherently political body) in law enforcement and the concomitant role of the law in providing for the legitimacy of Council action shows the intimate relationship between politics and law in contemporary world affairs.[139] There are, however, two key *ad bellum* concerns under such circumstances. The first is that states still maintain the right of unilateral countermeasures in response to breaches of community norms. This is similar to the idea of unilateral humanitarian intervention and should be governed by the same criteria (see above). An equally significant challenge, however, is that of encouraging states to act (or to accept their responsibility to protect community norms) where they have not suffered a material breach. For Cassese, while states still view state responsibility as a private matter arising within the legal framework of bilateral regulation, the direction of travel suggests that 'it is important for *forward looking legal means and instrumentalities* to be available to states'.[140] Again, the similarities with the moral, legal and political challenges of humanitarian military intervention are evident.

Turning to *in bello* considerations, the scale of devastation and the nature of the victims (predominantly civilians, among them a disproportionate number of women and children) raises a number of key moral questions. Together these issues ask whether and how sender states and organisations should be responsible for the suffering of individuals in the target state. There are several arguments that suggest that sanctions should be judged using the standards of human rights law, or humanitarian law or the law of countermeasures.[141] In each case the argument concerns the normative desirability of regulating a largely unregulated activity. This is not to say that the humanitarian challenges of economic coercion are not apparent to the international community. Indeed, the UN Security Council appends humanitarian exemptions to sanctions regimes and tasks a sanctions committee to oversee the impact of sanctions, and the UN General Assembly reports annually on the humanitarian effect of sanctions.[142] The UN Security Council has also recognised that it is bound by humanitarian principles and general principles of international law when acting under chapter VII.[143] Nevertheless, the humanitarian costs of sanctions remain high. The core moral issue concerns the collateral damage caused by economic sanctions, which, because of the methods used, can be far greater than that caused by the military instrument.[144] Collateral damage refers to damage caused to agents other than the intended target. If such damage is an unintended or unforeseeable consequence of a necessary act it may not be appropriate to hold the sender morally or legally responsible. However, sanctions purposefully target non-combatants. In the case of comprehensive regimes the whole point of the exercise is to coerce the target state into fulfilling its obligations by putting economic pressure on the entire population. A state, however rogue, is ultimately a collection of individuals, and we need to consider if it can be just to target those individuals. Some observers argue that such acts necessarily violate the UN Charter or key human rights rules. The justice of sanctions, argues Fausey, rests on a 'fixation on sovereignty', which 'results in the blind punishment of individuals not responsible for the behaviour which prompted the sanctions'.[145] While it is commonplace to ascribe moral and legal responsibility to states as entities,[146] it is vital to consider the extent to which the individuals that sanctions harm are legitimate targets of coercion. It is certainly the case that such individuals have certain non-derogable human rights. Marks shows that such rights are routinely violated by sanctions regimes. However, holding the sender legally responsible is difficult because neither the UN Security Council or the UN more broadly are party to treaties such as the ICESCR or the Convention on the Rights of the Child (CRC). Even if we were to think of the members of the UN as acting in a manner contrary to the object and purposes of their treaty obligations in respect of the ICESCR or CRC, the fact that all sanctions regimes contain humanitarian exemptions 'make it difficult to find wilful intent on the senders' part'.[147] While legal responsibility may be lacking, the question of the moral responsibility of senders is still a major issue for the UN General Assembly, the CESCR and many observers. It may simply be the case that the legal regime is inadequate. One response to this charge is that the responsibility lies with the target state – with the regime's leadership and the citizen body more broadly.[148] This line of argument is much stronger if the target state is democratic and we can assume that the citizens support the regime in question.[149] However, the vast majority of sanctions regimes do not target democratic states and this means not only that we cannot assume that the citizens support the regime, but that the 'trickle up' effect of sanctions, whereby the suffering of the population forces the regime to change, is less effective. Because of these moral challenges many scholars argue that just war principles and international humanitarian law should be applied to sanctions. In particular, the principles of necessity, proportionality and discrimination should provide a rigorous test of the justice of sanctions.

The emergence of a clear range of urgent and hierarchically superior community norms and increasing awareness of the humanitarian costs of measures short of war significantly alters the normative context in which we evaluate the justice of countermeasures and sanctions. The argument that economic sanctions must be used only in accordance with the principles of self-defence and the law of countermeasures seems well founded.[150] O'Connell goes further, arguing that developing the law of countermeasures to cover multilateral acts should also forgo the exceptions to the humanitarian limits on war found in international humanitarian law (whereby the limits on force recede as the need for greater force is required to meet the military objective) precisely because of the harm caused to civilians. Stricter considerations of necessity, proportionality and discrimination are warranted, and it may even be the case that the use of military force is morally preferable to a sustained sanctions regime, and that the established idea that 'conflict containment is the hierarchically superior value'[151] ought to be overturned. While considerations of the justice of war have been a long-standing part of the ethics of international politics, relatively little consideration has been given to other coercive acts. However, in the context of a highly legalised world order where the multilateral enforcement of community values is a crucial goal, the institutional and moral implications of sanctions suggest that such measures receive the same scrutiny as the use of force.

Notes

1 Hobbes, T., *Leviathan*, ed. C. B. Macpherson, London: Penguin, 1968, pp. 187–8.
2 Byers, M. and Chesterman, S., 'Changing the Rules about Rules? Unilateral Humanitarian Intervention and the Future of International Law' and Franck, T., 'Interpretation and Change in the Law of Humanitarian Intervention', both in J. Holzgrefe and R. Keohane (eds), *Humanitarian Intervention: Ethical, Legal and Political Dilemmas*, Cambridge: Cambridge University Press, 2003, pp. 177–203 and pp. 204–31, respectively; Walzer, *Arguing About War*; Wheeler, *Saving Strangers*; Kennedy, *Of War and Law*.
3 Kennedy, *Of War and Law*, p. 3.
4 Kennedy, *Of War and Law*, p. 45.
5 Kennedy, *Of War and Law*, pp. 91–6.
6 Kelsen, H., *General Theory of Law and State*, Clarke, NJ: The Law Book Exchange, 1945, p. 331. Also see Dinstein, Y., *War, Aggression and Self-Defence*, 5th edn, Cambridge: Cambridge University Press, 2011, pp. 65–75.
7 The National Security Strategy of the United States of America, September 2002, p. 16, available at: http://www.state.gov/documents/organization/63562.pdf.
8 Briggs, H. W., *The Law of Nations: Cases, Documents and Notes*, 2nd edn, London: Stevens, 1953, p. 976.
9 Available at: http://www.yale.edu/lawweb/avalon/imt/kbpact.htm, accessed 10 August 2012.
10 White, N. and Abass, A., 'Countermeasures and Sanctions', in M. Evans (ed.), *International Law*, 2nd edn, Oxford: Oxford University Press, 2006, pp. 509–30.

11 [1986] ICJ Rep. 14, para. 190.
12 [1996] ICJ Rep. 226, para. 47. For a detailed exploration of the issue of a threat of the use of force under Art. 2(4), see Green, J. and Grimal, F., 'The Threat of Force as an Action in Self-Defence under International Law', *Vanderbilt Journal of Transnational Law*, 44 (2011): 285–329, at pp. 289–98
13 Waxman, M., 'Cyber-Attacks and the Use of Force: Back to the Future of Article 2(4)', *Yale Journal of International Law*, 36 (2011): 421–59, at pp. 426–30.
14 2625(XXV), 24 October 1970, and A/RES/42/22, 18 November 1987.
15 Rosenstock, R., 'The Declaration of Principles of International Law concerning Friendly Relations: A Survey', *American Journal of International Law*, 65(5) (1971): 713–35, at pp. 724–5.
16 Paragraph 32(2)(a).
17 Macdonald, R. S., 'The Use of Force by States in International Law', in M. Bedjaoui (ed.), *International Law: Achievements and Prospects*, Dordrecht: Martinus Nijhoff, 1991, p. 720.
18 See Buchan, R., 'Cyber Attacks: Unlawful Uses of Force or Prohibited Interventions?', *Journal of Conflict and Security*, 17(2) (2012): 211–27, at pp. 215–16; Bowett, D., 'Economic Coercion and Reprisals By States', *Virginia Journal of International Law*, 13(1) (1972/3): 1–13.
19 Franck, T., 'Who Killed Article 2(4)? Or: Changing Norms Governing the Use of Force by States', *American Journal of International Law*, 64(5) (1970): 809–37.
20 Henkin, L., 'The Reports of the Death of Article 2(4) Are Greatly Exaggerated', *American Journal of International Law*, 65 (1971): 544–8.
21 Waxman, 'Cyber-Attacks and the Use of Force', pp. 421–59.
22 O'Connell, M., 'Cyber Security without Cyber War', *Journal of Conflict and Security*, 17(2) (2012): 187–209.
23 Contrast this position with that of O'Connell, 'Cyber Security without Cyber War', pp. 187–209.
24 Tsagourias, N., 'Cyber-attacks, Self-defence and the Problem of Attribution', *Journal of Conflict and Security Law*, 17(2) (2012): 229–44, at pp. 230–3; Buchan, 'Cyber Attacks', p. 217; Waxman, 'Cyber-Attacks and the Use of Force', pp. 421–59; Dinstein, *War, Aggression and Self-Defence*, p. 88.
25 USA International Strategy for Cyberspace: Prosperity, Security and Openness in a Networked World, May 2011, p. 14, available at: http://www.whitehouse.gov/sites/default/files/rss_viewer/international_strategy_for_cyberspace.pdf, accessed 26 August 2012.
26 Gray, C., 'The Use of Force and the International Legal Order', in M. Evans (ed.), *International Law*, 2nd edn, Oxford: Oxford University Press, 2006, pp. 593–7.

27 [1986] ICJ Rep. 14, para. 176.
28 Available at: http://avalon.law.yale.edu/19th_century/br-1842d.asp#web2, accessed 20 August 2012.
29 See the *Nicaragua* case, Merits, [1986] ICJ Rep. 14, para.194; *Legality of the Threat or Use of Nuclear Weapons*, Advisory Opinion, [1996] ICJ Rep. 226, para. 141; *Oil Platforms* case (*Iran* v. *USA*), [2003] ICJ Rep. 161.
30 Greenwood, 'International Law and the Pre-emptive Use of Force', p. 9.
31 Paragraph 189, available at: http://www.un.org/secureworld, accessed 20 August 2012.
32 Greenwood, 'International Law and the Pre-emptive Use of Force', pp. 12–16.
33 National Security Strategy of the United States of America, September 2002.
34 National Security Strategy of the United States of America, p. 15. See Reisman, W. M. and Armstrong, A., 'The Past and Future of the Claim of Preemptive Self-Defense', *American Journal of International Law*, 100 (2006): 525–50.
35 National Security Strategy of the United States of America, March 2006, p. 23.
36 Franck, T., 'Preemption, Prevention and Anticipatory Self-Defense: New Law Regarding Recourse to Force?', *Hastings International and Comparative Law Review*, 27 (2003/4): 425–35, at p. 428.
37 Franck, 'Preemption, Prevention and Anticipatory Self-Defense', pp. 429 and 433.
38 *Nicaragua* case, Merits, [1986] ICJ Rep. 103. See Art. 3(g) of the Definition of Aggression, UN General Assembly Resolution 3314(XXIX), 14 December 1974.
39 See Cassese, A., 'Terrorism is Also Disrupting Some Crucial Legal Categories of International Law', *European Journal of International Law*, 12(5) (2001): 993–1001, at pp. 995–8; Greenwood, 'International Law and the Pre-emptive Use of Force', pp. 16–18; Trapp, K., 'Back to Basics: Necessity, Proportionality, and the Right of Self-Defence Against Non-State Terrorist Actors', *International and Comparative Law Quarterly*, 50(1) (2007): 141–56; Tams, C., 'The Use of Force against Terrorists', *European Journal of International Law*, 20(2) (2009): 359–97; Steenberghe, R. van, 'Self-Defence in Response to Attacks by Non-State Actors in the Light of Recent State Practice: A Step Forward?', *Leiden Journal of International Law*, 23 (2010): 183–208.
40 Gray, 'The Use of Force and the International Legal Order', pp. 600–1; Harris, *Cases and Materials on International Law*, pp. 933–7. However, see Akehurst, M., 'The Use of Force to Protect Nationals Abroad', *International Relations*, 5 (1976/7): 3–23.
41 *Nicaragua* case, Merits, [1986] ICJ Rep. 103, paras 199–200.

42 See, 'In Larger Freedom: Towards Development, Security and Human Rights for All', Report, para. 126, A/59/2005, 21 March 2005.
43 Available at: http://www.unmultimedia.org/radio/english/2012/07/russia-and-china-veto-security-council-action-on-syria, accessed 27 August 2012.
44 UN General Assembly, Resolution 377 A(V), 3 November 1950.
45 Definition of Aggression, Art. 3, General Assembly Resolution 3314 (XXIX), 14 December 1974.
46 Article 3.
47 Article 4.
48 See Security Council, SC9000, 17 April 2007; Security Council, SC10332, 20 July 2011. Also see Penny, C. K., 'Greening the Security Council: Climate Change as an Emerging Threat to International Peace and Security', *International Environmental Agreements*, 7 (2007): 35–71; Scott, S. 'Securitizing Climate Change: International Legal Implications and Obstacles', *Cambridge Review of International Affairs*, 21(4) (2008): 603–19.
49 O'Connell, 'Cyber Security without Cyber War', pp. 205–6.
50 Repertoire of the Practice of the Security Council: Actions with Respect to Threats to the Peace, Breaches of the Peace, and Acts of Aggression (chapter VII), available at: http://www.un.org/en/sc/repertoire/actions.shtml#rel3, accessed 27 August 2012.
51 See, e.g., UN SC Resolution 1970 [2011] in respect of Libya.
52 Bothe, M., 'Security Council's Targeted Sanctions against Presumed Terrorists', *Journal of International Criminal Justice*, 6(3) (2008): 541–55, at p. 544.
53 Bothe, 'Security Council's Targeted Sanctions against Presumed Terrorists,' p. 544. See also Drezner, D., 'How Smart are Smart Sanctions?', *International Studies Review*, 5(1) (2003): 107–10.
54 See Fassbender, B., 'Targeted Sanctions Imposed by the UN Security Council and Due Process Rights', *International Organizations Law Review*, 3 (2006): 437–85; Milanovic, M., 'Al-Skeini and Al-Jedda in Strasbourg', *European Journal of International Law*, 23(1) (2012): 121–39, at pp. 133–8.
55 See Goldstone, R., 'International Criminal Tribunal for Former Yugoslavia: A Case Study in Security Council Action', *Duke Journal of Comparative and International Law*, 6 (1995/6): 5–10; Shraga, D. and Zacklin, R., 'The International Criminal Tribunal for Rwanda', *European Journal of International Law*, 7(4) (1996): 501–18.
56 Blokker, N., 'Is the Authorization Authorized? Powers and Practice of the UN Security Council to Authorize the Use of Force by Coalitions of the Able and Willing', *European Journal of International Law*, 11(3) (2000): 541–68.
57 UN Security Council Resolution 82, 1950.

58 UN Security Council Resolution 678, 1990.
59 UN Security Council Resolution 1973, 2011.
60 Dinstein, *War, Aggression and Self-Defence*, pp. 333–6.
61 Byers, M., 'Agreeing to Disagree: Security Council Resolution 1441 and Intentional Ambiguity', *Global Governance*, 10 (2004): 165–86.
62 See 'Attorney-General's Advice on the Iraq War: Resolution 1441', *International and Comparative Law Quarterly*, 54 (2005): 767–78.
63 Gray, C., *International Law and the Use of Force: Foundations of Public International Law*, 3ed edn, Oxford: Oxford University Press, 2008, pp. 354–69.
64 UN Report of the High-level Panel on Threats, Challenges and Change 'A More Secure World: Our Shared Responsibility', 2004, paras 84–8.
65 See http://www.un.org/en/peacekeeping/operations/current.shtml.
66 This creative way of interpreting the Charter provisions to permit peacekeeping is attributed to Dag Hammarskjöld, the second UN Secretary-General, see '60 Years of United Nations Peacekeeping', available at: http://www.un.org/events/peacekeeping60/60years.shtml, accessed 25 October 2012.
67 For current peacekeeping operations, see: http://www.un.org/en/peacekeeping/operations/current.shtml, accessed 25 October 2012.
68 See, e.g., Scheffer, D., 'United Nations Peace Operations and Prospects for a Standby Force', *Cornell International Law Journal*, 28(3) (1995): 650–60; Lilly, D., 'The Privatization of Peacekeeping: Prospects and Realities', *Disarmament Forum*, 3 (2000): 53–62; Zarate, J. C., 'Emergence of a New Dog of War: Private International Security Companies, International Law and the New World Disorder', *Stanford Journal of International Law*, 34 (1998): 75–162; Shearer, D., 'Outsourcing War', *Foreign policy*, 112 (1998): 68–82.
69 Tsagourias, N., 'Consent, Neutrality/Impartiality and the Use of Force in Peacekeeping: Their Constitutional Dimension', *Journal of Conflict and Security*, 11(3) (2006): 465–82.
70 Holzgrefe, J. L., 'The Humanitarian Intervention Debate', in J. L. Holzgrefe and R. Keohane (eds), *Human Intervention: Ethical, Legal, and Political Dilemmas*, Cambridge: Cambridge University Press, 2003, p. 18.
71 Report of the High-level Panel on Threats, Challenges and Change, 2004, para. 203.
72 ICISS Report, para. 4.17, available at: http://responsibilitytoprotect.org/ICISS%20Report.pdf, accessed 5 September 2012.
73 Holzgrefe, 'The Humanitarian Intervention Debate', p. 37.
74 Gray, 'The Use of Force and the International Legal Order', p. 595.
75 Holzgrefe, 'The Humanitarian Intervention Debate', pp. 38–40.
76 Gray, 'The Use of Force and the International Legal Order', p. 595.
77 Brownlie, *Principles of Public International Law*, 6th edn, pp. 710–12.

See also Simma, B., 'NATO, the UN and the Use of Force: Legal Aspects', *European Journal of International Law*, 10(1) (1999): 1–22.
78 Gray, 'The Use of Force and the International Legal Order', pp. 614–17.
79 Abass, A., *Regional Organisations and the Development of Collective Security: Beyond Chapter VIII of the UN Charter*, Oxford: Hart, 2004, pp. 52–9.
80 See Evans, M. A., *Just War Theory: A Reappraisal*, Edinburgh: Edinburgh University Press, 2005; Evans, M. A., 'Balancing Peace, Justice and Sovereignty in *Jus Post Bellum*: The Case of Just Occupation', *Millennium Journal of International Studies*, 36(3) (2008): 533–54.
81 Walzer, *Just and Unjust Wars*, pp. 51–3.
82 Walzer, *Just and Unjust Wars*, p. 34.
83 Walzer, *Just and Unjust Wars*, pp. 138–9.
84 Walzer, *Just and Unjust Wars*, p. 85.
85 Chesterman, S., *Just War or Just Peace: Humanitarian Intervention and International Law*, Oxford: Oxford University Press, 2001, pp. 121–8.
86 Evans, G., 'The End of the Argument: How We Won the Debate over Stopping Genocide', *Foreign Policy*, December 2011; Slaughter, A.-M., 'A Day to Celebrate but Hard Work Ahead', *Foreign Policy*, 18 March 2011. For a critical view, see Pollentine, M., 'Constructing the Responsibility to Protect', Ph.D. thesis, Cardiff University, 2012.
87 Walzer, 'The Moral Standing of States: A Response to Four Critics', p. 218.
88 Walzer, *Just and Unjust Wars*, pp. 87–91.
89 Wheeler, *Saving Strangers*, p. 35.
90 Luban, D., 'The Romance of the Nation State', *Philosophy and Public Affairs*, 9(4) (1980): 392–7, at p. 396.
91 Byers, and Chesterman, 'Changing the Rules about Rules?', p. 202.
92 Wheeler, *Saving Strangers*, p. 297.
93 Wheeler, *Saving Strangers*, pp. 275–81.
94 Wheeler, *Saving Strangers*, p. 281.
95 Byers and Chesterman, 'Changing the Rules about Rules?', p. 203.
96 Correll, H., 'To Intervene or Not: The Dilemma That Will Not Go Away', Keynote at Duke University, 19 April 2001, pp. 5–8.
97 Crawford and Olleson, 'The Nature and Forms of International Responsibility', pp. 463–4.
98 Wheeler, *Saving Strangers*, p. 41.
99 Wheeler, *Saving Strangers*, p. 34.
100 Walzer, *Just and Unjust Wars*, p. 85.
101 Walzer, *Just and Unjust Wars*, p. 75.
102 Walzer, *Arguing About War*, p. 137.
103 Buchanan, *Human Rights*, pp. 105–33.
104 Buchanan, *Human Rights*, p. 72.
105 Buchanan, *Human Rights*, p. 72.

106 Buchanan, *Human Rights*, p. 73.
107 See Doyle, M., *Striking First: Prevention and Preemption in International Conflict*, ed. S. Macedo, Princeton, NJ: Princeton University Press, 2008, pp. 62, 84; Shue, H., 'What Would Justified Preventative Military Attack Look Like?', in H. Shue and D. Rodin (eds), *Preemption: Military Action and Moral Justification*, Oxford: Oxford University Press, 2010, pp. 236–44, for qualified support of this view.
108 Reus-Smit, C., 'Liberal Hierarchy and the License to Use Force', *Review of International Studies*, 31 (S.I.) (2005): 72.
109 Reus-Smit, 'Liberal Hierarchy', p. 86.
110 Reus-Smit, 'Liberal Hierarchy', pp. 82–3.
111 Buchanan, *Justice, Legitimacy and Self-Determination*, p. 452.
112 Sutch, 'International Justice and the Reform of Global Governance', pp. 513–30.
113 Walzer, *Arguing About War*, pp. 171–91.
114 Walzer, *Arguing About War*, pp. 189–90.
115 Walzer, *Arguing About War*, p. 188.
116 Walzer, *Arguing About War*, p. 190.
117 Walzer, *Arguing About War*, p. 191.
118 Kennedy, *Of War and Law*, pp. 10–12, 88–144.
119 Kennedy, *Of War and Law*, p. 112.
120 Kennedy, *Of War and Law*, pp.139, 167.
121 Kennedy, *Of War and Law*, pp. 93–8.
122 Reisman W. M. and Stevick, D., 'The Applicability of International Law Standards to United Nations Economic Sanctions Programmes', *European Journal of International Law*, 9 (1998): 95.
123 Wight, N. and Abbas, A., 'Countermeasures and Sanctions', in M. Evans (ed.) *International Law*, Oxford: Oxford University Press, 2003, pp. 505–27.
124 Marks, S., 'Economic Sanctions as Human Rights Violations: Reconciling Political and Public Health Imperatives', *American Journal of Public Health*, 89(10) (1999): 1509–10.
125 Wight and Abbas, 'Countermeasures and Sanctions', p. 513.
126 Gowlland-Debbas, V., 'The Function of the United Nations Security Council in the International Legal System', in M. Byers (ed.), *The Role of Law in International Politics*, Oxford: Oxford University Press, 2000, pp. 281–312.
127 Cassese, *International Law*, p. 201.
128 Winkler, A., 'Just Sanctions', *Human Rights Quarterly*, 21 (1999): 133; Hufbauer, G., Schott, J., Elliot, K. and Oegg, B., *Economic Sanctions Reconsidered*, 3rd edn, Washington, DC: Peterson, 2009, pp. 20–41.
129 Gowlland-Debbas, 'The Function of the United Nations Security Council', p. 289.

130 Hufbauer *et al.*, *Economic Sanctions Reconsidered*, p. 159.
131 O'Connell, M., 'Debating the Law of Sanctions', *European Journal of International Law*, 13(1) (2002): 63–79.
132 Reisman and Stevick, 'The Applicability of International Law', pp. 102–20.
133 Marks, 'Economic Sanctions as Human Rights Violations', p. 1510. See also Cortright, D. and Lopez, G., 'Are Sanctions Just? The Problematic Case of Iraq', *Journal of International Affairs*, 52(2) (1999): 735–55, at pp. 741–2.
134 Drezner, D., 'Sanctions Sometimes Smart: Targeted Sanction in Theory and Practice', *International Studies Review*, 13 (2011): 96.
135 Hufbauer *et al.*, *Economic Sanctions Reconsidered*, p. 138.
136 Drezner, 'Sanctions Sometimes Smart', p. 102; Hufbauer *et al.*, *Economic Sanctions Reconsidered*, p. 141.
137 Hufbauer *et al.*, *Economic Sanctions Reconsidered*, pp. 138–9.
138 Cassese, *International Law*, pp. 200–1.
139 Gowlland-Debbas, 'The Function of the United Nations Security Council', pp. 277–313.
140 Cassese, *International Law*, p. 211 (original emphasis).
141 Marks, 'Economic Sanctions as Human Rights Violations'; O'Connell, 'Debating the Law of Sanctions'; Fausey, J., 'Does the United Nations' Use of Collective Sanctions to Protect Human Rights Violate its Own Human Rights Standards', *Connecticut Journal of International Law*, 10 (1994): 193–218; Gordon, J., 'A Peaceful, Silent, Deadly Remedy: The Ethics of Economic Sanctions', *Ethics and International Affairs*, 13(1) (1999): 123–42, Cortright and Lopez, 'Are Sanctions Just?', pp. 735–55, Reisman and Stevick, 'The Applicability of International Law Standards'; Winkler, 'Just Sanctions'.
142 Winkler, 'Just Sanctions', p. 134.
143 O'Connell, 'Debating the Law of Sanctions', p. 71.
144 Reisman and Stevick, 'The Applicability of International Law Standards', p. 93. For an alternative view, see Damrosch, L. (ed.), *Enforcing Restraint: Collective Intervention in Internal Conflict*, New York: Council on Foreign Relations, 1993, p. 300.
145 Fausey, 'Does the United Nations' Use of Collective Sanctions to Protect Human Rights Violate its Own Human Rights Standards', p. 197.
146 Erskine, T., 'Kicking Bodies and Damning Souls: The Danger of Harming "Innocent" Individuals while Punishing "Delinquent" States', *Ethics and International Affairs*, 24(3) (2010): 262–85.
147 Marks, 'Economic Sanctions as Human Rights Violations', p. 1511.
148 Winkler, 'Just Sanctions', p. 148.
149 Erskine, 'Kicking Bodies and Damning Souls', p. 277; Reisman and Stevick, 'The Applicability of International Law', p. 132.

150 Reisman and Stevick, 'The Applicability of International Law', p. 128. See also O'Connell, 'Debating the Law of Sanctions'.
151 Damrosch, *Enforcing Restraint*, p. 130.

CHAPTER EIGHT

| The Law of the Sea | Justice and the Common Heritage of Mankind |

From time immemorial the sea has served humankind in diverse ways. It has provided a link for transportation and trade between various states. In addition, through activities such as fishing, it serves as a source of food and, relatively more recently, it serves as a cache of tremendous offshore mineral resources for coastal states. These multi-functional uses of the sea have led over the years to the development of a body of norms to regulate the use and activities of the sea, and to delineate the powers and jurisdiction of states over various parts of the sea. This body of norms has been labelled as the '*International Law of the Sea*' or more simply the '*Law of the Sea*'. It is one of the long-lasting areas of international law.

For an understanding of the development of the law of the sea, it is perhaps useful to divide the development into two eras: the classical law of the sea and the modern law of the sea. The classical phase could be said to be the era when the input into the development of this most important branch of international law was limited to Western developed states. Anand describes the law of the sea as 'based on European State practices which were developed and consolidated during the last three centuries'.[1] On the other hand, the modern law of the sea could be said to be the phase with input from a wider, more diverse (both in terms of geographical location and economic development) number of states.

It has been argued that some aspects of classical law of the sea were unjust because it merely served the interests of the big maritime states in the North, sometimes to the detriment of developing states in the

South. For instance, the representative of Tanzania at the third United Nations Conference on the Law of the Sea (UNCLOS III), in respect of the freedom of the high seas, said:

> Freedom of the seas had ceased to serve the interests of international justice. It had become a catchword and an excuse for a few countries to exploit ruthlessly the resources of the sea, to terrorise the world and to destroy the marine environment. That type of freedom belonged to the old order and had outlived its time.[2]

The law of the sea is a staple element in the study of public international law, yet it remains underexplored by those interested in international politics. The recent history of the law of the sea, particularly provisions relating to the 'Area' of the deep seabed beyond sovereign jurisdiction, are at the heart of vital questions of environmental, economic development and security policy. These same provisions are also the locus of key debates on the nature of international law and justice. In the first sections of this chapter we explore the key components of the law of the sea before turning to an exploration of the ideal of the 'common heritage of mankind' as it was developed in UNCLOS III and codified in the 1982 Law of the Sea Convention (Part XI). The intention to treat the 'Area' of the deep seabed beyond sovereign jurisdiction as the common heritage of mankind was an exercise in global distributive justice (albeit one limited to the potential wealth of the 'global commons' of the deep seabed). It was an attempt to ensure that the developing world got an equal share of the mineral wealth of the deep seabed, despite the fact that only the developed states had any hope of developing the technology to reach those resources. The language of the treaty articulated a clear commitment to a conception of economic justice designed to manage the resources of the global commons equitably, and to address the injustice of the inequalities between the developed global North and the undeveloped, newly post-colonial South. It promised a new, just world order. In the later sections of the chapter we go on to explore the amendments to Part XI of the treaty in the 1994 Implementation Agreement that effectively undermined that normative ambition, and explore the implications of that decision for the politics of this and other global commons regimes (including the Arctic, Antarctic, space and the environment). Finally, we explore the impact this case has on our understanding of justice and the politics of international law.

Classical law of the sea: *mare clausum* versus *mare liberum*

A good starting point for tracing the development of classical law of the sea is the fifteenth century, when Pope Alexander VI by a Papal Bull in 1494, which was given legal effect through the Treaty of Tordesillas, drew a line dividing the seas between Portugal and Spain, the two predominant maritime powers at that time. This treaty was one of the earliest attempts to codify the law concerning the sea.[3] Other states such as Holland, because of their trading interests, in response to the Treaty of Tordesillas advocated for the doctrine of the freedom of the high seas. The Dutch state practice advocating for the freedom of the high seas is reflected in the writings of the famous Dutch jurist, Hugo Grotius, in his book, *Mare Liberum* (1609). This book has been described as 'the first and classic exposition of the doctrine of the freedom of the seas'.[4] Grotius published his book to defend the right of the Dutch (through the Dutch East India Company) to navigate in the Indian Ocean and other eastern seas over which Spain and Portugal claimed sovereignty in order to trade with India and the East Indies. This was therefore a situation in which the Portuguese and Spanish desired closed seas (*mare clausum*), while others like the Dutch desired open seas (*mare liberum*).[5]

England, under Elizabeth I, also challenged the claim by Spain and Portugal to sovereignty over the seas and advocated for freedom of the seas because the English were interested in having a share in the East India trade like the Dutch.[6] However, subsequently England under James I moved from the open sea policy of Elizabeth I to a closed sea policy. James I was more interested in curtailing the benefits accruing to the Dutch, who now had powerful merchant and fishing fleets, and therefore he pursued a policy of *mare clausum*. He commissioned an English man, John Selden, to make a strong case against *mare liberum*. In reply to Grotius' *Mare Liberum*, Selden wrote his treatise, *Mare Clausum, seu de Dominio Maris Libri Duo* (*The Closed Sea or Two Books concerning the Rule over the Sea*). This book was published in 1635 by the express command of the king to support the sovereignty of Britain over the seas around it. However, by the nineteenth century, when Britain had strengthened its maritime capability, thereby becoming a leading maritime power, it reverted again to a *mare liberum* policy, and has thereafter, along with other leading maritime powers, consistently pursued a policy of wanting as much of the seas as possible to be subject to freedom of the seas.[7]

By 1702, Cornelius van Bynkershoek, another Dutch jurist, in his book, *De Dominio Maris*, explained that the sovereignty of a coastal state over the sea was limited to a maritime belt (known presently as the territorial sea or waters) determined by the range of a cannon shot. The sea beyond the range of the cannon shot was to be regarded as high seas subject to the freedom of the high seas. Some jurists and states subsequently interpreted this rule (known as cannon shot rule) to mean that a coastal state could exercise sovereignty over a maritime belt three miles from the low-water mark.[8]

The above historical development gives an idea of the constant conflict between advocates of *mare liberum* (freedom of the high seas) and those of *mare clausum* (principle of sovereignty over the seas) that to this day permeates the law of the sea. According to Brown, the ascendancy of one over the other has over the years tended to reflect the interests of the predominant power of the day.[9]

UNCLOS I and II

In 1930 at The Hague codification conference an attempt was made by the League of Nations to codify the law of the sea, but nothing significant came out of this conference. The participating states were unable to reach an agreement on the breadth of the territorial sea.[10]

With the establishment of the United Nations, the first United Nations Conference on the Law of the Sea (UNCLOS I) was convened in 1957. This conference produced four Geneva Conventions adopted in 1958, namely, the Conventions on the Territorial Sea and Contiguous Zone, the High Seas, the Continental Shelf, and Fishing and Conservation of the Living Resources of the High Seas. There was also an optional protocol on dispute settlement. Despite the success of the 1958 conference, the parties failed to reach any agreement on two fundamental issues, namely, the breadth of the territorial sea and fishery limits. As a result, a second United Nations Conference on the Law of the Sea (UNCLOS II) was convened in 1960. It was to seek to resolve the outstanding issues from UNCLOS I. This conference, however, like its predecessor, failed to produce an agreement on the issue of the breadth of the territorial sea and fishery limits. It failed to produce any new conventions.[11]

The Law of the Sea

Modern law of the sea: prelude to UNCLOS III

From the 1960s, a number of developing states emerged as independent states and were able to garner an automatic majority in the UN General Assembly. At the time of UNCLOS I most of these states were still under colonial rule and did not have an opportunity to have a direct input into the formulation of classical law of the sea, including the 1958 Geneva Conventions. Consequently, these states were dissatisfied with the classical law of the sea, which they viewed as tilted in favour of the Western developed states.[12]

The developing states therefore pushed for a 'new' law of the sea that would incorporate their own interests. In a speech in 1967, the then Maltese representative at the General Assembly, Arvid Pardo, proposed that the deep seabed beyond national jurisdiction and the resources thereof should be declared as the common heritage of mankind and used for only peaceful purposes. This speech, in essence based on equal rights of all states to the sea and distributive justice, served as a rallying point for mainly developing states to push for a third Conference on the Law of the Sea. They succeeded in passing various resolutions at the UN General Assembly (including the Declaration of Principles Concerning the Seabed and the Ocean Floor and the Subsoil Thereof beyond the Limits of National Jurisdiction 1970), which culminated in third United Nations Conference on the Law of the Sea (UNCLOS III).[13]

UNCLOS III

Although UNCLOS III was a response to the need to accommodate the developing states unable to participate in the earlier efforts at formulating the law of the sea, it was also necessary to deal with some other outstanding issues. It not only needed to deal with the issue of the Area, which had assumed prominence with the speech of Arvid Pardo, and the improvement of technology opening up the possibility of mining the deep seabed, but also other outstanding issues from UNCLOS I and II, such as the breadth of the territorial sea and fishery zones. In addition, the fragmentation of the 1958 law of the sea conventions resulted in an uncoordinated law of the sea policy, whereby states had the latitude to choose to sign one convention and reject another. As a result, it was felt that there was a need for a single convention covering the various aspects of the law of the sea, since the problems of the sea are closely interrelated and ought to be considered as a whole.

This conference, involving diverse states from various parts of the globe, including a number of developing states, lasted for nine years (1973–1982) and ended with the adoption of the Law of the Sea Convention (LOSC) at Montego Bay, Jamaica, on 10 December 1982.[14]

After a very active participation at the UNCLOS III, the United States, under the Reagan administration, rejected the outcome of the conference – the Law of the Sea Convention 1982. The Reagan administration with its rather robust antagonism towards socialism rejected the convention due to the original Part XI provisions dealing with the deep seabed beyond national jurisdiction, which it felt incorporated central planning principles and introduced 'international socialism'.[15] Specifically, the United States, along with other developed states such as the United Kingdom and Germany, objected to the original Part XI provisions, especially in respect of the mandatory transfer of technology (Article 144), production limitations (Article 151) and review conference (Article 155). The United States also objected to the failure of the convention to provide it with a guaranteed seat on the Council of the International Seabed Authority (ISA) (Article 161). Although an Agreement Relating to the Implementation of Part XI of the United Nations Convention on the Law of the Sea 1994 (the 1994 Implementation Agreement, also known as the New York Agreement) has since addressed the concerns of the United States and other developed states, by effectively amending the original Part XI provisions to accommodate the above objections, the United States is yet to ratify the LOSC.[16]

The United States remains at present the only major maritime state that has failed to ratify the convention. Domestic politics and the constitutional provisions requiring the Senate to be involved in treaty ratification is the reason why the United States is yet to ratify this major Convention on the Law of the Sea. However, deliberations are ongoing in the Senate on the United States becoming a party to LOSC. The current tone appears to suggest that executive and the Senate Committee on Foreign Relations are now in support of America's accession to LOSC. In 2007, the then US president, George W. Bush, urged the Senate to act favourably so the United States could accede to the LOSC. It is probable that in the not too distant future the United States, the only authentic 'super power', will become a party to the LOSC.[17]

The President of the Conference, Ambassador Koh, at the final session of the UNCLOS III described this multilateral convention, which is a reasonably comprehensive elucidation of the law of the sea, as a 'Constitution for the Oceans'.[18] It was the result of a package deal involving trade-offs and compromise during UNCLOS III. As a single comprehensive document designed to achieve both the codification and progressive development of the law of the sea, it offers in one package different aspects of the law of the sea.[19] This, along with its almost universal ratification by 164 parties,[20] makes it undoubtedly the most significant treaty on the law of the sea. The LOSC covers a wide range of topics concerning the sea, including the limits and jurisdiction of coastal states over maritime zones, such as internal waters, territorial sea, exclusive economic zones (EEZ), continental shelf, high seas and the deep seabed beyond national jurisdiction (the Area). It also deals with navigational rights; legal status and exploitation of living and non-living marine resources; conservation and management of living marine resources; protection of the marine environment; marine research; and transfer of marine technology from developed states to developing states. Further, it provides for a compulsory dispute settlement mechanism. The sheer number of topics covered by the convention makes it impossible in a chapter of this length to cover all the topics. Neither does it allow for an all-inclusive analysis of the topics examined. We have therefore selected certain key topics, which in our view are of interest in understanding the development of the law of the sea, such as the relationship between the LOSC and other treaties related to the sea; certain key maritime zones, especially with respect to legal definitions, national claims and jurisdictional rights; and the institutions established under the LOSC.

Relationship between LOSC and other treaties related to the sea

Although the LOSC is without doubt the most important treaty on the law of the sea, it is by no means the only treaty affecting the sea. There are a number of other treaties governing the law of the sea. These treaties include the 1958 Geneva Conventions, which remain binding on a handful of states that are parties to the Geneva Conventions and not parties to the LOSC. As between states that are only parties to one or the other of the Geneva Conventions and states that are parties to both the relevant Geneva Convention and the LOSC, the appropriate Geneva Convention would apply. However, as between states that are parties to both the Geneva Conventions and the LOSC, the latter shall be the applicable treaty. The LOSC states that it 'shall prevail' over the Geneva Conventions in such cases.[21]

Apart from the 1958 Geneva Conventions, there are examples of other treaties that relate to the sea, such as the 1959 Antarctic Treaty, the 1974 International Convention for the Safety of Life at Sea (SOLAS) and the 2001 UNESCO Convention on the Protection of the Underwater Cultural Heritage. In respect of these other treaties, the LOSC states that it 'shall not alter the rights and obligations of States Parties which arise from other agreements compatible with this Convention [LOSC] and which do not affect the enjoyment by other States Parties of their rights or the performance of their obligations under this Convention'.[22] On the face of it, this implies that the LOSC would alter the rights and obligations of its states parties arising from other treaties that are incompatible with the LOSC provisions, thus making the LOSC a benchmark against which the compatibility of such other treaties to which the states parties to the LOSC are also parties can be measured. In so doing, the Article appears to suggest that the LOSC is higher in the hierarchy than other treaties relating to the sea. Nordquist, nevertheless, points out that this is a rather difficult provision of the LOSC that may give rise to disputes on interpretation.[23]

Overall, it is pertinent to emphasise that although the LOSC is undoubtedly a vital treaty, it is by no means the sole treaty dealing with the law of the sea. It is, however, in order, as is done in the sections below, to utilise the LOSC as a basis of analysis of the modern law of the sea because it encapsulates the subject.

Maritime zones

Baseline

The baseline is the line from which the breadth of the maritime zones, such as the territorial sea, contiguous zone, the exclusive economic zone and continental shelf are measured. As a rule, the baseline for measurement is the low-water line along the coast, which is marked on large-scale charts approved by the coastal states. In exceptional cases, where the coastline is deeply indented and cut into or if there is a fringe of islands along the coast in its immediate vicinity, the coastal state may measure the breadth by using the straight baselines method, which draws straight lines joining appropriate points in the coast.[24]

Internal waters

Internal waters are waters that lie landward of the baseline from which the territorial sea and other maritime zones are measured.[25] Internal waters include ports, bays, estuaries, rivers, lakes and any other waters on the landward side of the internal waters. The coastal state enjoys absolute sovereignty over internal waters. There is, therefore, no right of innocent passage for foreign ships. The only exception is in the case of internal waters, which ordinarily should be part of the territorial sea, but become part of internal waters because of the use of the straight baseline method.[26] Due to its absolute sovereignty, the coastal state may exercise jurisdiction, both civil and criminal, over foreign ships, subject to the rules of sovereign immunity of warships and non-commercial government ships. Nevertheless, the flag state of the foreign ship also has concurrent jurisdiction over acts or omissions committed on board the ship.

Recent developments in respect of the activities of pirates in the territorial waters of Somalia would appear to suggest that the UN Security Council, acting under its chapter VII powers, may authorise foreign ships to enter into the internal waters of a coastal state if it determines that this is needed to maintain international peace and security. It is suggested that this may even be done without the consent of the coastal state. The recent resolutions of the UN Security Council, for instance, Resolution S/RES/1816, 2 June 2008, and Resolution S/RES/1838, 7 October 2008, on the piracy situation in Somalia are in respect of the territorial sea and were passed with the consent of the Somalia Transitional Federal Government (TFG). However, nothing precludes the UN Security Council acting under its chapter VII powers from passing resolutions in respect of the internal waters also and even without the consent of the TFG. Article 2(7) of the UN Charter allows the Security Council to act under its chapter VII powers even in respect of matters within a state's domestic jurisdiction.

Territorial sea

The territorial sea is of vital importance to coastal states for both security and economic reasons. For instance, it acts as a sort of security buffer zone to protect the coastal state against sea-borne attack. It is not surprising, therefore, that historically the breadth of the territorial sea was measured based on the so-called cannon shot rule. Coastal states also have economic interests in this belt of the sea because of its potential to contain valuable resources such as oil and gas.

Territorial sea (sometimes also called 'territorial waters', 'marginal belt' or 'marginal sea') is that part of the sea that lies seaward from the baseline up to a limit of 12 nautical miles.[27] From the varying claims of different states, ranging from the rather narrow 3 nautical miles (mainly by developed maritime powers keen on restricting the areas of the sea within the sovereignty of the coastal state in order to have more 'open seas' subject to freedom of navigation) to the rather wide 200 nautical miles (mainly by developing states keen for more of the sea to be 'closed seas' in order to extend their sovereignty over the sea), the UNCLOS III was able to arrive at a compromise breadth of 12 nautical miles, a breadth now recognised under both the LOSC and customary international law.[28]

The right of a coastal state to territorial sea is automatic. As far back as 1951, a judge of the ICJ, Judge Arnold McNair in the *Anglo-Norwegian Fisheries* case, stated: 'International law does not say to a State: "You are entitled to claim territorial waters if you want them." No maritime State can refuse them. International law imposes upon a maritime State certain obligations and confers upon it certain rights arising out of the sovereignty which it exercises over its maritime territory.'[29] Due to its sovereignty over the territorial sea, the coastal state may exercise both criminal and civil jurisdiction over this belt of the sea.[30]

The coastal state exercises sovereignty not only in respect of the waters, but it extends to the bed and the subsoil as well as the airspace above the territorial sea.[31] For instance, aircraft have no right to fly over the territorial sea of another state without prior permission. The sovereignty of a coastal state is subject to the right of all foreign ships to enjoy innocent passage through the territorial sea. This right, which developed alongside the concept of the territorial sea, attempts to maintain a balance between the right of the coastal state to sovereignty and the right of all other states to enjoy navigation through the territorial sea. It has been incorporated both in the 1958 Territorial Sea Convention (TSC) and the LOSC.[32] Passage is defined as navigation through the territorial sea either for traversing it without entering into internal waters or for proceeding to or from internal waters.[33] Such passage is to be continuous and expeditious, though it may include stopping and anchoring, which are incidental to ordinary navigation or which are rendered necessary by *force majeure* or distress or for rendering assistance to persons, ships or aircraft in danger or distress.[34] A passage is innocent if it is not prejudicial to the 'peace, good order or security' of the coastal state.[35] The LOSC, however, unlike the earlier 1958 Convention, lists the activities that would make passage cease to be innocent, namely, the threat or use of force against the coastal state contrary to international law; weapons exercise or practice; espionage and propaganda against the defence or security of the coastal state; launching, landing or taking on board of any aircraft or military device; loading or unloading of commodity, currency or person contrary to the customs, fiscal, immigration or sanitary laws and regulation of the coastal state; unauthorised fishing and research or survey activities. In addition, it includes a rather omnibus clause – 'any other activity not having a direct bearing on passage' – which appears to suggest that the list of activities that may be regarded as making a passage cease to be innocent are not closed and exhaustive.[36] The United States and the then USSR, however, in a joint statement in 1989, obviously an attempt to restrict the power of coastal states to limit passage in their territorial seas, declared that the list of activities were exhaustive.[37]

It is not very clear if warships and ships carrying hazardous materials enjoy the right to innocent passage in the territorial sea of a coastal state, as there are divergent state practices on this. Some, such as the United States, insist that all ships, including warships, regardless of its cargo, armament or means of propulsion enjoy the right to innocent passage. Others insist that warships and ships carrying hazardous materials do not enjoy the right of innocent passage because they are inherently threatening to the 'peace, good order or security' of the coastal state. The practice of some other states, however, require such war ships or ships carrying hazardous materials to either obtain the prior consent of the coastal state or give prior notification before exercising the right to innocent passage. Clearly, practice on this issue is not uniform and is an example of state parties differing on the interpretation of provisions of the convention.[38]

Recent resolutions of the UN Security Council in respect of piracy in Somalia's territorial sea indicate that activities of ships, vessels or aircraft, which may not ordinarily fall within the LOSC definition of innocent passage, would be in order if authorised by the Security Council in exercise of its chapter VII powers.

Like the previous 1958 Convention on the Territorial Sea, under the LOSC adjacent or opposite states sharing common territorial sea are required to delimit it by agreement among themselves. In the event that they are unable to reach such agreement, a special procedure is used for delimitation known as the median or equidistance line, unless another boundary is justified by special circumstances (equidistance – special circumstance rule).[39]

Contiguous zone

The contiguous zone is that part of the sea over which the coastal state may exercise the control necessary to prevent and punish infringement of its customs, fiscal, immigration or sanitary laws and regulations within its territory or territorial sea. The coastal state, therefore, has rather limited rights for the purposes mentioned above over this belt of the sea falling short of the right to sovereignty.[40]

It is not obligatory for a coastal state to establish a contiguous zone. Previously under the 1958 Territorial Sea Convention the contiguous zone was not to extend beyond 12 nautical miles from the baseline. However, with the LOSC stating that the territorial sea could extend to a maximum breadth of 12 nautical miles, the contiguous zone has now been expanded to a maximum limit of 24 nautical miles from the baseline.

Continental shelf

The origin of the concept of the continental shelf (CS) may be traced back to the 1945 Proclamation by US President Truman. He declared that the natural resources of the subsoil and seabed of the CS beneath the high seas adjacent to the coasts of America are subject to its jurisdiction and control. The Proclamation, however, acknowledged that this claim did not affect the character of the waters above the CS as high seas and the right to freedom of navigation of foreign ships over these waters. The US claim was accompanied by similar widespread claims by other states, resulting in this concept emerging as part of customary international law.

The 1958 Convention on the Continental Shelf acknowledged that a coastal state had sovereign rights for the purpose of exploring and exploiting of natural resources in its CS. It defined the CS as the seabed and the subsoil of the submarine areas adjacent to the coastal state, but outside the territorial sea, up to a depth of 200 metres or beyond that limit up to the depth to which its technical capabilities allowed it to exploit (the so-called exploitability test) (Article 1). For a while, there was a debate about whether the rather vague 'exploitability' test permitted each coastal state to extend its CS shelf to include the seabed area *ad infinitum*, as long as there was technology available to exploit further. The better view is that the coastal state was permitted to exploit only the seabed and subsoil of the submarine area adjacent to its coast.[41]

However, by the UNCLOS III, especially with the emergence of a new maritime zone beyond national jurisdiction (the Area), the feeling was that there was need for more certainty regarding the scope of the CS. The LOSC defined the CS of a coastal state as the seabed and subsoil that extends beyond its territorial sea throughout the natural prolongation of its land territory to the outer edge of its continental margin, or in cases of states that do not have a broad continental shelf to a distance of 200 nautical miles from the baselines from which the breadth of the territorial sea is measured (Article 76(1)). This definition is largely based on a vital decision of the ICJ, the *North Sea Continental Shelf* case involving the delimitation of the CS of three coastal states: Federal Republic of Germany, Denmark and the Netherlands. In this case, the ICJ emphasised that the CS was the natural prolongation of a coastal state's land territory.[42]

The LOSC, therefore, while declaring that states that are not naturally endowed would be entitled to a CS up to a distance of 200 nautical miles from the baseline, does allow broad shelf states to have a CS extending beyond 200 nautical miles. It, however, limited such extended CS to a maximum of 350 nautical miles from the baselines (this limit does not apply to submarine elevations that are natural components of the continental margin, such as plateaux, rises, caps, banks and spurs) or 100 nautical miles from the 2,500-metre isobath. Two rather technical and complex methods are provided for establishing the outer limits of such extended CS, known as the Irish formula or the 1 per cent sediment thickness option and the Hedberg formula or foot of the slope (FOS) + 60 nautical miles.[43] The final outer limit of the extended CS beyond 200 nautical miles from the baseline is to be measured by straight lines not exceeding 60 nautical miles in length connecting all the fixed points.[44] Coastal states with extended CS are required under LOSC to make submissions in respect of the extended CS to a technical body established under the LOSC, the Commission on the Limits of the Continental Shelf (CLCS).[45]

It is pertinent to point out that the coastal state has rather limited rights over the CS, unlike the territorial sea. It merely exercises exclusive sovereign rights over the CS for the limited purpose of exploring and exploiting its natural resources. Natural resources include not only minerals and other non-living resources, such as oil and gas, but also living resources belonging to sedentary species. The latter is defined as organisms that at the harvestable stage are either immobile on or under the seabed or unable to move except in constant physical contact with the seabed or the subsoil.[46] Interestingly, this has been interpreted as include crabs but to exclude lobsters.[47]

In respect of the CS beyond 200 nautical miles broad-shelf states are required to make annual cash payments or contributions in kind at a specified rate from production. This specified rate takes effect only after the first five years of exploitation. From the sixth year, the rate of payment or contribution shall be 1 per cent, and this progressively increases by an additional 1 per cent for each subsequent year until it stabilises at 7 per cent in the twelfth year. Production does not include resources used in connection with exploitation. The payments or contributions are to be made to the International Seabed Authority (ISA), which is required to distribute them to state parties based on an equitable sharing formula, taking into account the interests and needs of developing states, particularly the least developed and the landlocked ones.[48]

A coastal state's right over the CS does not affect the legal status of the sub-adjacent waters and the airspace above the waters, and the freedom of navigation and other rights and freedoms of other states.[49] The regime of the CS would appear to be a functional one that seeks to reconcile the competing interests of coastal states' 'sovereign rights' to resource exploration and exploitation in its CS with the rights of other states to exercise the freedoms of the high seas.

Delimitation of the CS between adjacent or opposite states in view of the potential for the CS to contain vast valuable resources is a vital issue in international relations. Under LOSC, such states are to effect delimitation by treaty with a view to achieving an equitable solution. Pending such delimitation agreement, the states are encouraged, in a spirit of understanding and cooperation, to make an effort to enter into provisional arrangements of a practical nature that would be without prejudice to the final delimitation.[50] There are several examples of such provisional arrangements entered into by states.[51] In the event that the states are unable to reach an agreement within a reasonable period, they may resort to the dispute settlement mechanism. Under the 1958 Geneva Continental Shelf Convention (CSC), in the event of the absence of an agreement between the states the delimitation is to be determined by the equidistance–special circumstance principle.[52] The international courts, particularly the ICJ, in several cases, notably the *North Sea Continental Shelf* cases, decided that the equidistance–special circumstance method of delimiting the CS was a conventional rule and not a rule of customary international law. It decided that under CIL the appropriate method of achieving such delimitation is to seek to achieve equitable results. It, therefore, delimits such CS on equitable principles, which takes into account relevant circumstances (equitable principles–relevant circumstances rule). In practice, this rule appears to give the courts a rather wide discretion in determining in each case what criteria are to be selected in achieving the delimitation.[53]

Exclusive economic zone

The concept of the exclusive economic zone (EEZ) is of relatively recent origin. It is an area beyond, but adjacent to, the territorial sea, not extending beyond 200 nautical miles from the baselines. It includes the seabed and subsoil as well as the superjacent waters.[54] It emerged during the preparations for UNCLOS III, when African states put forward a proposal on the concept of the EEZ to the UN Seabed Committee in 1972.[55] The then Organisation of African Unity's (OAU) 1974 Declaration on Issues of the Law of the Sea affirmed that African states were entitled to claim an EEZ of 200 nautical miles from the baseline.[56] During the UNCLOS III, even before the coming into force of the LOSC, there was widespread acceptance of the concept of the EEZ, and it emerged as a rule of CIL. In the *Continental Shelf* (*Libya v. Malta*) case, the ICJ, even before the LOSC came into force, pointed out 'the institution of the exclusive economic zone . . . is shown by the practice of states to have become part of customary law'.[57]

The EEZ, like the CS, is a functional regime that gives the coastal state exclusive rights to exploit for natural resources, while at the same time allowing other states to exercise freedoms of the high seas as freedom of navigation, over flight and laying of submarine cables and pipelines.[58] A coastal state that has an EEZ has sovereign rights to explore and exploit, conserve and manage the natural resources, whether living or non-living, of the waters superjacent to the seabed and of the seabed and its subsoil, and with regard to other activities for the economic exploitation and exploration of the zone, such as the production of energy from the water, currents and winds. The important difference that the EEZ has over the CS is that the coastal state is allowed to explore and exploit both non-living and every living resource in the seabed and subsoil, as well as the waters superjacent to the seabed. In addition, the LOSC also emphasises the need for the coastal state to conserve and manage the natural resources in the EEZ.[59]

Unlike the CS, the coastal state is not obliged to have an EEZ. Further, there is provision for landlocked and geographically disadvantaged states to participate on an equitable basis in the exploitation of an appropriate part of the surplus living resources in the EEZ of coastal states of the same subregion or region. The latter arrangement is to be through bilateral, subregional or regional agreements between the states concerned. So far, it is estimated that about 126 states and territories have claimed a 200-mile EEZ.[60]

The same rule on delimitation of the CS between opposite or adjacent coastal states applies in the case of such in respect of the EEZ.[61]

High seas

The 1958 Geneva Convention on the High Seas (HSC), a codification of existing customary international law, defines the high seas as all parts of the sea not included in the internal waters or territorial sea.[62] It affirmed that the high seas are open to all states, with no state able to subject any part to its sovereignty. Further, it endorses the right of all states, both coastal and non-coastal, to have the freedoms of the high seas, such as the freedom of navigation, fishing, laying submarine cables and pipelines. The list of freedoms is obviously not exhaustive, as the convention mentions that there are other freedoms: 'which are recognised by the general principles of international law'.[63] At one point, there was a major debate about whether the freedoms under the 1958 Convention include the freedom to exploit the resources of the seabed and subsoil of what subsequently became known as the Area. Some like Kronmiller, Murphy and Brown argue that at one time deep seabed mining was one of the freedoms of the sea.[64] They point out that the provisions of the 1958 Convention made room for additional freedoms of the high seas recognised by international law, including the freedom of deep seabed mining. Brown, for instance, alludes to the ILC *travaux preparatoires*, which identified deep seabed mining as one of the freedoms of the high seas. He also argues that there was no rule under international law prohibiting deep seabed mining as a freedom of the seas.[65] Van Dyke and Yuen, as well as Mahmoudi, on the other hand, argue that the other freedoms mentioned by the Geneva Convention did not include the freedom of deep seabed mining.[66] Van Dyke and Yuen point out that there is no evidence in terms of state practice to show that deep seabed mining was established as a freedom of the high seas under CIL.[67] Mahmoudi argues that the other freedoms that the ILC had in mind when drafting Article 2 of the Geneva Convention were the freedom of scientific research and the freedom to undertake nuclear tests on the high seas for which there was sufficient state practice.[68] On the question of whether the freedom of the high seas could be extended to deep seabed mining because it was not expressly prohibited, he points out that for an act to be a rule under customary international law it must not only satisfy the status of non-prohibition, but must also be generally accepted by state practice. He further argued that though the *travaux preparatoires* of a treaty play a role in the interpretation of the treaty, it cannot replace the requisite state practice in determining whether a rule is customary international law.[69] Fortunately, this debate is not of practical consequence because the seabed and subsoil of the high seas and the resources therein have since LOSC been accepted to be the common heritage of mankind.

From the LOSC, which is substantially the same as the Geneva Convention, though developing on the latter, especially with the introduction of new maritime zones within a coastal state's national jurisdiction, the high seas is any part of the sea that is not within the limits of national jurisdiction of a coastal state. It further expands the list of freedoms, explicitly stated to include freedom of scientific research and the freedom to construct artificial islands and installations permitted under international law.[70]

Although it is clear under international law that all states have the freedom to fish on the high seas, this right is not absolute because of the need to conserve and manage the living stock of the high seas.[71] For instance, due to the LOSC not having comprehensive provisions dealing with the conservation and management of straddling and highly migratory fish stocks a Straddling Stock Conference was called in 1993. The outcome of this conference was an Agreement for the Implementation of the Provisions of the United Nations Convention on the Law of the Sea Relating to the Conservation and Management of Straddling Fish Sticks and Highly Migratory Fish Stocks 1995.[72] The Agreement, which currently has seventy-five state parties, is intended to promote cooperation between states to ensure that the right freedom of fishing in the high seas is balanced with the need for long-term conservation and sustainable use of straddling and highly migratory fish stocks.[73]

As a general rule, jurisdiction over a ship on the high seas is vested in the state where the ship is registered (the flag or national state). The

Geneva Convention, and subsequently the LOSC, however, requires that there must be a 'genuine link' between the flag state and the ship.[74] This requirement was to check the use of flags of convenience by certain ship owners who register in certain states, like Liberia and Panama, with which they have virtually no link in order to benefit from low taxation and avoid certain wage and maintenance standards that would be required by their actual home state. While ships like warships and ships owned or operated by a state used for purely governmental purpose are completely immune from the jurisdiction of any other state other than the flag state, there are some exceptions for other ships.[75] A warship may board or visit a foreign ship on the high seas if it has reasonable grounds to suspect that such ship is engaged in piracy, slave trade or unauthorised broadcasting. In the case of unauthorised broadcasting, the warship may board or visit only if its national state is the same as the person broadcasting, or the state where the transmissions can be received or the state where authorised radio communication is suffering interference. Further, a warship may board or visit another ship on the high seas if it is a ship without nationality or if, though flying a foreign flag or refusing to show its flag, the ship is in reality of the same nationality as the warship.[76] These exceptional powers of boarding or visiting a foreign ship are, however, required to be exercised with caution because an unfounded suspicion of any of the above would result in the national state of the warship having to compensate the foreign ship for any loss or damage sustained as a result.[77]

In addition, a coastal state may exercise jurisdiction over a foreign ship on the high seas that has committed an infraction of its laws through the right of hot pursuit, a right developed under CIL that was elaborated by both the High Seas Convention 1958 and the LOSC. The pursuit must start when the foreign ship or one of its boats is within the maritime zones within its national jurisdiction and continue uninterrupted outside these zones into the high seas. If the foreign ship is apprehended after the uninterrupted hot pursuit on the high seas, the coastal state may exercise jurisdiction over the foreign ship. However, it is unable to exercise such jurisdiction if the foreign ship enters the territorial sea of either its own state or a third state, since such right to hot pursuit immediately ceases.[78]

Further, a coastal state may exercise jurisdiction over a foreign shipping casualty in the high seas if it is a proportionate measure to protect its coastline from actual or threatened damage to its coastline or related interests, including fishing, from pollution or threaten of pollution from such casualty.[79] Churchill and Lowe further add that interference with a foreign ship may be justified if it is on the grounds of self-defence, necessity or pursuance to powers granted by special treaties.[80] Undoubtedly, another exception would be if such exercise of jurisdiction were in accordance with a resolution of the UN Security Council acting under its chapter VII powers; for instance, if such jurisdiction is necessary to enforce an embargo imposed by the Security Council in the exercise of its powers under Article 41 of the UN Charter.

Area

Part XI of the LOSC establishes a regime for the seabed and subsoil outside national jurisdiction (the Area).[81] It can be distinguished from the seabed and subsoil within national jurisdiction consisting of the territorial sea, EEZ and continental shelf. The Area assumed great prominence in the UNCLOS III mainly because certain key events, namely, the publicity given to the potential of the Area to contain valuable minerals; technological development that showed that the mining of such minerals could be accomplished; and the famous speech by Ambassador Arvid Pardo at the UN calling for this part of the sea and the resources therein to be declared as the common heritage of mankind.[82]

Although the initial focus was on polymetallic nodules, containing primarily manganese, nickel, copper and cobalt, recent scientific research has also aroused interest in other mineral resources in the Area. Such minerals include polymetallic sulphide deposits and cobalt-rich ferromanganese crusts. The polymetallic sulphides contain high concentration base metals such as zinc, lead and copper, as well as precious metals such as gold and silver. While cobalt-rich ferromanganese crusts are an important potential source of manganese, nickel, platinum, titanium, phosphorus, thallium, tellurium, zirconium, tungsten, bismuth and molybdenum.[83]

There has also been a call that attention should be given to methane (gas) hydrates in the Area. These are ice-like crystalline compounds consisting of gas (usually methane) and water molecules, which are widespread both on continental margins and in the Area. It is believed that the extraction of the hydrates could provide one of the most important energy sources for the future.[84]

Part XI of LOSC, consisting of five sections, along with some of the annexes, especially Annex III (Basic Conditions of Prospecting,

Exploration and Exploitation), Annex IV (on the Statute of the Enterprise) and Annex VI (Statute of the International Tribunal for the Law of the Sea, especially the part on the Seabed Disputes Chamber), detail a rather complex but unique regime for the Area. The Area and its resources are declared the common heritage of mankind and, therefore, not subject to claims of sovereignty by any state or subject to appropriation by any state or natural or juridical person and to be used only for peaceful purposes.[85]

Further, activities in the Area are to be carried out for the benefit of mankind as a whole represented by states irrespective of their geographical location or whether they are coastal or landlocked. In addition, the LOSC provides that in respect of activities in the Area special consideration should be given to the interests and needs of developing states and of peoples who have not attained independence or self-governing status.[86]

Mining in the Area is by a rather complex process known as the 'parallel system' or 'site-banking'. Under this system a state party or its entities or nationals, both natural and juridical (hereinafter 'the applicant'), seeking approval to carry out mining operations is required to make an application in respect of two sites of equal commercial value. Upon approval of such application, the applicant is authorised, based on the terms of the contract, to mine one site, while the other site is 'banked' for mining by the ISA through the Enterprise (the commercial operating arm of the ISA) or in association with developing states. This process anticipates mining by the applicant and the ISA working side by side.[87] Therefore, the original Part XI provided for the mandatory transfer of technology by developed states to the both the ISA and developing states interested in deep seabed mining and also provided access to finance on very liberal terms to the Enterprise (Annex III, Article 5). In addition, the original Part XI made provision for the adoption of production policies that limited exploitation of the resources of the Area in order to protect developing states that are land-based producers of these minerals.[88] Further, it allowed for a review conference that allowed in certain instances for an amendment to the Part XI provisions to be binding on states that have not consented to such amendment.[89]

Certain developed states objected to certain key terms of the original Part XI. To meet the concerns of these states an Implementation Agreement was adopted in 1994.

The Agreement, though called an Implementation Agreement, was actually an amending instrument.[90] The Agreement met the concerns of the developed states. Virtually all the developed states that initially refused to become parties to the LOSC, with the exception of the United States, have since done so.

The Agreement, among other things, amended the original Part XI provisions on the issue of mandatory transfer of technology, by now making it voluntary, it also removed the production limits and the liberal financial terms provided for the Enterprise, and further guaranteed that no proposal for amendment at the review conference would be binding on states without their consent. In addition, it amended the institutional framework by merging some institutions and including new institutions such as the Finance Committee.[91]

The 1994 Agreement, clearly intended to prevail over the original Part XI, states that: 'The provisions of this Agreement and Part XI shall be interpreted and applied together as a single instrument. In the event of any inconsistency between this Agreement and Part XI, the provisions of this Agreement shall prevail.'[92]

Institutions under LOSC

The LOSC, unlike its predecessor, the Geneva Conventions, established certain key institutions that have since played crucial roles in the development of the law of the sea. There are also certain institutions outside the institutional framework of the LOSC that play a vital role in the development of the law of the sea. These include the ICJ, with its numerous decisions in cases between states related law of the sea; the General Assembly, with its debates and various resolutions on issues related to the law of the sea; and the UN Secretary-General, with his now renowned annual report to the General Assembly on virtually all aspects of the law of the sea. This section would, however, focus on the key institutions set up by the LOSC, namely, the SPLOS, the CLCS, the ISA and the ITLOS.

Future projections on the law of the sea

The law of the sea has come a long way. From an area of international law developed by a few 'civilised' European states, it has become an area in which, as depicted by the UNCLOS III and the resultant LOSC

1982, now has the input of the generality of the international community, both developed and developing states. A number of key issues, such as the breadth of the territorial sea, upon which states were initially unable to arrive at an agreement, have since been resolved. New concepts such as the EEZ, the Area and its resources as the common heritage of mankind have emerged. Further, new international institutions, such as SPLOS, CLCS, ISA and ITLOS, have emerged as key actors in the area of the law of the sea.

The international community, under the auspices of the UN, has convened three major conferences, notably UNCLOS I, II and III, which have undoubtedly led to key developments in this crucial area of international law. The outcome of the UNCLOS III, the LOSC 1982, is a monumental piece of international law-making. The question arises as to whether the LOSC 1982 suffices to deal with twenty-first-century challenges affecting the sea. Is there a need at this point to convene an UNCLOS IV to carve out another comprehensive treaty on the law of the sea to cope with the challenges of the twenty-first century? The LOSC appears sufficiently flexible to cope with new challenges. In some regards, it operates as a sort of framework agreement that leaves room for states to enter into subsidiary treaties if there is a need to supplement and complement in order to deal with new challenges of the times. An example of this is the 1994 Implementation Agreement, which amends and complements the LOSC provisions on Part XI, which in most part was based on information available at the time the treaty was being carved out in the 1970s and 1980s. The flexibility of the LOSC makes it unlikely that states will embark in the near future on a major conference on the law of the sea in the form of UNCLOS IV. It would appear that the LOSC adopted in 1982 and still enjoying tremendous support from almost all states in the international community, with its almost universal ratification, is here to stay. Currently, the only major state outside the framework of this key treaty reflecting the new face of the law of the sea and described as the 'constitution of the seas' is the United States. From all indications this is it likely to change and the United States is likely to become a party in the near future.[93]

Justice and the common heritage of mankind

As we have seen the third United Nations Conference on the Law of the Sea (UNCLOS III) was convened in 1973 to deal with a number of unresolved issues (such as fishery zones and the breadth of the territorial sea) from earlier conferences, but the most controversial issue related to the area beyond national jurisdiction: the deep seabed beyond the continental shelf.[94] The reasons the Area (as it became known) assumed such significance can be found in a speech by Arvid Pardo, representative of Malta, in the UN General Assembly in 1967. Pardo, who was to become known as the Father of the Law of the Sea conference, argued that the existing law of the sea desperately needed amending in light of the increasing importance of the deep seabed. It is worth quoting in full one paragraph of the 123 that make up this famous speech:

> The known resources of the sea-bed and of the ocean floor are far greater than the resources known to exist on dry land. The sea-bed and the ocean floor are also of vital and increasing strategic importance. Present and clearly foreseeable technology also permits their effective exploitation for military or economic purposes. Some countries may therefore be tempted to achieve near-unbreakable dominance through predominant control over the sea-bed and ocean floor. This, even more than the search for wealth, will impel countries with the requisite technical competence to extend their jurisdiction over selected areas of the ocean floor. The process has already started and will lead to a competitive scramble for sovereign rights over the land underlying the world's seas and oceans, surpassing in magnitude and in its implications last century's colonial scramble for territory in Asia and Africa. The consequences will be very grave: at the very least a dramatic escalation of the arms race and sharply increasing world tensions, caused by the intolerable injustice that would reserve the plurality of the world's resources for the exclusive benefit of less than a handful of nations. The strong would get stronger, the rich richer, and among the rich themselves there would arise an increasing and insuperable differentiation between the two or three and the remainder. Between the very few dominant Powers, suspicions and tensions would reach unprecedented levels. Traditional activities on the high seas would be curtailed and, at the same time, the world would face the growing danger of permanent damage to the marine environment through radioactive and other pollution: this is the virtually inevitable consequence of the present situation.[95]

There are a number of issues raised in this extract. The core driver for a key range of concerns was the development of technology that would alter the potential uses of the deep seabed. The most significant issue here was the looming prospect of tapping the natural resources that could be found on and under the seabed. At the time the estimates were staggering. Minerals (especially manganese, iron, cobalt copper, nickel and lead) were estimated (for the Pacific alone) to be found in quantities that would support tens or hundreds of thousands of years of global consumption compared with the tens and hundreds of years worth of resources found on land. Oil and natural gas was thought to exist in the trillions of cubic feet. In addition to the natural wealth of the seabed, Pardo argued that the development of nuclear technology combined with advances in maritime technology made the prospect of military use of the seabed a near reality. Not only could nuclear submarines strike from anywhere, but the potential to site missile and missile defence systems and other fixed military installations on the seabed (particularly on mountain ranges) could lead to an undersea arms race. In addition, there were community issues, including the threat of environmental pollution from the disposal of radioactive waste. As the technology developed, so the challenges facing the regime covering the sea changed and Pardo predicted a highly destabilising struggle for control of the seabed. Importantly, all these concerns were framed by the politics of decolonisation.[96] Pardo's reference to the colonial scramble for territory and the insistence that the rush to conquer the ocean floor should take a different form were very significant. The newly independent states of Africa and Asia had had no part in the framing of the existing legal regime and many felt that it favoured the technologically advanced maritime states.[97] Pardo argued passionately that to allow the former colonial powers to simply divide the world's richest source of wealth between them would be a gross injustice of the same kind that was slowly being put right as their former colonies began to gain independence. In order to prevent this injustice (and to remedy existing ones) and to avoid the instability of a struggle to dominate the ocean floor, Pardo argued that the deep seabed should be considered as 'the common heritage of mankind' and that a new regime be developed to treat them as such.

The idea that the international community should treat the deep seabed as part of the common heritage of mankind (CHM) is an important one for a number of reasons. It is an idea that contrasts markedly with the predominantly 'Westphalian' manner in which all other aspects of international affairs are governed. It is an idea that articulates the need for a global and solidarist solution to a genuinely global challenge.[98] A CHM regime is a specific way of dealing with the global commons. Unowned territory can sometimes be thought of as *terra nullius*. *Terra nullius* could be appropriated by anyone who occupied and asserted legal control over the area. The idea of *terra nullius* was frequently invoked to justify the colonisation of large parts of the world.[99] Alternatively, unowned territory could be thought of as *res communis*. Such territory could not be appropriated by a state, but could be exploited for its resources by all. CHM is distinct in that it establishes a regime that does not permit unilateral exploitation, but manages any exploitation and ensures that any benefits are distributed to all.[100] The CHM ideal establishes an 'equity norm' and has been used in various guises to apply to other common areas such as outer space, the Arctic, the Antarctic and to issues such as climate change.[101] As Scott Shackelford notes:

> although no universal definition exists, most conceptions of the CHM share five primary points. First, there can be no private or public appropriation of the commons. Second, representatives for all nations must manage resources since a commons area is considered to belong to everyone. Third, all nations must actively share in the benefits acquired from exploitation of the resources from the common heritage region. Fourth, there can be no weaponry or military installations established in common areas. Fifth, the commons should be preserved for the benefit of future generations.[102]

Part XI of the Law of the Sea Convention established the idea that the seabed (the Area) should be governed as CHM. It established the ISA and its commercial arm, the Enterprise, to oversee equitable distribution of wealth, the mandatory transfer of marine technology, a favourable financing regime and the operation of a site-banking system of mining (see above). This 'constitution for the oceans' thus established a far-reaching redistributive mechanism to give expression to the idea that justice required that the international community treated the global commons in this manner both to ensure a fair distribution of the earth's bounty and to go some way to righting the wrongs of colonial occupation.

Part XI of the convention, however, was a significant reason for the fact that 130 states did not ratify the agreement.[103] The CHM regime was primarily supported by developing nations for whom this was the first time they could influence the direction of international legal development. Egede notes that the development of the CHM regime:

Justice and the Common Heritage of Mankind

Is only an aspect of a multifaceted conflict on different issues of international law, still ongoing and rehashed in various institutional fora such as the United Nations, World Trade Organisation (WTO), International Monetary Fund (IMF), and the World Bank, between developing states ... and developed states. On the part of African states, working together with other developing states, it is a fight for global equity and fairness in an international society and a clarion call for reform of rules and regulations governing the sea, which under classical international law leaned wholly in favour of the more developed states.[104]

However, the developed states, particularly the United States, the United Kingdom and Germany, had no intention of adhering to the new treaty and passed legislation that allowed businesses to begin exploration and mining of the seabed, and began negotiating with each other to ensure their concessions did not overlap.[105] At the same time, they took advantage of the articles establishing the EEZ, with the United States in particular declaring three billion acres of coastal seabed open for drilling.[106] In 1994, the New York Agreement modified the provisions of Part XI of the treaty in order to encourage the industrialised nations to ratify the convention. While the agreement reaffirmed the CHM principle, it effectively neutered the CHM ideal by providing a dominant voice for states actually engaged in mining in the Area, delaying the Enterprise and abolishing compulsory technology transfer. As Koskenniemi and Lehto note, the communitarian language was, by this point, mere rhetoric.[107] Nevertheless, as a consequence of the amendment all, bar the United States, acceded to the convention.

The amendment of the treaty is the core of the issue. The original CHM regime made some very strong statements about how the international community ought to deal with the global commons, and its ultimate failure has implications for other governance regimes and for the normative ideals that underpinned the CHM ideal. Concerns abound in relation to the military and commercial exploitation of outer space and the poles, and the failure to find a global solution also dogs the development of climate change negotiations.[108] Thinking about the political dynamics of CHM offers a stern test of the claim that justice is a core element of the normative structure of international society. The potential to mine the deep seabed provided a new challenge, and the fact that the UN was now populated by newly independent developing states added to that challenge. The CHM regime appeared to address both challenges, so why, we must ask, did the regime fail? Recognising that the law of the sea serves as key indicator of how the global commons might be governed in the future, Shackelford argues that:

> previous competing political and legal theories fail to adequately explain the transformation of sovereignty over the commons. The only notion that has both the explanatory and predictive power is that technological progress catalyzes changing political realities and thereby governance regimes over the commons.[109]

Shackelford is correct to argue that technological progress is a catalyst. The ability to efficiently exploit the regions adds an undeniable urgency to the question of how to govern the commons. Yet the choices that the international community makes when faced with this novel challenge need to be explained. To paraphrase Alexander Wendt's famous claim, technological advances are what states make of them. One way of viewing the fundamental disagreement between the developed and developing world in this context is to think about the cultural and ideological differences in the ways that the developed North and the developing South approach property rights in general. Shackelford, for example, argues that the establishment of a market-based solution to commons management is the traditional approach of the developed Western states.[110] In contrast, argues Egede, the idea of communal property is deeply embedded in African culture. The CHM regime:

> has significant similarity to the communal ownership of property by a village, community or family under native law and custom ... These African perceptions are antithetical to the western industrialised state's position of a more individualistic ownership of land and technology.[111]

The refusal of the United States and others to ratify the 1982 treaty was, in part, a matter of political and economic culture or ideology. Koskenniemi and Lehto show that for the US delegation in 1982, under President Reagan (whose administration viewed the CHM regime akin to 'international socialism') much of the negotiation aimed at the 'eradication of ideological impurity'. In response, the G77 and the East European group, despite the fact that the treaty was far from ideal from their perspective, also adopted an ideologically driven position affirming the justice of the New International Economic

Order (NIEO) and condemning the position of the developed West.[112] The argument was initially about the maximally efficient exploitation of the seabed. The neo-liberal position was that any non-market-based solution would be inefficient and would lead to the underexploitation of the Area – an aspect of the 'tragedy of the commons' thesis that is usually invoked to warn against overexploitation of an ungoverned commons.[113] Once the benefits of the seabed were found to be more limited than estimated, the ideological battle, argue Koskenniemi and Lehto, switched to the structures of the world economy as a whole: 'justice v. freedom, centralized v.. Market distribution, socialism v. Capitalism'.[114] However, because the anticipated resource dividend from the seabed was not to be as significant as estimated, the force of the argument abated. The retention of CHM language, albeit with a significant free-market amendment, was sufficient to bring all parties to agreement.

The central question of how to best manage the commons does not, however, simply dissipate. The prospect of mining in space – Halley's comet alone contains hydrocarbons to rival Earth's entire reserves[115] – or the rising attractiveness of exploiting the poles as alternative resources are depleted both raises the prospect of a resource dividend that can put the issue of general economic justice back on the table and raises questions concerning the environmental impact of challenges to existing commons regimes. We should also remember that the fact that the deep seabed may not provide the economic wherewithal to end poverty in the developing world does not mean that the issues surrounding the justice and injustice of global poverty simply go away. Yet the debate has moved on in a number of ways since the 1994 agreement. Since the end of the Cold War East–West and North–South relations have lost some of their ideological charge. Hurrell shows that with the intensification of globalisation:

> Many developing countries seemed to be abandoning the third world orthodoxies that shaped and inspired policy ... These policy reversals were perhaps most evident in the international political economy, when traditional bloc-type coalitions began to fragment and hard-line demands for revisions of dominant international economic norms began to give way to an emphasis on liberalisation and participation.[116]

Hurrell explains this set of facts by describing it as 'coercive socialization'. The hegemony of liberal ideals has not resulted in developmental equality. The legacy of colonialism results in a deeply uneven playing field meaning that, even if developing states want to 'play the game', questions of justice remain urgent. Okereke also pinpoints the hegemony of neo-liberal values in international society as a key reason for the failure of CHM and other equity norms to flourish in international society.[117] Indeed, he uses the example of the failure of Part XI of the 1982 treaty as evidence of the over-optimistic nature of the constructivist view that the world is becoming more susceptible to claims of justice such as those found in the CHM ideal. Okereke's analysis shows how important moral argument is in the debates concerning economic governance of the global commons. Nevertheless, the discussions of equity and justice, while prominent in the negotiations, are surface norms and the outcome of the debate is governed by the deeply entrenched background norms of international society that are stubbornly neo-liberal and market-oriented rather than justice-oriented.[118] The conflict between the clearly articulated equity norms of the CHM regime and the background norms of neo-liberalism do not mark the end of the debate. In fact, they open an opportunity for reflection on the justice of the economic governance of the global commons and by extension to economic governance more broadly. Importantly, this series of debates is increasingly internal to liberal thinking, although the barriers to presenting an egalitarian conception of global economic justice are still significant.

Liberalism, distributive justice and the law of the sea

The dominance of liberal economic ideals is a key part of the reason why the more egalitarian liberal conception of global justice does not play a stronger role in the development of regimes of economic governance. Within liberalism there are long-standing debates concerning distributive justice. The liberal tradition sees property ownership as the foundation of freedom. This is because property rights are thought necessary in order to give effective expression to all the other basic liberties. Throughout the history of liberal thought there are intense debates both about how property is acquired and how it is to be redistributed to ensure that all are guaranteed their basic liberties. John Locke, writing in the seventeenth century, argued that God gave the earth to mankind in common (an idea that speaks to the idea of the global commons we have been exploring here). However, the law of nature tells us that we must have the right to appropriate what we need to survive. We can go further and appropriate more than we need to survive because by mixing our labour with the world's resources we improve upon them and make more of the material necessities of life available. Locke goes on to argue that the development of property rights in society and a complex economy are thus based in nature and are a core element of the natural rights of man.[119] Importantly, however, there is proviso to all of this. Persons do have the right to acquire property as long as there is 'enough, and as good, left in common for others'.[120] If the liberal tradition had remained faithful to Locke's famous proviso then the idea of a CHM regime governing the global commons would make a great deal of sense from a liberal perspective. However, the dominant liberal position, in turning away from a natural law approach to rights, now treats justice (and therefore distributive justice) as something that arises within a scheme of social cooperation (where rights and duties are created) rather than in a state of nature. It is this, rather than any underlying aversion to distributive justice, that has erected barriers to a fuller discussion of the subject in liberal discourse. The *locus classicus* of the contemporary liberal egalitarian position is the political theory of John Rawls. In order to set out his theory of justice, Rawls uses a version of the social contract argument to show that justice requires that we organise and regulate the basic structure of society – those social institutions 'that assign fundamental rights and duties and shape the division of advantages that arises through social cooperation'[121] – so that each person has 'an equal right to the most extensive total system of basic equal liberties compatible with a similar system of liberty for all'. In order to give full effect to this first principle of justice Rawls argues that a just society requires a second principle:

> *Second Principle*: Social and economic inequalities are to be arranged so that they are both; (a) to the greatest benefit of the least advantaged, and (b) attached to offices and positions open to all under conditions of fair equality of opportunity.[122]

The first part of this second principle is called the difference principle because it permits differences in wealth, while attempting to maintain the social basis of equal basic liberties. However, when Rawls turned his attention to the international plane in *Law of Peoples* he argued that the difference principle does not apply. In *Political Liberalism* Rawls acknowledged that his theory of justice was a liberal theory of justice, worked out to apply to the basic structure of society in which a liberal public political culture prevailed. The *Law of Peoples*, however, was worked out to apply to international society. International society, Rawls argued, was neither a universal scheme of social cooperation nor liberal in its culture and, therefore, international justice (taken to apply to a plurality of independent peoples rather than individual members of scheme of social cooperation) would be rather different. Rawls' position disappointed many liberal commentators. As we saw in Chapter Five, Thomas Pogge offers strong, institutional–cosmopolitan reasons for demanding international economic justice. His argument demonstrates the centrality of economic rights to human rights more generally and points to the operation of global economic regimes and institutions as a key source of human rights violations and deprivations. Similarly, Allen Buchanan argues, contrary to Rawls, that transnational and international distributive justice is central to any just conception of international law.[123] For Buchanan, however, international society lacks the institutional capacity to sustain a distributive justice regime:

> due to current international *institutional incapacity*, which includes but is not restricted to a lack of enforcement capacity, there are serious limitations on the role that international law can now play in contributing to distributive justice. At present it is unrealistic to think that the international legal order can authoritatively formulate and implement comprehensive principles of distributive justice for relations among states or for assigning determinate distributive shares to individuals beyond a right to subsistence. This limitation has an important implication ... a moral theory of international law should acknowledge that for now states must be the primary arbiters and agents of distributive justice.[124]

The idea of institutional incapacity is important, but it does not apply to the governance of global commons regimes where, as we saw in the 1982 Law of the Sea Convention, international society did have the imagination to construct a regime that institutionalised equity norms. Buchanan argues that the CHM regime was part of an indirect attempt to establish global justice. It was indirect in that it left all other areas of the neo-liberal economic order intact and applied only to a specific, and rather unusual, economic field. It seemed to have the peculiar virtue of offering parties to the convention a blank canvas

Justice and the Common Heritage of Mankind

and a distinctly communal set of challenges. Commons regimes are the perfect proving ground for questions of distributive justice because of what appear to be unique characteristics. This claim to the *sui generis* nature of commons management is challenged in two key ways. Cosmopolitans, such as Buchanan and Pogge, want to draw parallels between commons regimes and the global economy more broadly. The core claim here is that the way that the globalised economy influences the benefits and burdens of international economic transaction is evidence of the existence of a global basic structure – a global society that must be regulated according to universal principles of justice (a global difference principle). For Buchanan, the institutional challenges to distributive justice mean that a comprehensive reworking of international political economy is some way off, but we do have obligations to support economic justice indirectly by focusing on regimes covering the global commons as well as intellectual property rights (on medicine and agricultural biotechnology for example), and human rights.[125] However, there is considerable pressure to treat the commons as just another type of free market. The source of this pressure is the core logic of a state-based system that embeds the idea that the international system is not a society in the relevant sense. Without society there is no basic structure to which the idea of justice applies and in which rights and responsibilities can be assigned. In particular, the state-based order imagines the ungoverned space that is the global commons as outside the basic structure to which the idea of justice applies. Even though there are good instrumental reasons for treating the global commons, the environment and the potential wealth of outer space as common to mankind, even though it is clear that the management of these areas has significant implications for established ideas of justice (especially human rights), the lack of a conception of global society entrenches the idea that the global free-market is somehow outside the broader normative framework of world affairs. The core idea that gets Rawls' difference principle off the ground is the thought that justice (the first virtue of social institutions) is to apply to the basic structure of society. For Rawls, this means that 'the political constitution, the legally recognized forms of property and the organization of the economy all belong to the basic structure'.[126] But international society has historically treated international political economy as being outside politics and, as globalisation forced the issue of regulation, has chosen to regulate it according to different normative ideals. The divergence of human rights politics and WTO politics, for example, belies the thought that there is a single global basic structure to which a coherent conception of justice applies. This is recognised by Rawls in his thinning out of the principles of justice appropriate to the 'law of peoples'. The cosmopolitan critics of Rawls are correct to point out the flaws in key elements of his reasoning, but the lack of consensus on matters of economic justice and of the relation between economic and social justice more broadly is a huge barrier to the establishment of distributive institutions. It also naturally privileges a neo-liberal economic agenda over other equity-based regimes.

Notes

1. Anand, R. P., *Origin and Development of the Law of the Sea: History of international Law Revisited*, The Hague: Martinus Nijhoff, 1982, p. 1.
2. UNCLOS III, *Official Records*, vol. I, p. 93, para. 67.
3. O'Connell, D. P., *International Law of the Sea*, Oxford: Clarendon Press, 1982, p. 2.
4. Anand, R. P., *International Law and the Developing Countries: Confrontation or Co-operation?* Dordrecht: Martinus Nijhoff, 1987, p. 53.
5. Anand, *International Law and the Developing Countries*, pp. 53–6.
6. Anand, *Origin and Development of the Law of the Sea*, p. 95.
7. Anand, *Origin and Development of the Law of the Sea*, p. 105; Brown, E. D., *The International Law of the Sea, Introductory Manual*, vol. 1, Aldershot: Dartmouth, 1994, p. 7.
8. Walker, W. L., 'Territorial Waters: The Cannon Shot Rule', *British Yearbook of International Law*, 22 (1945): 210–31.
9. Brown, *Seabed Energy and Minerals*, vol. 2, p. 14.
10. Wang, J., *Handbook on Ocean Law and Politics*, Westport, CT: Greenwood Press, 1992, pp. 23–5; Churchill, R. R. and Lowe, A. V., *Law of the Sea*, Manchester: Manchester University Press, 1999, pp. 13–15.
11. Dean, A. H., 'The Second Geneva Conference on the Law of the Sea: The Fight for Freedom of the Seas', *American Journal of International Law*, 54 (1960): 751–89; Wang, *Handbook on Ocean Law and Politics*, pp. 25–7; Churchill and Lowe, *Law of the Sea*, p. 15.
12. Brantley, H. T., 'Law of the Sea', *Harvard International Law Journal*, 14 (1973): 555–65, at p. 556.
13. Rembe, *Africa and the International Law of the Sea*, pp. 36–57.
14. UNCLOS III, *Official Records*, vol. XVI, pp. 152–67; Sebenius, J. K., *Negotiating the Law of the Sea*, Cambridge, MA: Harvard University Press, 1984.
15. Koskenniemi, M. and Lehto, M., 'The Privilege of Universality:

International Law, Economic Ideology and Seabed Resources', *Nordic Journal of International Law*, 65(3/4) (1996): 533–55, at p. 543.
16 Oxman, B. H., 'The 1994 Agreement and the Convention', *American Journal of International Law*, 88(4) (1994): 687–96; Brown, E. D., 'The 1994 Agreement on the Implementation of Part XI of the UN Convention on the Law of the Sea: Breakthrough to Universality?', *Marine Policy*, 19(1) (1995): 5–20.
17 Duff, J., 'A Note on the United States and the Law of the Sea: Looking Back and Moving Forward', *Ocean Development and International Law*, 35(3) (2004): 195–219; Bederman, D. J., 'The Old Isolationism and the New Law of the Sea: Reflections on Advice and Consent for UNCLOS', *Harvard International Law Journal Online*, 49 (2008): 21-7, available at: http://www.harvardilj.org/online. See also Centre for Oceans Law and Policy, at: http://www.virginia.edu/colp/los.html, accessed 26 October 2012.
18 Scott, S. V., 'The LOS Convention as a Constitutional Regime for the Oceans', in A. G. Oude Elferink (ed.), *Stability and Change in the Law of the Sea: The Role of the LOS Convention*, Leiden: Martinus Nijhoff, 2005, pp. 9–38.
19 Caminos, H. and Molitor, M. R., 'Progressive Development of International Law and the Package Deal', *American Journal of International Law*, 79 (1985): 871–90.
20 As at 7 November 2012.
21 Article 311.
22 Article 311(2).
23 Nordquist, M. (ed.), *United Nations Convention on the Law of the Sea 1982: A Commentary*, vol. V, The Hague: Martinus Nijhoff, 1982–2003, p. 240.
24 Articles 5 and 7.
25 Article 8.
26 Article 8(2).
27 Article 3. Brownlie, *Principles of Public International Law*, 6th edn, pp. 173–4.
28 Churchill and Lowe, *Law of the Sea*, pp. 77–81.
29 [1951] ICJ Rep. 116, at p. 160.
30 Articles 27 and 28.
31 Article 2(2).
32 TSC, 1958, Art. 14 and LOSC, 1982, Arts 2 and 17.
33 TSC, 1958, Art. 14(2) and LOSC, 1982, Art. 18(1).
34 TSC, 1958, Art. 14(3) and LOSC, 1982, Art. 18(2).
35 TSC, 1958, Art. 14(4) and LOSC, 1982, Art. 19(1).
36 LOSC, 1982, Art. 19(2).
37 (1989) 24 ILM 1444.
38 Churchill and Lowe, *Law of the Sea*, pp. 88–91; Churchill, R., 'The

Impact of State Practice on the Jurisdictional Framework Contained in the United Nations Convention on the Law of the Sea', in A. G. Oude Elferink (ed.), *Stability and Change in the Law of the Sea: The Role of the LOS Convention*, Leiden: Martinus Nijhoff, 2005, pp. 91–143.
39 LOSC, Art. 15.
40 LOSC, Art. 33.
41 Young, R., 'The Legal Regime of the Deep Sea Floor', *American Journal of International Law*, 62 (1968): 641–53; Finlay, L., 'The Outer Limit of the Continental Shelf: A Rejoinder to Professor Louis Henkin', *American Journal of International Law*, 64 (1970): 42–61; Henkin, L., 'A Reply to Mr Finlay', *American Journal of International Law*, 64 (1970): 62–72.
42 [1969] ICJ Rep. 3.
43 Article 76(4)(a)(i) and (ii).
44 Article 76(7).
45 Cook, P. and Carleton, C. (eds), *Continental Shelf Limits: the Scientific and Legal Interface*, Oxford: Oxford University Press, 2000; Mcdorman, T. L., 'The Role of the Commission on the Limits of the Continental Shelf: A Technical Body in a Political World', *International Journal of Marine and Coastal Law*, 17 (2002): 301–24; Egede, E., 'The Outer Limits of the Continental Shelf: African States and the 1982 Law of the Sea Convention', *Ocean Development and International Law*, 35 (2004): 157–78.
46 Article 77(1) and (4).
47 Wang, *Handbook on Ocean Law and Politics*, p. 60; Churchill and Lowe, *Law of the Sea*, pp. 151–2.
48 Article 82(2) and (4).
49 Article 78.
50 Article 83.
51 Ong, D. M., 'Joint Developments of Common Offshore Oil and Gas Deposits: "Mere" State Practice or Customary International Law?', *American Journal of International Law*, 93(4) (1999): 771–804.
52 CSC, 1958, Art. 6(2).
53 Churchill and Lowe, *Law of the Sea*, pp. 184–200.
54 Articles 55–77.
55 Rembe, *Africa and the International Law of the Sea*, pp. 116–23; Akintoba, T. O., *African States and Contemporary International Law: A Case Study of the 1982 Law of the Sea Convention and the Exclusive Economic Zone*, The Hague: Martinus Nijhoff, 1997, pp. 1–4.
56 UNCLOS III, *Official Record*, vol. III, pp. 63–5.
57 [1985] ICJ Rep. 13, at p. 74.
58 LOSC, Part V, Articles 55–75.
59 Articles 61–7.
60 Articles 69 and 70. Shaw, *International Law*, 6th edn, p. 583.

61 Article 74.
62 HSC, 1958, Art. 1.
63 HSC, 1958, Art. 2.
64 Kronmiller, T. G., *The Lawfulness of Deep Seabed Mining*, vols I and 2, London: Oceana Publications, 1980, pp. 369–418; Murphy, J., 'The Politics of Manganese Nodules: International Considerations and Domestic Legislation', *San Diego Law Review*, 16 (1979): 531–54, at pp. 536–8; Brown, *Sea-Bed Energy and Minerals*, pp. 14–22.
65 Brown, *Sea-Bed Energy and Minerals*, pp. 21–2.
66 Dyke, J. van and Yuen, C., 'Common Heritage v. Freedom of the High Seas?', *San Diego Law Review*, 19 (1982): 493–551, at pp. 501–14; Mahmoudi, S., *The Law of Deep Sea-Bed Mining: A Study of the Progressive Development of International Law Concerning the Management of the Polymetalic Nodules of the Deep Sea-Bed*, Stockholm: Almqvist & Wiksell, 1987, pp. 103–15.
67 van Dyke and Yuen, 'Common Heritage v. Freedom of the High Seas?', pp. 512–13.
68 Mahmoudi, *The Law of Deep Sea-Bed Mining*, p. 109.
69 Mahmoudi, *The Law of Deep Sea-Bed Mining*, pp. 112–15.
70 Articles 86 and 87.
71 LOSC, Pt VII, s. 2.
72 Anderson, D., 'The Straddling Stocks Agreement of 1995: An Initial Assessment', *International and Comparative Law Quarterly*, 45 (1995): 463–75.
73 See the United Nations Division for Ocean Affairs and Law of the Sea(DOALOS), list of ratifications, available at: http://www.un.org/Depts/los/convention_agreements/convention_overview_fish_stocks.htm, accessed 26 October 2012.
74 HSC, 1958, Art. 5 and LOSC, Art. 94.
75 LOSC, Arts 95 and 96.
76 LOSC, Arts 109 and 110.
77 LOSC, Art. 110(3).
78 LOSC, Art. 111.
79 LOSC, Art. 221.
80 Churchill and Lowe, *Law of the Sea*, pp. 216–20.
81 LOSC, Arts 133–91.
82 Ogley, R. C., *Internationalizing the Seabed*, Aldershot: Gower, 1984, pp. 12–24; Mahmoudi, *The Law of Deep Sea-Bed Mining*, pp. 26–36; Brown, *Sea-Bed Energy and Minerals*, pp. 49–151.
83 See ISA website, recent data on Polymetallic Sulphides and Cobalt-rich Ferromanganese Crusts, available at: http://www.isa.org.jm/en/home, accessed 26 October 2012.
84 Borgese, E. M., 'Caird Medal Address', *Marine Policy*, 25(6) (2001): 391–7, at p. 394.

85 LOSC, Arts 136, 137 and 141.
86 LOSC, Art. 140(1).
87 LOSC, Art. 153.
88 LOSC, Arts 150 and 151.
89 LOSC, Arts 154 and 155.
90 Brown, 'The 1994 Agreement on the Implementation of Part XI of the UN Convention on the Law of the Sea', pp. 5–20.
91 Annex, 1994 Agreement, ss. 1(4), 2(1) and 9.
92 Article 2.
93 [93] Nicholson, G., 'The Common Heritage of Mankind and Mining: An Analysis of the Law of the High Seas, Outer Space, the Antarctic and World Heritage', *New Zealand Journal of Environmental Law*, 6 (2002): 177–98, at p. 181.
94 Egede, E., *Africa and the Deep Seabed Regime: Politics and International Law of the Common Heritage of Mankind*, Heidelberg: Springer, 2011, p. 14.
95 UN General Assembly, official record of the 1515th Meeting of the first committee, pp. 12–13, para. 91.
96 Nicholson, G., 'The Common Heritage of Mankind and Mining: An Analysis of the Law of the High Seas, Outer Space, the Antarctic and World Heritage', *New Zealand Journal of Environmental Law*, 6 (2002): 177–98, at p. 181.
97 Egede, *Africa and the Deep Seabed Regime*, p. 10.
98 Shackelford, S., 'The Tragedy of the Common Heritage of Mankind', *Stanford Journal of Environmental Law*, 28 (2009): 109–67, at p. 113; Okereke, C., 'Equity Norms in Global Environmental Governance', *Global Environmental Politics*, 8(3) (2008): 25–50, at p. 36.
99 Boucher, *The Limits of Ethics*, pp. 116–32.
100 Egede, *Africa and the Deep Seabed Regime*, p. 57.
101 Okereke, 'Equity Norms', p. 31.
102 Shackelford, 'The Tragedy of the Common Heritage of Mankind', p. 111.
103 Shackelford, 'The Tragedy of the Common Heritage of Mankind', p. 127.
104 Egede, *Africa and the Deep Seabed Regime*, p. 30.
105 Chemillier-Gendreau, M., 'The Idea of the Common Heritage of Humankind and its Political Uses', *Constellations*, 9(3) (2002): 375–89, at p. 383.
106 Shackelford, 'The Tragedy of the Common Heritage of Mankind', p. 127.
107 Koskenniemi and Lehto, 'The Privilege of Universality', p. 535.
108 Shackelford, 'The Tragedy of the Common Heritage of Mankind', p. 130: Nicholson, 'The Common Heritage of Mankind and Mining', p. 188.

109 Shackelford, 'The Tragedy of the Common Heritage of Mankind', p. 113.
110 Shackelford, 'The Tragedy of the Common Heritage of Mankind', pp. 128–9.
111 Egede, *Africa and the Deep Seabed Regime*, p. 241.
112 Koskenniemi and Lehto, 'The Privilege of Universality', pp. 542–6
113 Shackelford, 'The Tragedy of the Common Heritage of Mankind', p. 118.
114 Koskenniemi and Lehto, 'The Privilege of Universality', p. 554.
115 Shackelford, 'The Tragedy of the Common Heritage of Mankind', p. 156.
116 Hurrell, *On Global Order*, p. 211.
117 Okereke, 'Equity Norms', p. 42.
118 Okereke, 'Equity Norms', p. 46. See also Okereke, C., *Global Justice and Neoliberal Environmental Governance*, London: Routledge, 2008b.
119 Locke, J., *Two Treatises of Government*, London: Everyman, 1989, para. 26.
120 Locke, *Two Treatises*, para. 27.
121 Rawls, J., 'The Basic Structure as Subject', *American Philosophical Quarterly*, 14(2) (1977): 159–65, at p. 159.
122 Rawls, *The Law of Peoples*, p. 226.
123 Buchanan, *Justice*, p. 193.
124 Buchanan, *Justice*, p. 193.
125 Buchanan, *Justice*, p. 193.
126 Rawls, 'The Basic Structure', p. 159.

Conclusion

We have not attempted to provide a comprehensive overview of public international law or of the politics of international law. Nevertheless, our sense of the ways in which complex normative questions arise in our legalised world order directed us to think about how legal, moral and political issues combine to force us beyond the comfortable parameters of academic disciplines. The character of contemporary international affairs requires that students of global politics confront the complexities of international law, while retaining the critical and creative skills to recognise the vital role of political and ethical judgement in interpreting, applying and amending the law. We do not underestimate the complexity of this task. Nor do we claim to have provided a template for the consideration of the questions we have explored. Rather, we have attempted to show how understanding the moral and political contours of the contemporary international legal order opens up vital questions – questions that can be broadly thought of as questions of justice and injustice – to critical scrutiny.

One of our goals has been to demonstrate just how deep the politics of international law must go into the constitution of international society if we are to begin to gain purchase on the urgent issues that frame international affairs. In the early chapters we explored questions of moral and political theory and legal doctrine before turning to the institutions and legal regimes that structure our globalised existence. We have emphasised how the practical and ethical challenges that arise in the operation of these institutions and regimes require critical engagement with fundamental questions of normative authority and moral desirability. This is not to deny the overarching context of power relations (or hegemony) in international politics. Rather, it is an attempt to explore the questions that arise when actors become dissatisfied with the configuration or effects of the power relations that are, of course, an inevitable aspect of politics. International law has evolved to become one of the fundamental institutions of global politics. It is hardly surprising, then, that we find urgent challenges framed by international law. As we examined calls for the reform of the UN, or the evolution of international human rights law and practice, or the operation of the coercive powers of the UN Security Council under chapter VII of the Charter we saw clear tensions emerging over questions of how to operationalise, develop or amend central aspects of international law. We portrayed these questions as questions of justice, and sought to explore the relationship between these questions and the development of law and politics. The urgency with which actors pursue questions concerning institutional reform, the use of sanctions or the distribution of the wealth of the common heritage of mankind stems from the sense of justice (more often injustice) that they experience and articulate when dealing with existing or potential normative frameworks, and it seemed to us to be vital to seek a way to bring together a rigorous study of international law and politics with an exploration of how claims to normative authority and moral desirability connect with that enterprise. As an intellectual experiment this approach has provided us with a stern challenge. Both law and IR (as academic disciplines) have long sought objectivity by distancing themselves from such questions. The post-war view of ethics as 'utopian', however, failed to understand the ways in which ethical questions drive political and legal questions, the ways in which they are thoroughly embedded in the practices of law and politics. The thought that such questions are embedded in practice underpinned the ways in which we chose to present and explore the moral and political debates. Requiring that ethical argument begins with the practices and institutions of international society does not, as we have seen, predetermine the outcome of those arguments. It does, however, direct us to those aspects of arguments about the justice or injustice of international politics that offer embedded or institutional moral reasons in support of their claims. This approach has enabled us to expose immensely rich normative contests and to explore their strengths and weaknesses. Arguments about the emerging normative importance of community norms (*erga omnes*) suggest shifts in the reasons why we might think that the whole international community have a real interest in matters

Conclusion

to which they are not directly connected. The emergence of a hierarchy of norms (perhaps treating core human rights claims as *jus cogens*) has the potential to encourage reforms in the ways we approach questions of poverty or the justice of economic or military sanctions. Arguments about the nature of the emerging constitutional structure of a legalised world order enable us to see the institutional and practical limits of cosmopolitan ambition while encouraging genuine reform in the name of global justice. This book has not resolved these normative contests (no book could). Rather it insists that normative judgement takes place in a specific time and place, creating political and moral opportunity by being engaged with the legalised world, and recognising the social, political and moral issues at stake. In making these claims and tracing them through debates in core areas of post-war international law we underpin the claim that the study of international politics and the study of international law are necessarily entwined, and that any such study requires a clear focus on questions of justice and injustice.

References

Abass, A. (2004), *Regional Organisations and the Development of Collective Security: Beyond Chapter VIII of the UN Charter*, Oxford: Hart.

Abbott, W., Keohane, R. O., Moravcsik, A., Slaughter, A.-M. and Snidal, D. (2002), 'The Concept of Legalization', in R. O. Keohane (ed.), *Power and Governance in a Partially Globalized World*, New York: Routledge.

Ackerman, B. (1994), 'Political Liberalisms', *Journal of Philosophy*, 41(7): 364–86.

Adler, E. (1997), 'Seizing the Middle Ground: Constructivism in World Politics', *International Relations*, 3(3): 319–63.

Akande, D. and Shah, S. (2011), 'Immunities of State Officials, International Crimes and Foreign Domestic Courts: A Rejoinder to Alexander Orakhelashvili', *European Journal of International Law*, 22(3): 857–61.

Akande, D. and Shah, S. (2010), 'Immunities of State Officials, International Crimes and Foreign Domestic Courts', *European Journal of International Law*, 21(4): 815–52.

Akehurst, M. (1982), *A Modern Introduction to International Law*, 4th edn. London: George Allen & Unwin, p. 115.

Akehurst, M. (1976/7), 'The Use of Force to Protect Nationals Abroad', *International Relations*, 5: 3–23.

Akehurst, M. (1974/5), 'Custom as a Source of International Law', *British Yearbook of International Law*, 47(1): 1–53.

Akintoba, T. O. (1987), *African States and Contemporary International Law: A Case Study of the 1982 Law of the Sea Convention and the Exclusive Economic Zone*, The Hague: Martinus Nijhoff.

Allesandri, E. (2008), 'World Order Re-Founded: The Idea of a Concert of Democracies', *International Spectator*, 43(1): 73–90.

Allott, P. (2000), 'The Concept of International Law', in M. Byers (ed.),

References

The Role of Law in International Politics, Oxford: Oxford University Press.

Alston, P. (1982), 'A Third Generation of Solidarity Rights: Progressive Development or Obfuscation of International Human Rights Law', *Netherlands International Law Review*, 29(3): 307–22.

Alvarez, J. E. (2006) 'International Organizations: Then and Now', *American Journal of International Law*, 100(2): 324–47.

Alvarez, J. E. (2005), *International Organizations as Law-makers*, Oxford: Oxford University Press.

Alvarez, J. E. (2003), 'Hegemonic International Law Revisited', *American Journal of International Law*, 97: 873–88.

Alvarez, J. E. (1994), 'Positivism Regained, Nihilism Postponed', *Michigan Journal of International Law*, 15: 747–84.

Anand, R. P. (1987), *International Law and the Developing Countries: Confrontation or Co-operation?*, Dordrecht: Martinus Nijhoff.

Anand, R. P. (1987), *Legal Regime of the Seabed and the Developing Countries*, The Hague: Sijthoff.

Anand, R. P. (1982), *Origin and Development of the Law of the Sea: History of international Law Revisited*, The Hague: Martinus Nijhoff.

Anderson, D. (1995), 'The Straddling Stocks Agreement of 1995: An Initial Assessment', *International and Comparative Law Quarterly*, 45: 463–75.

Anderson, K. (2000), 'The Ottawa Convention Banning Landmines, the Role of International Non-governmental Organizations and the Idea of International Civil Society', *European Journal of International Law*, 11(1): 91–120.

Armstrong, D. (ed.) (2009), *Routledge Handbook of International Law*, Abingdon: Routledge.

Armstrong, D., Farrell, T. and Lambert, H. (2007), *International Law and International Relations*, Cambridge: Cambridge University Press.

Asamoah, O. (1967), *The Legal Significance of the Declarations of the General Assembly of the United Nations*, The Hague: Martinus Nijhoff.

Ashley, R. (1988), 'Untying the Sovereign State: A Double Reading of the Anarchy Problematique', *Millennium: Journal of International Studies*, 17(2): 227–62.

'Attorney-General's Advice on the Iraq War: Resolution 1441' (2005), *International and Comparative Law Quarterly*, 54: 767–78.

Aust, A. (2007), *Modern Treaty Law and Practice*, 2nd edn, Cambridge: Cambridge University Press.

Aust, A. (1995), *Handbook of International Law*, Cambridge: Cambridge University Press (2nd edn, 2007).

Austin, J. (1995), *The Province of Jurisprudence Determined*, ed. W. E. Rumble, Cambridge: Cambridge University Press.

Ayer, A. J. (1936), *Language, Truth and Logic*, New York: Dover.

References

Barker, E. (2000), *International Law and International Relations*, London: Continuum.

Barsh, R. L. (1994), 'Indigenous Peoples in the 1990s: From Object to Subject of International Law', *Harvard Human Rights Journal*, 7: 33–86.

Baxter, R. R. (1965/6), 'Multilateral Treaties as Evidence of Customary International Law', *British Yearbook of International Law*, 41: 275–300.

Beck, R. J. (2009), 'International Law and International Relations Scholarship', in D. Armstrong (ed.), *Routledge Handbook of International Law*, Abingdon: Routledge, pp. 13–43.

Bederman, D. J. (2008), 'The Old Isolationism and the New Law of the Sea: Reflections on Advice and Consent for UNCLOS', *Harvard International Law Journal Online*, 49: 21–7, available at: http://www.harvardilj.org/online.

Bederman, D. J. (2001), *International Law in Antiquity*, Cambridge: Cambridge University Press.

Bellamy, A. J. (2005), *International Society and its Critics*, Oxford: Oxford University Press.

Berman, H. J. (1994/5), 'World Law', *Fordham International Law Journal*, 18: 1617–22.

Benvenisti, E. (2008), 'The Conception of International Law as a Legal System', *German Yearbook of International Law*, 50: 393–405.

Besson, S. (2010), 'Theorising the Sources of International Law', in S. Besson and J. Tasioulas (eds), *The Philosophy of International Law*, Oxford: Oxford University Press, pp. 163–86.

Best, G. (1999), 'Peace Conferences and the Century Of Total War: The 1899 Hague Conference and What Came After', *International Affairs*, 75(3): 619–34.

Bianchi, A. (2008), 'Human Rights and the Magic of *Jus Cogens*', *European Journal of International Law*, 19(3): 491–508.

Bianchi, A. (1999), 'Immunity versus Human Rights: The Pinochet Case', *European Journal of International Law*, 10(2): 237.

Bilder, R. (1969) 'Rethinking International Human Rights: Some Basic Questions', *Wisconsin Law Review*, 171(1): 171–217.

Blackstone, W. ([1765–1769] 1979), *Commentaries on the Laws of England*, vol. 4, Chicago, IL: University of Chicago Press.

Blokker, N. (2000), 'Is the Authorization Authorized? Powers and Practice of the UN Security Council to Authorize the Use of Force by Coalitions of the Able and Willing', *European Journal of International Law*, 11(3): 541–68.

Blum, Y. Z. (2005), 'Proposals for UN Security Council Reform', *American Journal of International Law*, 99(3): 632–49.

Bolton, J. R. (2000), 'Is there Really Law in International Affairs?', *Transnational Law and Contemporary Problems*, 10: 1–47.

Borgese, E. M. (2001), 'Caird Medal Address', *Marine Policy*, 25(6): 391–7.

Börzel, T. A. and Risse, T. (2000), 'Who is Afraid of a European Federation?

References

How to Constitutionalise a Multi-Level Governance System', NYU Jean Monnet Center for International and Regional Economic Law & Justice, Working Paper No. 7/00.

Bothe, M. (2008), 'Security Council's Targeted Sanctions against Presumed Terrorists', *Journal of International Criminal Justice*, 6(3): 541–55.

Boucher, D. (2009), *The Limits of Ethics in International Relations: Natural Law, Natural Rights and Human Rights in Transition*, Oxford: Oxford University Press.

Boucher, D. (1998), *Political Theories of International Relations: Thucydides to the Present*, Oxford: Oxford University Press.

Bowett, D. (1972/3), 'Economic Coercion and Reprisals By States', *Virginia Journal of International Law*, 13(1): 1–13.

Brantley, H. T. (1973), 'Law of the Sea', *Harvard International Law Journal*, 14: 555–65.

Brierly, J. L. (1963), *The Law of Nations: An Introduction to the Law of Peace*, ed. Sir Humphrey Waldock, 6th edn, Oxford: Clarendon Press.

Briggs, H. W. (1953), *The Law of Nations: Cases, Documents and Notes*, 2nd edn, London: Stevens.

Brolmann, C. (2011), 'International Organizations and Treaties: Contractual Freedom and Institutional Constraint', in J. Klabbers (ed.), *Research Handbook on International Organizations*, London: Elgar Publishers, pp. 285–312.

Brown, C. (2002) *Sovereignty, Rights and Justice: International Political Theory Today*, Cambridge: Polity Press.

Brown, C. (1993), *International Relations Theory: New Normative Approaches*, London: Harvester Wheatsheaf.

Brown, E. D. (2001), *Seabed Energy and Minerals: The International Legal Regime*, vol. 2: *Seabed Mining*, The Hague: Martinus Nijhoff.

Brown, E. D. (1995), 'The 1994 Agreement on the Implementation of Part XI of the UN Convention on the Law of the Sea: Breakthrough to Universality?', *Marine Policy*, 19(1): 5–20.

Brown, E. D. (1994), *The International Law of the Sea, Introductory Manual*, vol. 1, Aldershot: Dartmouth.

Brown, J. (1988), 'Diplomatic Immunity: State Practice Under the Vienna Convention on Diplomatic Relations', *International and Comparative Law Quarterly*, 37(1): 53–88.

Brown, M. M. (2008), 'Can the UN Be Reformed?', The John W. Holmes Lecture, *Global Governance*, 14(1): 1–12.

Brown, P. M. (1921), 'The Aaland Islands Question', *American Journal of International Law*, 15(2): 268–72.

Brownlie, I. (2003), *Principles of Public International Law*, 6th edn, Oxford: Oxford University Press.

Brownlie, I. (1998), *Principles of Public International Law*, Oxford: Clarendon Press.

Brownlie, I. (1982), 'Recognition in Theory and Practice', *British Yearbook of International Law*, 53: 197–201.

Buchan, R. (2012), 'Cyber Attacks: Unlawful Uses of Force or Prohibited Interventions?', *Journal of Conflict and Security*, 17(2): 211–27.

Buchanan, A. (2010), *Human Rights, Legitimacy and the Use of Force*, Oxford: Oxford University Press.

Buchanan, A. (2008), 'Human Rights and the Legitimacy of the International Order', *Legal Theory*, 14(1): 39–70.

Buchanan, A. (2004), *Justice, Legitimacy and Self-Determination: Moral Foundations for International Law*, Oxford: Oxford University Press.

Buchanan, A. (2003), 'Reforming the International Law of Humanitarian Intervention', in J. L. Holzgrefe and R. O. Keohane (eds), *Humanitarian Intervention: Ethical Legal and Political Dilemmas*, Cambridge: Cambridge University Press, pp. 130–73.

Buchanan, A. (2001), 'From Nuremburg to Kosovo: The Morality of Illegal International Legal Reform', *Ethics*, 111(4): 673–705.

Buchanan, A. and Keohane, R. (2006), 'The Legitimacy of Global Governance Institutions', *Ethics and International Affairs*, 20(4): 405–37.

Buchanan, A. and Keohane, R. (2004), 'The Preventive Use of Force: A Cosmopolitan Institutional Proposal', *Ethics and International Affairs*, 18(1): 1–22.

Buergenthal, T. (1988), 'International Human Rights Law and Institutions: Accomplishments and Prospects', *Washington Law Review*, 63(1): 1–19.

Bull, H. ([1977] 1995), *The Anarchical Society: The Study of Order in World Politics*, 2nd edn, Basingstoke: Palgrave Macmillan.

Burley, A. M. (1992), 'Law among Liberal States: Liberal Internationalism and the Act of State Doctrine', *Columbia Law Review*, 92: 1907–96.

Byers, M. (2004), 'Agreeing to Disagree: Security Council Resolution 1441 and Intentional Ambiguity', *Global Governance*, 10: 165–86.

Byers, M. (2002), 'A Decade of Forceful Measures Against Iraq', *European Journal of International Law*, 13(1): 21–41.

Byers, M. (ed.) (2000), *The Role of Law in International Politics*, Oxford: Oxford University Press.

Byers, M. (1999/2000), 'The Law and Politics of the Pinochet Case', *Duke Journal of Comparative and International Law*, 10: 415–41.

Byers, M. (1999), *Custom, Power, and the Power of Rules: International Relations and Customary International Law*, Cambridge: Cambridge University Press.

Byers, M. (1997), 'Conceptualising the Relationship between *Jus Cogens* and *Erga Omnes* Rules', *Nordic Journal of International Law*, 66: 211–39.

Byers, M. and Chesterman, S. (2003), 'Changing the Rules about Rules? Unilateral Humanitarian Intervention and the Future of International Law', in J. Holzgrefe and R. Keohane (eds), *Humanitarian Intervention:*

Ethical, Legal and Political Dilemmas, Cambridge: Cambridge University Press, pp. 177–203.

Cali, B. (ed.) (2010), 'International Law for International Relations: Foundations for Interdisciplinary Study', in *International Law for International Relations*, Oxford: Oxford University Press.

Cameron, I. (1985), 'First Report of the Foreign Affairs Committee of the House of Commons', *International and Comparative Law Quarterly*, 34: 610–20.

Caminos, H. and Molitor, M. R. (1985), 'Progressive Development of International Law and the Package Deal', *American Journal of International Law*, 79: 871–90.

Caney, S. (2005), *Justice Beyond Borders: A Global Political Theory*, Oxford: Oxford University Press.

Caplan, L. (2003), 'State Immunity, Human Rights and *Jus Cogens*: A Critique of the Normative Hierarchy Theory', *American Journal of International Law*, 97(4): 741–81.

Carothers, T. (2008), 'Is a League of Democracies a Good Idea?', Carnegie Endowment for International Peace, Policy Brief No. 59, available at: http://www.carnegieendowment.org/events/index.cfm?fa=eventDetail&id=1137.

Carr, E. H. ([1939] 2001), *The Twenty Years Crisis: 1919–1939*, London: Palgrave Macmillan.

Cassese, A. (2005), *International Law*, 2nd edn, Oxford: Oxford University Press.

Cassese, A. (2001), *International Law*, Oxford: Oxford University Press.

Cassese, A. (2001), 'Terrorism is Also Disrupting Some Crucial Legal Categories of International Law', *European Journal of International Law*, 12(5): 993–1001.

Cassese, A. (2000), 'The Martens Clause in International Law: Half a Loaf or Simply Pie in the Sky?', *European Journal of International Law*, 11(1): 187–216.

Cerna, C. (1994), 'Universality of Human Rights and Cultural Diversity: Implementation of Human Rights in Different Socio-Cultural Contexts', *Human Rights Quarterly*, 16: 740–52.

Charney, J. (1985), 'The Persistent Objector and the Development of Customary International Law', *British Yearbook of International Law*, 56: 1–24.

Charney, J. (1983), 'Transnational Corporations and Developing Public International Law', *Duke Law Journal*, 32(4): 748–88.

Charnovitz, S. (2006), 'Nongovernmental Organizations and International Law', *American Journal of International Law*, 100(2): 348–72.

Charnovitz, S. (1997), 'Two Centuries of Participation: NGOs and International Governance', *Michigan Journal of International Law*, 18: 183–286.

Checkel, J. (1997), 'International Norms and Domestic Politics: Bridging the Rationalist–Constructivist Divide', *European Journal of International Relations*, 3(4): 473–95.

Chemillier-Gendreau, M. (2002), 'The Idea of the Common Heritage of Humankind and its Political Uses', *Constellations*, 9(3); 375–89.

Cheng, B. (1965), 'United Nations Resolutions on Outer Space: "Instant" International Customary Law?', *Indian Journal of International Law*, 5: 23–112.

Chesterman, S. (2001), *Just War or Just Peace: Humanitarian Intervention and International Law*, Oxford: Oxford University Press.

Chetail, V. (2003), 'The Contribution of the International Court of Justice to International Humanitarian Law', *International Review of the Red Cross*, 85: 235–69.

Christenson, G. (1987), 'The World Court and *Jus Cogens*', *American Journal of International Law*, 81(1): 93–101.

Churchill, R. (2005), 'The Impact of State Practice on the Jurisdictional Framework Contained in the United Nations Convention on the Law of the Sea', in A. G. Oude Elferink (ed.), *Stability and Change in the Law of the Sea: The Role of the LOS Convention*, Leiden: Martinus Nijhoff, pp. 91–143.

Churchill, R. R. and Lowe, A. V. (1999), *Law of the Sea*, Manchester: Manchester University Press.

Clausewitz, C. von (1976), *On War*, ed. and trans. M. Howard and P. Paret, Princeton, NJ: Princeton University Press.

Cohen, J. (2010), 'Sovereignty in the Context of Globalization: A Constitutional Pluralist Perspective', in S. Besson and J. Tasioulas (eds), *The Philosophy of International Law*, Oxford: Oxford University Press, pp. 261–80.

Cook, P. and Carleton, C. (eds) (2000), *Continental Shelf Limits: the Scientific and Legal Interface*, Oxford: Oxford University Press.

Corbett, P. E. (1971), *The Growth of World Law*, Princeton, NJ: Princeton University Press.

Corbett, P. E. (1925), 'The Consent of States and the Sources of the Law of Nations', *British Yearbook of International Law*, 6: 20.

Correll, H. (2001), 'To Intervene or Not: The Dilemma That Will Not Go Away', Keynote at Duke University, 19 April.

Cortright, D. And Lopez, G. (1999), 'Are Sanctions Just? The Problematic Case of Iraq', *Journal of International Affairs*, 52(2): 735–55.

Cox, R. (1981), 'Social Forces, States and World Orders: Beyond International Relations Theory', *Millennium: Journal of International Studies*, 10(2): 126–55.

Crawford, J. R. (2006), *The Creation of States in International Law*, 2nd edn, Oxford: Oxford University Press.

Crawford, J. (1976/7), 'The Criteria for Statehood in International Law', *British Yearbook of International Law*, 48: 93–182.

Crawford, J. and Grant, T. (2007), 'International Court of Justice', in T. G.

References

Weiss and S. Daws (eds), *The Oxford Handbook on the United Nations*, Oxford: Oxford University Press, pp. 193–213.

Crawford, J. and Koskenniemi, M. (eds) (2012), *The Cambridge Companion to International Law*, Cambridge: Cambridge University Press.

Crawford, J. and Koskenniemi, M. (2012) 'The Contexts of International Law', in J. Crawford and M. Koskenniemi (eds), *The Cambridge Companion to International Law*, Cambridge: Cambridge University Press.

Crawford, J. and Olleson, S. (2003), 'The Nature and Forms of International Responsibility', in M. Evans (ed.), *International Law*, Oxford: Oxford University Press.

Cutler, C. (2001), 'Critical Reflections on the Westphalian Assumptions of International Law and Organization: A Crisis of Legitimacy', *Review of International Studies*, 27: 133–50.

Daadler, I. and Lindsay, J. (2007), 'Democracies of the World Unite', *Public Policy Research*, 14(1): 47–58.

D'Amato, A. (1985), 'Is International Law Really "Law"?', *Northwestern Law Review*, 79: 1293–314.

D'Amato, A. (1982), 'The Concept of Human Rights in International Law', *Columbia Law Review*, 82(6): 1110–59.

D'Amato, A. (1971), *The Concept of Custom in International Law*, New York: Cornell University Press.

Damrosch, L. (2011), 'Changing the International Law of Sovereign Immunity through National Decisions', *Vanderbilt Journal of Transnational Law*, 44: 1185–200.

Damrosch, L. (ed.) (1993), *Enforcing Restraint: Collective Intervention in Internal Conflict*, New York: Council on Foreign Relations.

Danilenko, G. (1991), 'International *Jus Cogens*: Issues of Law-Making', *European Journal of International Law*, 2: 42–65.

Dean, A. H. (1960), 'The Second Geneva Conference on the Law of the Sea: The Fight for Freedom of the Seas', *American Journal of International Law*, 54: 751–89.

Diehl, J. (2008), 'A "League" by Other Names', *Washington Post*, 19 May.

Dinstein, Y. (2011), *War, Aggression and Self-Defence*, 5th edn, Cambridge: Cambridge University Press.

Dixon, M. (2007), *International Law*, 6th edn, Oxford: Oxford University Press.

Dixon, M. and McCorquodale, R. (2003), *Cases and Materials on International Law*, 4th edn, Oxford: Oxford University Press.

Donnelly, J. (2007), 'The Relative Universality of Human Rights', *Human Rights Quarterly*, 29(2): 281–306.

Donnelly, J. (2006), 'The Virtues of Legalization', in S. Meckled-García and B. Cali (eds), *The Legalization of Human Rights: Multidisciplinary Perspectives on Human Rights and Human Rights Law*, London: Routledge, p. 71.

Donnelly, J. (1984), 'Cultural Relativism and Universal Human Rights', *Human Rights Quarterly*, 6(4): 400–19.

Doyle, M. (2008), *Striking First: Prevention and Preemption in International Conflict*, ed. S. Macedo, Princeton, NJ: Princeton University Press.

Drezner, D. (2011), 'Sanctions Sometimes Smart: Targeted Sanction in Theory and Practice', *International Studies Review*, 13: 96–108.

Drezner, D. (2003), 'How Smart are Smart Sanctions?', *International Studies Review*, 5(1): 107–10.

Duff, J. (2004), 'A Note on the United States and the Law of the Sea: Looking Back and Moving Forward', *Ocean Development and International Law*, 35(3): 195–219.

Dyke, J. van and Yuen, C. (1982), 'Common Heritage v. Freedom of the High Seas?', *San Diego Law Review*, 19: 493–551.

Egede, E. (2011), *Africa and the Deep Seabed Regime: Politics and International Law of the Common Heritage of Mankind*, Heidelberg: Springer.

Egede, E. (2007), 'Bringing Human Rights Home: An Examination of the Domestication of Human Rights Treaties in Nigeria', *Journal of African Law*, 51(2): 249–84.

Egede, E. (2004), 'The Outer Limits of the Continental Shelf: African States and the 1982 Law of the Sea Convention', *Ocean Development and International Law*, 35: 157–78.

Egede, E. (2004), 'The Nigerian Territorial Waters and the 1982 Law of the Sea Convention', *International Journal of Marine and Coastal Law*, 19(2): 151.

Egede, E. (2000), 'The New Territorial Waters (Amendment) Act 1998: Comments on the Impact of International Law on Nigerian Law', *African Journal of International and Comparative Law*, 12: 84–104.

Elias, O. (1995), 'The Nature of the Subjective Element in Customary International Law', *International and Comparative Law Quarterly*, 44: 501–20.

Elias, T. O. (1972), 'Modern Sources of International Law', in W. Friedmann, L. Henkin, O. J. Lissitzyn and P. C. Jessup (eds), *Transnational Law in a Changing Society: Essays in Honour of Philip C. Jessup*, New York: Columbia University Press.

Erskine, T. (2010), 'Kicking Bodies and Damning Souls: The Danger of Harming "Innocent" Individuals while Punishing "Delinquent" States', *Ethics and International Affairs*, 24(3): 262–85.

Evans, G. (2011), 'The End of the Argument: How We Won the Debate over Stopping Genocide', *Foreign Policy*, December.

Evans, G. (1994), 'Co-operative Security and Intra-State Conflict', *Foreign Policy*, 96: 3–20.

Evans, M. A. (2008), 'Balancing Peace, Justice and Sovereignty in *Jus Post Bellum*: The Case of Just Occupation', *Millennium Journal of International Studies*, 36(3): 533–54.

References

Evans, M. A. (2005), *Just War Theory: A Reappraisal*, Edinburgh: Edinburgh University Press.

Evans, M. (ed.) (2003) *International Law*, Oxford: Oxford University Press.

Falk, R. (2007), 'What Comes after Westphalia: The Democratic Challenge', *Widener Law Review*, 13: 243–54.

Falk, R. (2000), *Human Rights Horizons: The Pursuit of Justice in a Globalizing World*, London: Routledge.

Falk, R. (1985), 'The Grotian Quest', in S. Mendlovitz, F. Kratochwil and R. Falk (eds), *International Law: A Contemporary Perspective*, Boulder, CO: Westview, pp. 36–42.

Falk, R. (1974), 'The Global Environment and International Law: Challenge and Response', *University of Kansas Law Review*, 23: 385.

Falk, R. (1966), 'On the Quasi-Legislative Competence of the General Assembly', *American Journal of International Law*, 60: 782–91.

Fassbender, B. (2006), 'Targeted Sanctions Imposed by the UN Security Council and Due Process Rights', *International Organizations Law Review*, 3: 437–85.

Fassbender, B. (1998), *UN Security Council Reform and the Right of Veto: A Constitutional Perspective*, The Hague, Kluwer Law.

Fassbender, B. (1998), 'The United Nations Charter as Constitution of the International Community', *Colombia Journal of Transnational Law*, 36: 529–619.

Fausey, J. (1994), 'Does the United Nations' Use of Collective Sanctions to Protect Human Rights Violate its Own Human Rights Standards', *Connecticut Journal of International Law*, 10: 193–218.

Finlay, L. (1970), 'The Outer Limit of the Continental Shelf: A Rejoinder to Professor Louis Henkin', *American Journal of International Law*, 64: 42–61.

Finnemore, M. and Sikkink, K. (1998), 'International Norm Dynamics and Political Change', *International Organization*, 50(4): 887–917.

Finnemore, M. and Toope, S. (2006), 'Alternatives to "Legalization": Richer Views of Law and Politics', in B. Simmons and R. Steinberg (eds), *International Law and International Relations*, Cambridge: Cambridge University Press, pp. 188–204.

Fitzmaurice, G. G. (1956), 'The Foundations of the Authority of International Law and the Problem of Enforcement', *Modern Law Review*, 19(1): 1–13.

Fitzmaurice, M. (2002), 'Third Parties and the Law of Treaties', *Max Planck Yearbook of United Nations Law*, 6: 37–137.

Foot, R., Gaddis, J. L. and Hurrell, A. (eds) (2003), *Order and Justice in International Relations*, Oxford: Oxford University Press.

Forsythe, D. P. (2005), *Human Rights in International Relations*, 2nd edn, Cambridge: Cambridge University Press.

Fox, H. (2006), 'International Law and Restraints on the Exercise of

Jurisdiction by National Courts of States', in M. Evans (ed.), *International Law*, 2nd edn, Oxford: Oxford University Press.

Fox, H. (2002), *The Law of State Immunity*, Oxford: Oxford University Press.

Fox, H. (1999), 'The Pinochet Case (No. 3)', *International and Comparative Law Quarterly*, 48(3): 687–702.

Franck, T. (2003/4), 'Preemption, Prevention and Anticipatory Self-Defense: New Law Regarding Recourse to Force?', *Hastings International and Comparative Law Review*, 27: 425–35.

Franck, T. (2003), 'Interpretation and Change in the Law of Humanitarian Intervention', in J. Holzgrefe and R. Keohane (eds), *Humanitarian Intervention: Ethical, Legal and Political Dilemmas*, Cambridge: Cambridge University Press, pp. 204–31.

Franck, T. (1995), *Fairness in International Law and Institutions*, Oxford: Oxford University Press.

Franck, T. (1990), *The Power of Legitimacy Among Nations*, Oxford: Oxford University Press.

Franck, T. (1989), 'Is Justice Relevant to the International Legal System', *Notre Dame Law Review*, 64: 945–63.

Franck, T. (1988), 'Legitimacy in the International System', *American Journal of International Law*, 82(4): 702–59.

Franck, T. (1970), 'Who Killed Article 2(4)? Or: Changing Norms Governing the Use of Force by States', *American Journal of International Law*, 64(5): 809–37.

Freeman, M., 'Putting Law in its Place: An interdisciplinary Evaluation of National Amnesty Laws', in S. Meckled-García and B. Cali (eds), *The Legalization of Human Rights: Multidisciplinary Perspectives on Human Rights and Human Rights Law*, London: Routledge, 2006, p. 51.

Frost, M. (1996), *Ethics in International Relations: A Constitutive Theory*, Cambridge: Cambridge University Press.

Gardam, J. (2001), 'The Contribution of the International Court of Justice to International Humanitarian Law', *Leiden Journal of International Law*, 14: 349–65.

Gardbaum, S. (2008), 'Human Rights as International Constitutional Rights', *European Journal of International Law*, 19(4): 749–68.

Glennon, M. (1991), 'The Constitutional Power of the United States Senate to Condition its Consent to Treaties', *Chicago-Kent Law Review*, 67: 533–70.

Goldsmith, J. and Posner, E. (2005), *The Limits of International Law*, Oxford: Oxford University Press.

Goldstein, J., Kahler, M., Keohane, R. and Slaughter, A.-M. (2000), 'Introduction: Legalization and World Politics', *International Organization*, 54(3): pp. 1–15.

Goldstone, R. (1995/6), 'International Criminal Tribunal for Former

References

Yugoslavia: A Case Study in Security Council Action', *Duke Journal of Comparative and International Law*, 6: 5–10.

Goodrich, L. M. (1947), 'From League of Nations to United Nations', *International Organization*, 1(1): 3.

Gordon, J. (1999), 'A Peaceful, Silent, Deadly Remedy: The Ethics of Economic Sanctions', *Ethics and International Affairs*, 13(1): 123–42.

Gowlland-Debbas, V. (2000), 'The Function of the United Nations Security Council in the International Legal System', in M. Byers (ed.), *The Role of Law in International Politics*, Oxford: Oxford University Press, pp. 277–314.

Gray, C. (2008), *International Law and the Use of Force: Foundations of Public International Law*, 3ed edn, Oxford: Oxford University Press.

Gray, C. (2006), 'The Use of Force and the International Legal Order', in M. Evans (ed.), *International Law*, 2nd edn, Oxford: Oxford University Press, pp. 593–7.

Green, J. and Grimal, F. (2011), 'The Threat of Force as an Action in Self-Defence under International Law', *Vanderbilt Journal of Transnational Law*, 44: 285–329.

Greenwood, C. (2003), 'International Law and the Pre-emptive Use of Force: Afghanistan, Al-Qaida, and Iraq', *San Diego International Law Journal*, 4: 7–37.

Gross, L. (1948), 'The Peace of Westphalia 1648–1948', *American Journal of International Law*, 42(1): 20–41.

Guzman, A. (2005/6), 'Saving Customary International Law', *Michigan Journal of International Law*, 27: 115–76.

Guzman, A. T. and Meyer, T. L. (2010), 'International Soft Law', *Journal of Legal Analysis*, 2(1): 171–225.

Hannum, H. (1995/6), 'The Status of the Universal Declaration of Human Rights in National and International Law', *Georgia Journal of International and Comparative Law*, 25: 287–395.

Harris, D. J. (2004), *Cases and Materials on International Law*, 6th edn, London: Sweet & Maxwell.

Harris, P. (2010), *World Ethics and Climate Change: From International to Global Justice*, Edinburgh: Edinburgh University Press.

Hart, H.L.A. (1997), *The Concept of Law*, Oxford: Clarendon Press.

Hart, H. L. A. (1994), *The Concept of Law*, with Postscript, ed. P. A. Bulloch and J. Raz, 2nd edn, Oxford: Oxford University Press.

Hathaway, O. and Koh, H. 2005. *Foundations of International Law and Politics*, New York: Foundation Press.

Heinrich, D. (1992), 'The Case for a United Nations Parliamentary Assembly', unaltered edition of the first printing by the World Federalist Movement, October, made available by the German Committee for a Democratic UN, June 2003, available at: http://www.wfm-igp.org/site/files/UNPA1992-Heinrich.pdf.

Henkin, L. (1979), *How Nations Behave*, 2nd edn, New York: Columbia University Press.

Henkin, L. (1971), 'The Reports of the Death of Article 2(4) Are Greatly Exaggerated', *American Journal of International Law*, 65: 544–8.

Henkin, L. (1970), 'A Reply to Mr Finlay', *American Journal of International Law*, 64: 62–72.

Henkin, L. (1959), 'The Treaty Makers and the Law Makers: The Law of the Land and Foreign Relations', *University of Pennsylvania Law Review*, 107(7): 903–36.

Higgins, R. (1994), *Problems and Process: International Law and How we Use It*, Oxford: Clarendon Press.

Higgins, R. (1978), 'Conceptual Thinking about the Individual in International Law', *British Journal of International Studies*, 4: 1.

Higgins, R. (1963) *The Development of International Law through the Political Organs of the United Nations*, Oxford: Oxford University Press.

Hillemanns, C. F. (2003), 'UN Norms on the Responsibilities of Transnational Corporations and Other Business Enterprises with regard to Human Rights', *German Law Journal*, 4(10): 1065–80.

Hillgenberg, H., 'A Fresh Look at Soft Law', *European Journal of International Law*, 10(3) (1999): 499.

Hobbes, T. (1968), *Leviathan*, ed. C. B. Macpherson, London: Penguin.

Hollis, D. (2005), 'Why State Consent Still Matters: Non-State Actors, Treaties and the Changing Sources of International Law', *Berkeley Journal of International La*w, 22 (2005): 137–74.

Holzgrefe, J. L. (2003), 'The Humanitarian Intervention Debate', in J. L. Holzgrefe and R. Keohane (eds), *Human Intervention: Ethical, Legal, and Political Dilemmas*, Cambridge: Cambridge University Press, p. 18.

Holzgrefe, J. L. and Keohane, R. O. (eds) (2003), *Humanitarian Intervention: Ethical Legal and Political Dilemmas*, Cambridge: Cambridge university Press.

Hoof, G. J. H. van (1983) *Rethinking the Sources of International Law*, Deventer: Kluwer Law.

Hudson, M. (1932), *Progress in International Organization*, Oxford: Oxford University Press, p. 83.

Hufbauer, G., Schott, J., Elliot, K. and Oegg, B. (2009), *Economic Sanctions Reconsidered*, 3rd edn, Washington, DC: Peterson.

Hurrell, A. (2007), *On Global Order: The Constitution of International Society*, Oxford: Oxford University Press.

Hurrell, A. and Kingbury, B. (eds) (1992), *The International Politics of the Environment*, Oxford: Oxford University Press.

Ijalaye, D. (1971), 'Was "Biafra" at Any Time a State in International Law?', *American Journal of International Law*, 65: 551–9.

Ikenberry, G. J. and Slaughter, A.-M. (2006), 'Forging a World of Liberty Under Law: US National Security in the Twenty First Century', Final

References

Report of the Princeton Project on National Security, available at: http://www.princeton.edu/~ppns/report/FinalReport.pdf.

Independent International Commission on Kosovo (2000), *The Kosovo Report: Conflict, International Response, Lessons Learned*, Oxford: Oxford University Press.

Jackson, R. (2003), *The Global Covenant*, Oxford: Oxford University Press.

Janis, M. (1987/8), 'The Nature of *Jus Cogens*', *Connecticut Journal of International Law*, 3: 359–63.

Janis, M. W. (1984), 'Jeremy Bentham and the Fashioning of International Law', *American Journal of International Law*, 78(2): 405–18.

Jenks, C. W. (1958), *The Common Law of Mankind*, London: Stevens.

Jennings, R. and Watts, A. (eds) (1996) *Oppenheim's International Law*, vol. 1, 9th edn, New York: Longman.

Jessup, P. C. (1956), *Transnational Law*, New Haven, CT: Yale University Press.

Johnstone, I. (2008), 'Legislation and Adjudication in the UN Security Council: Bringing down the Deliberative Deficit', *American Journal of International Law*, 102(2): 275–308.

Jonah, J. O. C. (2007), 'Secretariat Independence and Reform' and 'Secretary-General', in T. G. Weiss and S. Daws (eds), *The Oxford Handbook on the United Nations*, Oxford: Oxford University Press, 2007, pp. 160–74 and 175–92, respectively.

Kaldor, M. (2003), 'The Idea of Global Civil Society', *International Affairs*, 79(2): 583–93.

Kagan, R. (2008), *The Return of History and the End of Dreams*, London: Atlantic Books.

Kagan, R. (2008), 'The Case for a League of Democracies', *Financial Times*, 13 May.

Kammerhofer, J. (2004), 'Uncertainty in the Formal Sources of International Law: Customary International Law and Some of its Problems', *European Journal of International Law*, 15(3): 523–53.

Kelly, J. P. (1999/2000), 'The Twilight of Customary International Law', *Virginia Journal of International Law*, 40: 449–544.

Kelsen, H. (1945/6), 'Sanctions in International Law under the Charter of the United Nations', *Iowa Law Review*, 31: 499–543.

Kelsen, H. (1945), *General Theory of Law and State*, Clarke, NJ: The Law Book Exchange.

Kennedy, D. (2006), *Of War and Law*, Princeton, NJ: Princeton University Press.

Kennedy, D. (2004), *The Dark Side of Virtue: Reassessing International Humanitarianism*, Princeton, NJ: Princeton University Press.

Keohane, R. (2002), *Power and Governance in a Partially Globalized World*, London: Routledge.

References

Keohane, R. (1989), *International Institutions and State Power: Essays in International Relations Theory*, Boulder, CO: Westview.

Keohane, R. (1984), *After Hegemony: Cooperation and Discord in the World Political Economy*, Princeton, NJ: Princeton University Press.

Kissinger, H. (2001), 'The Pitfalls of Universal Jurisdiction', *Foreign Affairs*, 80(4): 86–96.

Klabbers, J. (2009), *An Introduction to International Institutional Law*, 2nd edn, Cambridge: Cambridge University Press.

Klabbers, J. (2004), 'Constitutionalism Lite', *International Organizations Law Review*, 1: 31–58.

Koh, H. (2005), 'Why do States Obey International Law', in O. Hathaway and H. Koh (eds), *Foundations of International Law and Politics*, New York: Foundation Press, pp. 12–25.

Koh, H. (1998/9), 'How is International Human Rights Law Enforced?', *Indiana Law Journal*, 74: 1397–1417.

Koh, H. (1996/7), 'Why do Nations Obey International Law?', *Yale Law Journal*, 106: 2599–659

Korsgaard, C. (1996), *The Sources of Normativity*, Cambridge: Cambridge University Press.

Koskenniemi, M. (2011), *The Politics of International Law*, Oxford: Hart.

Koskenniemi, M. (2007), 'The Fate of Public International Law: Between Technique and Politics', *Modern Law Review*, 17(1): 4.

Koskenniemi, M. (2006), *From Apology to Utopia: The Structure of International Legal Argument*, Cambridge: Cambridge University Press.

Koskenniemi, M. (2004), *The Gentle Civilizer of Nations: The Rise and Fall of International Law 1870–1960* Hersch Lauterpacht Memorial Lectures, Cambridge: Cambridge University Press.

Koskenniemi, M. (1997), 'Lauterpacht: The Victorian Tradition in International Law', *European Journal of International Law*, 8: 215.

Koskenniemi, M. and Lehto, M. (1996), 'The Privilege of Universality: International Law, Economic Ideology and Seabed Resources', *Nordic Journal of International Law*, 65: 533–55.

Krasner, S. (1982), 'Structural Causes and Regime Consequences: Regimes as Intervening Variables', *International Organization* 36(2): 185–206.

Kratochwil, F. (2009), 'Legal Theory and International Law', in D. Armstrong (ed.), *Routledge Handbook of International Law*, Abingdon: Routledge, pp. 55–67.

Kratochwil, F. (2000), 'How do Norms Matter?', in M. Byers (ed.), *The Role of Law in International Politics: Essays in International Relations and International Law*, Oxford: Oxford University Press.

Kratochwil, F. (1989), *Rules, Norms and Decision: On the Conditions of Practical and Legal Reasoning in International Relations and Domestic Affairs*, Cambridge: Cambridge University Press.

References

Kronmiller, T. G. (1980), *The Lawfulness of Deep Seabed Mining*, vols I and 2, London: Oceana Publications.

Kunz, J. (1945) 'The Meaning and the Range of the *Norm Pacta Sunt Servanda*', *American Journal of International Law*, 39(2): 180–97.

Lauterpacht, H. (1982), *The Development of International Law by the International Court*, Cambridge: Cambridge University Press.

Lauterpacht, H. (1977), *International Law: Collected Papers*, vol. 3, ed, E. Lauterpacht, Cambridge: Cambridge University Press.

Lauterpacht, H. (1970), *International Law, Collected Papers*, ed. E. Lauterpacht, Cambridge, Cambridge University Press.

Lauterpacht, H. (1953), Report to the International Law Commission', *Yearbook of the International Law Commission*, 2: 90.

Lillich, R. (1995/6), 'The Growing Importance of Customary International Human Rights Law', *Georgia Journal of International and Comparative Law*, 25: 1–30.

Lilly, D. (2000), 'The Privatization of Peacekeeping: Prospects and Realities', *Disarmament Forum*, 3: 53–62.

Linklater, A. and Suganami, H. (eds) (2006), *The English School of International Relations: A Contemporary Reassessment*, Cambridge: Cambridge University Press.

Lipstein, K. (1981), *Principles of the Conflict of Laws: National and International*, The Hague: Kluwer Law.

Locke, J. (1989), *Two Treatises of Government*, London: Everyman, para. 26.

Lowe, V. (2007), *International Law*, Oxford: Oxford University Press.

Lowe, V. (2000), 'The Politics of Law-Making: Are the Method and Character of Norms Creation Changing?', in M. Byers (ed.), *The Role of Law in International Politics*, Oxford: Oxford University Press, pp. 208–66.

Luban, D. (1980), 'The Romance of the Nation State', *Philosophy and Public Affairs*, 9(4): 392–7.

Luck, E. (2007), 'Prospects for Reform: Principal Organs', in T. Weiss and S. Daws (eds), *The Oxford Handbook on the United Nations*, Oxford: Oxford University Press, pp. 654–5.

Luck, E. C. (2005), 'How Not to Reform the United Nations', *Global Governance*, 11: 407–14.

Lukashuk, I. I. (1989), 'The Principle *Pacta Sunt Servanda* and the Nature of Obligation Under International Law', *American Journal of International Law*, 83(3): 513–18.

Macdonald, R. S. (1991), 'The Use of Force by States in International Law', in M. Bedjaoui (ed.), *International Law: Achievements and Prospects*, Dordrecht: Martinus Nijhoff, pp. 717–41.

Mahmoudi, S. (1987), *The Law of Deep Sea-Bed Mining: A Study of the Progressive Development of International Law Concerning the*

Management of the Polymetallic Nodules of the Deep Sea-Bed, Stockholm: Almqvist & Wiksell.
Malone, D. M. (2007), *International Struggle over Iraq: Politics in the United Nations Security Council 1980–2005*, Oxford: Oxford University Press.
Manner, G. (1952), 'The Object Theory of the Individual in International Law', *American Journal of International Law*, 46(3): 428–49.
Månsson, K. (2007), 'Reviving the "Spirit of San Francisco": The Lost Proposals on Human Rights, Justice and International Law to the UN Charter', *Nordic Journal of International Law*, 76: 217–39.
Marks, S. (1999), 'Economic Sanctions as Human Rights Violations: Reconciling Political and Public Health Imperatives', *American Journal of Public Health*, 89(10): 1509–13.
McCain, J. (2007), 'An Enduring Peace Built on Freedom: Securing America's Future', *Foreign Affairs*, November/December, available at: http://www.foreignaffairs.org/20071101faessay86602/john-mccain/an-enduring-peace-built-on-freedom.html.
McCorquodale, R. (2006), 'Beyond State Sovereignty: The International Legal System and Non-State Participants', *International Law: Revista Colombiana de derecho internacional*, 8: 103–59.
Mcdorman, T. L. (2002), 'The Role of the Commission on the Limits of the Continental Shelf: A Technical Body in a Political World', *International Journal of Marine and Coastal Law*, 17: 301–24.
McWhinney, E. (1969), 'Canadian Federalism and the Foreign Affairs and Treaty Making Power: The Impact of Quebec's "Quiet Revolution"', *Canadian Yearbook of International Law*, 7: 3–32.
Mearshiemer, J. (2001), *The Tragedy of Great Power Politics*, New York: W. W. Norton.
Meckled-García, S. and Cali, B. (eds) (2006), 'Lost in Translation: The Human Rights Ideal and international Human Rights Law', *The Legalization of Human Rights: Multidisciplinary Perspectives on Human Rights and Human Rights Law*, London: Routledge, p. 12.
Menon, P. K. (1992), 'The International Personality of Individuals in International Law: A Broadening of the Traditional Doctrine', *Journal of Transnational Law and Policy*, 1: 151–82.
Meron, T. (2006), *The Humanization of International Law*, The Hague: Martinus Nijhoff.
Meron, T. (2000), 'The Humanization of Humanitarian Law', *American Journal of International Law*, 94(2): 239–78.
Meron, T. (2000), 'The Martens Clause, Principles of Humanity, and the Dictates of Public Conscience', *American Journal of International Law*, 94(2): 78–89.
Meron, T. (1986), 'On a Hierarchy of Human Rights', *American Journal of International Law*, 80(1): 1–23.

References

Mertus, J. (2009), *The United Nations and Human Rights: A Guide for a New Era*, 2nd edn, New York: Routledge.

Milanovic, M. (2012), 'Al-Skeini and Al-Jedda in Strasbourg', *European Journal of International Law*, 23(1): 121–39.

Mohamed, A. A. (1999), 'Individual and NGO Participation in Human Rights Litigation before the African Court of Human and Peoples' Rights: Lessons from the European and Inter-American Courts of Human Rights', *Journal of African Law*, 43(2): 201–13.

Morgenthau, H. J. ([1948] 2005), *Politics Among Nations: The Struggle For Power and Peace*, Boston, MA: McGraw Hill.

Morris, J. (2000), 'UN Security Council Reform: A Counsel for the 21st Century', *Security Dialogue*, 31: 265–77.

Mulligen, J. van (2011), 'Global Constitutionalism and the Objective Purport of the International Legal Order', *Leiden Journal of International Law*, 24: 277–304.

Murphy, J. (1979), 'The Politics of Manganese Nodules: International Considerations and Domestic Legislation', *San Diego Law Review*, 16: 531–54.

Mutua, M. (2001), 'Savages, Victims and Saviors: The Metaphor of Human Rights', *Harvard International Law Journal*, 42: 201–45.

Mutua, M. (1999), 'The African Human Rights Court: A Two-Legged Stool?', *Human Rights Quarterly*, 21: 342–63.

Nagel, T. (2005). 'The Problem of Global Justice', *Philosophy and Public Affairs*, 33(2): 113–47.

Nardin, T. (2008), 'Theorizing the International Rule of Law', *Review of International Studies*, 34: 385–401.

Nardin, T. (2000), 'International Pluralism and the Rule of Law', *Review of International Studies*, 26(5): 96–110.

Nardin, T. (ed.) (1992), *Traditions of International Ethics*, Cambridge: Cambridge University Press.

Nardin, T. (1983), *Law, Morality and the Relations Between States*, Princeton, NJ: Princeton University Press.

Neff, S. (2003), 'A Short History of International Law', in M. Evans (ed.), *International Law*, Oxford: Oxford University Press.

Neumann, I. (2003), 'The English School on Diplomacy: Scholarly Promise Unfulfilled', *International Relations*, 17(3): 341–69.

Nicholson, G. (2002), 'The Common Heritage of Mankind and Mining: An Analysis of the Law of the High Seas, Outer Space, the Antarctic and World Heritage', *New Zealand Journal of Environmental Law*, 6: 177–98.

Nordquist, M. (ed.) (1982–2003), *United Nations Convention on the Law of the Sea 1982: A Commentary*, vol. V, The Hague: Martinus Nijhoff.

Nowak, M. (2007), 'The Need for a World Court of Human Rights', *Human Rights Law Review*, 7(1): 251–9.

Nowrot, K. (1998/9), 'Legal Consequences of Globalization: The Status of Non-Governmental Organizations under International Law', *Global Legal Studies Journal*, 6: 579–645.
O'Brien, J. (2001), *International Law*, London: Cavendish Press.
O'Connell, M. (2012), 'Cyber Security without Cyber War', *Journal of Conflict and Security*, 17(2): 187–209.
O'Connell, M. (2002), 'Debating the Law of Sanctions', *European Journal of International Law*, 13(1): 63–79.
O'Connell, D. P. (1982), *International Law of the Sea*, Oxford: Clarendon Press.
O'Neill, O. (1996), *Towards Justice and Virtue: A Constructive Account of Practical Reason*, Cambridge: Polity Press.
O'Neill, O. (1987), 'Abstraction, Idealization and Ideology in Ethics', in J. Evans (ed.), *Moral Philosophy and Contemporary Problems*, Cambridge: Cambridge University Press, pp. 55–69.
Ogley, R. C. (1984), *Internationalizing the Seabed*, Aldershot: Gower.
Okereke, C. (2008a), 'Equity Norms in Global Environmental Governance', *Global Environmental Politics*, 8(3): 25–50.
Okereke, C. (2008b), *Global Justice and Neoliberal Environmental Governance*, London: Routledge.
Ong, D. M. (1999), 'Joint Developments of Common Offshore Oil and Gas Deposits: "Mere" State Practice or Customary International Law?', *American Journal of International Law*, 93(4): 771–804.
Oppenheim, L. (1996), *International Law*, vol. I, eds Sir R. Jennings and Sir A. Watts, 9th edn, Oxford: Oxford University Press.
Oppenheim, L. (1955), *International Law: A Treatise*, 8th edn, New York: Longmans Green.
Oppenheim, L. (1905), *International Law*, vol. I, London: Longmans.
Oppenheim, L. and Roxburg, R. (1920), *International Law: A Treatise*, vol. I, London: Longmans.
Orakhelashvili, A. (2012), 'Jurisdictional Immunities of the State (*Germany v. Italy, Greece Intervening*),' *American Journal of International Law*, 106(3): 609–16.
Orakhelashvili, A. (2008), 'State Immunity and Hierarchy of Norms: Why the House of Lords Got It Wrong', *European Journal of International Law*, 18(5): 955–70.
Orakhelashvili, A. (2006), *Peremptory Norms in International Law*, Oxford: Oxford University Press.
Orakhelashvili, A. (2000/1), 'The Position of the Individual in International Law', *California Western International Law Journal*, 31: 241–76.
Osiander, A. (2001), 'Sovereignty, International Relations and the Westphalian Myth', *International Organization*, 55(2): 251–87.
Oxman, B. H. (1994), 'The 1994 Agreement and the Convention', *American Journal of International Law*, 88(4): 687–96.

References

Parker, K. (1988/9), '*Jus Cogens*: Compelling the Law of Human Rights', *Hastings International and Comparative Law Review*, 12: 411–65.

Parry, C. (1965), *The Sources and Evidences of International Law*, Manchester: Manchester University Press.

Patterson, A. (2008), 'Act of State Doctrine is Alive and Well: Why Critics of the Doctrine are Wrong', *University of California Davis Journal of International Law and Policy*, 15: 111–55.

Paulus, A. (2009), 'International Law and International Community', in D. Armstrong (ed), *Routledge Handbook of International Law*, Abingdon: Routledge, pp. 44–54.

Paust, J. J. (1996), *International Law as Law of the United States*, Durham, NC: Carolina Academic Press.

Penny, C. K. (2007), 'Greening the Security Council: Climate Change as an Emerging Threat to International Peace and Security', *International Environmental Agreements*, 7: 35–71.

Peters, A. (2006), 'Compensatory Constitutionalism: The Function and Potential of Fundamental International Norms and Structures', *Leiden Journal of International Law*, 19: 579–610.

Peterson, M. J. (2006), *The UN General Assembly*, London: Routledge.

Pettit, P. (2006), 'Rawls' Peoples', in R. Martin and D. Reidy (eds), *Rawls's Law of Peoples: A Realistic Utopia?*, Oxford: Blackwell, pp. 38–55.

Pogge, T. (2012), 'Divided Against Itself: Aspiration and Reality of International Law', in J. Crawford and M. Koskenniemi (eds), *The Cambridge Companion to International Law*, Cambridge: Cambridge University Press, pp. 373–97.

Pogge, T. (2008), '"Assisting" the Global Poor', in T. Pogge and K. Horton (eds), *Global Ethics: Seminal Essays*, St Paul, MN: Paragon.

Pogge, T. (2002), *World Poverty and Human Rights*, Oxford: Polity Press.

Pogge, T. (1992), 'Cosmopolitanism and Sovereignty', *Ethics*, 103(1): 48–75.

Pollack, M. A. (2005), 'Theorizing the European Union: International Organization, Domestic Polity or Experiment in New Governance?', *Annual Review of Political Science*, 8: 357–98.

Pollentine, M. (2012), 'Constructing the Responsibility to Protect', PhD thesis, Cardiff University.

Potter, P. B. (1945), 'Origin of the Term International Organization', *American Journal of International Law*, 39: 803–6.

Price, R. and Reus-Smit, C. (1998), 'Dangerous Liaisons? Critical International Theory and Constructivism', *European Journal of International Relations*, 4(3): 259–94.

Pustogarov, V. V. (1999), 'The Martens Clause in International Law', *Journal of the History of International Law*, 1: 125–35.

Qi, D. (2008), 'State Immunity, China and its Shifting Position', *Chinese Journal of International Law*, 7(2): 307–37.

Ramesh, R. (2008), 'Paradise Almost Lost: Maldives Seek to Buy a New

Homeland', *The Guardian*, Monday, 10 November, available at: http://www.guardian.co.uk/environment/2008/nov/10/maldives-climate-change.
Rawls, J. (1999), *The Law of Peoples*, Cambridge, MA: Harvard University Press.
Rawls, J. (1993), *Political Liberalism*, New York: Columbia University Press.
Rawls, J. (1977), 'The Basic Structure as Subject', *American Philosophical Quarterly*, 14(2): 159–65.
Rawls, J. (1971), *A Theory of Justice*, Cambridge, MA: Harvard University Press.
Rayfuse, R. (2009), 'W(h)ither Tuvalu? International Law and Disappearing States', University of New South Wales Faculty of Law Research Series, available at: http://law.bepress.com/unswwps/flrps09/art9.
Reisman, M. (1994), 'Amending the UN Charter: The Art of the Feasible', *American Society of International Law Proceedings*, 88: 108–15.
Reisman, W. M. and Armstrong, A. (2006), 'The Past and Future of the Claim of Preemptive Self-Defense', *American Journal of International Law*, 100: 525–50.
Reisman W. M. and Stevick, D. (1998), 'The Applicability of International Law Standards to United Nations Economic Sanctions Programmes', *European Journal of International Law*, 9: 86–141.
Rembe, N. (1980), *Africa and the International Law of the Sea: A Study of the Contribution of the African States to the Third United Nations Conference on the Law of the Sea*, The Hague: Sijthoff & Noordhoff.
Reus-Smit, C. (2005), 'Liberal Hierarchy and the License to Use Force', *Review of International Studies*, 31(S.I.).
Reus-Smit, C. (2005), 'The Constructivist Challenge after September 11', in A. Bellamy (ed.), *International Society and its Critics*, Oxford: Oxford University Press, pp. 81–94.
Reus-Smit, C. (ed.) (2004), *The Politics of International Law*, Cambridge: Cambridge University Press.
Reus-Smit, C. (1999), *The Moral Purpose of the State: Culture, Social Identity and Institutional Rationality in International Relations*, Princeton, NJ: Princeton University Press.
Reus-Smit, C. (1997), 'The Constitutional Structure of International Society and the Nature of Fundamental Institutions', *International Organization*, 51(4): 555–91.
Roberts, A. E. (2001), 'Traditional and Modern Approaches to Customary International Law: A Reconciliation', *American Journal of International Law*, 95: 757–91.
Roberts, P. and Sutch, P. (2004), *An Introduction to Political Thought*, Edinburgh: Edinburgh University Press.
Robertson, G. (2003), *Crimes Against Humanity*, London: Penguin.
Rodgers, R. S. (1967), 'The Capacity of States of the Union to Conclude

References

International Agreements: The Background and Some Recent Developments', *American Journal of International Law*, 61: 1021–28.

Roling, B. V. A. (1960), *International Law in an Expanded World*, Amsterdam: Djambatan.

Rorty, R. (1993), 'Human Rights, Rationality and Sentimentality', in S. Shute and S. Hurley (eds), *On Human Rights: The Oxford Amnesty Lectures*, New York: Basic Books, pp. 175–202.

Rosenstock, R. (1971), 'The Declaration of Principles of International Law concerning Friendly Relations: A Survey', *American Journal of International Law*, 65(5): 713–35.

Rosenthal, G. (2007), 'Economic and Social Council', in T. G. Weiss and S. Daws (eds), *The Oxford Handbook on the United Nations*, Oxford: Oxford University Press, pp. 136–48.

Rossitto, A. (1987), 'Diplomatic Asylum in the United States and Latin America: A Comparative Analysis', *Brooklyn Journal of International Law*, 13: 111–35.

Rubin, A. (1997), *Ethics and Authority in International Law*, Cambridge: Cambridge University Press.

Ruggie, J. (2002) *Constructing the World Polity: Essays on International Institutionalization*, London: Routledge.

Scheffer, D. (1995), 'United Nations Peace Operations and Prospects for a Standby Force', *Cornell International Law Journal*, 28(3): 650–60.

Schermers, H. G. (1997), 'We the Peoples of the United Nations', *Max Planck Yearbook of United Nations Law*, 1: 111.

Schreuer, C. (1993), 'The Waning of the Sovereign State: Towards a New Paradigm for International Law?', *European Journal of International Law*, 4: 447–71.

Schutter, O. de (2012), 'Human Rights and the Post-Carbon Economy', Oxford Amnesty lecture.

Scott, S. (2008), 'Securitizing Climate Change: International Legal Implications and Obstacles', *Cambridge Review of International Affairs*, 21(4): 603–19.

Scott, S. V. (2005), 'The LOS Convention as a Constitutional Regime for the Oceans', in A. G. Oude Elferink (ed.), *Stability and Change in the Law of the Sea: The Role of the LOS Convention*, Leiden: Martinus Nijhoff, pp. 9–38.

Scott, S. V. (2004), *International Law in World Politics: An Introduction*, Boulder, CO: Lynne Rienner.

Sebenius, J. K. (1984), *Negotiating the Law of the Sea*, Cambridge, MA: Harvard University Press.

Shackelford, S. (2009), 'The Tragedy of the Common Heritage of Mankind', *Stanford Journal of Environmental Law*, 28: 109–67.

Sharp, P. (2009), *Diplomatic Theory of International Relations*, Cambridge: Cambridge University Press.

Shaw, M. (2008), *International Law*, 6th edn, Cambridge: Cambridge University Press.
Shaw, M. (2003), *International Law*, Cambridge: Cambridge University Press.
Shearer, D. (1998), 'Outsourcing War', *Foreign policy*, 112: 68–82.
Shelton, D. (2006), 'Normative Hierarchy in International Law', *American Journal of International Law*, 100(2): 291–323.
Shoenbaum, T. (2006), *International Relations, The Turn Not Taken: Using International Law to Promote World Peace and Security*, Cambridge: Cambridge University Press.
Shraga, D. and Zacklin, R. (1996), 'The International Criminal Tribunal for Rwanda', *European Journal of International Law*, 7(4): 501–18.
Shue, H. (2010), 'What Would Justified Preventative Military Attack Look Like?', in H. Shue and D. Rodin (eds), *Preemption: Military Action and Moral Justification*, Oxford: Oxford University Press, pp. 222–46.
Sieghart, P. (1986), *The Lawful Rights of Mankind: An Introduction to the International Legal Code of Human Rights*, Oxford: Oxford University Press.
Simma, B. (1999), 'NATO, the UN and the Use of Force: Legal Aspects', *European Journal of International Law*, 10(1): 1–22.
Simma, B. and Alston, P. (1988/9), 'The Sources of Human Rights Law: Custom, *Jus Cogens* and General Principles', *Australian Yearbook of International Law*, 12: 82–108.
Simmons, B. and Steinberg, R. (eds) (2006), *International Law and International Relations*, Cambridge: Cambridge University Press.
Simpson, G. (2012), 'International Law in Diplomatic History', in J. Crawford and M. Koskenniemi (eds), *The Cambridge Companion to International Law*, Cambridge: Cambridge University Press, pp. 25–46.
Sinclair, A. and Byers, M. (2007), 'When US Scholars Speak of "Sovereignty" What Do They Mean?', *Political Studies*, 55(2): 318–40.
Singer, P. (1972), 'Famine, Affluence, and Morality', *Philosophy and Public Affairs*, 1(3): 229–43.
Skouteris, T. (2011), 'The Force of a Doctrine: Art. 38 of the PCIJ Statute and the Sources of International Law', in F. Johns, R. Joyce and P. Sundhya (eds), *Events: The Force of International Law*, London: Routledge.
Slaughter, A.-M. (2011), 'A Day to Celebrate but Hard Work Ahead', *Foreign Policy*, 18 March.
Slaughter, A.-M. (2007), 'Plugging the Democracy Gap', *International Herald Tribune*, 30 July.
Slaughter, A. and Burke-White, W. (2006), 'The Future of International Law is Domestic (or, the European Way of Law)', *Harvard International Law Journal*, 47(2): 327–52.
Slaughter Burley, A.-M. (1993), 'International Law and International Relations Theory: A Dual Agenda', *American Journal of International Law*, 87(2): 205–39.

References

Sloane, R. (2002), 'The Changing Face of Recognition in International Law: A Case Study of Tibet', *Emory International Law Review*, 16: 107–86.

Smith. S., Booth, K. and Zalewski, M. (1996), *International Theory: Positivism and Beyond*, Cambridge: Cambridge University Press.

Sohn, L. (1997), 'Important Improvements in the Functioning of the Principal Organs of the United Nations that can be made without Charter Revision', *American Journal of International Law*, 91: 652–62.

Sohn, L. (1982), 'The New International Law: Protection of the Rights of Individuals Rather than States', *American University Law Review*, 32(1): 1–64.

Sohn, L. (1977), 'The Human Rights Law of the Charter', *Texas International Law Journal*, 12: 129–40.

Sornarajah, M. (1982), 'Problems in Applying the Restrictive Theory of Sovereign Immunity', *International and Comparative Law Quarterly*, 31(4): 661–85.

Spiermann, O. (2005), *International Legal Argument in the Permanent Court of International Justice: The Rise of the International Judiciary*, Cambridge: Cambridge University Press.

Starke, J. G. (1936), 'Monism and Dualism in the Theory of International Law', *British Year Book of International Law*, 17: 66–81.

Steenberghe, R. van (2010), 'Self-Defence in Response to Attacks by Non-State Actors in the Light of Recent State Practice: A Step Forward?', *Leiden Journal of International Law*, 23: 183–208.

Sutch, P. (2012), 'Human Rights and the Use of Force: Assertive Liberalism and Just War', *European Journal of Political Theory*, 11(2): 172–90.

Sutch, P. (2012), 'Normative IR Theory and the Legalization of International Politics: The Dictates of Humanity and of the Public Conscience as a Vehicle For Global Justice', *Journal of International Political Theory*, 8(1): 1–24.

Sutch, P. (2009), 'International Justice and the Reform of Global Governance: A Reconsideration of Michael Walzer's International Political Theory', *Review of International Studies*, 35: 513–30.

Sutch, P. (2001), *Ethics, Justice and International Relations: Constructing an International Community*, London: Routledge.

Sutch, P. and Elias, J. (2007), *The Basics: International Relations*, London: Routledge.

Szasz, P. C. (2002), 'The Security Council Starts Legislating', *American Journal of International Law*, 96(4): 901–5.

Talmon, S. (2005), 'The Security Council as World Legislature', *American Journal of International Law*, 99(1): 175–93.

Tams, C. (2009), 'The Use of Force against Terrorists', *European Journal of International Law*, 20(2): 359–97.

Tay, S. (1996), 'Human Rights, Culture, and the Singapore Example', *McGill Law Journal*, 41: 743–80.

References

Terris, D., Romano, C. and Swigart, L. (2007), *The International Judge: An Introduction to the Men and Women Who Decide the World's Cases*, Oxford: Oxford University Press.
Téson F. (1998), *A Philosophy of International Law*, Boulder, CO: Westview.
Téson, F. R. (1992), 'The Kantian Theory of International Law', *Columbia Law Review*, 92: 53–102.
Thakur, R. (2010), 'Law, Legitimacy and United Nations', *Melbourne Journal of International Law*, 11: 1–26.
Tharoor, S. (2008), 'This Mini League of Nations would Cause only Division', *The Guardian*, 27 May.
Tharoor, S. (2001), 'Are Human Rights Universal?', *New Internationalist Magazine*, March 2001.
Thomas, K. R. (2006), 'The Changing Status of International Law in English Domestic Law', *Netherlands International Law Review*, 53(3): 371–98.
Thirlway, H. (2006), 'The International Court of Justice', in M. Evans (ed.), *International Law*, 2nd edn, Oxford: Oxford University Press, p. 561.
Thirlway, H. (2003) 'The Sources of International Law', in M. Evans (ed.), *International Law*, Oxford: Oxford University Press.
Thirlway, H. (1972), *International Customary Law and Codification: An Examination of the Continuing Role of Custom in the Present Period of Codification of International Law*, Leiden: Sitjhoff.
Ticehurst, R. (1997), 'The Marten's Clause and the Laws of Armed Conflict', *International Review of the Red Cross*, 37: 125–34.
Tinker, C. (1995), 'The Role of Non-state Actors in International Law-making during the UN Decade of International Law', *American Society of International Law Proceedings*, 89 (1995): 177–80.
Tomuschat, C. (1993), 'Obligations Arising for States Without or Against their Will', *Recueil des Cours*, 241(IV): 195–374.
Trapp, K. (2007), 'Back to Basics: Necessity, Proportionality, and the Right of Self-Defence Against Non-State Terrorist Actors', *International and Comparative Law Quarterly*, 50(1): 141–56.
Tsagourias, N. (2012), 'Cyber-attacks, Self-defence and the Problem of Attribution', *Journal of Conflict and Security Law*, 17(2): 229–44.
Tsagourias, N. (2006), 'Consent, Neutrality/Impartiality and the Use of Force in Peacekeeping: Their Constitutional Dimension', *Journal of Conflict and Security*, 11(3): 465–82.
Ulfstein, G. (2008), 'Do We Need a World Court of Human Rights?', in O. Engdahl and P. Wrange (eds), *Law at War: The Law as it Was and the Law as it Should, Liber Amicorum Ove Bring*, The Hague: Martinus Nijhoff.
UKMIL, *British Yearbook of International Law*, 70 (1999): 408.
Vagts, D. F., 'Rebus Revisited: Changed Circumstances in Treaty Law', *Columbia Journal of Transnational Law*, 43 (2004): 459–76.
Veuthey, M. (2003), 'Public Conscience in International Humanitarian Action', *Refugee Survey Quarterly*, 22: 198–201.

References

Waever, O. (1996), 'The Rise and Fall of the Inter-paradigm Debate', in S. Smith, K. Booth and M. Zalewski (eds) (1996), *International Theory: Positivism and Beyond*, Cambridge: Cambridge University Press, pp. 149–85.

Waldock, H. M. (1962), 'General Course on Public International Law', *Hague Recueil*, 106(11): 1–252.

Waldron, J. (1987), *Nonsense upon Stilts: Bentham, Burke and Marx on the Rights of Man*, London: Taylor & Francis.

Walker, W. L. (1945), 'Territorial Waters: The Cannon Shot Rule', *British Yearbook of International Law*, 22: 210–31.

Wallace, R. M. (2002), *International Law*, 4th edn, London: Sweet & Maxwell.

Wallensteen, P. and Grusell, H. (2012), 'Targeting the Right Targets? The UN Use of Individual Sanctions', *Global Governance*, 18: 207–30.

Walzer, M. (2004), *Arguing About War*, New Haven, CT: Yale University Press.

Walzer, M. (1997), *On Toleration*, New Haven, CT: Yale University Press.

Walzer, M. (1992), *Just and Unjust Wars: A Moral Argument with Historical Illustrations*, New York: Basic Books.

Walzer, M. (1990), 'Nation and Universe', *The Tanner Lectures on Human Values XI 1989*, ed. G. Peterson, Salt Lake City: University of Utah Press.

Walzer, M. (1983), *Spheres of Justice: A Defence of Pluralism and Equality*, Oxford: Blackwell.

Walzer, M. (1980), 'The Moral Standing of States: A Response to Four Critics', *Philosophy and Public Affairs*, 9(18): 209–29.

Wang, J. (1992), *Handbook on Ocean Law and Politics*, Westport, CT: Greenwood Press.

Warbrick, C. (2003), 'States and Recognition in International Law', in M. Evans (ed.), *International Law*, Oxford: Oxford University Press, pp. 205–68.

Watson, A. (1992), *The Evolution of International Society: A Comparative Historical Analysis*, London: Routledge.

Watson, A. (1987), 'Hedley Bull, States Systems and International Societies', *Review of International Studies*, 13: 147–53.

Watson, A. (1982), *Diplomacy: The Dialogue Between States*, London: Routledge.

Waxman, M. (2011), 'Cyber-Attacks and the Use of Force: Back to the Future of Article 2(4)', *Yale Journal of International Law*, 36: 421–59.

Wedgwood, R. (2003), 'The Fall of Saddam Hussein: Security Council Mandates and Preemptive Self-defense', *American Journal of International Law*, 97: 576–84.

Wedgwood, R. (1999), 'Responding to Terrorism: The Strikes Against bin Laden', *Yale International Law Journal*, 24: 559–76.

Wellens, K. (2003), 'The UN Security Council and New Threats to the Peace: Back to the Future', *Journal of Conflict and Security Law*, 8(1): 15–70.
Weller, M. (2009). 'The Struggle for an International Constitutional Order', in D. Armstrong (ed.), *Routledge Handbook of International Law*, Abingdon: Routledge, pp. 179–94.
Wellman, C. (2000), 'Solidarity, The Individual and Human Rights', *Human Rights Quarterly*, 22: 639–57.
Weiss, T. G. (2005), 'An Unchanged Security Council: The Sky Ain't Falling', *Security Dialogue*, 36: 367.
Weissbrodt, D. and Kruger, M. (2003), 'Norms on the Responsibilities of Transnational Corporations and other Business Enterprises with Regard to Human Rights', *American Journal of International Law*, 97(4): 901–22.
Wendt, A. (2006), 'Driving with the Rearview Mirror: On the Rational Science of Institutional Design', in B. Simmons and R. Steinberg (eds), *International Law and International Relations*, Cambridge: Cambridge University Press.
Wendt, A. (1992), 'Anarchy is What States Make of It: The Social Construction of Power Politics', *International Organization*, 46: 391–425.
Westlake, J. (1904), *International Law*, vol. I, Cambridge, Cambridge University Press.
Weston, B. (1984), 'Human Rights', *Human Rights Quarterly*, 6: 257–83.
Wet, E. de (2006), 'The International Constitutional Order', *International and Comparative Law Quarterly*, 55: 51–76.
Wet, E. de (2006), 'The Emergence of International and Regional Value Systems as a Manifestation of the Emerging International Constitutional Order', *Leiden Journal of International Law*, 19: 611–32.
Wet, E. de (2004) *The Chapter VII Powers of the United Nations Security Council*, Oxford: Hart.
Wheeler, N. (2001), *Saving Strangers: Humanitarian Intervention in International Society*, Oxford: Oxford University Press.
White, N. and Abass, A. (2006), 'Countermeasures and Sanctions', in M. Evans (ed.), *International Law*, 2nd edn, Oxford: Oxford University Press.
Wight, M. (1994), *International Theory: The Three Traditions*, Leicester: Leicester University Press.
Wight, M. (1979), *Power Politics*, Leicester: Leicester University Press.
Wight, M. (1966), 'Why Is There No International Theory', in H. Butterfield and M. Wight (eds), *Diplomatic Investigations: Essays in the Theory of International Politics*, London: Allen & Unwin.
Wight, N. and Abbas, A. (2003).'Countermeasures and Sanctions', in M. Evans (ed.), *International Law*, Oxford: Oxford University Press, pp. 505–28.
Wilde, R. (2007), 'Trusteeship Council', in T. G. Weiss and S. Daws (eds), *The Oxford Handbook on the United Nations*, Oxford: Oxford University Press, pp. 149–59.

References

Wildhaber, L. (1974), 'External Relations of the Swiss Cantons', *Canadian Yearbook of International Law*, 12: 211.

Williams, G. (1945), 'International Law and the Controversy Concerning the Word "Law"', *British Year Book of International Law*, 22: 146–53.

Wilson, C. L. (1996), 'Changing the Charter: The United Nations Prepares for the Twenty-first Century', *American Journal of International Law*, 90(1): 115.

Winkler, A. (1999), 'Just Sanctions', *Human Rights Quarterly*, 21: 133–55.

Wouters, J. and Duquet, S. (2011), 'The EU, EEAS and Union Delegations and International Diplomatic Law: New Horizons', Leuven Centre for Global Governance Studies, Working Paper No. 62.

Wouters, J. and Ruys, T., 'Security Council Reform: A New Veto for a New Century', Egmont Paper No. 9, Royal Institute for International Relations (IRRI-KIIB), Brussels, August 2005, p. 5, available at: http://www.egmontinstitute.be/paperegm/ep9.pdf.

Yee, S. (2009), 'Notes on the International Court of Justice, Part 2: Reform Proposals Regarding the International Court of Justice – A Preliminary Report for the International Law Association Study Group on United Nations Reform', *Chinese Journal of International Law*, 8(1): 181–9.

Young, R. (1968), 'The Legal Regime of the Deep Sea Floor', *American Journal of International Law*, 62: 641–53.

Zarate, J. C. (1998), 'Emergence of a New Dog of War: Private International Security Companies, International Law and the New World Disorder', *Stanford Journal of International Law*, 34: 75–162.

Zechenter, E. (1997), 'In the Name of Culture: Cultural Relativism and the Abuse of the Individual', *Journal of Anthropological Research*, 53(3): 319–47.

Zwaan, J. W. de (1999), 'The Legal Personality of the European Communities and the European Union', *Netherlands Yearbook of International Law*, 30: 75–113.

Index

acts, unfriendly, 262–3, 284
adoption, 24, 50–1, 56, 62, 67, 81, 93, 189–90, 311, 325
Africa, 95, 139–40, 148, 187, 212, 246, 290, 328–9, 338, 340, 342–3
African Charter on Human and Peoples' Rights, 184, 187, 192, 209
African States and Contemporary International Law, 95, 140, 320, 331, 340
African Union *see* AU
agents, diplomatic, 232–4, 236
aggression, 156, 266–7, 273, 275–6, 283–4, 297–301
AICHR (ASEAN Intergovernmental Commission on Human Rights), 193
Alvarez, José, 50, 88, 94–5, 107, 130
American Convention on Human Rights, 192
Anand, Ram, 95, 306, 338
Arab Charter on Human Rights, 193
Armstrong, David, 29, 42–4, 87, 174, 299
ASEAN (Association of Southeast Asian Nations), 193
ASEAN Intergovernmental Commission on Human Rights (AICHR), 193
Assange, Julian, 233–4, 253

AU (African Union), 108, 140, 142, 155, 272
Aust, Anthony, 40, 56, 89–91
Austin, John, 14–15, 40

bag, diplomatic, 232, 235–6
basic rights, 162, 194, 204–5
basic structure, 163, 335–7
Baxter, Richard, 67, 92–3
Beitz, Charles, 123
belt, maritime, 309
Bentham, Jeremy, 12, 40, 183, 209
Biafra, 129
bilateral treaties, 54, 56–7, 119
Blackstone, William, 7, 9, 12, 40
Bolton, John, 14–15, 40
Brownlie, Ian, 49, 62, 65, 87, 89, 91–2, 111, 129, 131, 202, 209, 301, 339
Buchanan, Allen, 37–8, 45, 82, 97, 111, 121, 123–4, 131, 133, 135, 160–8, 175–7, 201–2, 206, 212, 247–8, 285–7, 302–3, 336–7, 343
Bush Doctrine *see* National Security Strategy (NSS)
Byers, Michael, 87, 93–4, 96, 279, 297, 302

Carr, E. H., 2, 9, 26–9, 42, 49, 77–9, 88, 96
Cassese, Antonio, 89, 92–3, 95–6, 177, 213, 294–5, 299, 303–4

375

Index

challenges
  global, 4, 6, 156, 221–2
  human rights-based, 194
Chapter VII powers, 18, 41, 134, 141–2, 158, 170, 266, 269–70, 276, 291, 295, 300, 314, 316, 324, 345
Chesterman, Simon, 279, 297, 302
Chetail, Vincent, 212–13
CHM regime *see* Common Heritage of Mankind
CHR (Commission on Human Rights), 146–7, 192, 237–8
civilians, 273–5, 282, 295, 297
CLCS (Commission on the Limits of the Continental Shelf), 318, 326–7, 340
climate change, 103, 221–2, 250, 300, 330
coalition of democratic states, 166, 168, 287
coalition of rights-respecting states, 169, 286
coercion, 256, 258, 260, 262, 264, 266, 268, 270, 272, 274, 276, 278, 280, 282, 284, 286, 288, 290, 292, 294, 296, 298, 300, 302, 304
Cohen, Jean, 155, 158, 175
Cold War, 16, 101, 167, 190, 240, 257–8, 268–9, 271, 274, 276, 292
collective sanctions, 291, 304
comity, 64, 226–7
Commission on Human Rights *see* CHR
Commission on the Limits of the Continental Shelf *see* CLCS
Common Heritage of Mankind, 66, 94, 148, 186–7, 306–7, 309–11, 313, 315, 317, 319, 321–5, 327, 329–37, 339, 341–3, 345
community, national, 6, 119
community interests, 203–4, 291
community values, 2, 81–2, 205, 292, 294–5, 297, 345
compliance, 2, 15, 17–18, 31, 73, 81–3, 149, 182, 190, 236, 269, 291
conferences, diplomatic, 55, 217, 220
conflict, 18, 22–4, 65, 112, 144, 154, 156, 160, 163, 176–7, 205–6, 219, 231, 256–7, 262, 273–5, 290, 294, 298, 301, 303, 334
conflict of laws, 22
consent, 8, 11, 16, 30, 46, 53, 56–7, 59–60, 63, 68, 80–1, 84, 90–1, 118, 142, 150, 158–9, 202, 205, 234–5, 270, 301, 314, 326, 339
constitutional monism, human rights-based, 168
Constitutional Structure of International Society, 34, 74–6, 96, 126, 134, 151–9, 168, 206, 242, 244–5, 248
constitutionalism, 4, 125–6, 152, 157, 159, 175
constructivists, 29, 33–4, 36–8, 76, 244, 334
contiguous zone, 309, 313, 317
continental shelf, 61, 64, 67, 91–3, 309, 312–13, 317–21, 324, 328, 340
  extended, 318
Continental Shelf Convention (CSC), 319, 340
core values, 2–3, 126, 163, 167, 246
Correll, Hans, 281–2, 302
cosmopolitanism, 77, 80–1, 113–14, 121–3, 126, 131, 135, 159–62, 180, 194–5, 198–200, 205, 218, 221–2, 247, 249, 279, 337
countermeasures
  law of, 258, 295–6
  unilateral, 291, 294
countermeasures and sanctions, 17, 260, 291–2, 294, 296–7, 303
courts
  municipal, 21, 69, 230
  national, 6, 63, 225, 251
  regional, 193
critical theory, 32–3, 85, 240, 247
Cultural Relativism, 183, 209
customary international law, 8, 24, 48, 51–3, 58, 61–5, 67–9, 71, 87, 91–3, 95, 101, 165, 167, 189, 191, 197, 199, 203, 224, 231–2, 234, 236, 261, 264, 271–2, 315, 317, 320–3, 340
cyberspace, 262–3, 298, 300

D'Amato, Anthony, 17, 40–1, 62, 64, 91, 93, 182, 209

Damrosch, Lori, 251–2, 304–5
de-formalisation, 125–6, 156–7
death penalty, 185, 190
deep seabed mining, 321–2, 325, 341
delimitation, 58, 317–21
democracies, league of, 135, 160–3, 165–8, 175–6, 248–9, 286–7
developing countries, 95, 140, 186–8, 228, 261, 306, 310–12, 319, 325, 327, 331, 333–4, 338
development of international law, 48, 82, 88, 94–5, 119, 203, 217
difference principle, 335, 337
dignity, 182, 189, 226–8, 234
diplomacy, 134, 214–19, 221, 238–47, 249–50, 254
  collective, 220
  legalisation of, 214, 216
  legalised, 216–17, 238, 249
  multilateral, 217, 243
  open, 219
  traditional, 217, 219, 221, 239
diplomacy and justice, 214–15, 217, 219, 221, 223, 225, 227, 229, 231, 233, 235, 237, 239, 241, 243, 245, 247, 249, 251, 253, 255
diplomatic communications, 216, 218, 220, 222–4, 226, 228, 230, 232, 234, 236, 238, 240, 242, 244, 246, 248, 250, 252, 254
discrimination, racial, 66, 190–1
disputes, peaceful settlement of, 104, 150–1
distributive justice, global, 194–5, 198, 307, 310, 334–7
Dixon, Martin, 48, 55, 62, 72, 87, 89–91, 95, 102, 127–8, 223, 250, 252
domestic analogy, 21–2
domestic law, 16–18, 22–4, 31, 42, 54, 230

economic, social and cultural rights, 184, 186–90, 194–7, 200
Economic and Social Council *see* ECOSOC
Economic Community of West African States (ECOWAS) *see* ECOWAS (Economic Community of West African States)

economic justice, 307, 337–8
ECOSOC (Economic and Social Council), 136, 146, 169–70, 172–3, 194
ECOWAS (Economic Community of West African States), 272
ECtHR (European Court of Human Rights), 110, 126, 192, 230–1, 252
EEZ (exclusive economic zones), 312–13, 320–1, 324, 327, 331, 340
enforcement, 17–18, 41, 80, 82, 119, 142, 192, 224, 260, 272, 288, 291
English School, 26, 35, 37–8, 77, 80, 96, 114, 118, 216, 218, 239–40, 244
erga omnes obligations, 66–7, 93, 201, 204–5
ethics, 1–3, 5, 7–8, 10, 25–30, 35, 37, 72, 84, 86, 96, 122, 131–2, 162, 169, 176, 180, 209, 254, 258–9, 297, 304, 342, 345
EU (European Union), 20, 54, 107–8, 130, 155, 165
European Convention on Human Rights, 23, 192
European Court of Human Rights *see* ECtHR
European Union *see* EU
exclusive economic zones *see* EEZ
exercise of jurisdiction, 226, 231, 251, 314, 323
'Ezulwini Consensus', 140, 170–1

Falk, Richard, 37, 45, 82, 94, 97, 219–20, 222, 250
Fassbender, Bardo, 153–6, 171, 174–5, 300
force, 45, 87, 132, 176–7, 256–7, 259, 261, 263, 265, 267, 269, 271, 273, 275, 277, 279, 281, 283, 285, 287, 289, 291, 293, 295, 297–303, 305
forum state, 224, 230
fragmentation of international law, 113, 125–6, 152, 156–7, 218–19, 310
France, 78, 104, 160, 169–70, 269
Franck, Thomas, 14, 36, 40, 44, 96–7, 262, 282, 297–9

Index

freedom of navigation, 315, 317, 319–21
Freeman, Michael, 179, 208–9
Frost, Mervyn, 97, 207, 213
fundamental freedoms, 184, 188–9, 192–3

Gardbaum, Stephen, 155, 175
General Assembly, 54, 62, 70, 95, 101, 127, 136–8, 140–1, 143–7, 149–50, 156, 170–2, 189, 196, 218, 235, 237, 266, 270, 310, 326
General Assembly resolutions, 49–50, 71, 92, 171, 173, 189
general international law, 20, 55, 65, 154
Geneva Conventions, 72, 294, 309–10, 312–13, 321–3, 326
genocide, 66, 75–6, 93, 117, 142, 150, 156, 174, 178, 190–1, 200, 222, 267, 278–80, 293–4
global commons, 148, 186, 307, 330–5, 337
Global Constitutionalism, 157, 174
global justice, 5, 8, 44, 77, 96, 112, 122, 180, 194, 198, 222, 239, 250, 334, 336, 346
Gowlland-Debbas, Vera, 292, 303–4
Grotius, Hugo, 52, 115, 308
Guzman, Amy, 61, 64, 72, 91–2, 95

Hague conferences, 216–17
Hart, H. L. A, 40–1, 46, 87, 97, 302
Henkin, Louis, 18, 41, 90, 94, 262, 298, 340
hierarchy of norms, 82, 154, 203–4, 210, 346
Higgins, Rosalyn, 52–3, 88–9, 91, 94–5, 109, 128, 130, 182, 185, 209
High Commission on Human Rights, 192
high seas, 307–9, 312, 317, 319–23, 328, 341–2
HLP Report, 137–40, 142–50, 169–73
Hobbes, Thomas, 27, 73, 256, 297
HRC (Human Rights Council), 137, 146–7, 173, 192
human rights, 3–4, 7, 23, 38, 45, 51, 82–3, 88, 97, 112–13, 116–18, 122–6, 131–4, 146, 158–9, 161–2, 165–8, 178–213, 220–2, 230, 247–50, 252, 267–8, 282–3, 285–9, 293–4, 302–3, 336–7
 basic, 124, 162–3, 194–5, 202, 204–5, 286
 gross violations of, 142, 202, 205, 271, 280, 293
 legalisation of, 178–80
 moral, 197
 non-derogable, 201, 296
 normative authority of, 180, 194
 politics of, 169, 180, 337
 protection of, 20, 123, 135, 146–7, 181, 188, 191, 193, 206, 285
 role of, 123, 248
 universal, 118, 184, 209, 259
human rights abuses, 206, 280
Human Rights and *jus cogens*, 250
human rights-based conception of institutional legitimacy, 124, 193, 286
Human Rights Committee, 190
Human Rights Council *see* HRC
human rights courts, 192, 212, 221, 248
 established regional, 192
human rights enforcement, 192, 288
human rights institutions, 124, 147, 178
human rights law, 75, 112, 125–6, 162, 178, 191, 208–9, 211, 222, 258, 289, 295
human rights norms, 38, 77, 80, 82, 123, 156, 158, 162, 167, 178, 201–2, 204–6, 258, 277, 287
human rights violations, 3, 99, 192, 194, 198, 200, 230, 271, 286, 303–4, 336
 gross, 230
humanitarian atrocity, 249, 280–2
humanitarian law, international, 72, 96–7, 202, 212–13, 257–8, 293, 295–7
humanitarian military intervention, 8, 117, 163–5, 169, 176–7, 195, 205, 216, 241, 249, 258, 270–1, 273–4, 276–83, 286, 295, 297
Hurrell, Andrew, 37, 42, 44–5, 96, 111, 118–21, 123, 131–2, 207, 213, 250, 333, 343

Index

IAEA (International Atomic Energy Agency), 174
IBRD (International Bank for Reconstruction and Development), 174
ICAO (International Civil Aviation Organization), 174
ICC (International Criminal Court), 16, 18, 75, 110, 203, 216, 220, 231, 238
ICCPR (International Covenant on Civil and Political Rights), 58, 153, 189–90, 196, 204, 294
ICESCR (International Covenant of Economic, Social and Cultural Rights), 72, 153, 186–7, 189–90, 196, 200, 296
ICISS (International Commission on Intervention and State Sovereignty), 271, 301
ICJ (International Court of Justice), 6, 18–19, 47–8, 51–2, 57, 59, 61–8, 70, 75, 86, 89, 99–100, 102, 108, 126–7, 149–51, 156, 173–4, 191, 204, 212–13, 223, 227, 231–3, 237, 261, 264–5, 291, 315, 318, 320, 326
ICSID (International Centre for Settlement of Investment Disputes), 110
ICTR (International Criminal Tribunal for Rwanda), 16, 18, 110, 231, 268
IDA (International Development Association), 174
IFAD (International Fund for Agricultural Development), 174
IFC (International Finance Corporation), 174
IHL *see* international humanitarian law
IHRL *see* International human rights law
ILC (International Law Commission), 50, 66, 88, 93, 191, 235–6, 253, 291, 322
illegal international legal reform, 163
IMF (International Monetary Fund), 174, 197, 331
immunities, 222–4, 227–38, 251–2
  consular, 223
  diplomatic, 223, 232, 236, 253
immunities of international organisations, 223, 236
IMO (International Maritime Organization), 174
In Larger Freedom Report *see* HLP Report
injustice, 5, 7, 34, 37, 39, 111–12, 114, 116–18, 124–5, 127, 178–81, 183, 185, 187, 189, 191, 193, 195, 197, 199, 201, 203, 205, 207, 209, 211, 213, 216–17, 241, 248–9, 256, 307, 329, 333, 344–6
institutional moral reasoning, 9, 38, 122, 152, 161–6, 181, 202
institutional reforms, 122–4, 137, 150, 163, 198, 206, 288, 345
institutionalism, 31, 33, 80–2
institutions, fundamental, 74–5, 96, 214, 244, 345
instruments, constitutional, 134, 154
Inter-American Commission on Human Rights, 193
Inter-American Court of Human Rights, 193
Inter-Paradigm Debate, 43
internal conflicts, 163, 259, 267–70
international community, 3, 6, 11, 19–20, 22, 27–8, 36, 47–8, 50–2, 76–7, 80–1, 97, 100, 104, 117, 134–5, 143–5, 147–9, 151, 153, 155–7, 161, 163, 169, 173–5, 183–4, 194, 199–200, 205–7, 278–80, 282, 290, 294–5, 327, 329–32
International Constitutional Order, 159, 174–5
International Constitutional Rights, 175
International Covenant of Economic, Social and Cultural Rights *see* ICESCR
International Covenant on Civil and Political Rights *see* ICCPR
International Criminal Court *see* ICC
International Criminal Tribunal for Rwanda *see* ICTR
International Customary Law and Codification, 88, 91
International Development Association (IDA), 174
international ethics, 79–80, 110, 131–2

379

Index

international human rights law, 51, 110, 112, 119, 168, 178, 180–2, 201, 209–11, 345
international humanitarian law (IHL), 72, 110, 212–13, 257–8, 296
international institutions, 34, 118, 122, 156, 162, 215
international justice, viii, 3, 5–7, 9–10, 25, 32, 37, 57, 66, 74, 113–14, 132, 181, 195, 206, 303, 307, 336
international law
    classical, 99, 331
    creation of, 48–51, 69
    definition of, 7, 12
    formal sources of, 73, 75
    modern, 12, 114
    private, 22
    progressive development of, 67, 204
    rapid development of, 81, 214
International Law Commission *see* ILC
international legal order, 26, 37, 39, 74, 83, 111–12, 117, 120, 123, 125, 134, 153, 161–2, 174, 197, 199, 201–2, 204, 206, 249, 283, 287, 298–9, 301–2, 336, 344
International Monetary Fund *see* IMF
international order, 26, 65, 76, 79, 118, 123, 153–4, 197, 199, 226, 288
international organisations, 9, 11, 13, 21, 31, 43, 48–51, 53–4, 56–7, 59, 81, 88–91, 96, 99–100, 107–9, 112, 130, 135, 153, 156, 169, 223, 226, 236, 247, 254, 285
    practice of, 49, 62–3
international personality *see* personality
international political theory, 35, 39, 96, 111, 113, 132
international relations (IR), vii, 1–3, 5, 7, 9–10, 12, 19, 25–6, 28–9, 31–2, 37, 42–4, 62, 71–2, 75, 78, 80, 87–8, 92, 96–8, 114, 117, 122, 127, 180, 213, 239–42, 254, 261
International Seabed Authority *see* ISA
international society, 3–4, 8, 10, 15–16, 19, 21, 26, 36–8, 48, 74, 76–83, 86–7, 96–8, 111, 113–16, 118–19, 127, 132, 134, 151, 157, 159, 165, 200, 207–8, 214–16, 220, 240–4, 246–9, 272–3, 287–8, 334, 336–7
    constitution of, 86, 154, 179, 201, 344
    normative structure of, 38, 82, 125, 247, 331
international theory, 34, 43, 131, 180, 239, 242, 254
intervention *see* humanitarian military intervention
Iraq, 18, 41, 94, 167, 258, 265, 269, 277, 292–3, 304
ISA (International Seabed Authority), 107, 148, 311, 319, 325–7, 330
ITU (International Telecommunication Union), 174

Jackson, Robert, 44, 157–60, 175
Janis, Mark, 40, 65, 93
Jessup, Philip C., 13, 40, 42, 94
jurisdiction, 93, 99, 112–13, 119–20, 126, 150, 183, 186, 190, 196, 204–5, 223, 225–8, 231, 235, 251, 306, 312, 317, 322–4, 328
jurisdictional immunities, 231, 251–3
jus ad bellum, 158, 260, 272–5
jus cogens, 19, 55, 65–7, 75, 93, 156, 191, 204–5, 211, 230–1, 250, 252, 261, 346
jus in bello, 207, 260, 273–5, 284
just war theory, 256, 272, 274–5, 279, 282, 285, 292, 294, 302
justice
    human rights-based conception of, 124, 162, 165, 194, 201
    natural, 84
    observance of, 7, 12
    political conception of, 180–1, 202, 207
    principles of, 7, 116, 180–1, 241, 337–8
    social, 116, 338
justice and international law, 210
justice and international relations
justice claims, 85, 127, 193, 249, 334
justifications
    political, 8
    public, 38, 152

Kennedy, David, 2, 9, 83, 85, 97, 179, 209, 289, 297, 303

Keohane, Robert, 32, 43, 82, 96–7, 135, 160, 175–6, 285, 297, 301
Koskenniemi, Martti, 84–5, 89, 97, 125–6, 131, 133, 212, 242, 249, 254, 331–3, 338, 342–3

Lauterpacht, Hersch, 10, 39, 66, 89, 94, 227, 251
law
  classical, 158, 306, 308, 310
  common, 13, 15
  general principles of, 48, 66, 68, 119, 154, 191
  modern, 306, 310, 313
  municipal, 22–3, 28, 55
  national, 23–4
  natural, 65, 116, 183, 203, 245–6, 254
  rule of, 7, 26–7, 62–4, 74, 82, 115–16, 122, 155, 188, 216–17, 222
  soft, 47, 51, 72, 75, 83, 95, 178
Law of Nations, 11, 39, 297
Law of Peoples, 44, 131, 181, 195, 207–8, 212–13, 335–6, 338, 343
Law of the Sea Convention *see* LOSC
League of Nations, 27–8, 42, 47, 59, 78–9, 103, 135–6, 144, 150, 169, 217–18, 260, 309
legal order, 4, 23, 31, 73, 77, 79–83, 108, 119–20, 124–5, 127, 157, 162, 194, 197, 201, 208
legal persons *see* personality
legalisation of world politics, viii, 1–5, 12, 24, 31–2, 43–4, 79, 82, 95–6, 126, 152, 208, 213, 216, 222, 229, 234, 257
legalised world order, 3–4, 7, 26, 30–1, 77, 86, 120–1, 289, 297, 344, 346
legitimacy, 2, 8, 33, 36–8, 45, 47, 74–6, 82, 94, 96–7, 119–23, 127, 131, 133, 137, 141, 157, 159–63, 168–9, 199, 205, 216, 244, 257, 273, 277, 281, 285, 287, 289, 294
Locke, John, 334–5, 343
LOSC (Law of the Sea Convention), 50, 55–7, 60, 107, 130, 148, 173, 224, 252, 307, 310–13, 315–27, 330, 336, 339–42
Luban, David, 279, 302

Mahmoudi, Said, 321–2, 341
mare clausum, 308–9
mare liberum, 308–9
maritime powers, 308
maritime zones, 312–14, 323
Martens Clause, 71–2, 75, 95–6, 203–4, 212–13, 244, 249, 279
material sources, 48–9
Meron, Theodore, 82, 95–7, 178, 203, 205, 208, 210, 212–13
metavalues, 75–6, 244, 246
MNCs, 48, 50, 99–100, 110
Montevideo Convention on Rights and Duties of States, 93, 101
moral agency, 113–14, 117–18
moral equality principle, 162, 165
moral theory of international law, 38, 162, 336
morality, 5–6, 25–6, 64, 78, 115, 120, 132, 162–3, 176, 180, 212, 241, 257, 282, 288
Morgenthau, Hans J., 2, 9, 26, 28–9, 42, 218–19, 250
multilateral treaties, 54, 56–60, 67, 92–3, 294
multilateralism, 75, 206, 214, 217, 220, 244–6, 248, 287–8

Nardin, Terry, 37, 45, 97, 114–16, 131–2
nation state, 31, 111, 113, 118, 302
national jurisdiction, 95, 148, 310–12, 318, 322–4, 328
National Security Strategy (NSS), 258–9, 265, 283–4, 297, 299
nations
  civilised, 68
  law of, 11–13, 24
natural duty of justice argument, 168
natural law theory, 6, 30, 35, 182
natural persons, 98, 110–14, 117
navigation, 315, 317, 319–21
negotiations, 55–6, 214, 216–19, 261, 332, 334
new diplomacy, 217, 220, 222–3, 238–9, 246–7
New Stream of international law scholarship, 83
NGOs (non-governmental organisations), 20, 48, 50–1, 88, 100, 110, 112, 131, 145, 216, 220

Index

Nicaragua, 67, 92–3, 261, 264–5, 299
non-governmental organisations *see* NGOs
non-intervention, 124, 158, 167, 195, 205, 207–8, 274, 276–7, 279, 287, 290
non-justiciability, 225–6
non-state actors, 11–13, 20, 22, 31, 36, 47–51, 72, 81, 88, 98–100, 110, 119, 135, 265, 299
normative authority, 5, 7–8, 25–6, 30, 34–6, 46–7, 49, 51, 53, 55, 57, 59, 61, 63, 65, 67, 69, 71, 73, 75–7, 79–83, 85–7, 89, 91, 93, 95, 97, 152, 159, 181, 247, 344–5
normative claims, 6–8, 30, 35, 37, 39, 83, 152–3, 157, 216, 241, 247
normative hierarchy, 83, 86, 93–5, 97, 213, 231
normativity, 7–9, 34, 84, 152
norms, 13, 20–1, 32, 38–9, 51–3, 55, 65–7, 81–3, 88, 120, 154, 156, 179, 202–7, 215, 230, 238, 245–6, 252, 275, 287, 292, 346
  body of, 11–13, 19, 306
  communal, 80, 206
  fundamental, 66, 165
  human rights-based, 204
  settled, 207
  social, 33–4, 118, 152
  superior, 47, 204–5, 231–2
  systemic, 245
North Sea Continental Shelf cases, 61, 64, 67, 91–3, 318, 320
NSS *see* National Security Strategy

OAS (Organisation of American States), 272
obligations, 11, 15, 18, 20, 24, 31, 41, 49, 54–5, 57–8, 61, 66–8, 73–4, 76, 78, 82–3, 89–90, 98, 105, 111, 113, 150, 154, 161, 191, 194, 196–8, 200, 202–4, 208, 214, 221, 268–9, 290–1, 313
ocean floor, 148, 310, 328–9
O'Connell, Mary, 292–3, 296, 298, 300, 304–5, 338
Okereke, Chukwumerije, 334, 342–3
omnilateralism, 219–20, 222, 247
opinio juris, 52, 61–2, 64–5, 72, 92, 189, 203

Oppenheim, Lassa, 10, 39, 41, 93, 105, 129
order, normative, 8, 39, 115, 119, 285

P-5 members, 101, 138, 141–3, 266, 276
Pacific Settlement of Disputes, 138, 141, 269
pacta sunt servanda, 73, 78–9, 89
Pardo, Arvid, 310, 328–9
PCIJ (Permanent Court of International Justice), 47, 57, 78, 87, 130, 149
peace-building, post-conflict, 144, 273
peacekeeping, 269–70, 288, 301
Permanent Court of International Justice *see* PCIJ
personality, 51, 98, 100, 107–9, 112, 116, 118
Peters, Anne, 155–9, 175
Pinochet Case, 252
pluralism, 4, 76, 80–2, 84, 114–15, 118, 124–7, 132, 157, 160, 205–6, 218, 220–1, 238–9, 241–4, 247, 288
  constitutional, 159
  institutionalised, 118
pluralist world order, 75, 118, 121
Pogge, Thomas, 122–3, 131–3, 194–5, 197–200, 202, 206, 212, 215, 221, 248–9, 255, 336–7
political theory, 5, 7–9, 34–5, 37, 132, 161, 179–80, 195, 239–40, 274–5, 335, 344
political theory of international law, 38, 86
politics of international law, 1, 3, 5–6, 8, 10, 25–7, 32, 34, 36, 43–5, 73, 96–7, 118, 127, 131, 133, 152, 168, 180, 201, 208, 254–5, 257, 307, 344
population, 71, 101–3, 105, 275, 295
positivism, 29–30, 32, 35, 43, 84
Pot, Pol, 271
poverty, 3, 117, 124, 194–5, 197–200, 215, 238, 248–9, 333, 346
power, 2–4, 7, 9, 13, 16, 18, 27–30, 34, 39, 43, 47, 50, 54, 69, 71, 82, 85, 87, 96–7, 99, 106, 108, 112–15, 120, 122–3, 125–7, 138, 141–2,

158–60, 168–9, 222–3, 249, 265–6, 268–71, 324
power politics, 2–3, 26, 28, 33, 43, 84, 113, 120, 159, 215, 219, 254, 345
practical association, 115, 244, 247
preemption, 264, 283, 299, 303
premises, diplomatic, 232–3
preventative self-defence, 8, 168, 258, 265, 274, 283–4
primary rules, 73, 75, 154
principles
  constitutional, 119–20, 135, 157, 160, 206
  general, 48–9, 66, 68, 119, 154, 191, 211, 226, 295, 321
procedural justice, 245–6, 287
property, 81, 223–5, 229, 233, 332, 334–5, 337
proportionality, 275–6, 291–2, 294, 296–7, 299
public international law, 1, 22, 25, 46, 71, 81, 83, 87, 89, 91–3, 110–11, 131, 133, 161, 203, 209, 273, 301, 307, 339, 344
public opinion, 142–3, 203, 281

ratification, 56–7, 187, 190, 311, 330–2, 341
Rawls, John, 44, 131, 181, 195, 197, 207–9, 212–13, 335–8, 343
Rayfuse, Rosemary, 102–3, 128
realism, 3, 25, 29, 32, 49, 77–9, 82, 116, 239–40
recognition, 19, 35, 67–8, 86, 104–6, 129, 131, 148, 163, 179, 207, 279, 282, 288
Red Cross, 212–13, 289
regional human rights treaties, 192
religion, 35, 183, 185, 189
reservations, 58–60, 83, 90, 191, 203, 237
resolutions, 16, 41, 62, 70–1, 85, 88, 128, 173, 243, 265–9, 280–1, 300–1, 314, 316, 324
resources, natural, 66, 160–1, 163, 190, 196, 317, 319–21, 329
responsibility
  aggravated, 292, 294
  legal, 112, 296
Reus-Smit, Christian, 34, 37, 39, 43–5,

74, 85, 96–7, 111, 132, 208, 239, 244–8, 254–5, 287, 303
rights, 11, 28, 57–8, 66, 93, 96, 99, 101–2, 104, 108–11, 113, 115, 117–18, 124, 131, 178–91, 193–4, 196–200, 204, 218, 221, 223, 273, 275, 279, 285–6, 289, 296, 300, 313, 315, 319, 335, 337
  civil, 194, 196–7
  international, 98–100, 108
  natural, 181–3, 197, 335
  negative, 186, 196
  positive, 186, 196
  second-generation, 186–8, 196, 200
  third-generation, 186, 194, 196, 210, 212
rights of individuals, 113, 179, 183, 187, 210, 273, 279
rules
  general, 28–9, 31, 57, 67, 70, 215, 322
  particular, 7, 69, 84
  secondary, 46, 73–4, 76, 154
  tertiary, 73

sanctions, vi, 15, 17, 41, 110, 134, 164, 167, 207, 244, 257–9, 261, 263, 265, 267–9, 271, 273, 275, 277, 279, 281, 283, 285, 287, 289–97, 299–301, 303–5, 345
  justice of, 293, 295–6, 303–4
sanctions committee, 293–5
Second World War, 2, 26, 28, 110, 135–6, 138, 141, 181, 188, 208, 214, 222, 260, 273
Secretariat, 136, 143, 148–9, 173
Secretary-General, 137, 140, 143, 145, 148–9, 169, 173
security, 27, 71, 87, 108, 110, 125–6, 135, 137–9, 141, 146, 149, 151, 158–9, 162, 172, 185, 192, 260, 263, 266–9, 272–3, 275–6, 291–3, 298, 300–2, 314, 316
Security Council *see* UN Security Council
Security Council Reform *see* UN Security Council Reform
Selden, John, 52, 308
self-defence, 263–6, 270–1, 280, 282–3, 296, 298, 324

Index

self-determination, 45, 66, 97, 117–18, 120, 122, 131, 133, 148, 156, 164, 176–7, 181, 186, 188, 191, 195, 207–8, 212, 277–8, 287, 293, 303
Shackelford, Scott, 330, 332, 342–3
Shelton, Dinah, 86, 93–5, 97, 213
Simma, Bruno, 153, 211, 302
Slaughter, Anne-Marie, 12, 17, 40–1, 43, 96–7, 175–6, 302
smart sanctions, 267, 293, 300
society
  the basic structure of, 335–7
  global, 38, 76, 111, 113, 337
society of states, 11, 19, 100, 207, 218, 243
solidarism, 81, 114, 118–20, 126–7, 221, 239–40, 279–80
solidarity rights *see* rights, third-generation
Somalia, 104, 277, 292, 314, 316
sources, new, 72, 201
sovereign, 15, 27, 73, 163, 199, 201, 223–7, 229–30, 232, 247, 252, 259–60
sovereign equality, 47, 119, 158, 165, 224, 287
sovereign immunity, 69, 214, 222–4, 226–7, 230, 251–2, 314
sovereign jurisdiction, 307
sovereign powers, 50, 121, 225
sovereign rights, 167, 195, 226, 262, 317, 319–20, 328
sovereign states, 4, 11, 30, 32, 44, 50, 80, 82–3, 100, 110–11, 113–16, 119–20, 129, 131, 158–9, 206–7, 217, 224–5, 247, 275–6, 288
sovereignty, 19, 66, 81–3, 96, 101, 104, 113, 117, 119, 125, 131, 155, 159, 165, 167, 175, 200–2, 206–7, 223, 228, 238, 244–7, 254, 259, 287, 302, 308–9, 315, 317, 321, 325, 332
  absolute, 314
  coastal state exercises, 315
special rapporteur, 66, 192, 237–8
state-centrism, 114
state consent, 30, 47, 66, 75, 80–1, 88, 119, 124, 165, 167, 201–2, 206
state failure, 124, 280

state immunity, 224, 231, 250, 252
  head of, 3, 217
state of nature, 4, 115–16, 256, 335
state power, 43, 82, 117, 124, 249
state practice, 21, 24, 47, 49, 52, 61–5, 68–9, 72, 84, 92, 184, 189, 253, 270, 272, 320, 322, 340
state responsibility, 291, 295
state system, 100, 112–13
statehood, 100–6, 117, 124, 128, 202
states
  act of, 225–6
  civilised, 11
  delinquent, 71, 290, 304
  equality of, 76, 195, 226
  failed, 104, 148, 273
  flag, 314, 323
  head of, 222, 230
  host, 232–3
  independence of, 117, 158
  injured, 260
  international community of, 11, 20, 65–6, 105
  intervening, 286, 290
  maritime, 315
  modern, 207, 245–6
  moral standing of, 113, 116
  morality of, 112, 115
  reserving, 60
  sovereign equality of, 4, 110
subjects of international law, 39, 88, 98–100, 102, 104, 106, 108–10, 112, 114, 116, 118, 120, 122, 124, 126, 128, 130, 132, 153
subsidiary organs, 143, 146–7, 170

territorial sea, 309–10, 312–18, 320–1, 323–4, 327–8
Territorial Sea Convention *see* TSC
territory, defined, 101–2, 105
territory of states, 271, 284
terrorism, international, 124, 188, 258–9, 265, 268, 274–7, 283–6, 289, 299–300
TFG (Transitional Federal Government), 314
Theory of Justice, A, 195
Thirlway, Hugh, 62, 73, 87–9, 91, 96, 174, 212
Tomuschat, Christian, 41, 153–4
Toope, Stephen, 33, 44, 208

Index

torture, 66, 185, 190, 196, 230–1, 275
Transitional Federal Government (TFG), 314
Transnational Corporations, 51, 88
treaties, 8, 11, 14–15, 18, 22, 24–5, 28, 46–51, 53–61, 65–8, 72–3, 75, 78–9, 81, 83, 86, 88–91, 93, 99, 106–7, 130, 150, 155, 158, 165, 189–91, 204, 214, 224, 226, 307–8, 312–13, 322, 331–2
  constituent, 54, 99, 153, 155, 237
  law-making, 54–5
  law of, 72, 77
  sanctity of, 77–8
tribunals, international, 28, 65–6, 110, 181, 325
Trusteeship Council, 147–8, 170, 173
TSC (Territorial Sea Convention), 315, 317, 339

UDHR (Universal Declaration of Human Rights), 50–1, 119, 178–9, 185, 189, 193–5, 199, 202–3, 210–11
UHMI (unilateral humanitarian military intervention), 80, 270–2
UK government, 233–5
UN (United Nations), 3, 6, 11, 18–20, 41, 54, 70, 94–5, 99–101, 107–8, 127–8, 134–41, 144–51, 153, 155–61, 163–5, 168–74, 176, 188–90, 192, 217–18, 220, 237–8, 243, 248–9, 260–3, 271–2, 280–1, 290, 292, 296, 331
UN Charter, 6–7, 11, 28, 41, 67, 70, 76, 94, 99, 104, 107–8, 119, 127–8, 134, 136–9, 141–50, 153–9, 161, 163–6, 168–70, 172–5, 178, 188–9, 192, 210–11, 214, 237, 248, 260–4, 266–72, 275–6, 280–2, 291, 295, 302
UN Convention on Jurisdictional Immunities of States, 229
UN General Assembly, 141, 144, 172, 192, 295–6, 300, 310, 328, 342
UN member states, 144, 194
UN Protection Force (UNPROFOR), 282
UN Security Council, 16, 18, 41, 50, 70–1, 76, 88, 95, 101, 110, 124, 128, 135–44, 150, 159–61, 164, 166, 168–71, 192, 202, 218, 258, 263, 265–72, 276, 280–1, 287, 290–2, 294–6, 300–1, 314, 316, 324
UN Security Council Reform, 135, 160, 169–71, 286
UN Secretary-General, 137, 140, 146–7, 169, 326
UN system, 81, 160–1, 165–6, 273
UNCLOS, 309–10, 327, 339
UNCLOS III, 50–1, 55, 307, 310–12, 315, 318, 320, 324, 326–7, 338, 340
UNESCO (United Nations Educational, Scientific and Cultural Organization), 174
UNICEF (United Nations Children's Fund), 107, 293
UNIDO (United Nations Industrial Development Organization), 174
unilateral humanitarian military intervention *see* UHMI
United Kingdom, 16, 21, 23, 54, 57, 69, 75, 141, 170, 226, 234, 269, 292
United Nations *see* UN
United Nations Children's Fund (UNICEF), 107, 293
United Nations Convention on Jurisdictional Immunities, 224
United Nations Educational, Scientific and Cultural Organization (UNESCO), 174
United Nations General Assembly Millennium Declaration, 7
United Nations High Commissioner for Human Rights, 211
United Nations Industrial Development Organization (UNIDO), 174
United Nations Resolutions on Outer Space, 92
United States of America, 14, 16–17, 21, 24, 27, 42, 56, 69, 75, 101, 105, 141, 170, 187, 190, 220, 259, 263, 265, 269, 275, 283–4, 287, 290, 292, 297, 299, 311, 316, 326–7, 331–2, 339
United States of America Foreign Sovereign Immunities Act, 224

385

Index

Universal Declaration of Human Rights *see* UDHR
Universality of Human Rights, 210
UNPROFOR (UN Protection Force), 282
USSR, 101, 170, 316
utopianism, 26–8, 30, 77, 79

values
  common, 19–20
  fundamental, 86, 156, 160
  universal, 4, 220–2, 247
Vasak, Karel, 185, 194, 196
VCDR (Vienna Convention on Diplomatic Relations), 153, 232–6
VCLT (Vienna Convention on the Law of Treaties), 19, 53, 55–60, 65–6, 89–91
veto power, 101, 128, 138–43, 158, 160, 164, 166, 171, 192, 218–19, 266, 269–70, 280
Vienna Convention on Diplomatic Relations *see* VCDR
Vienna Convention on the Law of Treaties *see* VCLT

Walzer, Michael, 116–18, 131–2, 273–5, 277–9, 282–3, 285, 288, 297, 302–3

war, 5, 71–2, 79, 120, 131–2, 178, 181, 199, 211, 219, 222, 226, 243, 256–60, 272–6, 282–6, 289–90, 293, 296–8, 301–3
war convention, 273–5
waters, 142, 309, 314–15, 317, 319–20
  internal, 312, 314–15, 321
  territorial, 314–15, 338
Watson, Adam, 127, 219–20, 243–4, 246, 249–50, 254
Weiss, Thomas, 140, 170, 172–3, 176
Wendt, Alexander, 33–4, 43–4
Wheeler, Nicholas, 97, 177, 279–82, 297, 302
Wight, Martin, 131, 239–41, 254, 303
Wilson, Woodrow, 27, 173
Wolfke, Karol, 69, 94
World Conference on Human Rights, 51, 210
World Court of Human Rights, 211
world order treaties, 153–4, 168
World Summit Outcome, 140, 143, 145, 147, 149–51, 170–4
WTO (World Trade Organization), 20, 108, 155, 197, 199, 215, 331